CONTRACT, STATUS, AND FIDUCIARY LAW

Contract, Status, and Fiduciary Law

Edited by
PAUL B MILLER
and
ANDREW S GOLD

OXFORD
UNIVERSITY PRESS

OXFORD
UNIVERSITY PRESS

Great Clarendon Street, Oxford, OX2 6DP,
United Kingdom

Oxford University Press is a department of the University of Oxford.
It furthers the University's objective of excellence in research, scholarship,
and education by publishing worldwide. Oxford is a registered trade mark of
Oxford University Press in the UK and in certain other countries

First Edition published in 2016
Impression: 1

Published in the United States of America by Oxford University Press
198 Madison Avenue, New York, NY 10016, United States of America

British Library Cataloguing in Publication Data
Data available

Library of Congress Control Number: 2016957568

ISBN 978–0–19–877919–3

Printed and bound by
CPI Group (UK) Ltd, Croydon, CR0 4YY

For my parents, Paul and Louise Miller, with love and gratitude—P.B.M.
For my brother, Matthew Gold, who makes us proud—A.S.G.

Acknowledgements

We gratefully acknowledge financial assistance provided by Dean Daniel Jutras on behalf of the McGill University Faculty of Law, as well as Prof Robert Leckey, Centre Director, on behalf of the Paul-André Crépeau Centre for Private and Comparative Law at McGill University. We are appreciative of logistical and administrative support provided by Manon Berthiaume, Anne-Sophie Hulin, and Libby Parker. And we are grateful to Evan Fox-Decent, Scott Hershovitz, Daniel Markovits, James Penner, and Alexandra Popovici for their participation in the Contract, Status, and Fiduciary Law workshop held at McGill University in November 2015.

Table of Contents

IV. CONTRACT AND STATUS WITHIN THE FIRM

V. THE FIDUCIARY STATE AND THE INSTITUTION OF CONTRACT

List of Contributors

Aditi Bagchi is Professor of Law at Fordham University School of Law

Hanoch Dagan is the Stewart and Judy Colton Professor of Legal Theory and Innovation at Tel Aviv University Faculty of Law

Andrew S Gold is Professor at DePaul University College of Law

John CP Goldberg is Eli Goldston Professor of Law at Harvard Law School

Matthew Harding is a Professor of Law and Deputy Dean of the Melbourne Law School at the University of Melbourne

Gregory Klass is Professor of Law, Georgetown University Law Center

Paul B Miller is Associate Professor at the McGill University Faculty of Law

Margaret Jane Radin is Faculty of Law Distinguished Research Fellow at the University of Toronto Law School; Henry King Ransom Professor of Law, Emerita, University of Michigan Law School; and the William Benjamin Scott and Luna M Scott Professor of Law, Emerita, Stanford University Law School

Irit Samet is Reader in Private Law at the Dickson Poon School of Law, King's College London

Elizabeth S Scott is Harold R Medina Professor of Law at Columbia Law School

Emily L Sherwin is the Frank B Ingersoll Professor of Law at Cornell Law School

D Gordon Smith is Dean and also Glen L Farr Professor at the Brigham Young University Law School

Lionel D Smith is Sir William C Macdonald Professor at the McGill University Faculty of Law

Stephen A Smith is the James McGill Professor at the McGill University Faculty of Law

Benjamin C Zipursky is the James H Quinn '49 Chair in Legal Ethics and Professor of Law at Fordham University School of Law

Introduction

Paul B Miller and Andrew S Gold***

Contractual and fiduciary relationships are the two dominant legal forms of interaction through which persons can pursue individual and shared interests. Contract law is sometimes distinguished from fiduciary law on the basis that, where under contract law persons pursue their respective interests independently, fiduciary law provides means to pursue individual or common interests in a dependent or interdependent way. There is something to this rendering. Yet, the impulse to fasten upon this and other points of difference between contract and fiduciary law risks creating the false suggestion that the boundaries—doctrinal, conceptual, and normative—between the fields are fixed rather than fluid.

The chapters in this volume show that the intersection between contractual and fiduciary relationships is vital to understanding both subjects. Most prior work that compares contract principles to fiduciary principles has focused on the question whether fiduciary relationships are, at their core, contractual.[1] As a consequence, many significant questions have been overlooked. By considering the areas of overlap between these fields, the contributors to this volume open up a range of new topics for consideration. For example, one contributor suggests that, properly understood, the fiduciary duty of loyalty is not actually concerned with loyalty, properly so called. Another suggests that contract and status exist along a continuum, with fiduciary relationships falling in between these two categories. Yet others provide new insights into the nature of voluntary undertakings and their significance in contract and fiduciary law.

* Paul B Miller is Associate Professor of Law, McGill University Faculty of Law.
** Andrew S Gold is Professor, DePaul University College of Law.

[1] For a classic statement of the contractarian view, see FH Easterbrook and DR Fischel, 'Contract and Fiduciary Duty' (1993) 36 Journal of Law & Economics 425. It should be noted, however, that the argument may also go in the reverse direction. Arguably, there are cases in which fiduciary understandings are being used to theorize contracts. For discussion, see Daniel Markovits, 'Theories of the Common Law of Contracts' *Stanford Encyclopedia of Philosophy* (Fall 2015 Edition), <http://plato.stanford.edu/archives/fall2015/entries/contracts-theories/>.

The work collected here reflects a reality in which contract and fiduciary law, while distinctive, are deeply intertwined. The fact that contract and fiduciary law are intertwined can be appreciated from the perspective of either field. Many relational contracts, for example, implicate fiduciary relationships.[2] Furthermore, whether a contract is relational or otherwise, in many settings its subject matter is the provision of fiduciary services (eg, retainer agreements with lawyers, employment contracts with corporate officers, and agency contracts with agents). Equally, many fiduciary relationships are premised on an underlying contract for fiduciary services. This is especially true of commercial and professional fiduciary relationships.[3]

The relevance of status to contemporary contract and fiduciary law is, perhaps, less obvious. Private law scholars are most accustomed to thinking of status in historical terms, reflecting the influence of the work of Henry Maine.[4] Maine famously argued that English common law at the time of his writing had come to reflect broader social changes; in particular, the gradual erosion of rigid social structures premised on family and social statuses (in which statuses themselves mediated social and legal standing and interactions) and the replacement of these with more fluid social structures in which contract and associated values were harnessed in support of development of industrialization and the growth of markets. With the benefit of hindsight, scholars have questioned Maine's sweeping historical opposition of status and contract.[5] Contract scholars have, for example, suggested that the implication of terms on the basis of contract-type, convention, and/or industry practice shows that contract law is partly status-based (or, at least, status-informed).[6] Many, perhaps most, fiduciary relationships are established on the footing of contract. Yet many of these relationships are considered in law to be presumptively fiduciary as a matter of status, given the incidents of the relationship or the role occupied by the fiduciary.[7] Contract and status likewise have an important, if complex, bearing on the content and enforcement of fiduciary duties.

Following Maine's presentation of status and contract in oppositional terms, some have suggested that fiduciary law's reliance on status distinguishes it from contract.[8] But here, too, the reality is more complex. An alternative view that makes room for such complexity is that (a) at a general level, status figures differently in contract and fiduciary law, being more prominent in the latter than in the former; (b) to the extent that many contracts for fiduciary service attract fiduciary

[2] CJ Goetz and RE Scott, 'Principles of Relational Contracts' (1981) 67 Virginia L Rev 1089.

[3] Recognition of the frequent co-incidence of contractual and fiduciary relationships does not imply that there will normally be total or even substantial overlap of contractual and fiduciary terms, or that these terms will have co-equal significance in achievement of the objectives of the parties.

[4] HS Maine, *Ancient Law* (John Murray, 1861).

[5] RH Graveson, *Status in the Common Law* (Athlone Press, 1953); G MacCormack, 'Status: Problems of Definition and Use' (1984) 43 Cambridge Law Journal 361.

[6] N Isaacs, 'The Standardizing of Contracts' (1917) 27 Yale Law Journal 34.

[7] J Glover, 'The Identification of Fiduciaries' in P Birks (ed), *Privacy and Loyalty* (Oxford University Press, 1997).

[8] D Markovits, 'Sharing *Ex Ante* and Sharing *Ex Post*: The Non-Contractual Basis of Fiduciary Relations' in AS Gold and PB Miller (eds), *Philosophical Foundations of Fiduciary Law* (Oxford University Press, 2014).

impositions on the basis of status, it follows that peculiarly *fiduciary* statuses are invariably of significance to contract *and* fiduciary law; and (c) to the extent that the coincidence of contractual and fiduciary relationships is reflected in the terms governing them (being that these will be derived from contract and fiduciary law), peculiarly fiduciary statuses will influence contracting norms and behaviour within these relationships (eg, the fiduciary status of corporate offices places constraints on self-dealing transactions).

Clearly contract and fiduciary law are intertwined, and are connected in a way that implicates status. In our view, the fact of their being intertwined profoundly influences the way in which contract and fiduciary law contribute to conditions of social and economic prosperity.

Given that contract, status, and fiduciary law have a significant bearing upon one another, it should not be surprising that some scholars have already attempted to explain their relationship, doctrinally, conceptually, and normatively. Existing work tends to be aimed not at explaining the interaction of contract, status, and fiduciary law but instead at determining which of contract and fiduciary law is ascendant or dominant relative to the other.[9]

Tamar Frankel was amongst the first to provide a sustained analysis of the interface between contract and fiduciary law. In an influential article in which she sought to establish the distinctiveness of fiduciary law, Frankel emphasized historical and normative points of divergence between status, contract, and fiduciary law.[10] Following Maine, Frankel explained status as involving non-voluntary relationships between dependents (ie., incapable persons) and power-holders rooted in primary social groups (and especially families). She treated contract as consensual, mutually self-interested exchange. Frankel suggested that fiduciary relationships involve a limited kind of dependency, in which one person actively entrusts another with powers over their affairs or property.

Frankel understood status, contract, and fiduciary relationships as mutually exclusive modes of interaction that are not merely distinct but are historically and normatively rivalrous. In Frankel's rendering, status relationships invariably involve domination of a dependent by a superior for the latter's own ends or interests; contractual relationships involve mutually self-interested pursuit by the parties of their own independent purposes; and fiduciary relationships implicate ministerial relationships in which a person is entrusted with power for the sake of another. Each mode of interaction is viewed as doctrinally and conceptually distinctive and as normatively divergent by virtue of engaging opposed values (eg, inequality, trust, and vulnerability vs equality, autonomy, and independence). For that reason, Frankel has long been critical of accounts that aim at the assimilation of contract and fiduciary law.[11]

[9] But see J Getzler, 'Ascribing and Limiting Fiduciary Obligations: Understanding the Operation of Consent' in AS Gold and PB Miller (eds), *Philosophical Foundations of Fiduciary Law* (Oxford University Press, 2014).
[10] T Frankel, 'Fiduciary Law' (1983) 71 Cal L Rev 795.
[11] T Frankel, 'Fiduciary Duties as Default Rules' (1995) 74 Or L Rev 1209; T Frankel, *Fiduciary Law* (Oxford University Press, 2010).

Frankel's effort to establish the distinctiveness of fiduciary law was challenged by the rise of a contractarian analysis of fiduciary duties.[12] The contractarians ignored status but articulated a deeply influential account of fiduciary duties as contractual duties (ie, as gap-filling terms in long-term agency contracts featuring information asymmetries and high transaction costs). Where Frankel was interested in fiduciary law as such, the contractarians approached fiduciary duties as a problem for economic theories of firms and other economic organizations. Facing claims that fiduciary duties cannot be accommodated within contractarian theories of the corporation and the trust, the contractarians developed accounts that characteristically (a) rejected the doctrinal, conceptual, and normative distinctiveness of fiduciary duties; (b) analysed fiduciary duties in reductive terms as a special kind of contractual duty; and (c) asserted the supremacy of contract in establishing the terms governing fiduciary relationships. Each of these characteristic claims has inspired broad scholarly attention, further work within the contractarian paradigm, and extensive criticism.

Seeking to avoid the excesses of contractarianism while retaining the appeal held by its voluntarist foundations, in more recent but influential work, James Edelman has argued that fiduciary and contractual duties are best understood as varieties of voluntary obligation, premised on voluntary undertakings.[13] Edelman suggests that a voluntarist approach can explain commonalities between fiduciary and contract law without the interpretive sin of reductionism. For example, the foundational significance of consent to contractual and fiduciary duties is revealed in judicial attention to construction of the terms of fiduciary and contractual undertakings. Equally, Edelman argues, a voluntarist approach focused on undertakings can explain the significance of status in contract *and* fiduciary law.[14] On Edelman's view, status is nothing more or less than a consideration for judges in placing a proper construction on an undertaking. The presence of an underlying position or relationship of status is material to judicial construction to the extent that it shapes the parties' mutual expectations about the character of the undertaking (eg, whether it is fiduciary or 'merely' contractual) and its content (eg, what is required by way of performance of the undertaking).

Each of the above-mentioned accounts has highlighted and addressed important questions concerning the subject matter of this book. For example, Frankel's work has shown that fiduciary law is uniquely concerned with relationships in which one person exercises power for or on behalf of another in circumstances that involve dependency and vulnerability. Additionally, Frankel recognized genuine normative tension between the values that underlie status, contract, and fiduciary law,

[12] FH Easterbrook and DR Fischel, 'Contract and Fiduciary Duty' (1993) 36 Journal of Law & Economics 425; HN Butler and L Ribstein, 'Opting Out of Fiduciary Duties: A Response to the Anti-Contractarians' (1990) 65 Wash L Rev 1; JH Langbein, 'The Contractarian Basis of the Law of Trusts' (1995) 105 Yale Law Journal 625.

[13] J Edelman, 'When Do Fiduciary Duties Arise?' (2010) 126 Law Quarterly Review 302.

[14] J Edelman, 'The Role of Status in the Law of Obligations: Common Callings, Implied Terms, and Lessons for Fiduciary Duties' in AS Gold and PB Miller (eds), *Philosophical Foundations of Fiduciary Law* (Oxford University Press, 2014).

respectively. The contractarians, for their part, were amongst the first to notice that many, if not most, fiduciary relationships are formed on the basis of contract. They also recognized fundamental questions concerning the interaction between fiduciary and contract law in the specification of terms governing relationships that are at once fiduciary and contractual. Finally, they highlighted essential functional synchronicities between contract and fiduciary law (notably, their respective contribution to facilitation of long-term relationships involving cooperation and coordination in pursuit of shared or joint ends). Edelman, in turn, recognized the importance of fresh analysis of the role played by status in contract and fiduciary law respectively, and he helpfully showed how legal statuses might figure in modern law in ways not captured by the supposition (common since Maine) that legal statuses merely inscribe social statuses.

While these and other accounts indicate the importance of theoretical questions at the interface of contract and fiduciary law, the relative isolation in which contract and fiduciary theorists have worked has meant a missed opportunity for deep, cross-cutting analysis enriched by mutual engagement. This volume aims to remedy that. The work of our contributors collectively suggests the value of philosophical analysis that traverses, investigates, and sometimes boldly re-imagines conventionally drawn boundaries between private law fields. Equally it offers profound new insights into fiduciary law, contract law, and the ragged edge of doctrinal, conceptual, and normative dividing lines and points of intersection that lie between them.

Some of our authors take up unresolved philosophical questions raised by previous work. Thus, for example, several chapters query whether fiduciary duties are profitably understood as premised on undertakings. Other chapters revisit the characteristic claims of contractarians. Here, our contributors make significant advances in established debates. But, equally, several chapters address new questions and promise to engender lively new debates. For example, some offer original accounts of statuses, offices, and roles, and explain how these concepts figure in contract and fiduciary law. Others offer insights into the significance of differences between law and equity for our understanding of the structure of contract and fiduciary law. Yet other authors expand the scope of cross-cutting analysis fostered by this volume, suggesting new ways of conceptualizing the relationship between fiduciary law and tort law, or between contract, fiduciary, and property law.

While the chapters gathered here cover a remarkable variety of themes, taken collectively they mark a significant shift in thinking. In the extant literature, there is a tendency to view contract and fiduciary law in oppositional terms (eg, by exclusive emphasis on points of doctrinal or normative divergence) or in reductive terms (with one category of obligation conceived of as subordinate normatively and doctrinally to the other). Our contributors, by contrast, challenge the reader to consider the fluidity and porosity of boundaries between these fields, and to consider how certain concepts (eg, status) and values (eg, autonomy) animate relationships and institutions that are facilitated by contract law, fiduciary law, tort law, and other frameworks of social interaction and cooperation.

In this introduction, we provide a brief thematically organized overview of the present volume. Our descriptions of chapters are necessarily incomplete.

Nevertheless, we hope that this introduction will reveal the philosophical interest of the questions identified by our contributors and the value of the intriguing, often provocative, answers that they offer.

I. Contract, Status, and Fiduciary Relationships

Some of the most difficult philosophical questions at the interface of contract and fiduciary law concern the role of contract and status in the formation of fiduciary relationships, the ascription of fiduciary duties, and determination of the scope and terms of fiduciary liability.

If one accepts, contra the contractarian view, that fiduciary relationships are distinctive, one must still confront the fact that many fiduciary relationships are formed contractually and fiduciary mandates and duties are susceptible to being defined (in part, at least) by contract. Thus there are significant philosophical questions concerning the nexus between fiduciary and contractual relationships. For example, to what extent do methods of formation of fiduciary relationships matter to our understanding of their basic nature? When a given relationship is both fiduciary and contractual, how are fiduciary and contractual duties accommodated to one another for the purpose of realizing the law's ends and the parties' own expectations for their relationship?

Other questions concern the role of status in the identification of fiduciary relationships and the imposition of fiduciary and contractual duties. Even where formed contractually, relationships are characterized by law in most cases as fiduciary not (or not just) because the parties have intended that characterization. Instead, the fiduciary characterization arises as a result of fiduciary status having been attributed to the kind of relationship they have. Status mediates the interaction of contract and fiduciary law by establishing a legal presumption that relationships of a particular kind are of a fiduciary character. Thus, the classical fiduciary relationships—trustee–beneficiary, director–corporation, agent–principal, lawyer–client, and so on—are recognizable as such precisely on the basis of long-established fiduciary status. The centrality of status in the identification of fiduciary relationships raises a unique set of philosophical questions. For example: what, exactly, does fiduciary status signify? How does status interact with contract in determining the legal nature of particular relationships? How can status-based imposition of fiduciary duties be reconciled with the notion that fiduciary duties also, ordinarily, arise on the basis of consent?

In his contribution, Paul Miller provides a novel account of the idea of fiduciary status. Miller begins by situating fiduciary status relative to other conceptions of status. Statuses, he explains, can be social, moral, or legal in nature. Sometimes these particular statuses need to be understood in relationship to one another. For example, Miller notes that many legal statuses have historically encoded social statuses, including morally pernicious ones that reflect discriminatory attributions of social rank to persons, based on group characteristics. While noting that it is important to attend to interactions of, and differences between, social, moral, and legal conceptions of status, Miller argues that all statuses have common conceptual properties and serve parallel functions in the normative systems in which they are generated and used. According to Miller, a status provides categorical designation of the normative position of a person, relationship, or group in a normative system for the purpose of facilitating the efficient and effective operation of the system. Statuses designate by picking out (or by purporting to pick out) normatively salient qualities of persons, relationships, or groups for the purposes of distinguishing persons in terms of normative entitlements and/or burdens (eg, in attributing rights, duties, powers, or liabilities to persons). Because reliance on a status invariably involves reliance on simplifying assumptions about the normative position of the persons to whom they apply, and because these assumptions are inherently contestable empirically and normatively, statuses can be (and historically often have been) deficient, either in general or in use.

Drawing on this account, Miller explains the idea of status peculiar to fiduciary law. Fiduciary status is a form of legal status attaching to broad kinds of relationship. More specifically, attributions of fiduciary status mean that a given (often non-legal) kind of relationship is treated in law as being of a certain formal legal type. Status-based identification differs fundamentally from fact-based identification, whereby particular relationships are assessed for evidence that they possess formal properties that define the legal type. As is true of other status concepts, reliance on fiduciary status enables actors (here, the courts) in a normative system to manage systemic complexity by generating and/or relying upon assumptions about the normative position of persons and relationships. Miller argues that fiduciary status is best understood as being based juridically on the supposition that designated kinds of relationship (eg, agent–principal, trustee–beneficiary, director–corporation) are typified by possession of formal properties that, in turn, typify fiduciary relationships.[15] Where attributions of status are properly made on this basis, and are invoked from a critical posture (ie, in recognition that designations of normative position made on the basis of status are necessarily merely provisional, conceptually and normatively), their use is legitimate. However, Miller cautions that habitual reliance on time-worn attributions of status can generate complacency and blindness to the inherent limitations of status-based reasoning. Where judges are heedless of these limitations, they can be led to unjust or rationally indefensible results.

In their chapter, Hanoch Dagan and Elizabeth Scott critically examine the tendency to treat status and contract in oppositional terms. They trace it to 'binaristic' abstract conceptions of status and contract, respectively. On these conceptions, legal status is an ascribed (rather than undertaken) designation that is 'innate, comprehensive, and inalienable', whereas contract is an arms-length exchange of value between equals premised on their mutual consent. Dagan and Scott follow

[15] See also PB Miller, 'The Fiduciary Relationship' in AS Gold and PB Miller (eds), *Philosophical Foundations of Fiduciary Law* (Oxford University Press, 2014) and PB Miller, 'Justifying Fiduciary Duties' (2013) 58 McGill LJ 969.

Maine in the assumption that legal statuses are paradigmatically hierarchical and hereditary. So construed, it is understandable that status and contract should be viewed as doctrinally and normatively divergent. Yet, as Dagan and Scott recognize, an oppositional perspective on status and contract runs into difficulty when confronted with fiduciary relationships. That is because many fiduciary relationships are formed on the basis of contract yet are also mediated by immutable rules of the sort ordinarily associated with status. Fiduciary law thus seems to straddle contract and status without fitting into either category and without explicitly reconciling tensions between them. Fiduciary law thus has a 'seemingly confusing hybrid nature'.[16]

According to Dagan and Scott, the confusion can be resolved through recognition that between the poles of status and contract lie the intermediate conceptions of the office and contract type. This is the terrain within which fiduciary relationships lie. Dagan and Scott explain that offices and contract types are analogues of status and of the liberal ideal of contract, which exhibit some of the features of each without associated conceptual and normative inflexibility. An office is, like a status, subject to 'immutable rules' that include 'core obligations [which are] not fully assignable', yet, unlike statuses, offices are normally voluntarily undertaken (and so are not innate) and are circumscribed (and so not comprehensive). By contrast, a 'contract type' is a variety of contract that is typified, as it were, through a detailed set of more-and-less sticky default rules reflecting different sets of values (adjusted to type).[17] According to Dagan and Scott, most fiduciary relationships arise neither as a matter of status nor as a matter of contract (of the liberal ideal category), but instead arise either by way of office or contract type. As they put it, 'fiduciary law … presents a micro-cosmos of the office-to-contract type divide.'[18] By way of illustration, Dagan and Scott explain that the parent–child fiduciary relationship is premised on parents' occupation of an office with fixed obligations that cannot be derogated from by contract. Equally, they argue, commercial fiduciary relationships such as that between an investment professional and client are best analysed as a contract type with fiduciary incidents, some of which can be derogated from by contract.

In his chapter, Matthew Harding provides a critical analysis of Edelman's voluntarist account of fiduciary duties, clarifying the significance of undertakings in the ascription and delimitation of fiduciary duties. Like Miller, Harding emphasizes the role of status in the identification of fiduciary relationships, and he offers an original account of the basis of attributions of fiduciary status.

Harding begins by clarifying the nature of undertakings. He explains that all undertakings entail voluntary commitment to norms that are the subject of the undertaking. In the case of fiduciary undertakings, these are norms to act in the

[16] Hanoch Dagan and Elizabeth S Scott, 'Reinterpreting the Status–Contract Divide: The Case of Fiduciaries' at p 51 in this volume.

[17] See also H Dagan and MA Heller, *The Choice Theory of Contracts* (Cambridge University Press, forthcoming March 2017).

[18] Dagan and Scott, (n 16) at p 62.

interests of beneficiaries. Having clarified that, Harding counters Edelman's suggestion that undertakings are a necessary and sufficient condition for the ascription of fiduciary duties. In showing that undertakings are not a necessary condition, Harding notes that in some cases (notably, parent–child fiduciary relationships) fiduciary duties are imposed simply in consequence of the formation of a relationship of recognized fiduciary status, and so irrespective of party consent. In demonstrating that undertakings are not a sufficient condition, Harding highlights cases that establish that relationships—however formed—must have certain properties to be deemed fiduciary (notably, the fiduciary must be in receipt of power and discretion under the relationship). Harding concludes that 'undertakings to serve others' interests are fiduciary only in the sense that they may number among the reasons why the law recognises a person as a fiduciary.'[19]

Harding then considers the significance of status in fiduciary law. He notes that many fiduciary relationships are considered such on a prima facie basis due to an attribution of fiduciary status to entire categories of relationship. Harding suggests that fiduciary status is premised—in part, at least—on the social roles occupied by fiduciaries in these relationships. Social roles undergird status because they are a locus for patterned expectations of behaviour in conformity with fiduciary norms. Social roles, according to Harding, come with 'pre-packaged' fiduciary norms (eg, norms entailing service of the interests of others). As such, voluntary occupation of a social role grounds a generalized expectation that the role-occupant has committed to abidance of fiduciary standards of behaviour. Fiduciary status is properly attributed to entire categories of relationship that implicate social roles on this basis.

II. Contractual and Fiduciary Obligations

The above-referenced chapters focus on how contract and status factor in the formation and judicial identification of fiduciary relationships. Other philosophical questions go to the nature of, and relationships between, contractual and fiduciary obligations. There is, for example, the question how contractual and fiduciary relationships are made to accommodate one another through specification by contract, by fiduciary law, or otherwise, of terms going to the performance of contracts and of fiduciary mandates. At a still higher level of generality are questions concerning the place of contract and fiduciary law, respectively, in broader systems of private law, including systems of law and equity. Questions of this sort are addressed by the next set of chapters.

The contribution by Gregory Klass addresses several questions concerning the relationship between fiduciary and contractual obligations, and challenges the assumption (implicit on contractarian and voluntarist accounts) that fundamental

[19] Matthew Harding, 'Fiduciary Undertakings' at p 80 in this volume.

insights about fiduciary obligations may be arrived at by treating them as, or as analogous to, contractual duties.

Klass begins by analysing the content of contractual and fiduciary obligations. Klass expresses strong scepticism of the supposition that contract law can explain the content of fiduciary duties. Contractual obligations, Klass explains, are binding for content-independent reasons. That is, they are binding not because of what, specifically, they require by way of compliance, but rather because they have been generated in the right way (eg, because they were agreed to). Furthermore, content-dependent constraints on the *generation* of contractual obligations (ie, constraints that bear on the process of contracting) reflect 'no more than the *minima moralia* of the marketplace'. Fiduciary obligations, by contrast, are content-dependent and the hallmark duties of care and loyalty reflect robust expectations of other-regarding behaviour. Klass is also critical of the suggestion that the content of fiduciary obligations is subject to specification by the courts on the basis of hypothetical contract analysis. He explains that the normative appeal of this form of analysis turns not on consent, as such, but instead on it directing attention to the welfare effects of possible specifications of the content of obligations. From the perspective of welfare economics, there can be powerful reasons to prefer obligations with content specified by way of mandatory rules or sticky defaults, in which case the criteria for determining the content of obligations are located in general normative theory rather than in contract as such.

Klass proceeds to consider the significance of the fact that fiduciary and contractual obligations can sometimes be traced to the same source or causative event, whether consent or contract.[20] He begins by questioning the standard conceptualization of the source of contractual obligations. Klass explains that while contract law has a power-conferring function realized through recognition of the capacity of persons to undertake new obligations through agreement, equally fundamental is contract law's duty-imposing function through which obligations arise irrespective of party consent.[21] This insight both diminishes the conceptual and normative power of the suggestion that fiduciary obligations can be assimilated to contractual ones on the basis that they are undertaken rather than imposed, while also indicating that fiduciary law might, like contract law, have a power-conferring and duty-imposing function. Turning his attention to the source of fiduciary obligations, Klass notes that, while some fiduciary relationships (and thus attendant obligations) are premised on consent, others are recognized by law irrespective of consent. Further, even where required, consent does not necessarily have the significance sometimes attributed to it. Klass explains that, for consensual fiduciary relationships that are distinctively legal in nature (eg, trustee–beneficiary, agent–principal relationships), fiduciary law appears to recognize fiduciary obligations largely on the basis of power-conferring rules (because these relationships are formed precisely in order to occasion fiduciary

[20] The language of causative event comes from the work of Peter Birks. See, for example, P Birks, *Unjust Enrichment* (2nd ed, Oxford University Press, 2005).

[21] See also G Klass, 'Three Pictures of Contract: Duty, Power, and Compound Rule' (2008) 83 NYU L Rev 1726.

obligations). By contrast, consensual fiduciary relationships that have a non-legal character (eg, doctor–patient, priest–parishoner relationships) likely attract fiduciary obligations on the basis of duty-imposing rules. These relationships are formed for reasons other than a desire to occasion fiduciary obligations, suggesting that the law has independent reasons for imposing them. In short, fiduciary and contractual obligations equally may originate in consent or in law, but this does not suggest that fiduciary and contractual obligations have a special relationship by virtue of sharing a common source. Many different kinds of obligations arise by virtue of consent or are mandated by law for other reasons. If, as seems likely, the reasons for imposing fiduciary obligations are different from the reasons for imposing contractual obligations, we'd be better off clarifying the nature of those reasons.

Klass concludes his chapter by considering the significance of the fact that fiduciary and contractual obligations have mutability in common. Klass acknowledges that some fiduciary obligations, in some fiduciary relationships, are defaults, and asks what this implies about the law's reasons for imposing them and for calibrating their 'stickiness' as it does. Klass observes first that the mere fact of mutability does not in itself tell us anything about the law's reasons for recognizing an obligation that is mutable. He then notes that default rules and altering rules (the latter being key to calibration of the mutability of a default) can be choice-promoting, but equally they can be choice-inhibiting, expressing the significance of general societal interests. Here, too, Klass notes, is space for divergence of contract and fiduciary law despite superficial similarity. Even though each body of law makes allowance for mutability of obligations, and may do so for similar reasons (ie, those rooted in respect for autonomy), in other cases they allow and/or limit mutability for reasons that are distinctive, reflecting the different social and economic functions and values implicated by fiduciary and contractual relationships, respectively.

In his chapter, Lionel Smith also addresses questions of broad compass concerning the relationship between fiduciary and contractual obligations. Smith begins by clarifying and questioning the claims of contractarians as to the similarities between fiduciary and contractual obligations. He notes that many contractarians have based broad assertions about the 'contractual' nature of fiduciary obligations on the fact that they can be modified by contract. Smith argues that these assertions are fundamentally misconceived; one is unable to sustain any particular conclusion about the nature of, or justification for, a given legal obligation on the basis that it can or cannot be modified by contract. Many legal obligations can be varied by contract (eg, certain tort duties), but the juridical and normative bases of the obligations lie elsewhere. Smith also considers blanket assertions that fiduciary and contractual obligations have a common source in contractual agreement. He rejects this suggestion outright, pointing to several examples of fiduciary relationships that cannot plausibly be construed as founded on contract.

Smith next addresses the claims of the voluntarists.[22] Smith acknowledges that voluntarist theories, to the extent that they locate the source and reasons for

[22] Amongst whom, in addition to Edelman, Smith counts Robert Sitkoff. See R Sitkoff, 'An Economic Theory of Fiduciary Law' in AS Gold and PB Miller (eds), *Philosophical Foundations of Fiduciary Law* (Oxford University Press, 2014).

recognition of fiduciary duties in the mere fact of the fiduciary's consent, have broader explanatory power than do contractarian theories. However, Smith argues that they are untenable as well. Smith suggests that some voluntarist writings elide differences between consent and contract with a view to propping up contractarianism, ignoring the doctrinal and normative significance of these differences. For pure voluntarists like Edelman, there is the separate question of what to make of the significance of undertakings to the ascription of fiduciary obligations. Smith suggests that undertakings have less significance, doctrinally, than they have been taken to have by Edelman. He emphasizes that in many cases, the fiduciary nature of a relationship and attendant obligations are determined as a matter of law; the undertaking of the fiduciary goes only to show that his participation in the relationship is voluntary.

Smith concludes by noting that while contract and consent cannot explain *away* fiduciary obligations, they are nevertheless clearly important to fiduciary law. He explains that some—but not all—fiduciary relationships are formed by contract, and a larger proportion—but again, not all—of fiduciary relationships are premised on consent. Smith also allows that the content and enforcement of certain fiduciary duties, in certain fiduciary relationships, can be adjusted by contract or consent. But like Klass, Smith suggests that recognition of these points doesn't get us closer to answering the most fundamental of philosophical questions; namely, what makes a relationship fiduciary, and why the law imposes the duties it does on these relationships.[23]

Irit Samet's chapter addresses questions similar to those entertained by Klass and Smith, but does so from the perspective of the relationship between law and equity. According to Samet, contractarian theory can be profitably understood as a fusionist project: a project that denies the conceptual and normative salience of traditional doctrinal distinctions between law and equity and that calls for incorporation of equitable and legal doctrine. Samet acknowledges that contractarians don't explicitly frame their views in this way. However, she says that contractarian arguments are fusionist in substance inasmuch as they assert doctrinal fusion, or counsel same.

Samet is highly critical of contractarianism, so interpreted. She argues that fiduciary obligations are conceptually, doctrinally, and normatively distinctive, and that they are distinctively equitable. Samet identifies several interpretive problems facing contractarianism. Amongst other things, she argues that the contractarians are incapable of explaining non-contractual fiduciary relationships, the mandatory nature of many fiduciary duties, the distinctive content of the fiduciary duty of loyalty, and generous gain-based fiduciary remedies.

[23] These issues are taken up in L Smith, 'Fiduciary Relationships: Ensuring the Loyal Exercise of Judgement on Behalf of Another' (2014) 130 Law Quarterly Review 608 and L Smith, 'Can We Be Obliged to be Selfless?' in AS Gold and PB Miller (eds), *Philosophical Foundations of Fiduciary Law* (Oxford University Press, 2014).

Samet thinks that while contractarianism fails as an interpretive project, it is more fundamentally a normative project. Of course, interpretive and normative ambitions often coincide in the expression of argument. And Samet provides one telling illustration of this tendency. Contractarians, she points out, tend to say little about the idea of loyalty at work in fiduciary law, and what they do say is normatively deflationary. As interpreted by contractarians, loyalty requires little more than that the fiduciary commit herself to some material advancement of the interests of the beneficiary; it requires little by way of self-sacrifice. Indeed, as Samet points out, some contractarians suggest that fiduciary loyalty norms are premised on expectations of mutual benefit from fiduciary relationships. Samet demonstrates that this is not only a bad interpretation of fiduciary loyalty, it is misleading in its suggestion that, doctrinally and normatively, contractual and fiduciary obligations are roughly equivalent in the way that they structure expectations in contractual and fiduciary relationships. The unearned payoff of this interpretive error for contractarians is that an unwitting reader might assume the normative equivalence of contractual and fiduciary relationships and obligations. It is this possibility that Samet warns most urgently against.

Samet argues that the duty of loyalty is doctrinally more complex and normatively more robust than indicated by the contractarians. Consistent with its origins in the conscience-based jurisdiction of equity, the content of the duty of loyalty is specified by moral norms that require other-regarding behaviour that is utterly foreign to contract law.[24] While parties to ordinary contracts are entitled, and indeed expected, to behave with mutual self-interest, the duty of loyalty commits the fiduciary to suppress self-interest in faithful service of the interests of a beneficiary. Samet suggests that the expectation of self-sacrifice reflects the distinctive moral salience of fiduciary relationships. Where parties to a contract are presumed to be on an equal footing, parties to a fiduciary relationship are presumed to be on unequal footing due to the power that a fiduciary receives and holds on trust for the beneficiary. According to Samet, widespread failure to recognize the distinctive moral values implicated by fiduciary relationships and duties would mean loss of public trust in fiduciary relationships and institutions.

In her chapter, Emily Sherwin also analyses fiduciary law and contract through the lens of the relationship of law and equity, but she does so by considering how each deals with a core normative problem—one commonly thought to have necessitated the development of equity. This is the problem of 'how to reconcile general rules with particular justice'.

Equity is conventionally understood as supplementing or amending law as necessary to achieve 'particular justice' in circumstances where the law fails to do so owing to its generality. On this understanding, and recognizing that fiduciary duties arose primarily in the context of equity, one might expect Sherwin to show

[24] See also I Samet, 'Fiduciary Loyalty as Kantian Virtue' in AS Gold and PB Miller (eds), *Philosophical Foundations of Fiduciary Law* (Oxford University Press, 2014) and I Samet, 'Guarding the Fiduciary's Conscience' (2008) 29 Oxford Journal of Legal Studies 763.

how fiduciary law, being equitable in the traditional sense, interacts with formal rules of contract law (eg, through correction or supplementation of those rules). Instead, Sherwin suggests that contract and fiduciary law have both had to address the balancing problem and that they have done so differently.

Sherwin argues that, generally speaking, efforts at balancing must address the following exigencies: (a) ensuring that the coordination benefits of legal rules are achieved; (b) providing adequate means for achievement of particular justice through judicial discretion; and (c) ensuring that these mechanisms do not distort the law or otherwise undermine its coordination benefits.[25]

Sherwin argues that contract law achieves this balance by establishing formal legal rules governing the formation of contracts—providing needed coordination benefits by making it clear 'what actions are need to create an obligation'—while making space for the achievement of particular justice through broad equitable standards that modify application of default legal rules in the enforcement of contracts. Thus, Sherwin explains, the courts may refuse enforcement of a contract on the basis of mistake, in certain circumstances. Discretionary limitations on enforcement like this 'exemplify Aristotle's conception of equity as correction of errors that result from the generality of rules'. They don't pose a threat to the ends served by legal rules because, being remedial, they operate 'at the fringe of lay understandings of law'.

Sherwin suggests that fiduciary law strikes the balance differently, with a skew toward formal legal rules. According to Sherwin, fiduciary law addresses its formal legal rules not to relationship formation but, instead, to defining the obligations of the fiduciary. She points, in particular, to the broad and generally stringent no-profit and no-conflict rules by which fiduciary loyalty is judged. She also points to the strict enforcement and burdensome character of gain-based fiduciary remedies, contrasting the remedial rigidity of fiduciary law with the flexibility generated by judicial discretion in contract remedies. Sherwin suggests that there is 'pressure' for increased equitable discretion in fiduciary remedies (especially where profit-stripping remedies have been granted against fiduciaries who acted in good faith) but this has yet to result in equitable adjustment to, or correction of, the law. Somewhat ironically, then, and certainly surprisingly, Sherwin's account suggests that fiduciary law is less equitable than contract law.

III. Loyalty and Morality across Contract, Fiduciary, and Tort Law

The next series of papers provides insights into the relations between fiduciaries and their beneficiaries, with a focus on the duty of loyalty. Contract theory can

[25] Sherwin elsewhere frames the problem of balancing the demands of law and morality. See L Alexander and E Sherwin, *The Rule of Rules: Morality, Rules, and the Dilemmas of Law* (Duke University Press, 2001).

shed light on fiduciary loyalty in more than one way. Loyalty is often seen as an essential feature of fiduciary relationships, and there is an ongoing debate whether legally enforceable expectations of loyalty can arise from contract alone. On some views, contract duties are fundamentally different in kind from loyalty duties. In order to assess these claims, we need to understand the basis of both contractual and fiduciary obligations. Recent work in contract theory can also give us new insights into the broader significance of loyalty in those settings where it is legally required. Whether or not loyalty is properly seen as contractual, parallels between contract and loyalty obligations may tell us a great deal.

For contract theorists, a crucial concern is whether contract law should reflect or otherwise take into account promissory morality. For example, Seana Shiffrin argues that contract law should make room for promissory morality given the overlap between contractual and promissory relationships. On her view, the law should accommodate the extra-legal duties that people undertake when they enter into a contract.[26] Like contracts, fiduciary relationships can implicate both legal and extra-legal practices. Andrew Gold's chapter notes that a fiduciary will often owe both legal and extra-legal loyalty duties, and in many cases the extra-legal loyalty duties will be deeply felt. Yet, there are important complications in the fiduciary setting. For one thing, loyalties are not necessarily moral; in some cases an expression of loyalty can even be morally noxious. We shouldn't assume that if we accommodate extra-legal loyalty we are invariably accommodating morally desirable behaviour. In addition, loyalty is a multi-faceted practice, with significant variations across types. If we accommodate one type of loyalty, we may fail to accommodate another type.

Even if loyalty is not moral, Gold suggests we have reasons to accommodate extra-legal forms of loyalty, given the central role loyalty plays in our ground projects, the settings in which loyalty involves deeply felt commitments, and the various ways in which loyalty connects with personal life decisions. The distinct types of loyalty practice, however, mean that we cannot just pick an overarching legal category of loyalty and hope for convergence with the extra-legal. The law will inevitably diverge from loyalty practices outside the law. Instead, variety in forms of loyalty calls for legal doctrine that will enable choices. Gold proposes a number of mechanisms for accommodating extra-legal loyalty duties, such as vagueness in the law or the availability of contractual modifications. On the other hand, these distinctive mechanisms may each respond to different reasons for accommodation. As he suggests, determining how best to accommodate loyalty will also require us to figure out why we want to accommodate.

Stephen Smith's chapter offers an important contrast. Rather than argue that fiduciary loyalty diverges from extra-legal loyalty, Smith contends that the 'loyalty' required by fiduciary law isn't really properly conceptualized as a form of loyalty. As he argues: 'not only is loyalty not a central concern of fiduciary law, it is not a

[26] See Seana Valentine Shiffrin, 'The Divergence of Contract and Promise' (2007) 120 Harv L Rev 708.

concern at all.'[27] Fiduciaries have a responsibility to perform their fiduciary mandates, but this is not the same thing as being loyal; indeed, in many cases it may be impossible for fiduciaries to be loyal. In part, this is because loyal relationships require a shared history—one cannot instantly become loyal to someone, yet fiduciary relationships implicate legally enforced obligations from the instant they are formed. There is also another challenge: loyal actors must act for the right motive. When we act loyally, we must be motivated at least partly by a prior commitment to our beneficiary. The classic no-conflict rule, however, is strikingly insensitive to motivation.

Drawing on these premises, Smith then offers related insights about other areas of fiduciary law, including the no-conflict rule, the no-profit rule, and the characteristic disgorgement remedies that courts provide. In doing so, he reaches a striking conclusion: most fiduciary law is best understood as a branch of contract law after all. In many cases, the fiduciary's mandate is contractual in the standard sense; in other cases, the mandate is at least voluntarily undertaken. Drawing on an analysis of how implied-in-fact duties work in the context of undertakings, Smith suggests that the core no-conflict duties in fiduciary law are implied-in-fact terms.

On Smith's view, the no-conflict rule is not designed to promote or support loyalty as loyalty is ordinarily understood outside the law. What most beneficiaries will want is for fiduciaries to perform their mandates properly, whatever their motives might be. Supposing that beneficiaries do not care about their fiduciaries' motives, Smith plausibly questions whether the law does, or should, seek such loyalty. In other words, there are reasons to doubt whether the no-conflict rule is designed to support loyalty in its ordinary, extra-legal sense. Smith suggests, instead, that the no-conflict rule is best understood as imposing a prophylactic duty, with the aim of increasing the likelihood that fiduciaries will comply with their mandates. The no-profit rule, in turn, can be seen as part of the no-conflict rule—and it too imposes a prophylactic duty.

Disgorgement remedies raise very interesting challenges under this approach. Smith rejects the deterrence rationale for disgorgement, and he also questions the primary right-based approaches developed by Paul Miller and Lionel Smith. Prophylactic duties have very distinctive features: their breach never results in a loss that is not otherwise compensable. As Smith argues, the point of a prophylactic duty is to decrease the risk that another duty will be breached. If the remedies for breach of a prophylactic duty are limited to compensatory damages, the prophylactic duty will be effectively unenforceable. How, then, should courts value a beneficiary's right that her fiduciary not make an unauthorized profit? Smith offers an answer that has broad implications: he suggests that disgorgement of profits provides an 'objective and proportionate representation of the infringed right'. The resulting account not only provides an important analysis of fiduciary law, it also

[27] Stephen A Smith, 'The Deed, Not the Motive: Fiduciary Law Without Loyalty' at p 213 in this volume.

offers new insights into the nature and purpose of prophylactic duties and the remedies for their breach.

John Goldberg and Benjamin Zipursky address a distinctive feature of fiduciaries' loyalty obligations. As they note, the loyalties that fiduciaries owe to their beneficiaries may generate conflict with other duties they owe to other persons, including the duties of care they owe to third parties. Focusing on doctor–patient and lawyer–client relationships, they provide a detailed analysis of the case law, demonstrating how the presence of a fiduciary loyalty duty may limit duties of care. For example, in a series of cases, parents have sued therapists for negligently causing children to recover false memories of sexual abuse by a parent. Courts are divided, but, in many cases, courts have found that a therapist treating a child owes no duties to the child's parents. This, in turn, raises a tort theory puzzle.

As these examples indicate, there are cases of professional misconduct in which what appears to be a privity limitation is barring claims based on injuries to third parties—cases which Goldberg and Zipursky refer to as 'triangular torts'. In other settings, tort law has rejected a privity rule, as evidenced in decisions like *MacPherson v Buick*. How should we explain the outcome in these cases? One possibility is that courts are simply applying a multi-factor policy analysis to determine that duties aren't owed to third parties. Goldberg and Zipursky suggest a different interpretation: 'the fiduciary nature of professionals' duties is given dispositive or near-dispositive weight'.[28]

Goldberg and Zipursky's reading also offers an interesting account of the reasons why fiduciary duties might diminish or crowd out other duties. The philosopher Bernard Williams famously suggested that certain relationships may call for heightened duties to individuals within those relationships. To use Williams' example, a man who has the ability to save only one of two people from drowning—one of whom is his wife—may have a duty to save his wife.[29] Goldberg and Zipursky emphasize that, in such cases, '*X's* special relationship to Y might not only intensify *X's* duties to Y, but might also diminish what would otherwise be *X's* duties to Z.'[30] On their view, tort law involves a similar phenomenon: the special relationship that fiduciaries participate in not only gives them heightened duties to their beneficiaries, it may curtail duties owed to third parties.

IV. Contract and Status within the Firm

The next two chapters focus on fiduciary relationships within the firm—a classic setting for both contractual and fiduciary obligations. One of the most fundamental

[28] John CP Goldberg and Benjamin C Zipursky, 'Triangular Torts and Fiduciary Duties' at p 263 in this volume.

[29] Bernard Williams, 'Persons, Character and Morality' in his *Moral Luck: Philosophical Papers 1973–80* (Cambridge University Press, 1980) at 1.

[30] Goldberg and Zipursky, (n 28) at p 266.

relationships within the firm is that between employers and employees. Aditi Bagchi looks into the nature of employees' loyalty duties, duties that courts sometimes describe as fiduciary and sometimes describe as contractual. As she points out, the effect of a loyalty duty on an employee's wellbeing is potentially great: employment relationships may dominate the lives of most employees, thus differing from many fiduciary settings. Bagchi concludes that as a general matter these loyalty duties are best understood as contractual. Moreover, she grounds employee loyalty in a particular type of contract term: the implied covenant of good faith and fair dealing.

As Bagchi indicates, the employer–employee relationship can be understood as a status-based relationship. She notes, however, that the modern view of employment status is only justified when it is protective of employees. Moreover, she emphasizes that different types of employees have very different degrees of power, and accordingly employee loyalty duties may appropriately vary with their role and responsibilities in the firm. There are employees who should be identified as fiduciaries: elite employees whose decisions cannot readily be regulated by clear decision rules ex ante, and whose decisions are not effectively policed by employers. For most employees, however, she suggests a non-fiduciary obligation. On Bagchi's view, 'we should impute only the loyalty requirements that are implicitly required under contract to preserve value for the employer in the face of potential opportunism.'[31]

Yet there are multiple ways in which an employee's loyalty could be understood as contractual. As Bagchi recognizes, loyalty could be an implied contractual term based on public policy, or it could be read into employment contracts in light of the parties' words and conduct. Bagchi suggests that the best interpretation is to see the employee's contractual duty of loyalty as a corollary of the duty of good faith and fair dealing. This view has the advantage of accounting for both the loyalty duty's mandatory nature and its mutability in light of specific contract terms. Bagchi also suggests that this contractual duty of loyalty should be read narrowly, and with particular consideration of the powers that employers have over employees in a given relationship. For example, in cases of at-will employment, she argues that a duty of loyalty should have limited scope since termination can already discipline employee behaviour. On this view, where employment agreements also limit employees' legal remedies for unlawful terminations, the duty of loyalty should be even more constrained. And, by the same token, where employment contracts give the employer wide discretion over an employee's obligations, the duty of loyalty ought to be correspondingly curtailed. The result is a duty of loyalty, but in a form that differs in important respects from the classic fiduciary version, and which is sensitive to asymmetries of power as they exist in particular employer–employee relationships.

Gordon Smith connects fiduciary relationships to the theory of the firm. Drawing on the property rights theory of the firm, Smith suggests that fiduciary law is a response to risks of opportunism that arise when one party exercises discretion over the critical resources of another. Accordingly, a key focus of this analysis is

[31] Aditi Bagchi, 'Exit, Choice, and Employee Loyalty' at p 273 in this volume.

the definition of a resource. Resources, for the purposes of fiduciary law, cover more than tangible assets, and in fact they extend beyond property in the legal sense—confidential information is an important example. On the other hand, there are limits to what counts as a resource. Human capital does not generally qualify, as it is not subject to the fiduciary's discretion. The resulting range of contexts potentially implicating fiduciary relationships is quite broad, but not unbounded.

With this framework in place, Smith then identifies a key difference between fiduciary law and contract law: the duties imposed on fiduciaries 'are not designed to fill gaps in [the parties'] contract, but rather to protect the resources of the beneficiary'.[32] Indeed, from this perspective, one of the striking features of fiduciary law is what it shares with a different private law institution: the law of property. Fiduciaries have a broad discretion over resources that belong to the beneficiary, and this discretion is similar to the discretion possessed by an owner. At the same time, this ownership-like authority over another's resources is constrained by duties that are personal to the fiduciary. For Smith, fiduciary law has both contract-like and property-like features, with fiduciary law ultimately being a hybrid institution.

Smith's account provides insights into the content of fiduciary duties, the nature of the wrong when a breach occurs, and the characteristic remedies provided by fiduciary law. Fiduciary loyalty, for example, is understood in light of the concern that a fiduciary will take advantage of her discretion over the beneficiary's resources. The duty of loyalty is responsive to the risk that fiduciaries will engage in self-interested behaviour, misusing their discretion. In many cases, such behaviour will result in the fiduciary acquiring resources—including opportunities—that properly belong to or should belong to the beneficiary. Accordingly, a breach is often explicable as a form of misappropriation (although in non-loyalty cases it may instead involve imposition of harm on the beneficiary). Disgorgement remedies, in turn, are designed to deprive a disloyal fiduciary of any gains from misappropriation of a beneficiary's resources.

V. The Fiduciary State and the Institution of Contract

Finally, we can analyse the relation between contract law and fiduciary law from a political theory perspective. Contract principles are an established source of insights into the State's obligations to its citizens, not to mention its claim to authority. Recently, theorists have developed a series of fiduciary accounts of the State and of public-office holders. One of the key things that the State provides for, however, is contract law itself. The idea that the State is a fiduciary gives us a distinctive framework for assessing contract law, both as it exists and also as it might be reformed.

Margaret Jane Radin's contribution considers what contract law should look like if the State is understood as a fiduciary to its citizens. From this perspective,

[32] D Gordon Smith, 'Firms and Fiduciaries' at p 307 in this volume.

fiduciary principles ought to govern how the State shapes contract law doctrine, and in particular they indicate that the State must protect the right to a redress of grievances. A central focus of Radin's paper is the harm caused by mass-market boilerplate when it results in large-scale removal of legal rights to redress. Radin contends that certain rights should be market-inalienable, which means that they should be permanently in the care of the State as a fiduciary for its people. Her central claim is that legal rights to redress fall into this market-inalienable category. She develops three bases for this view: a commitment to the rule of law; the protection of basic human rights; and the need for solutions to coordination problems.

From a rule of law perspective, she contends that mass-market boilerplate that limits access to public redress of grievances 'undermines the value of equality before the law and abrogates the responsibility of the State to prevent the exercise of arbitrary power'.[33] One implication of these claims is that boilerplate should not just be assessed in terms of contractual formation and consent. Her human rights argument focuses on individual autonomy, freedom of speech, and privacy. She argues that in different ways each may be implicated by mass-market boilerplate (eg, if boilerplate undermines a practice of private ordering, or if boilerplate requires non-publication of critical comments about a product). Her coordination argument focuses on the ways in which rights enacted by the State can solve coordination problems. Radin contends that a fiduciary State will not allow mass-market terms that undermine a collective commitment to rule-based social coordination.

Interestingly, Radin's account also calls for an application of fiduciary principles at multiple levels. In developing the argument that the State should protect against the effects of mass-market boilerplate, she concludes that the recipients of boilerplate rights deletions are 'in the position of the unfairly disappointed beneficiary of a fiduciary relationship'.[34] But she also describes public fiduciary principles at the level of office holders. In Radin's view, 'American constitutional law, under a principle of fundamental fairness, holds that every injured party must have her day in court. American constitutional law is in the guardianship of the courts.'[35] From this perspective, the courts occupy a distinctively fiduciary role—that of guardianship—and they have a distinctive beneficiary as well. In other words, contracts are not only significant from the perspective of the fiduciary State, they are also significant from the perspective of fiduciary judges.

Contract, status, and fiduciary law intersect in multiple ways. As the chapters in this volume show, fiduciary relationships can be understood as contract-based or status-based, and as both contract- and status-based. Understanding the implications can tell us a great deal that is of equal interest for contract and fiduciary law. There is, of course, a longstanding divide between contractarian and anti-contractarian

[33] Margaret Jane Radin, 'The Fiduciary State and Private Ordering' at p 320 in this volume.
[34] Ibid at p 325.
[35] Ibid at p 327.
For an account of judges as fiduciaries to the people (rather than to constitutional law), see Ethan J Leib and others, 'A Fiduciary Theory of Judging' (2013) 101 Cal L Rev 699.

approaches to fiduciary law. While the present volume offers new insights for that debate, many of the chapters contend with quite different issues. It is the interaction of contract and fiduciary principles that these chapters seek to understand.

As is true of private law more generally, some of the most difficult questions arise along the boundaries between fields. Attending to these questions produces interesting insights. For example, it may well be the case that fiduciary loyalty isn't really a form of loyalty properly so called. Or, that fiduciary relationships involve a type of loyalty that curtails tort law duties of care. Or, that fiduciary relationships occupy multiple places along a continuum between status and contract. Fiduciary status, in turn, may take both legal and extra-legal forms, and loyalty obligations may stem from both law and society. For that matter, on some views loyalty obligations may fall into multiple legal categories—perhaps they can be fiduciary or contractual, depending on the context.

Fiduciary law is increasingly recognized as a distinct field, with its own unique concerns. Yet, in various settings—ranging from employment law, to professional relationships between doctors and patients or lawyers and clients, to political theory—it is the interactions between fiduciary and other fundamental principles that raise the most pressing and significant conceptual and normative challenges. This volume aims to clarify what is at stake, and in the process to offer new insights into fiduciary law and surrounding fields.

PART I

CONTRACT, STATUS, AND FIDUCIARY RELATIONSHIPS

1

The Idea of Status in Fiduciary Law

Paul B Miller

I. Introduction

Fiduciary law, like so many other areas of law, relies on formal methods of categorization of particulars. It does so in part for reasons that are common. Methodical categorization enables legal actors to recognize and sort social phenomena in ways that generate meaning or make sense of social patterns with which the law is confronted. Furthermore, in many cases methodical categorization is integral to the law's aims, including its aims to effectively regulate and coordinate human behaviour, to provide stable, intelligible forms of interaction and association, and to ensure consistency and coherence in the law and its enforcement.

Fiduciary law relies specifically on methods of relationship categorization. In determining whether fiduciary liability rules apply, a court must first decide whether there was a fiduciary relationship. The law can and does rely on a number of methods of categorization in making this determination, some of which are familiar and relatively well understood. But, strikingly, the most prominent one is not. In most cases, fiduciary law relies on status as a method of relationship categorization.[1] The prominence of status-based categorization in fiduciary law should be obvious. Most jurists, to the extent that they are familiar with fiduciary law at all, know that it involves the imposition of a duty of loyalty in certain kinds of relationship. These kinds of relationship have fiduciary status inasmuch as the parameters of the kind are thought to be dispositive of the question whether or not the relationship is fiduciary. The average jurist, if asked who or what a fiduciary is, would likely refer to kinds of relationship that have recognized fiduciary status. She would refer to relationships between lawyers and clients, directors and corporations, agents and principals, and trustees and beneficiaries. If asked *why* these kinds of relationship have fiduciary status—or, perhaps, why others do not—our jurist may have

[1] Some think that fiduciary relationships are incomprehensible absent reference to status and that fiduciary law's reliance on status marks an essential point of distinction between it and contract law. See, notably, Daniel Markovits, 'Sharing *Ex Ante* and Sharing *Ex Post*: The Non-Contractual Basis of Fiduciary Relations' in Andrew S Gold and Paul B Miller eds, *Philosophical Foundations of Fiduciary Law* (Oxford University Press, 2014) 209.

difficulty providing a satisfactory answer. She might even be genuinely puzzled precisely because status dominates the categorization of relationships in fiduciary law. Attributions of status are, after all, everywhere in evidence in fiduciary law—in legislated fiduciary standards, as much as in judge-made law.

For all its prominence, the idea of status in fiduciary law is nevertheless perplexing for several reasons, all going to a lack of clarity surrounding the concept.[2] First, the juridical basis of attributions of fiduciary status is opaque. Second, the precise juridical effects of an attribution of status are uncertain (that is, the effect of an attribution of status on legal reasoning and, specifically, on determinations of liability). Third, the social, economic, and other functions of fiduciary status are largely unknown. Fourth, the relationship between fiduciary status and contract is unclear, particularly in respect of their respective implications for the formation of fiduciary relationships and justification of fiduciary duties. Finally, the relationships between fiduciary and other forms of status (legal and otherwise) are unclear.

This chapter examines the idea of status in fiduciary law. Its primary aim is to explain and defend the claim that attributions of status in fiduciary law are inherently provisional, conceptually and normatively. Attributions of fiduciary status are provisional conceptually in that they (a) presume the coherence of a concept of the fiduciary relationship; (b) make necessary (if indirect) reference to that concept; and (c) and are therefore contestable conceptually (ie, the reference may be imperfect). They are provisional normatively in that their legitimacy turns on (a) the cogency of the attribution of status to a particular kind of relationship, and to a given relationship treated as an instantiation of that kind; and (b) the actual normative salience of properties of relationships thought to justify the attribution of fiduciary status in general.

In order to make these points, I shall address fiduciary status from several perspectives. I begin, in Section II, by explaining the nature of fiduciary status and by contrasting it with other status concepts. I proceed, in Section III, to consider the functions served by attributions of fiduciary status. In Section IV, I canvass different views about the basis of fiduciary status and offer a novel account of my own. The conclusion summarizes the argument and suggests some of its implications.

II. Fiduciary and Other Statuses

A. Statuses in general

Any attempt to clarify fiduciary status is immediately confronted with the problem that status concepts have different meanings, and are used in different ways, in the law and more broadly. All conceptions of status arguably reflect a struggle to

[2] Of course, legal statuses are in general perplexing, as Austin recognized in observing—no doubt, with a healthy measure of overstatement—that: '[t]o determine precisely what a Status is … [is] the most difficult problem in the whole science of jurisprudence.' John Austin, *Lectures on Jurisprudence* (John Murray, 1885) 389–90.

overcome limitations of human rationality; in particular, in our perceived (perhaps, in many cases, real) need to make and rely upon simplifying assumptions about the normative position of others in developing, participating in, and otherwise making use of complex normative systems (systems through which we attempt to bring about political, social, and/or moral order).

It is sometimes assumed, incorrectly, that all statuses are attributions of normative standing made of others irrespective of their will and that statuses are thus invariably in tension with respect for individual autonomy and related values in law (including freedom of contract). In fact, many statuses are achieved rather than ascribed, whether they are actively sought and formally conferred, or voluntarily undertaken with little ceremony. But whether a particular status is ascribed or achieved, its normative meaning and implications are not determined by the person who achieves or is assigned it.[3] Statuses reflect a prevailing need or desire of society to make simplifying assumptions about the normative position of others and for that reason the attribution, meaning and precise normative implications of statuses are socially mediated (either through diffuse channels or in a structured way through social, legal, and political institutions). Even where a valued status is achieved by a person entirely through her own efforts, the status is valued almost entirely because of the social meaning attached to it, and conditions of achievement are socially determined.

Statuses can be differentiated by type as being derived from law, from moral principles, or from social structures and/or practices. In other words, a particular status may be a legal status, a moral status, or a social status.[4] To better appreciate differences between these kinds of status, it may be useful to attend to the following dimensions of status concepts: (a) what attribution of the kind of status involves in

[3] Hence the humour in efforts, real or feigned, by persons to devise titles, positions, or other tokens of status or rank for themselves.

[4] While I think it is possible, and important, to distinguish legal statuses from social and moral ones, I do not mean to imply that these statuses are invariably or even generally mutually exclusive. Indeed, there is good reason to believe that certain legal statuses are, and ought to be, informed by a proper appreciation of moral status (eg, the legal status of personality ought to be afforded to beings with a moral claim of recognition as persons, and it is a sad fact that law and morality have historically diverged on this point). Similarly, history reveals that in some cases legal statuses have institutionalized pernicious social ones and in doing so have underwritten conflicts between legal and moral status. See generally Jack M Balkin, 'The Constitution of Status' (1997) 106 Yale Law Journal 2313 at 2314: 'law is usually complicit in the preservation of existing social structure' and at 2325: 'law often directly reflects social status or helps preserve status markers. Sometimes law helps constitute hierarchies of social status directly. Examples are nineteenth century doctrines regarding slaves. Jim Crow laws, laws against miscegenation, and rules about the comparative political and property rights of men and women.' Equally, as Balkin and others have shown, some struggles for legal status—eg, for the status of marriage—are best understood as elements of broader conflict over social status. Balkin, ibid, at 2320: 'many of the struggles that define America's "culture wars" … are really battles over social status and social structure. The combatants are fighting over whether an existing form of social stratification will prevail or be transformed.' Finally, it should be recognized that in some cases legal statuses that have no direct corollary in social status nevertheless have distinctive social meanings. Consider, for example, social meanings attached to the legal status of a bankrupt or a felon. For an account of legal status that (in my view, wrongly) assimilates it with social status, see Rehbinder's discussion of status as a Weberian 'ideal type'. Manfred Rehbinder, 'Status, Contract, and the Welfare State' (1971) 23 Stan L Rev 941, 942.

the normative system(s) in which the status figures; (b) what, in general, ideas of status of that kind might designate within these normative system(s); (c) the kinds of properties of persons, relationships, or groups that particular statuses might make reference to in defining normative positions for the purposes of the normative system(s) in which they figure; (d) the kinds of normative implication that can be borne by attributions of status; and (e) the social origins and sites for determining the meaning and attribution of statuses.

B. Social status

We may begin with a familiar kind of status—social status. Social statuses reflect efforts to categorize persons, relationships, and social groups by position in a social structure. Many sociologists consider social statuses to be core, constitutive elements of social structures.[5] It is conceivable that in a truly egalitarian society, social status could denote normative position by reference to the kind of social role performed by a person, relationship or group, and as such simply reflect differentiation in social organization without implying anything about relative social value (and, in turn, the esteem due to a person, relationship, or group). Nevertheless, as Balkin and others have shown, even in democratic societies with a robust commitment to equality, attributions of social status often create and perpetuate structural social inequality.

As is true of all forms of status, social statuses are relatively stable across time, reflect relative differentiation (ie, statuses are defined in relation to one another), and are based on implicit or explicit conditions of attribution. Unlike other forms of status, social statuses are a product of diffuse channels in society at large and may over time be contested and revised to reflect broader changes in law, public opinion, and conventional morality.

Social statuses are wider ranging than other forms of status in terms of the kinds of normative position they denote, and in terms of what positioning by status invites us to assume about the normatively salient properties of persons, relationships, and groups. Marxists have tended to emphasize socioeconomic status (personal wealth and economic class), employment status (prestige or reputation), and relationships of production in economic organization (status and hierarchy in the workplace). Others have noted that social statuses have, historically, been assigned on the basis of age, race, ethnicity, gender, sexual orientation, religious affiliation, language, physical appearance and ability, education, employment, social affiliations and involvements, professional and personal achievements, and family structure: bases

[5] See R Linton, *The Study of Man* (Appleton-Century, 1936); E A Shils and H Goldhamer, 'Types of Power and Status' (1939) 45 American Journal of Sociology 267; Michael Argyle, 'The Concepts of Role and Status' (1952) The Sociological Review 39; W Goldschmidt, 'Social Class and the Dynamics of Status in America' (1955) 57 American Anthropologist 1209; Gottfried Lang, 'The Concepts of Status and Role in Anthropology: Their Definition and Use' (1956) 17 American Catholic Sociological Review 206; and Frederick Bates, 'Position, Role, and Status: A Reformulation of Concepts' (1956) 34 Social Forces 313.

of social differentiation some of which are, unsurprisingly, amongst the most widely recognized grounds of discrimination. Indeed, the correlation between attributions of social status and discriminatory attitudes and behaviour explains the wariness that most now bear toward social practices that invoke or place reliance on differentiation by social status.

The implications of social statuses are complex in part because of wide variation between kinds and social origins of social statuses, ongoing contestation and social change in respect of some statuses, and differences in the social functions of various social statuses. In some cases, social positions designated by social statuses may be mere markers of social identity and/or grounds for differentiation by social function, but, in many cases, status is treated as a basis for attribution of value, and for communication of social judgement (whether the attribution of value supports equal treatment of persons within or between statuses or, as has more often been the case, is understood as a basis for treating people in a discriminatory fashion, as more or less worthy of respect, acceptance, and/or admiration). Social status therefore ordinarily denotes normative position as a matter of social rank in light of attributions of value made by society as a matter of conventional morality. Given that social statuses embed attributions of value made as a matter of conventional morality, the meaning and ascription of value to a particular status is susceptible to change wrought by associated shifts in conventional morality.

C. Moral status

While the idea of social status is familiar, the notion of moral status may be less so. Claims about status in morality tend to be rather narrow. In most circumstances, moral statuses are posited as constraints on the invocation of, or reliance on, social statuses, or otherwise as giving reason for reform or rejection of a social status. Moral status, so understood, provides a vantage point for the critique of social statuses precisely because posited criteria of moral status depart from conclusions of conventional morality that support social statuses. Contrasting claims of moral status with brute (and often discomfiting) social facts about social statuses often reveals conventional morality to be illogical and insidious. Indeed, these accounts give reason for questioning entire social practices of assigning social statuses (and of tolerating status-based social structures) on the basis of conventional morality.

Consistent with this, moral status is often presented as a levelling concept; as one the acceptance of which entails denying the moral salience of distinctions between persons, relationships, or groups made as a matter of social status in favour of some universal measure of moral status (ie, some moral reason or set of reasons for equal consideration and treatment). Thus Jeremy Waldron has invoked the idea of the equal moral status of persons (reflecting an innate claim we all have to equal dignity and respect) in justifying principles of equality that forbid discrimination and support human rights.[6]

[6] Waldron, for example, appeals to the idea of equal moral status as a basis for, or entailment of, (it is unclear which) the principle of moral equality: 'the principle of basic equality commits us to the

Turning our attention from the use that has been made of ideas of moral status, we may briefly note the following points of comparison. First, as is true of statuses in general, attributions of moral status reflect an underlying preoccupation with categorization (in particular, with the actual moral salience of bases for designating—and so describing—the moral position of persons, relationships, and groups in one way or another). Second, as is again true of other forms of status, moral statuses refer to the normative position of a person, relationship, or group relative to others to whom that status, or related statuses, might apply. This is true regardless whether status is invoked as a levelling concept or as a basis for signifying morally salient differences in position. Thus, for example, Waldron's invocation of the idea of moral status is intended to signify an innate moral equality in the normative position of all persons, while attributions of different ranks of achieved (and, more controversially, ascribed) moral status purport to define normative positions held by persons or groups in an ordinal way.[7]

Moral status is often (problematically, for reasons that will become clear in Section III) invoked without reference to its moral basis and associated moral reasons for recognition and attribution of the status. That being said, claims about moral status implicitly refer to morally salient properties of *persons* (eg, their rationality or sentience), *relationships* (especially the special moral character or value of relationships of friendship and kinship), and *groups* (eg, a group's moral status as historically oppressed and so worthy of heightened moral consideration by virtue of the unjust historical attribution of diminished social status). The precise normative implications of moral statuses depend on the kind of status and whether it is ascribed or achieved. Where ascribed moral status is invoked as a levelling concept, it is (as noted earlier) often taken to imply the innate and inherently equal moral value of the persons, relationships, or groups to which it applies. Where moral status is invoked as designating morally salient differences, it implies the existence of moral reasons supporting differentiation by status. Whatever the implications of a particular moral status, they are, unlike social statuses, not contingent upon extant social structures and the presuppositions of conventional morality. Instead, moral status is something that all moral agents are properly concerned with, in respect of themselves and in respect of others, and attribution and recognition of moral status may be understood as an ineliminable feature of individual moral judgement.

ideal of a single-status moral community. We all have the same moral status … We are all on the same footing morally, irrespective of race, sex, birth, wealth, or national or communal membership … The idea of single moral status conveys that we all have the same basic moral rights and we labor under the same array of basic moral duties.' Jeremy Waldron, 'Does "Equal Moral Status" Add Anything to Right Reason?' (2011) NYU School of Law Public Law Research Paper No. 11–52 at 2, online: <http://papers.ssrn.com/sol3/papers.cfm?abstract_id=1898689>. See also Jeremy Waldron, *Dignity, Rank, and Rights* (Oxford University Press, 2012) at 57: 'I think it is part of our modern notion of law that almost all … gross status differences have been abandoned. We have adopted the idea of a single-status system, evolving a more or less universal status—a more or less universal legal dignity—that entitles everyone to something like the treatment before law that was previously confined to high-status individuals.'

[7] Waldron, 'Equal Moral Status' (n 6) and Waldron, *Dignity, Rank, and Rights* (n 6).

D. Legal status

Legal statuses, like other statuses, are categories that designate the normative position of persons, relationships, and groups (including associations and organizations) within a complex normative system – the legal system. Perhaps because legal statuses are familiar features of legal systems, they have sometimes been used as a reference point in theoretical analyses of social and moral statuses.[8] But this is unfortunate because legal statuses are distinctive[9] and their distinctiveness matters in understanding the ways in which legal statuses interact with social and moral statuses.

Whereas social and moral statuses denote normative position as a matter of social perception[10] and moral judgement, legal statuses do so juridically. To say this is not merely to observe (tritely) that such statuses are recognized by law; legal statuses are juridical in the further and more fundamental sense of being constituted juridically. That is, they are defined in terms of juridical concepts within a normative system that is itself constructed juridically and which must function (at least in part) for legal or juridical ends. Legal statuses, so understood, denote the normative position of persons, relationships, or groups through categorical allocation of different set packages of jural standing(s) and relations. More specifically, legal statuses may denote the jural standing of persons by delineating the legal capacities they have relative to a norm (ie, normative status) of full personal legal capacity (as is true of the statuses attributed to children and corporations). Additionally or alternatively, legal statuses may be a basis for the attribution of specific sets of legal powers, rights, and privileges, or liabilities, duties, and disabilities to persons on the basis of their personality as such or on the basis of the relationships, associations, or other groups to which they belong.[11] The fact that legal statuses are so constituted should

[8] Waldron recognizes that legal conceptions of status diverge from moral ones, and his argument that a kind of universal moral status underlies human rights seems to commit him to the view that moral statuses have a normative salience independently of posited legal ones. Yet Waldron places considerable reliance on legal statuses in adumbrating the idea of moral status. See Waldron, 'Equal Moral Status' (n 6) at 2: 'Obviously the idea of status that is used here is a legal concept, and its use in the moral context is based on analogies with its use in the legal context.' See also Waldron, *Dignity, Rank, and Rights* (n 6) at 36 and 47. As I shall explain below, it is not obvious that any conception of status can be normatively basic in the way that he assumes.

[9] As Jack Balkin recognized, (n 4) at 2324: '[L]awyers have their own concept of "status" which is used in a number of different contexts and forms the basis of many different doctrines … the legal and sociological concepts are importantly different.' Balkin is correct that social and legal statuses differ but errs in differentiating them according to whether the status is ascribed to an individual or a group. According to Jack Balkin, legal status is a property of individuals whereas social status is a property of groups, and of individuals solely in respect of their membership in socially stratified groups. This is simply untrue. The law ascribes legal statuses to groups, from families to corporations. And similarly certain social statuses—and especially achieved ones—are ascribed to individuals in recognition of individual rather than group properties (eg, a powerful, resilient, and strategic fighter may be ascribed the status 'good fighter' without there being a defined social group 'good fighters'; the ascription of that status turns on personal qualities possessed by an individual that are marked by the status granted to her).

[10] Jack Balkin (n 4) at 2321: 'Social status is the degree of prestige and honor that individuals or groups enjoy. The prestige involves the approval, respect, admiration, or positive qualities imputed to a person or group.'

[11] Compare Waldron, 'Equal Moral Status' (n 6) at 4: 'A status comprises a set of rights, duties, capacities, incapacities, and liabilities which the law has determined should be borne by people of a certain class or in a situation or predicament.'

be evident from even brief consideration of well-known modern legal statuses (eg, the individual status of a minor or a bankrupt, the relational status of marriage, or the institutional status of a charity). Consider the legal status of minors. This status includes limitations on legal capacity that curtail the minor's ability to make legally effective decisions and to participate in certain legal institutions; it similarly gives rise to limitations on the enjoyment or exercise of certain legal rights, powers and privileges (eg, the right to vote or the privilege of driving) and supports the suspension of certain liabilities and duties (eg, the liability to certain forms of criminal punishment and the duty to perform jury service).

Legal statuses also differ from other statuses in the manner in which they are constructed, attributed, contested, and revised. Moral and social statuses largely develop organically and informally, reflecting the influence of a variety of factors that shape individual moral judgement and conventional morality. Legal statuses, by contrast, are the product of the law and of legal institutions, as is consistent with the fact that they denote normative positions for the purposes of the law as a normative system. Of course, social statuses (and, arguably, implicit claims of moral status) are often incorporated in the law, and the law accordingly frequently becomes a site for social, moral, and political conflict over status. But legal statuses are determined as a matter of positive law and as such by, and within, legal institutions.

Unsurprisingly, given that legal statuses are a product of law, the processes of constructing, applying for, and/or attributing, and challenging the construction and/or attribution of legal statuses, are highly formal and are ritualized in the way that other legal proceedings are. Thus, for example, the legal statuses of a charity, bankrupt, felon, and minor have been developed in an incremental way by courts and legislators over centuries. The semantics of statuses are carefully honed in law, partly because of the deliberative processes through which they are constructed, and partly because legal statuses serve important technical functions in the law and in legal processes. The attribution and contestation of legal statuses is also usually distinctively deliberate, involving formal legal transactions or proceedings that signal, in part, public ratification of the attribution of status or public notice of same. So, for example, the civil status of marriage is formalized not merely through social rituals reflecting its social significance but also through bureaucratic processes reflecting its legal significance (eg, the issuance and registration of marriage licences). Similarly, the status of a minor is formalized not merely in the express provisions of law through which the status and its implications are articulated, but also in processes through which the status is challenged or made subject to a petition for partial suspension (eg, a teenager's petition for a declaration of emancipation).

Fiduciary status is, evidently, a legal status. It is a normative position defined juridically, primarily in terms of the powers, duties, and liabilities of the fiduciary.[12] While some legal statuses are attributed to persons and groups, fiduciary status is

[12] Though, because the status applies to the fiduciary ordinarily in virtue of her relationship to a beneficiary or benefactor, it is also a basis for the attribution of primary and secondary rights relative to the mandate undertaken by the fiduciary.

an attribution made of relationships.[13] Some fiduciary statuses are established by common law, others by statute. But the normative implications of fiduciary status are uniform; it entails designation of a particular kind of relationship (eg, doctor-patient) as being of a particular legal form (ie, fiduciary relationship), with the usual normative implications for our understanding of the juridical situation of the parties.

III. The Functions of Fiduciary Status

We have said that all status concepts provide categorical designation of the normative position of persons, relationships, or groups in normative systems. All status concepts are, for better or for worse (and, unfortunately, it has often been the latter), borne of our need or desire to categorize (to place, order, and organize) people. Equally, for ease of categorization, attributions of status involve (embed, and invite) simplifying assumptions about matters material to the normative position they designate. So far, so good. But, one might object, there is residual ambiguity. I have said that statuses are categorical designations of normative position in normative systems. But how, exactly, do statuses designate? And what do they designate? Answering these questions is critical to understanding how statuses function.

We may address the latter question quickly because it does not admit of a general answer. Different statuses designate different things about the normative position of the person, relationship, or group to whom or to which they apply. In some cases it might not be clear what, exactly, a status designates (in which case we have reason to question reliance on it). In other cases, customary usage of a status concept may provide a reliable indication of what it designates. In still other cases, it will be impossible to concisely say what a status designates because it designates a complex array of propositions about the normative position of persons, relationships, or groups encompassed by it. Because it is not possible to give a general answer to the question what statuses designate, we need not be detained by this issue at present. However, it is important to recognize that we would not progress very far in our effort to understand fiduciary status if we were unable to say what *it* designates. This question is therefore taken up in Section IV, below.

[13] Interestingly, on Maine's account, status was understood restrictively in terms of powers and privileges attached to membership and positions within the hierarchical structure of families. Thus, he claimed that, 'All the forms of Status taken notice of in the Law of Persons were derived from, and to some extent are still coloured by, the powers and privileges anciently residing in the Family.' Henry Maine, *Ancient Law* (John Murray, 1861) 170. Status in this sense is ascribed rather than acquired and is possessed only in virtue of one's membership within a group, such as a family, that itself is the primary bearer of legal and/or social standing. Maine's widely cited claim that progressive societies are marked by the ascendance of contract and diminution of status as modes of social and legal ordering is widely misinterpreted and overextended because scholars have failed to realize that his conception of status is focused narrowly on ascribed legal statuses linked to the family as a unit of social and legal organization. On this latter point, see Geoffrey MacCormack, 'Status: Problems of Definition and Use' (1984) 43 Cambridge Law Journal 361, 362–63.

We may now consider the question of the sense in which statuses designate. This question, fortunately, does admit of a general answer. There is an obvious sense in which statuses designate categorically—ie, they define a normative position, a position to which persons or groups are assigned through the attribution of status. For example, the legal status of a bankrupt designates that the person to whom it attaches is (because he has been declared to be) a bankrupt. But statuses designate in a deeper and more interesting sense than this. They designate not merely a normative position but also *concepts* (a concept, or network of concepts) associated with the definition of that position and *reasons* (moral, juridical, and otherwise) for the existence and attribution of the status (ie, for defining the normative position in a particular way, and for believing that the status is salient in general and as applied to particular persons, relationships, and groups).[14] It is for this reason that I have said that attributions of fiduciary status entail conceptually and normatively provisional claims about the relationships to which they attach.[15]

Of course, in some cases, a particular status may not designate particularly well. It may be, for example, that the conceptually provisional claims embedded in the attribution of status will prove dubious due to the incoherence of the concept(s) designated by the status, or due to conceptual error in the attribution of the status in a particular case. Equally, and perhaps more obviously, the normatively provisional claims embedded in an attribution of status may be indefensible. It may be that purported reasons for recognizing an entire status designation are bad or worse, and/or these reasons may be defeated by competing normative considerations in general or in a particular case. Troublingly, these frailties often go unnoticed. All status designations are presented as legitimate (ie, as meaningful and justifiable) categorizations.[16] But recognition of their inherent limitations suggests that status concepts should be invoked only from a critical, reflective posture: one in which it is recognized that status can only be premised on provisional claims about the normative position of the persons, relationships, or groups to which or to whom it is attributed.

Having clarified how status concepts in general function semantically and normatively, we are now in a position to consider the particular functions served by the idea of status in fiduciary law.

[14] This way of construing the abstract function of status concepts is, I think, consistent with Waldron's suggestion that they are abbreviating concepts: 'In law … status seems to operate as an abbreviating concept: it sums up information about a person's legal or moral position.' Waldron, 'Equal Moral Status' (n 6) at 3.

[15] To the extent that status designations entail *simplifying* assumptions, it might seem to go without saying that the conceptual and normative entailments of a particular status designation will often be quite complex; all the more so in conceptually elaborate normative systems like formal legal systems.

[16] Waldron, referring to the status of 'alien' explains: 'the idea of alienage [as a legal status] tells us something about the *rationale* of these provisions [those that apply to aliens by virtue of their status, including the liability to deportation]; it makes sense of them; it indicates their *ground or reasons*. And the same is true of all statuses … Their primary structural presence in the law is *justificatory*: it works to package certain arrays of rights, duties, etc., under the auspices of *a certain entrenched concern* in the law.' 'Equal Moral Status' (n 6) at 8.

A. Juridical functions

We may begin by considering the juridical functions of fiduciary status. Recalling that all status concepts are categorization devices, the primary juridical function of fiduciary status is that of facilitating categorization of the kinds of circumstances in which fiduciary principles arise.

I have noted that reliance on any status concept entails acceptance of simplifying assumptions (in the form of implicit provisional conceptual and normative claims) about the normative position occupied by the persons, relationships, or groups to which or to whom a status is attributed. These assumptions operate (ie, are relied upon, and so permit status designations to function normally) at two levels, at least. The first is semantic: statuses are a tidy way of encapsulating the often complex semantic relationship between normative concepts that together fully articulate the normative position denoted by status. Statuses simplify semantically by giving us a provisional conceptual characterization of the normative position held by a person, relationship, or group, thereby relieving us of the burden of fully articulating (for ourselves or for others) our conceptualization of that position in each and every case in which we might have to refer to it. The second level at which status concepts function is deliberative: statuses simplify (narrow) practical reasoning, inviting those who rely upon them to bypass questions concerning the characterization of the normative position of a person, relationship, or group in favour of questions relating to the normative consequences of occupation of that position in a particular case.

Fiduciary statuses involve simplifying assumptions that operate (and so permit the status concept to function, juridically) at both levels. A well settled designation of fiduciary status generates a strong presumption that particular relationships falling within the kind to which status attaches are themselves fiduciary relationships. Recourse to fiduciary status in these cases involves semantic simplification in the sense that courts need not explain precisely what it means to say that a particular relationship is fiduciary. It involves deliberative simplification in that reliance on status permits the court to bypass legal questions pertaining to the characterization of the parties' relationship in favour of different questions pertaining to the legal terms governing it (eg, questions concerning the interpretation and application of fiduciary duties, the availability and calculation of fiduciary remedies, and so on).

As noted earlier, fiduciary status attaches to particular kinds of relationship, many of which are now considered (if for no other reason than by virtue of time-worn status) to be quintessentially fiduciary (eg, trustee–beneficiary, agent–principal, and director–corporation relationships). In any event, the juridical effect of the attribution of fiduciary status to a kind of relationship is that presumptive fiduciary characterization is thereby extended to each and every particular relationship that falls within the kind. Thus, through the gradual extension of fiduciary status to several kinds of relationship, the courts needn't ask in most fiduciary cases what it means to say that a relationship is fiduciary. Furthermore, for the most part, the courts remain oblivious to the merely provisional nature of conceptual and normative claims embedded in attributions of fiduciary status (consistent with patterned acceptance of the simplifying assumptions embedded in attributions of status). Courts thus rarely ask, for example, whether it is meaningful to speak of fiduciary relationships as such, or about the reasons underlying the fiduciary characterization of particular relationships or kinds of relationship. They simply accept that it is meaningful and justifiable to speak of relationships as fiduciary and that a given relationship is fiduciary as a matter of status.

The juridical functions of legal statuses are primordial. Nevertheless, legal statuses do not exist in a vacuum. They are interpreted and applied informally in social contexts, much as they are formally in legal ones. Furthermore, history provides powerful illustrations of the interdependence of legal and social statuses. Legal statuses can encode social statuses for social or political purposes, and the law has a sorry history of encoding just those social statuses that are most objectionable. Equally, however, legal statuses inform social norms, structures and practices, and can generate parallel social statuses (consider the social stigma attached to the legal statuses of the bankrupt or felon). It is thus worth briefly considering the possible social and economic functions of fiduciary status.

B. Social and economic functions

Some of the social functions of fiduciary status are generic. As is true of reliance on other status concepts, reliance on attributions of fiduciary status eases cognitive burdens generated by actual normative complexity. But fiduciary status seems likely to have distinctive social functions as well.

As noted above, fiduciary statuses designate the legal nature of the relationship between persons in particular kinds of relationship. This default characterization means that relationships falling within the kind to which status attaches will ordinarily be treated in law as being of a fiduciary character, and as such will be subject to legal duties that collectively make it more likely that the fiduciary will prove true to the objects of her mandate. Where a designation of fiduciary status is (a) relatively well settled as a matter of authority, and (b) this fact is relatively widely known, the simplifying assumptions that a status invites juridically are likely to have corollaries for the social behaviour of those who may participate in, or engage with, fiduciary relationships in the law's shadow. Amongst these assumptions, a rather obvious one might be that it is (more) rational to trust in the behaviour of (if not the motivation) of others with whom one is contemplating entering a relationship founded on trust. If one can be relatively certain that the relationship will attract fiduciary impositions, demonstration of trust will be (more) warranted as fiduciary status alone gives the would-be fiduciary (additional) reason to behave in a trustworthy way. If fiduciary status provides a rational warrant of trustworthiness (even if only in a conditioned and limited way), it seems likely to influence the prudential reasoning and behaviour of persons considering whether to entrust care of their person or property to another.

Fiduciary status also likely has important economic functions. The simplifying assumptions invited by all status concepts promise cognitive efficiencies. Fiduciary status further promises associated institutional efficiencies by saving judges (and litigants) the trouble of developing and analysing duplicative arguments about the legal characterization to be placed on the kinds relationship to which attributions of status have been made. These efficiencies are almost certain to be correlated with economic efficiencies. The social costs of fiduciary litigation may be reduced to the extent that judges are spared the necessity of engaging in time consuming, and ordinarily redundant, legal analysis. The personal costs of fiduciary litigation for individuals may be reduced to the extent that fiduciary status relieves lawyers of the burden of developing intricate legal arguments about whether a particular relationship is fiduciary or not. Furthermore, fiduciary status may reduce information and transaction costs for parties considering entering relationships or undertakings in which one is to be granted discretionary power over the person or property of another. Finally, the expressive dimension of fiduciary status may generate efficiencies to the extent that a known status may be taken to be a reliable signal (for the parties' own sake) of their mutual expectation that all residual pecuniary gains resulting from their relationship (ie, gains other than those for which the fiduciary has contracted) will accrue to the beneficiary alone.

C. The functional limits of fiduciary status

The functions of fiduciary status discussed thus far reflect its nature as a status concept that designates a normative position by means of simplifying assumptions about the normatively salient properties of the relationships to which it attaches. We will return, in Section IV, to the question *what* fiduciary status designates, normatively. But we need first to consider the functional limits of fiduciary status. As we shall see, these limits also illustrate features that fiduciary status enjoys in common with other status concepts. The functional utility *and* limits of fiduciary status are equally a product of its capacity to reliably designate the presence of a fiduciary relationship.

The limits of fiduciary status are not always well appreciated. Indeed, courts have worried openly that undue reliance on status-based reasoning renders fiduciary law inflexible and insensitive both to its underlying principles and to tensions generated by the diversity of contexts in which fiduciary principles arise. But that needn't be the case. Even as a matter of doctrine, where the significance of fiduciary status is most obvious, the importance of status-based reasoning can be overstated. The limits of status-based reasoning are clearly illustrated in cases that lie at or beyond the margins of fiduciary status.

Consider first cases that are beyond status. These are cases in which the parties have not argued that theirs is a relationship of fiduciary status (and, often, could not plausibly argue for a novel attribution of status) but nevertheless maintain that it *is* fiduciary. Courts routinely decide cases like this, and do so by a methodology that involves a marked departure from status-based reasoning. In cases of this sort, courts analyse material facts pertaining to the relationship between the parties looking for hallmarks of a fiduciary relationship. These are cases of so-called ad hoc or *fact-based* relationship characterization, and they provide a clear illustration of the limits of fiduciary status: status designations are justified and are useful only where normatively salient features of persons, relationships, or groups conform to patterns that support a designation of normative position by status.

Now consider cases at the margins of status. One such category of case is that involving atypical relationships that fall within kinds of relationship with fiduciary status but which have idiosyncratic features that differentiate them materially from the archetypal relationship of that kind. Examples include cases featuring limited partners in limited partnerships (whose position is contrasted with that of general or managing partners), or doctors conducting non-invasive examinations of patients for insurers' or employers' purposes. Cases like this destabilize the application of established attributions of fiduciary status because they implicate departures from typical relational form that are, or might be, pertinent to proper application of a seemingly settled attribution of fiduciary status.[17] Reference to status is incapable of resolving doubt over how these cases should be decided; indeed, these cases are difficult precisely because they raise questions about the bases and extent of existing attributions of status.

Other cases test fiduciary status from the margins in a different way and raise important questions about the attribution of fiduciary status as such. Amongst these are cases involving disagreement about the propriety of a (usually, new or relatively recent) attribution of fiduciary status to a given kind of relationship (eg, whether parent–child and physician–patient relationships warrant fiduciary status). In these cases, the question is not whether relationships falling within a kind can sometimes be fiduciary; it is whether the kind itself merits fiduciary status because it is typically or, somehow, inherently fiduciary. A concept of status cannot be called upon in answering these questions because statuses are mere designations of normative position. Functionally, there is nothing for the concept of status to do in these cases, juridically or otherwise, because they involve questions about the appropriateness of an attribution of status rather than the ritual invocation of same.

The parts of fiduciary law that lie beyond fiduciary status are important because they remind us of the hazards of uncritical reliance on status concepts. Designations of fiduciary status are functionally valuable to the extent that they reliably signify the normative position of relationships to which the status attaches. But the prevalence of status-based reasoning can dull the mind to its inherent limitations. Status is always and everywhere a mere badge; a label devised for the purposes of categorization, driven by considerations of ease and expediency.[18] To understand a particular status—what *specifically* it signifies about a person, relationship, or group—one must look beyond it to what the status asks and invites us to *assume* about persons

[17] See John Glover, 'The Identification of Fiduciaries' in Peter Birks (ed), *Privacy and Loyalty* (Clarendon Press, 1997) 269, 270: 'recognition that there are accepted categories of fiduciaries does not take one far toward predicting the next extension of the fiduciary canon.'

[18] As Waldron recognized: 'Abbreviations can be helpful for certain practical purposes but it seems odd to invoke an abbreviation as a way of explicating something which is supposed to be fundamental.' 'Equal Moral Status' (n 6) at 3.

whose position is denoted by it, and further consider whether the normative implications that are to be attached to a position designated by status are justified. Failure to recognize the inherent limitations of status concepts will mean that we become blind to the risk (or reality) that our categorizations are faulty morally, empirically, or otherwise.

IV. Juridical Bases of Fiduciary Status

As we have seen, cases at the margins of fiduciary status force us to confront questions of *what* fiduciary status designates, conceptually and normatively. The question about conceptual designation has a simple answer; fiduciary status designates the presence of the fiduciary relationship (ie, a conceptually distinctive form of legal relationship).[19] But it is less clear what fiduciary status designates normatively; ie, the reasons(s) that justify characterizing a relationship as fiduciary. Fiduciary status is most often invoked unreflectively, but examination of case law and commentary reveal several distinct claims about the juridical bases of fiduciary status. I shall presently consider two possible (but ultimately implausible) bases of fiduciary status before considering a third which is, I think, capable of explaining not only where attributions of fiduciary status are warranted, but also why the margins of fiduciary status are defined by law as they are.

A. The incapacity of the beneficiary

One popular view holds that fiduciary status is premised on the legal incapacity of beneficiaries. On this view, fiduciary status is warranted on the basis that incapable persons are *ipso facto* unable to consent to the establishment of a fiduciary relationship (in contrast to ad hoc characterization, where evidence of mutual consent is essential). It is further thought to be justified on the basis of the protection fiduciary duties provide for dependent persons in relationships in which they must, by virtue of their incapacity, place trust in, or rely on, others. Fiduciary duties are, in turn, framed as a direct response to normatively salient features of the position of the beneficiary as an incapable person, notably, his inability to act autonomously in and through law to protect and advance his interests. The hallmark fiduciary duty of loyalty forbids fiduciaries from self-interested behaviour in all events, but in the context of relationships of fiduciary status, it forbids exploitation of vulnerabilities specifically occasioned by legal incapacity.

The suggestion that the incapacity of beneficiaries underlies fiduciary status is most clearly expressed in Kantian private law theory. The Kantians treat contract and fiduciary law as categorically distinct modes of private ordering. Fiduciary law governs relationships in which persons are incapable of consenting to interactions

[19] Paul B Miller, 'The Fiduciary Relationship' in Andrew S Gold and Paul B Miller (eds), *Philosophical Foundations of Fiduciary Law* (Oxford University Press, 2014) 63.

in which others act for them; incapacity is the juridical ground of a need of fiduciary representation. It is assumed, by contrast, that if a person enjoys full legal capacity, her voluntary interactions with others will take place on the footing of contract alone. A person with formal capacity to contract is assumed to have the actual capacity to protect and advance her interests through contract, and so to be without need of the protections that fiduciary law affords beneficiaries. Consider Arthur Ripstein's work, drawing on Kant's writings on legal status.[20] According to Ripstein:

> The category of status is just the category of cases in which persons find themselves in a relationship in which one party is not in a position to consent to the modification of the terms of that relationship. As a result, the other party is not allowed to enlist the nonconsenting party in the pursuit of his or her own ends ... There are many ... examples that fit this pattern. The legal relation between a fiduciary and a beneficiary is one such case.[21]

The suggestion here—that relationships of fiduciary status are of a piece with other relationships of status, being premised on the legal incapacity of a dependent—is not entirely far-fetched. Certainly attributions of fiduciary status have been made of kinds of relationship in which beneficiaries can be safely presumed legally incapable. Relationships between parents and children, and directors and corporations, come to mind. Furthermore, the suggestion that the incapacity of beneficiaries underlies fiduciary status resonates with leading analyses of legal status. As Graveson has explained, 'Maine himself excluded from his [conception of status] those personal conditions which resulted, immediately or remotely, from agreement'[22] because he 'favoured the generally accepted basis of status relationship[s], namely, the inability of persons subjected to status to form a judgment on their own interests'.[23]

Nevertheless, Ripstein errs in relying on this conception of status. I say this for two reasons. First, status concepts cannot reasonably be restricted to relationships featuring legal incapacity. While this blinkered view of legal status enabled Maine to highlight important changes in legal constructions placed on family relationships, it meant excluding statuses that must be based juridically on considerations other than personal legal capacity. One need only consider the (modern) status of marriage, or the statuses of a bankrupt, permanent resident, citizen, or felon,

[20] Specifically, Kant's discussion of 'rights to persons [that are] akin to rights to things' in his *Doctrine of Right*. See Immanuel Kant (Mary Gregor, trans and ed), *The Metaphysics of Morals* (Cambridge University Press, 1996).

[21] Arthur Ripstein, 'Authority and Coercion' (2004) 32 Philosophy & Public Affairs 2, 18. See also Arthur Ripsteim, *Force and Freedom* (Harvard University Press, 2009) 72–6. On the demarcation of fiduciary from contractual relationships, see Arthur Ripstein, 'Kant's Legal and Political Philosophy' in Thomas Hill (ed), *A Companion to Kant's Ethics* (Blackwell, 2009) 155: 'Contract covers the case in which parties interact interdependently and consensually ... In cases of contract, one person has the use of another's powers, as specified by their agreement, without having possession of the other person. Relations of status are the mirror image of contractual relations, because in relations of status one person has the possession of another but *not* the use of a person. Such relationships are possible when people interact interdependently, but non-consensually.'

[22] R H Graveson, 'The Movement from Status to Contract' (1941) 4 MLR 261, 262.

[23] Graveson (n 22) at 267.

to appreciate this. Second, it is simply incorrect to suggest that beneficiaries can safely be presumed incapable in all, or even most, relationships of fiduciary status. On the contrary, in most relationships they must be presumed fully capable. Just consider the implications of the Kantian view for our understanding of fiduciary relationships between business partners. Partnerships conduct business on the basis of reciprocal relationships of legal agency between the partners. These relationships give rise to reciprocal fiduciary duties which enjoin each partner to act for the mutual benefit of the partners collectively. If fiduciary status really were premised on the incapacity of beneficiaries, we would have to assume that partners are legally incapable of acting for their fellow partners (which is absurd, as it implies that partnerships are inherently inert) or that the relationship is not one of fiduciary status (which is untrue).

The recognition that legal incapacity cannot serve as a uniform juridical basis of fiduciary status[24] disrupts overly tidy Kantian thinking about the boundaries between fiduciary and contract law. The Kantians would have us believe that fiduciary status is imposed by law, but only where made necessary by the incapacity of a dependent, leaving to contract the full gamut of relationships of consensual exchange. The reality is, of course, far more complex. Many (but not all) fiduciary relationships are premised on the mutual consent of the parties, and sometimes this consent is given through contract. Furthermore, consent (and contract) underlie the formation of ad hoc fiduciary relationships, but equally are implicated in the formation of status-based fiduciary relationships. In such cases, fiduciary characterization of the kind of relationship is an imposition of law, but the decision whether to enter a relationship of that kind is normally contingent on establishment of common will between the parties.[25] Contract and consent are thus means by which particular relationships of status may be formed, much as they are modes of undertaking or entering into other relationships, offices, or positions to which a legal status is attached (as is reflected in consent rituals such as swearing oaths of office and making vows of marriage).

[24] One might argue that the Kantian approach can be rehabilitated by extending the meaning of 'incapacity' to include factual as well as legal bases of incapacity. Indeed, Evan Fox-Decent has written eloquently along these lines in his *Sovereignty's Promise: The State as Fiduciary* (Oxford University Press, 2011). Unfortunately, there are several problems with this approach. First, factual capacities differ from legal capacities in many respects, including their origins, inhibiting features or effects (with the inhibitory effect of factual incapacities varying remarkably and legal incapacity being generally absolute), and likely normative salience. Second, there is little reason to think that factual incapacities are stable across relationship types, and, indeed, there is much reason to think that they will be highly variable, making factual incapacity far less suitable a juridical basis for uniform status designations. And finally, most writing on factual incapacity in fiduciary relationships—including that of Fox-Decent—treats it as a material implication of the dependency engendered by an existing fiduciary relationship. In which case factual incapacity is (perhaps) a consequence of fiduciary relationships and not a basis for status-based relationship characterization.

[25] Graveson appreciated this point as one that holds for contractual undertakings of positions of status more generally: 'A confusion of thought is apparent in Maine's refusal to regard as status legal conditions resulting from agreements of certain kinds ... for it is not the agreement itself which secures the status, but the State alone when the agreement has been both made and performed according to its terms.' Graveson (n 22) at 262.

B. The social role of the fiduciary

Another popular view suggests that fiduciary status is based on judicial assessment of the social importance of social roles[26] occupied by fiduciaries. Proponents of this view point out that some of the best-known status-based fiduciary relationships feature fiduciaries who occupy prominent social roles. Proper performance of fiduciary mandates in these contexts is an essential element of role performance. Just consider the roles occupied by fiduciaries like parents, lawyers, physicians, and corporate officers. Each of these roles has undeniable social importance. The quality of modern health care depends considerably on the trust patients routinely place in physicians to protect their health. Investors risk capital in corporations on the understanding that executives will manage the entity soundly with a view to maximizing firm value and shareholder return. Similar points could be made about roles occupied and performed by other fiduciaries. The point that adherence to fiduciary strictures promotes role integrity also seems beyond serious doubt: a lawyer, physician, or corporate officer could hardly be understood as living up to their roles without demonstrating loyalty to those who rely on them in the performance of their roles.

For these reasons, it has been suggested that fiduciary statuses are role-based; status is reserved for relationships in which the fiduciary occupies an important social role, and, at least in the context of these relationships, fiduciary principles have role-based justification. Put simply, they make it more likely that fiduciaries will meet role-based expectations and accordingly support forms of trust (and associated social practices) requisite to fulfilment of social and economic functions allocated to persons through roles.

The notion that fiduciary status is role-based is reflected in some judicial commentary on the importance of fiduciary roles in social institutions. For example, in *Hodgkinson v Simms*, Justice La Forest reasoned that '[t]he desire to protect and reinforce the integrity of social institutions and enterprises is prevalent throughout fiduciary law … the law has recognized the importance of instilling in our social institutions and enterprises some recognition that not all relationships are characterized by a dynamic of mutual autonomy.'[27] In analysing the question whether financial advisors should be considered fiduciaries as a matter of status, Justice La Forest placed considerable weight on role-related expectations of advisors.

[26] What is a social role, exactly, and how does it figure in the law? Social theorists have suggested that like statuses, roles are generalizations, but ones focused on the particular social functions performed by persons occupying a particular social position, rather than (in contrast with statuses) their ordinal positioning in a social system. On this view, the occupation and performance of a social role may be a means by which to achieve an acquired social status, but the status one enjoys is a function of the esteem with which the role is held, while the role itself is defined primarily in terms of its social function and associated norms of role-related behaviour. Rehbinder explains: 'We understand role as the sum of all rules of conduct imposed by society on the holder of a certain social position … A role represents a normative generalization … Law does not regulate the legal relationships of the person but rather the legal relationships of the merchant, the employee, or the tenant.' Rehbinder (n 4) at 951.

[27] *Hodgkinson v Simms* [1994] 3 SCR 377 at 422.

Independently, prominent fiduciary scholars have also suggested that fiduciary status is role-based.[28]

This line of argument is congenial to certain social theorists' views about the ways in which basic units of social structure—including, notably, social institutions, statuses, and roles—have come to be reflected in the law.[29] Much work of social theory analyses social roles alongside social statuses and considers the extent to which roles embed statuses, including patterns of social inequality that social statuses perpetuate. But some have argued that, as social roles and statuses have become increasingly differentiated (ie, as social roles, and the processes of defining role-related expectations, have become liberated from rigid social statuses), social roles have taken on increased significance in the law.[30] The notion that fiduciary status is role based seems to dovetail nicely with the suggestion that the law more generally is increasingly role oriented as it becomes less 'formal' and more 'social'.[31]

[28] See, for example, P D Finn, 'The Fiduciary Principle' in T G Youdan (ed), *Equity, Fiduciaries and Trusts* (Carswell, 1989) at 50–1, who (in analysing the question whether advisory relationships should be considered fiduciary as a matter of status) suggests that social roles influence the reasonable expectations of the parties to relationships: 'It does seem to be the case, here, that our ready acceptance of a fiduciary expectation is coloured by … our perception of the social importance of the advisory function itself.' See also Leonard Rotman, *Parallel Paths: Fiduciary Doctrine and the Crown-Native Relationship in Canada* (University of Toronto Press, 1996) at 152, asserting in general that 'the law of fiduciaries is focused on a desire to preserve and protect the integrity of socially valuable or necessary relationships' and Donald Bayliss, 'Breach of Confidence as a Breach of Fiduciary Obligations: A Theory' (2000–2002) 9 Auckland U L Rev 702, 737: 'It is generally accepted that fiduciary relationships are protected by law because they are relationships with sufficient social utility to warrant such protection.'

[29] It resonates especially well with Graveson's definition of legal statuses, which suggests that statuses are rooted in recognition of the social importance of various kinds of relationship: 'Status is now defined as a special condition of a continuous and institutional nature, differing from the legal position of the normal person, which is conferred by law and not purely by the act of the parties, *whenever a person occupies a position of which the creation, continuance or relinquishment and the incidents are of sufficient social and legal concern.*' Graveson (n 22) at 2.

[30] Older work of social theory treats social roles and statuses as essentially intertwined. See, for example, Ralph Linton, who claimed that, 'A status, in the abstract, is a position in a particular pattern … as distinct from the individual who may occupy it, [the status] is simply a collection of rights and duties … *A role represents the dynamic aspect of a status.* The individual is socially assigned to a status and occupies it with relation to other statuses. When he puts the rights and duties which constitute the status into effect, he is performing a role.' Ralph Linton (n 5) at 113–14 (emphasis added); see also Talcott Parsons: 'Role is the dynamic aspect of status, the behavior[al] counterpart of the ideal or expected position defined by status.' Talcott Parsons, *Essays in Sociological Theory, Pure and Applied* (The Free Press, 1949) 43.

[31] Radbruch explains a purported shift from formal to social law in the following terms: 'Social law is based … on a structural change in legal thought, on a new concept of man: Social law is a law that is tailored to the concrete, socialized human being … social law makes apparent the individual particularity, the social position of power and powerlessness.' Gustav Radbruch, 'Vom Individualistischen zum Sozialen Recht' in (1930) 13 *Hanseatische Rechts- Und Gerichts-Zeitschrift* 459–60 (trans Rehbinder, n 4, at 950). Rehbinder observes that in many respects, and particularly in evidencing concern for the interests of individuals as employees, consumers, tenants, spouses, children, and the like, the law 'considers man within his social context … [and] undertakes the regulation of his legal relationship, but it differentiates according to the subject's position in the social system … [more specifically, the law refers] to a concrete partial aspect of his social relationships—the law relates to a man as a holder of a specific social role.' Rehbinder (n 4) at 951.

This notwithstanding, the claim that fiduciary status is role based is implausible. Doubtless social roles are *relevant* to fiduciary law. The occupation of social roles by fiduciaries may inform the expectations of the parties to some fiduciary relationships upon relationship formation, inform judicial construction of certain fiduciary mandates, and factor in evaluation of the performance of fiduciaries in some cases. Equally, as noted earlier, fiduciary law is relevant to social roles, inasmuch as respect for fiduciary strictures lies at the core of the social meaning attached to these roles (eg, our conception of the devoted physician, or of the lawyer as steadfast advocate). Nevertheless, the suggestion that social roles underlie fiduciary status in general is untenable for a couple of reasons.

First, the claim is implausible as a matter of interpretation. In some relationships fiduciaries *do* occupy important and well-defined social roles.[32] But in many they do not. Indeed, in some status-based relationships, fiduciaries can occupy different social roles and perform role-related social functions that seem likely to differ in social importance. Consider relationships between trustees and beneficiaries, or agents and principals. Trustees and agents perform important, and relatively well-understood *legal* functions. But their social roles are less clear and in any event are not uniform. A given trustee may be a trusted family friend administering a testamentary trust, in which case his specifically legal role is occupied largely as a result of his independent social role and relationship to the settlor. Another trustee may be an expert financial manager charged with administration of a large pension fund, engaged for her management expertise and known (if at all) by her beneficiaries only through her performance in managing the fund. Agents even more obviously occupy different roles and perform various functions, from the familiar (eg, real estate agent or employee) to the abstruse (eg, holder of a power of attorney). Given that many fiduciary relationships either do not implicate clearly defined social roles, or implicate several different ones, social roles seem incapable of supplying a cohesive juridical basis for fiduciary status.

Second, the view that fiduciary status is based on social roles assumes that roles are normatively simple. This assumption is questionable. As Judith Andre has shown, close analysis reveals role morality to be normatively complex.[33] The complexity is a function of a number of things. To begin with, genuine role-related obligations are role-specific; they reflect a patterned set of expectations relating to the performance of a particular social role in the social contexts in which the role figures.[34] Variability in the normative implications of roles make them an unlikely

[32] However, even in these cases it is interesting that attributions of status have been challenged, notwithstanding the undoubted importance of the role occupied by the fiduciary (consider, for example, differences of opinion on whether fiduciary status is appropriately attributed to physician–patient relationships).

[33] Judith Andre, 'Role Morality as a Complex Instance of Ordinary Morality' (1991) 28 American Philosophical Quarterly 73. See also Cass Sunstein, 'Social Norms and Social Roles' (1996) 96 Colum L Rev 903, 921: 'Consider the following social roles: doctor, employee, waiter, law school dean, wife, friend, pet-owner, colleague, student. Each of these roles is accompanied by a remarkably complex network of appropriate norms. The network is not easily reduced to rules.'

[34] For example, a police officer may be said to have a role-related obligation to respond to the cries of distress of a bystander, even if off-duty; a director of a corporation has a role-related obligation to review

basis for normative generalizations of the sort entailed by attributions of status. Additionally, to the extent that the normativity of role-related obligations is a function of the nature and importance of particular roles, roles can only provide contingent and variable justification for associated obligations in any event. While some social roles have obvious social value,[35] others have no value at all and, indeed, the role may be socially and morally pernicious (eg, gender roles reflecting the institutionalization of patriarchy).[36] Whether or not roles give good (much less sufficient) reasons for recognizing and acting on particular role-related obligations will depend on the characteristics of the role and its actual social value.

C. Presumed formal properties of the relationship

Apart from the difficulties already mentioned with the view that fiduciary status is based on the incapacity of beneficiaries or the social roles of fiduciaries, there is another, namely, that each would base the attribution of status on considerations pertinent to the normative position of either party to a fiduciary relationship rather than upon considerations material to their relationship as such.

Partly for this reason, I think that the most plausible account of fiduciary status understands it as based on the presumed presence of formal properties of fiduciary relationships.[37] This account holds that fiduciary status is properly attributed where relationships of a particular kind are typified by possession of formal properties enjoyed by all fiduciary relationships. The appropriateness of adherence to an established attribution of fiduciary status in particular cases is thus a function of the accuracy of the construction placed on the typical properties of a kind of relationship *and* the categorization of a particular relationship within the kind to which the status is attached (ie, whether it possesses the properties of fiduciary relationships typically present in the kind of relationship in question).

a business plan before an upcoming meeting at which it will be discussed; a physician has a role-related obligation to inform her patient of new information material to the patient's treatment, and so on.

[35] Some have suggested that roles reliably generate role obligations by virtue of their connection with morally valuable institutions (eg, families, the state, regulated professions and the like) and our role-related participation in them. See Michael Hardimon, 'Role Obligations' (1994) 91 Journal of Philosophy 333, 333: 'Role obligations … illustrate the existence and importance of a dimension of the moral life largely unnoticed by the ethical mainstream: the dimension that is lived through social institutions.' Others have suggested that role obligations are a form of associative obligation arising in connection with one's occupation of roles in associations, political and otherwise. See Ronald Dworkin, *Law's Empire* (Harvard University Press, 1986) 196. Of course some fiduciaries occupy roles in institutions in this sense, and some fiduciaries occupy roles in associations, but many do not and in any case this analytical move further deflects the burden of justification of fiduciary status from roles to the institutions or associations in which they figure.

[36] Andre (n 33) at 79: '[Roles] can institutionalize injustice, they can make demeaning treatment standard. Sometimes, perhaps often, we should break from our roles, deny them and try to change them … Because roles can be dangerous … we must sometimes ask … Should this role exist at all? Is it permissible or positively good or even morally necessary? Is it, on the other hand, regrettable or even deplorable?'

[37] Properties which together define, conceptually, what a fiduciary relationship is, and are integral to our understanding of the justification of the legal incidents of fiduciary status.

An attraction of this account is that it offers a way of viewing fact-based and status-based methods of relationship characterization as mutually consistent. Under a fact-based approach, the court must determine whether a *given* relationship is fiduciary on the basis of its possession of the formal properties of fiduciary relationships. By comparison, under a status-based approach the courts may bypass the question whether a particular relationship actually has the formal properties of a fiduciary relationship on the basis of a presumption, formalized by the attribution of status, that it does insofar as it falls within a kind of relationship typified by possession of these properties. Consistent with the provisional nature of the conceptual and normative claims implicit in attributions of status, courts must revert to fact-based assessment where a designation of status is questioned or otherwise is evidently questionable.[38]

The argument that fiduciary status is based on the presumed presence of formal properties of fiduciary relationships is also consistent with judicial opinion in the (admittedly few) cases in which courts have commented on the matter. For example, in *Guerin v Canada*, the Supreme Court of Canada was faced with the novel question whether the federal government was in a relationship of fiduciary status with aboriginal persons on the basis of powers it held over aboriginal lands. In entertaining this question, Justice Dickson observed:

It is sometimes said that the nature of fiduciary relationships is both *established and exhausted* by the standard categories of agent, trustee, partner, director, and the like. I do not agree. *It is the nature of the relationship, not the specific category of actor involved that gives rise to the fiduciary duty*. The categories of fiduciary, like those of negligence, should not be considered closed.[39]

[38] And the courts have acknowledged this. For example, in *Hodgkinson v Simms* (n 27) at 436, it was cautioned by the dissent that status designations are presumptive only and can mislead if not openly questioned: 'The second consideration which may act as a false indicator of a fiduciary obligation is the "category" into which the relationship falls. Professional relationships like doctor-patient and lawyer-client often possess fiduciary aspects. But equally, many of the tasks undertaken pursuant to these relationships may not be trust-like or attract a fiduciary obligation.' See also *Lac Minerals Ltd v International Corona Resources Ltd* [1989] 2 SCR 574 at 597: 'the nature of the relationship may be such that, notwithstanding that it is usually a fiduciary relationship, in exceptional cases it is not' and Glover (n 17) 269: 'Fiduciaries of the familiar sort are sometimes said to be with "accepted categories" of fiduciary relationship ... Calling these relationships "accepted" means no more than that the courts habitually invest them with a fiduciary consequence ... Claims of beneficiaries who stand within an "accepted" category of relationship are just like the claims of any other fiduciary beneficiary. Defendants are brought within the court's range of reliable inference, subject to special circumstances obtaining.'

[39] *Guerin v Canada* [1984] 2 SCR 335 at 341 (emphasis supplied). See also *Frame v Smith* [1987] 2 SCR 99, 134–35 per Justice Wilson: 'In the past the question whether a particular relationship is subject to a fiduciary obligation has been approached by referring to categories of relationships in which a fiduciary obligation has already been held to be present. Some recognized examples of these categories are relationships between directors and corporations, solicitors and clients, trustees and beneficiaries, agents and principals, life tenants and remaindermen, and partners. As well, it has frequently been noted that the categories of fiduciary relationship are never closed ... *An extension of fiduciary obligations to new "categories" of relationship presupposes the existence of an underlying principle which governs the imposition of the fiduciary obligation*' (emphasis supplied).

In a later case involving a novel claim of fiduciary status—*Lac Minerals v International Corona Resources*—Justice La Forest explained the basis of fiduciary status in the following terms:

Much of the confusion surrounding the term 'fiduciary' stems, in my view, from its undifferentiated use … [There are cases in which the question is whether a] certain class of relationship … [is] a category, analogous to directors and corporations, solicitors and clients, trustees and beneficiaries, and agents and principals, the existence of which relationship would give rise to fiduciary obligations … [Here, t]he focus is on the identification of relationships in which, *because of their inherent purpose or their presumed factual or legal incidents*, the courts will impose a fiduciary obligation on one party to act or refrain from acting in a certain way.[40]

Courts have even from time to time cautioned against unreflective reliance on uncontroversial designations of fiduciary status, emphasizing that attention must be paid to *actual* properties of the relationship between the would-be beneficiary and fiduciary. For example, in the Australian case, *Beach Petroleum v Kennedy*, the Court noted that:

Even in the case of a solicitor-client relationship, long accepted as a status based fiduciary relationship, *the duty is not derived from status*. As in all such cases, the *duty is derived from what the solicitor undertakes, or is deemed to have undertaken, to do in the particular circumstances*.[41]

An implication of the argument that I've been developing is that a sound understanding of fiduciary status requires that one be able to identify formal properties of fiduciary relationships and explain their normative salience. As I shall explain, I have elsewhere provided an account of the formal properties of fiduciary relationships and I think this account is serviceable here.[42] However, my primary aim presently is not to establish the merits of a particular way of thinking about fiduciary relationships. It is, instead, to emphasize our inevitable need for such an account. Some authors have pointed to the prevalence of status-based reasoning in fiduciary law as an indication that conceptual analysis of fiduciary relationships is unnecessary, futile, or pointless.[43] Our inquiry thus far suggests the opposite; these analyses

[40] *Lac Minerals* (n 38) 646–47 (emphasis supplied). See also *Hodgkinson v Simms* (n 27) at 378 in which the majority of the court reiterated the point that fiduciary status is based on the properties of fiduciary relationships and offered an account of same: 'The term fiduciary is properly used in two ways. The first describes certain relationships having as their essence discretion, influence over interests, and an inherent vulnerability. *A rebuttable presumption arises out of the inherent purpose of the relationship* that one party has a duty to act in the best interests of the other party. The second, slightly different use of fiduciary exists where fiduciary obligations, though not innate to a given relationship, arise as a matter of fact out of the specific circumstances of that particular relationship.'

[41] *Beach Petroleum v Kennedy* (1999) 48 NSWLR 1, 188 (Spigelman CJ, and Sheller and Stein JJA). Cited and discussed in James Edelman, 'The Role of Status in the Law of Obligations: Common Callings, Implied Terms, and Lessons for Fiduciary Duties' in Andrew S Gold and Paul B Miller (eds), *Philosophical Foundations of Fiduciary Law* (Oxford University Press, 2014) 21.

[42] Miller (n 19); Paul B Miller, 'Justifying Fiduciary Duties' (2013) 58 McGill LJ 969; Paul B Miller, 'Justifying Fiduciary Remedies' (2013) 63 University of Toronto Law Journal 570.

[43] Matthew Conaglen, 'The Nature and Function of Fiduciary Loyalty' (2005) 121 Law Quarterly Review 452; Peter Birks, 'The Content of Fiduciary Obligation' (2000) 34 Israel L Rev 3.

are essential, for otherwise we have no reason for confidence in the attributions of fiduciary status upon which much of fiduciary law is constructed, and no way of productively addressing questions about the appropriateness of attributions of fiduciary status.

I wish to allow for the possibility of multiple plausible accounts of the formal properties of fiduciary relationships. Nevertheless, the burden of establishing that *some* such account is implicit in the very idea of fiduciary status must be discharged presently. I will thus briefly show how my own theory of fiduciary relationships—the fiduciary powers theory—explains fiduciary status. If this theory proves helpful, we shall have good reason to think that a plausible account of the formal properties of fiduciary relationships is necessary to make sense of fiduciary status and its limitations.

The fiduciary powers theory holds that all fiduciary relationships are characterized by the fiduciary's possession of discretionary powers derived from the person of a beneficiary or benefactor (individually, or on a collective basis) and devoted to objects specified by the beneficiary or benefactor. Fiduciary powers are, on this view, originally innate or acquired personal powers held by individuals as legal persons in their own right, ordinarily exercised by them as they see fit for objects they specify.[44] Fiduciary relationships are formed when these powers are devolved upon a fiduciary in a mandate under which they are to be exercised for specific objects.

The fiduciary powers theory generates a unique account of fact- and status-based methods of identifying fiduciary relationships. Consistent with the theory, under the fact-based approach courts must determine whether the relationship before them is one in which the alleged fiduciary held fiduciary powers (again, discretionary powers derived from the person of a beneficiary or benefactor, being expressly or impliedly granted for the purpose of advancing the interests of a beneficiary or for pursuit of abstract purposes specified by a benefactor). The theory suggests that attributions of fiduciary status will be appropriate where a given kind of relationship is one in which would-be fiduciaries typically hold and exercise fiduciary powers. Supposing that most status categories of fiduciary relationship rest on accurate typification, it will normally be unnecessary for a court to consider whether a given relationship of fiduciary status actually features a grant of fiduciary power. But where status is questioned or is questionable, the court ought to directly consider whether the relationship (in fact, or in type) possesses the formal properties that fiduciary status designates. In short, it must determine whether (a) notwithstanding the validity of the attribution of status to a kind of relationship, in a particular atypical relationship the purported fiduciary was not in possession of fiduciary powers; or (b) an existing but now questioned attribution of status is appropriate based on whether enjoyment of fiduciary powers really is typical of that kind of relationship; or (c) a kind of relationship not presently recognized as enjoying fiduciary

[44] Of course, in many cases personal powers may be exercised without any objects or ends having been made explicit; they may not even be conscious.

status should be attributed status, again on the basis that enjoyment of fiduciary powers is typical in a relationship of that sort.

To be convincing, an account of fiduciary relationships must not only be interpretively sound; it must also be capable of supporting a normative theory of fiduciary liability. That is, one must be able to locate in the account some reason(s) for the particular legal norms that fiduciary relationships occasion. As explained elsewhere, the fiduciary powers theory roots the hallmark fiduciary duty of loyalty and distinctive gain-based fiduciary remedies in the beneficiary or benefactor's personal interest in fiduciary power as a means (ie, a legal mechanism of purposive action) derived from their legal personality and subject to disposition at their will for objects of their choice. On this view, the very nature and derivation of fiduciary powers supply reasons for the particular norms that the law attaches to fiduciary relationships. Whether or not one accepts the fiduciary powers theory, it should by now be evident that some such account is necessary to make sense of the provisional normative claim implicit in attributions of fiduciary status; namely, that it is right that one party to a relationship be legally compelled to faithfully serve the ends of the other.

V. Conclusion

To a large extent, fiduciary principles are applied in reliance on attributions of fiduciary status to particular kinds of relationship. Indeed, as noted earlier, if a non-specialist jurist were asked to describe fiduciary law as a field she might simply gesture to kinds of relationship that have recognized fiduciary status. Our experience of fiduciary law through fiduciary status is only reinforced by the piecemeal way in which fiduciary law is taught in law schools (ie, as refracted through the necessarily circumscribed lenses of trust law, corporate law, agency law, family law, and so on). It should therefore be unsurprising that status is sometimes treated as foundational in fiduciary law, as though one might know all that one needs to know (or all that it is possible to know) about fiduciary relationships by familiarizing oneself with particular attributions of fiduciary status.

I have argued here that the idea of status in fiduciary law does not, and cannot, bear the weight of these claims. Status concepts are inherently provisional, being mere designations that invite and entail simplifying assumptions about the normative position of a person, relationship or group in a normative system. Being provisional, it is analytically impossible for statuses (fiduciary or otherwise) to be conceptually or normatively basic. The suggestion otherwise is not just erroneous; as history has proven, it is also dangerous. Employed defensibly, statuses denote genuinely normatively salient features that typify the position of persons, relationships, or groups in a normative system. But statuses are often devised or attributed in ways that are defective morally and/or analytically. The risk of illegitimacy is made worse by the nature of status concepts and the ways in which they function. All statuses embed and invite assumptions about normatively salient characteristics of persons, relationships or groups; accepting these assumptions means that one may overlook normatively salient differences rooted in contexts over which statuses offer a gloss. Fresh judgement is sacrificed (perhaps, in some cases, necessarily) for the sake of convenience and economy of effort. These features of status concepts generate serious risks of idleness or corruption of judgement. These risks can be minimized only by working with status concepts from a posture of critical awareness—a posture in which it is recognized that categorization by status is valuable and valid only to the extent that the status reliably designates a normative position defined by genuinely normatively salient properties of the persons or groups to which the status designation applies.

2

Reinterpreting the Status–Contract Divide

The Case of Fiduciaries

*Hanoch Dagan and Elizabeth S Scott**

I. Introduction

This essay uses a perplexing puzzle in the emerging theoretical literature on fiduciary law in order to rethink and indeed reconstruct the status vs contract conceptual framework. The puzzle springs from the seemingly confusing hybrid nature of fiduciary law. 'Many, perhaps most, fiduciary relationships are established on the footing of contract', and contract has 'an important, if complex, bearing on the content and enforcement of fiduciary duties'. But most fiduciary relationships 'are considered in law to be presumptively fiduciary as a matter of status, given the incidents of the relationship or the role occupied by the fiduciary', and this status seems to also significantly affect the fiduciary duties' content and enforcement.[1] So does this dichotomy create too simplistic a taxonomy?

Instead of addressing these questions directly, we begin, in Section II, with a conceptual inquiry questioning the traditional uses (and abuses) of the status–contract divide, which permeates legal analyses of categories of cooperative interpersonal interactions in which one party has particular obligations to the other. We elucidate the extreme interpretations of status as innate, comprehensive, and inalienable, and of contract as a wholly open-ended framework, which have been used as foils in some scholarly debates. While neither is wrong, they are both, we argue, usually unhelpful because neither presents core cases of interpersonal relationships in a liberal polity. We therefore highlight (in Section III) two intermediate stations along the spectrum between these two extremes: offices and contract types.

* Respectively, Stewart and Judy Colton Professor of Legal Theory and Innovation, Tel-Aviv University Buchmann Faculty of Law, and Harold R. Medina Professor of Law, Columbia Law School. Thanks to Avihay Dorfman, Chris Essert, Evan Fox-Decent, Andrew Gold, Scott Hershovitz, Adam Hofri-Winogradow, Greg Klass, Shelly Kreiczer-Levy, Ethan Leib, Daniel Markovits, Paul Miller, Irit Samet, Steve Smith, and Ben Zipursky for their helpful comments and to David Griffin for superb research assistance.

1 Paul B Miller and Andrew S Gold, 'Introduction' at p 2 in this volume.

Like status, an office also typically implicates the parties'—or at least one of the parties'—personal identity, and its features are also largely non-negotiable; at times it is also inalienable. But it is less comprehensive and, most importantly, it is not necessarily innate. By the same token, alongside the open-ended contract, a liberal private law offers people a rich menu of contract types and property institutions from which they can choose in shaping and reshaping their interpersonal interactions. Unlike the idea of an open-ended contract—and similarly to offices—each contract type is shaped by an animating principle, so that (most of) its rules can be understood and justified by reference to such functional or normative 'DNA'.[2] Unlike with offices, however, contract types are more instrumental so the bulk of these rules are negotiable; they offer defaults which can be rejected or adjusted by the pertinent actors to fit to their own goals and preferences.

Introducing the alternatives of offices and contract types enriches our understanding of the status-to-contract framework vis-à-vis the innate status vs open-ended contracting binarism. Furthermore, our use (in Section IV) of two core examples of fiduciaries—parents and financial fiduciaries—as typical examples of offices and contract types (respectively), facilitates a preliminary account of the main implications of this choice and the most important considerations that should inform it. We hope that our expanded taxonomy will help ensure that fiduciary scholars avoid the highly artificial dichotomy that affected the legal fields in which the status–contract divide has been most extensively invoked, namely, family law and employment law, and that our account of offices and contract types can refine some of the immediate concerns and debates of fiduciary scholarship. This account may also have broader implications, because in liberal law innate status and open-ended contracting are marginal cases, and most of the drama occurs in between offices and contract types.

II. Between Innate Status and Open-Ended Contract

'The movement of the progressive societies has been uniform in one respect', announced Sir Henry Maine more than one hundred and fifty years ago: it has been 'a movement *from Status to Contract*'.[3] Whereas this famous dichotomy of status and contract plays a significant role in numerous debates in family law, labour law, and fiduciary law (among others), its key concepts—status and contract—are oftentimes not sufficiently elucidated. Contract seems the easier, or at least more familiar, concept, so we begin with status, remembering John Austin's dictum that '[t]o determine precisely what a *status* is, is in my opinion the most difficult problem in the whole science of jurisprudence.'[4]

[2] Thus, although most of the rules of our case study of contract type—the law of financial fiduciaries—are defaults, this doctrine nicely responds to its autonomy-enhancing role of allowing people to safely delegate to experts the task of money management. See *infra* Section IV.C.

[3] Henry Sumner Maine, *Ancient Law* (1st edn 1861, J M Dent & Sons Ltd, 1917) 99–100.

[4] John Austin, *Lectures on Jurisprudence or the Philosophy of Positive Law* (3rd ed, Robert Campbell, 1896) 401.

Maine seemed to have understood status along the lines we mentioned earlier, namely, as innate (based on fixed characteristics) and thus also both comprehensive and inalienable. This explains his strong proposition that by and large statuses—like 'the Slave', 'the Female under Tutelage', or 'the Son [of full age] under Power'—have 'no true place in the law of modern European societies'.[5] The remaining cases, such as '[t]he child before years of discretion, the orphan under guardianship, the adjudged lunatic', are thus for Maine 'exceptions ... which illustrate the rule', because they are all 'subject to extrinsic control on the single ground that they do not possess the faculty of forming a judgment on their own interests; in other words, that they are wanting in the first essential of an engagement by Contract.'[6]

Maine's conception of status is extremely narrow: status, in his view, is not only innate, comprehensive, and inalienable, but also 'purely a matter of *incapacity*'.[7] It arises out of 'accidents of birth' or 'circumstances which lie beyond the control and choice of the individual', and it depends solely on 'defect of judgment'.[8] The equation of status with incapacity is rare,[9] but Maine's caste-like understanding of status isn't. As an ideal-type, a status-based society is said to be one in which individuals are 'rigidly bound into a hierarchic group' and their rights and obligations derive from such involuntary associations.[10] Status, in this view, 'connotes an element of social and legal differentiation between categories of persons', because it stands for 'the sum total of the powers and disabilities, the rights and obligations, which society confers or imposes upon individuals irrespective of their own volition'.[11]

Neither Maine nor other scholars who followed his discussion of the status-to-contract narrative denied that all legal orders have some elements of status; in contemporary societies citizenship may be the least disputed example.[12] But with this caste-like understanding of status as a foil, many join Maine in both documenting 'the rise of contractualization' and celebrating it 'as a triumph of individual freedom and equality'.[13] This celebration is especially understandable given the unhappy legacy of 'the attribution of status' in the common law, which signified 'not normality but abnormality',[14] so that '[w]omen, lunatics, blacks, Indians, and others have been limited from time to time in their legal rights and capacities simply by reason of their sex, color, ethnic background, or mental abilities.'[15] Indeed, if a 'universe based on status' denotes that 'rights and duties are set at birth [and] viewed as

[5] Maine (n 3) at 99–100. [6] Ibid at 100.

[7] Carleton Kemp Allen, 'Status and Capacity' (1930) 46 LQR 277, 286.

[8] Ibid at 283, 286.

[9] Indeed, many cases of incapacity—notably our case study of parenthood—are now governed by what we are calling office, rather than status. See, *infra*, text accompanying n 50.

[10] Manfred Rehbinder, 'Status, Contract, and the Welfare State' (1971) 23 Stan L Rev 941, 942.

[11] O Kahn-Freund, 'A Note on Status and Contract in British Labour Law' (1967) 30 MLR 635, 636.

[12] See, eg, Kahn-Freund (n 11) at 686, 689; but see Ayelet Shachar, *The Birthright Lottery: Citizenship and Global Inequality* (Harvard University Press, 2009).

[13] Jill Elaine Hasday, 'The Canon of Family Law' (2004) 57 Stan L Rev 825, 834.

[14] R H Graveson, *Status in the Common Law* (1953) 5.

[15] Howard O Hunter, 'An Essay on Contract and Status: Race, Marriage, and the Meretricious Spouse' (1978) 64 Va L Rev 1039, 1043.

inexorable because they attend relationships understood as natural' or 'follow the perceived natural order of things',[16] liberalism's basic tenets imply a preference for 'the world of contract', in which in theory 'nothing is inevitable' because 'individuals are putatively equal and, as such, can design or at least negotiate the terms of their own interactions.'[17] This is exactly why, if law subscribes to liberalism's injunctions against reliance on illegitimate factors, such as those just mentioned, status becomes a very narrow category.

But Maine's observation that society tends to shift from status to contract and that this shift is properly deemed progress is of course highly disputed.[18] While the historical debate is far beyond the scope of this essay, it is important for our purposes to identify the conception of contract on which this strong dissent relies. These critics, who particularly dispute the contractual understanding of employment and marriage, challenge the idea that these relationships are appropriately understood to be purely self-interested exchanges based on equal bargaining power. Their (explicit, or more frequently implicit) conception of contract is of a wholly open-ended, empty framework.[19] Some critics then point to 'a counter-narrative of the persistence of status rules denying individuals choice about the structure of their relationships.'[20] Thus, it has been argued that '[o]nly for a relatively short period of history was the employment relationship treated as purely contractual', so that '[t]he rights and responsibilities of the parties were left to contractual determination.'[21] But this 'concept of the employment relationship as a purely contractual exchange of services for wages' declined with a 'new regulation of the employment relationship [which] has been described as a return to status, although a status of a new kind'.[22] Though the set of familiar immutable rules in employment law is not 'as strict and all-comprehensive as those of the master and servant regulation,' it seems sufficiently removed from the open-ended contract to lead commentators to conclude that '[f]or typical employment, trends definitely point in the direction of a status type relationship', thus indicating 'a movement "from status to contract and back."'[23]

Resisting contract as the organizing conception of employment or marriage is understandable if, but only if, contract is conceptualized as an open-ended

[16] Janet L Dolgin, 'Status and Contract in Surrogate Motherhood: An Illumination of the Surrogacy Debate' (1990) 38 Buff L Rev 516, 517.

[17] Janet L Dolgin, 'The Family in Transition: From Griswold to Eisenstadt and Beyond' (1994) 82 Geo LJ 1519, 1526.

[18] See, eg, Graveson (n 14) at 50; Morris R Cohen, 'The Basis of Contract' (1933) 46 Harv L Rev 553, 558. But see, eg, E Allan Farnsworth, 'The Past of Promise: An Historical Introduction to Contract' (1969) 69 Colum L Rev 576, 581–82.

[19] See, eg, Milton C Regan, Jr, *Family Law and the Pursuit of Intimacy* (New York University Press, 1993) 1–2.

[20] Hasday (n 13) at 834.

[21] Frances Raday, 'Status and Contract in the Employment Relationship' (1989) 23 Israel L Rev 77, 77–8.

[22] Ibid at 78.

[23] Reinhold Fahlbeck, 'Flexibility: Potentials and Challenges for Labor Law' (1998) 19 Comp Lab L & Pol'y J 515, 527–8. See also, eg, Gillian Demeyere, 'Human Rights as Contract Rights: Rethinking the Employer's Duty to Accommodate' (2010) 36 Queen's L J 299.

framework, which is indifferent to *systemic* inequality between the parties and to the identitarian nature of their relationships. Thus, it has been argued that when based on a 'rhetoric of universal free will', contract cannot 'account adequately' for the inequality of employers and employees.[24] While courts 'characterize the unfavorable circumstances that many employees face as the product of unequal bargaining power … bargaining power disparity does not capture the moral problem raised by inequality in the employment relation', which 'encompasses one's level of economic resources, leisure, and discretion', and is thus best understood 'in terms of status'.[25] Marriage, even equal marriage, can also hardly fit in. Although contractual to an extent, marriage—the union of equals defined by mutual care, obligation, and self-identification—cannot be easily accommodated within the open-ended conception of contract.[26]

The failure of this conception of contract, however, is not limited to the contexts of employment and marriage, but rather applies much more broadly.[27] Understanding contract solely as an open-ended framework is hardly autonomy-enhancing, given the transaction (and other) costs that parties would face if they were to design from scratch their reciprocal undertakings;[28] further, and just as important, it improperly dismisses the identitarian significance of certain long-term voluntary relationships.[29] Indeed, while the option of open-ended contracting is a significant feature of liberal law, the implication that this specific form of contract lies at the conceptual core of contract law is both descriptively wrong and normatively disappointing.

A liberal contract law can, and in fact by and large does, perform its core role as one of society's main autonomy-enhancing devices by providing—in addition to its respect to parties' open-ended agreements—a divergent repertoire of contract types for people to choose from. Indeed, given the diversity of acceptable human goods from which autonomous people should be able to choose and their distinct constitutive values, the state must recognize a sufficiently diverse set of robust frameworks for people to organize their life. This liberal commitment to personal autonomy by fostering diversity and multiplicity is relevant to private law because given the endemic difficulties of both transaction costs and 'obstacles of the imagination', many of these frameworks cannot be realistically actualized without the support of viable legal institutions. The liberal state should thus enable individuals to pursue valid conceptions of the good by *proactively* providing a multiplicity of options. A structurally pluralist private law—our private law—follows suit by including diverse categories of property institutions and contract types, each incorporating a different value or different balance of values.[30]

[24] Aditi Bagchi, 'The Myth of Equality in the Employment Relation' (2009) Mich St L Rev 579, 579, 602 (2009).

[25] Ibid at 579–80.

[26] See, generally, Regan (n 19).

[27] See also Nathan Isaacs, 'The Standardizing of Contracts' (1917) 27 Yale LJ 34, 47 ('There is … much to be gained by the further standardizing of the relations in which society has an interest, in order to remove them from the control of the accident of power in individual bargaining').

[28] See Rehbinder (n 10) at 955.

[29] See Regan (n 19) at 89, 94, 117.

[30] See, generally, Hanoch Dagan and Michael A Heller, *The Choice Theory of Contracts* (Cambridge University Press, forthcoming 2017); Hanoch Dagan, 'Pluralism and Perfectionism in Private Law'

III. On Offices and Contract types

One may criticize the way friends of contract and of status use the corner cases of innate status and open-ended contracts (respectively) as foils that artificially boost their positions.[31] But these moves are not sheer rhetorical excesses. After all, while the legitimate scope of the universe of status is certainly disputable, even perfectly liberal societies must ascribe to some people (say, babies) a status understood as innate, comprehensive, and inalienable. By the same token, while a liberal contract law must take seriously the task of forming a sufficiently diverse repertoire of contract types, it should not fall back to the pre-liberal understanding of contract in which the state only supports its own favoured forms of interaction; quite the contrary, as we have just noted, although the residual category of open-ended contracting does not exhaust or even properly represent the core of contract, it is indispensable to liberal contract law because it allows people to reject the state's suggestions and decide for themselves how to mold their interpersonal interactions.[32]

Thus, neither innate status nor open-ended contracts are a caricature. But at least in a liberal private law neither presents a core case, which may explain why they can hardly be used as ideal types that offer viable alternatives to choose from. For the status/contract apparatus to properly serve the analytical role it seems to play in fields like family, employment, and fiduciary law, it must include further categories that fall short of innate status and are yet not as empty as the open-ended contract.[33] In this section we attempt to introduce such categories—office and contract type—and broadly articulate their main features. The next section puts these constructs to work in the context of fiduciary law.

The need for something along the lines of the concept of office as we understand it emerges from many attempts to define status that find its restricted understanding too narrow since it excludes categories which 'are matters of choice'.[34] Because 'a "contract" may lead to the assumption of a socially imposed status rather than to one that is the creation of the contracting parties,'[35] some authors suggested we

(2012) 112 Colum L Rev 1436. See also Joseph Raz, *The Morality of Freedom* (Oxford University Press, 1986) 133, 162, 265, 372, 395, 398. Nothing in the emphasis on contract types (or property institutions) implies that contract (or property) is not a viable category. See Hanoch Dagan, 'Doctrinal Categories, Legal Realism, and the Rule of Law' (2015) 164 U Pa L Rev 1889.

31 By the same token, one may criticize the way Maine's work figures in these debates. See J. Russell VerSteeg, 'From Status to Contract: A Contextual Analysis of Maine's Famous Dictum' (1988) 10 Whittier L Rev 669, 669–72.

32 See Dagan and Heller (n 30), chapter 8.

33 Cf. Elizabeth S Scott, 'Rehabilitating Liberalism in Modern Divorce Law' (1994) Utah L Rev 687.

34 Allen (n 7) at 284. See also, eg, Graveson (n 14) at 34, 36, 38.

35 See Hunter (n 15) at 1044. See also, eg, Lenore J Weitzman, *The Marriage Contract* (Free Press, 1981) xix–xxi; Hendrik Hartog, 'Marital Exits and Marital Expectations in Nineteenth Century America' (1991) 80 Geo L.J. 95, 97–8; Orly Lobel, 'The Slipperyness of Stability: Contracting for Flexible and Triangular Employment Relationships in the New Economy' (2003) 10 Tex Wesleyan L Rev 109, 127–29.

ought to 'see status as an institution, entered into voluntarily, but without individualized redefinition of the institution.'[36] This approach indeed underlies two of the classical definitions of status as 'the condition of belonging to a particular class of persons to whom the law assigns certain capacities or incapacities or both',[37] and as 'a special condition of a continuous and institutional nature, differing from the legal position of the normal person, which is conferred by law and not purely by the act of the parties, whenever a person occupies a position of which the creation, continuance or relinquishment and the incidents are a matter of sufficient social or public concern.'[38]

These broader definitions are in many ways innocuous. But they might have contributed to 'the conceptual confusion between two phenomena as different as the imposition of rights and duties irrespective of the volition of the person concerned' on the one hand, and the shaping of the parties' relationships by 'mandatory norms which cannot be contracted out' into which he or she can freely enter, on the other hand.[39] This confusion is consequential in ways that we have already noted, because 'it may be one explanation for the ... tendentious inclination to link [every manifestation of the latter] phenomenon with "status," that hall-mark of a "non-progressive" society'.[40]

In order to avoid this confusion, and because status in its narrower understanding is not an empty category, a different term is needed. Office seems to fit well partly because of its legacy and partly because it was recently used for identifying the 'anti-contractarian' position in the theoretical debate as to the nature of fiduciaries. The idea of an office, Joshua Getzler noted, 'comes from the classical Roman concept of an *officium*, a standard set of primary duties pertaining to a person with recognized responsibilities. The nature of that office will then accent and shape all the relevant duties of the officeholder, both positive and negative'; it will 'color, intensify, and constrain all dealings, simply by virtue of the position or personality of the actors'.[41] Office seems to capture what critics of Maine want to highlight when they point out status-like features that typify certain quarters of modern law, while avoiding the implication of them being necessarily hereditary or hierarchic.

In an important attempt to escape the conceptual confusion noted above (but one that unfortunately has not greatly influenced the literature), Manfred Rehbinder used the term, 'role', which he borrowed from sociology, for similar—but not identical—purposes. Role is 'the sum of all rules of conduct imposed by society on the holder of certain social position', which define 'a model of conduct' that prescribes 'what characteristics one must have' and 'what kind of conduct is expected of him'.[42] Rehbinder acknowledges that, unlike the innate status, individuals

[36] Katharine B. Silbaugh, 'Marriage Contracts and the Family Economy' (1998) 93 Nw U L Rev 65, 115.

[37] Allen (n 7) at 288. [38] Graveson (n 14) at 2. [39] Kahn-Freund (n 11) at 640.

[40] Ibid at 642.

[41] Joshua Getzler, 'Ascribing and Limiting Fiduciary Obligations' in Andrew S Gold and Paul B. Miller (eds), *Philosophical Foundations of Fiduciary Law* (Oxford University Press, 2014) 39, 42–43.

[42] Rehbinder (n 10) at 951–52.

voluntarily undertake roles, but he insists that '[f]reedom of the individual today consists less in a freedom of role creation than in a freedom' to 'choose among positions and behavioral standards, created and safeguarded by the state'.[43] And once a role has been chosen, its 'role expectations' affect the choosing individual 'through two means: first, through the psychological act of internalization of its behavioral expectations, which are then considered right and just; second, through a system of positive or negative sanctions.'[44]

We endorse Rehbinder's proposition as to the significance of this broad spectrum between innate status and open-ended contract in liberal private law, and our analysis of these cases will also assume the complex interaction of incentives and internalized cultural expectations he observed. But Rehbinder's proposed category is still overbroad as it includes not only ' "must"-expectations' and ' "should"-expectations', but also ' "may"-expectations', thus encompassing also 'the law of sales', which 'regulate[s] the roles of the buyer and the seller'.[45] We thus offer a more fine-grained taxonomy, which subdivides Rehbinder's capacious understanding of 'roles' into offices and contract types. As we hope to (begin to) demonstrate in the remainder of this essay, offices and contract types are not fortuitous packages of possible configurations of the different sticks that distinguish the innate status from the freestanding contract, but rather coherent structures with distinct integrities.

Offices, as we have already mentioned, typically implicate individuals' identities and often involve asymmetrical vulnerability given the parties' asymmetrical capacity for autonomous choice.[46] They are thus by and large neither negotiable nor assignable, giving rise to duties with 'a depth or intensity that would not be owed by a shopkeeper or a plumber on whom a customer relies for goods and services'.[47] By contrast, contract types—a term coined by one of us in a co-authored work with Michael Heller on contract theory—accounts for Rehbinder's claim that even categories of voluntary interactions, like sales (or suretyship, bailment, insurance, etc.), which are largely instrumental and typically adjustable by the parties, nonetheless embody a set of state-created and safeguarded expectations.

Indeed, unlike its Willistonian conceptualization, contract law is not a simple, unified body of doctrine. Rather, alongside the normatively important but

[43] Ibid at 955. As he notes, other commentators discussed this phenomenon by distinguishing between 'ascribed status and achieved status'. Ibid at 954.

[44] Ibid at 953.

[45] Ibid. There are further aspects in which we do not subscribe to Rehbinder's discussion. Notably, we are not committed to the view that each office and contract type reflects a 'role-based morality' at least not in the way he conceived of this term. Each, to be sure, has its animating principle that colors its rules and gives it its unique character. But that regulative principle is not necessarily derivative of a socially defined role and at least some of these (notably regarding contract types) may be (at least to an extent) functional.

[46] Our characterization of office admittedly implies that offices may be affected by the status of one of the parties. This observation, however, does not undermine the significance of distinguishing office from status; quite the contrary, it shows that this distinction can be analytically helpful by suggesting that we may think differently about (for example) the powers of a parent that derive from the child's status (and its attendant incapacities) and those that do not.

[47] Getzler (n 41) at 43.

practically marginal category of open-ended contracting, contract law is a loose umbrella covering a rather diverse set of contract types. Contract law actively empowers people to form collaborative voluntary arrangements—both discrete and impersonal as well as long-term and relational—by providing a broad menu of divergent background regimes for such risky undertakings in the various relevant spheres of contracting: home; intimacy; work; and commerce. Each such contract type is guided by a robust animating principle that reflects a specific balance of the possible utilitarian and/or communitarian goods people can gain from contractual activity in this specific contractual sphere. Such a structurally pluralist contract law, as we have typified it above, follows liberalism's ultimate commitment to people's autonomy in two ways: it presumptively subscribes to the familiar freedom of contract prescription, which sanctions bargaining for terms *within* a contract (this presumption may be rebutted in cases of asymmetrical vulnerability, but even in these cases, a liberal contract law usually prefers sticky defaults over mandatory rules); *and* it also follows the 'freedom of contract*s*' injunction: the freedom to choose from *among* a range of normatively-attractive, already-existing contract types.[48]

Many of the existing debates as to the status vs contract—descriptive or normative—classification of marital or employment positions can be reformulated as addressing the choice between office and contract type, or more precisely among the range of more refined permutations that lies in between these two ideal types. This reformulation is helpful because, at least typically, neither side to these debates supports innate status or open-ended contract, so that arguing against either of these foils cannot do any real work.[49] But the significance of introducing our fine-grained continuum as an alternative to the familiar status-contract binarism is not only in setting aside irrelevant arguments. Rather, its more important contribution is in focusing our attention on the choice between office and contract type (or, again, among the various options along their continuum), which is the real choice for many of our current practices. This focus is important because (as the discussion above implies and our extended treatment of the fiduciaries case study further demonstrates) it helps refine what is at stake: what are the main implications of our choice—the question of immutability and the possibility of outsourcing—and what are its most important justifications, which turn largely on both the identitarian-instrumental divide (alluded to earlier) and the significance and salience of concerns of asymmetrical vulnerability.

Before we turn to fiduciary law, it may be helpful to return to the category of incapacity, which was originally emphasized by Maine,[50] and can now be properly appreciated. Categories of cases of incapacity inevitably involve the identity

48 See Dagan and Heller (n 30).

49 It is also helpful because it provides a satisfying way to sidestep the seemingly unavoidable but radically unsatisfying alternative of 'deconstruct[ing] the status/contract distinction, replacing it … with the idea of a "marriage system" that is irretrievably ambivalent as between status and contract'. Janet Halley, 'Behind the Law of Marriage (I): From Status/Contract to the Marriage System' (2010) 6 Unbound: Harv J Legal Left 1, 4.

50 See *supra* text accompanying nn 7–9.

the incapacitated party and are thus 'naturally' governed under the office category,[51] rather than the contract-type one.[52] The question of whether there are other categories of cases that should be similarly governed—think of employees or of spouses—depends upon our conceptualization of these putative categories along the identitarian-instrumental continuum. In a liberal society, which insists that even our identities should be to some extent chosen, it is unsurprising that identitarian categories that do not involve incapacity are situated in-between office and contract type, with some degree of immutability and non-assignability that is more than what we find in contract-types but less than what typifies offices.[53]

IV. Varieties of Fiduciary Relationships

A. The Monistic Positions

Fiduciary law, to which we (finally) turn, provides a rich case study for our theoretical observations. To be sure, while no one (to the best of our knowledge) argues that fiduciaries fit into the category of innate status,[54] the other pole of the status-to-contract spectrum did surface in the theoretical analyses of fiduciary law. Some lawyer economists, notably Frank Easterbrook and Daniel Fischel, argued along these lines that 'fiduciary' is simply the term law attaches to 'some contractual relations' when 'transaction costs reach a particularly high level', so that fiduciary relations do not raise any 'distinctive and interesting questions' and '[f]iduciary duties are not special duties'.[55] But this position has been severely criticized,[56] and is rarely defended in contemporary debates as to the nature of fiduciary law,[57] which should not be surprising given that even a view that disputes or dismisses any office-like

[51] In other words, what makes these cases typical examples of an office is both the characteristics of the beneficiary (being incapable) and the position assumed by the fiduciary.

[52] Cf Paul B Miller, 'The Idea of Status in Fiduciary Law' (at p 39–41 in this volume) (Kantians are correct to argue that incapacity is *a* ground of a need for fiduciary representation, but wrong to limit fiduciary law to relationships featuring incapacity).

[53] For the same reason, a liberal polity may be obligated to facilitate more forms of identitarian categories—such as non-conjugal aspiring families (eg, multigenerational groups and voluntary kin groups)—that offer more options, and thus choice. See Elizabeth S Scott and Robert E Scott, 'From Contract To Status: Collaboration and The Evolution Of Novel Family Relationships' (2015) 115 Colum L Rev 293, 369–73.

[54] Indeed, once status is limited along the lines of our discussion in the previous sections of this essay, it becomes, as Lionel Smith argues, 'part of the law of persons', and thus irrelevant to fiduciary law. Lionel Smith, 'Contract, Consent, and Fiduciary Relationships' (this volume).

[55] Frank H Easterbrook and Daniel R Fischel, 'Contract and Fiduciary Duty' (1993) 36 JL & Econ 425, 427, 438. See also, eg, John Langbein, 'The Contractarian Basis of the Law of Trusts' (1995) 105 Yale LJ 625.

[56] See, eg, Hanoch Dagan and Sharon Hannes, 'Managing Our Money: The Law of Financial Fiduciaries as a Private Law Institution' in *Philosophical Foundations of Fiduciary Law* (n 41) at 91, 101–02.

[57] Thus, in his recent restatement of the economic theory of fiduciary law Robert Sitkoff acknowledges that fiduciary duties have distinctive features. See Robert H Sitkoff, 'An Economic Theory of Fiduciary Law' in *Philosophical Foundations of Fiduciary Law* (n 41) at 197.

features of fiduciary law would likely understand fiduciary law as a contract type, and not an open-ended contract.

Indeed, the real action lies elsewhere, in the choice between office and contract type.[58] Lionel Smith and Daniel Markovits may represent the former position.[59] Although the parties 'voluntarily assume the fiduciary role', their obligations, Smith argues, 'are determined by the law', rather than by 'the particular undertaking that was given by a particular party'.[60] Thus, 'while entering the relationship is voluntary and consensual, the consent of those who enter the relationship is not what determines the content of the obligations.'[61] This characterization nicely fits that of Markovits who insists that 'fiduciary relations are not merely creatures of the parties' intentions but instead establish and reflect status-like orders.'[62] These orders—one example Markovits uses is of guardianship, which he describes as a 'jointly but asymmetrically pursued project of … constituting the ward's self-conception', which 'can become one of the great sources of meaning in the lives of both guardian and ward'—are far removed from 'the model of contract', because they are not only 'means for serving antecedent ends', but are also valuable 'in themselves'.[63]

James Edelman, by contrast, supports a conception of fiduciaries which falls squarely into our category of contract types. 'Fiduciary duties', he argues, 'are not duties which are imposed by law nor are they necessarily referable to a relationship or status'; rather, they 'arise in the same manner as any other express or implied term: by construction of the scope of voluntary undertakings.'[64] Fiduciary duties are 'based upon consent', and can therefore be contractually 'modified' and 'moulded', and 'cannot be superimposed upon a contract to alter its intended operation.'[65] This view, which on its face resembles Easterbrook and Fischel's, in fact reflects the contract-type conception of fiduciaries, because, as Edelman recently clarified, 'the relationship [] provides crucial context for the construction' of fiduciary undertakings, which both 'serve[] as a basis from which an implication can be drawn

[58] For another position, which conceptualizes fiduciary law as 'a well-designed union of penalty default and standard efficient default rules', see Getzler (n 41) at 61.

[59] See also, eg, Paul Miller, 'The Fiduciary Relationships' in *Philosophical Foundations of Fiduciary Law* (n 41) at 63, 67, who argues that 'the kind-status of a relationship … determines whether fiduciary duties apply to it'. For a detailed analysis and critique of Miller's position, which indeed unduly typifies fiduciary law as a whole based on an account of office-like cases of fiduciaries, see Dagan and Hannes (n 56) at 95–99.

[60] Lionel Smith, 'Fiduciary Relationships: Ensuring the Loyal Exercise of Judgment on Behalf of Another' (2014) 130 LQR 608, 613.

[61] Ibid. As Smith notes, '[t]his is not unusual; … when the law attaches features to a legal relationship, parties may have a choice as to whether or not they enter the relationship, but they do not necessarily have the ability to vary its features.' Ibid at 614.

[62] Daniel Markovits, 'Sharing Ex Ante and Sharing Ex Post: The Non-Contractual Basis of Fiduciary Relationships' in *Philosophical Foundations of Fiduciary Law* (n 41) at 209, 224.

[63] Ibid at 223–24. As an aside, we do not share Markovits' account of the guardian–ward relationship as identity-shaping, at least when it is freestanding (as opposed to cases in which the guardian is the parent, but then the identitarian category is parenthood). It is thus not surprising to us that, unlike parents, appointed guardians can be more readily substituted.

[64] James Edelman, 'When Do Fiduciary Duties Arise?' (2010) 126 LQR 302, 302.

[65] Ibid at 302–03.

in [the fiduciary's] undertaking' and 'shape[] the understanding that a reasonable person will have of their conduct.'[66]

Both positions are coherent and both can point to ample evidence in fiduciary law to support their descriptive power.[67] But neither deserves a hegemony throughout the vast terrain of fiduciary law.[68] In fact, fiduciary law as we understand it presents a micro-cosmos of the office-to-contract-type divide. Within fiduciary law we can find both offices and contract types, as well as intermediate configurations between these ideal types.[69] In order to illustrate this claim we use two typical examples: parenting for office and financial fiduciaries for contract type. The following discussion of these important categories heavily draws on prior works we have separately published, co-authored with Robert Scott and Sharon Hannes, respectively.[70] Thus, it does not purport to provide a comprehensive account of either doctrine, but can focus on the task at hand: gaining a more robust understanding of the different options presented by offices and contract types.

B. Parents

Law's traditional understanding of the parent–child relationship was premised on the 'natural' rights of parents.[71] Parents, particularly fathers as heads of household, had extensive legal authority over the lives of their children.[72] This was of course a classic example of hereditary and hierarchic status (no coincidence that it was the one on which Maine focused): the authority of biological parents was not dependent on behaviour that promoted the child's interest and was lost only by abandonment

[66] James Edelman, 'The Role of Status in the Law of Obligations' in *Philosophical Foundations of Fiduciary Law* (n 41) at 21, 34. For this reason, a court may assume, in this view, 'as a heuristic of private law that parties will *expect* to incorporate as implied or imputed terms those regular duties ascribed by general law or practice or the custom of a trade'. Getzler (n 41) at 49.

[67] To be sure, as the text which follows implies, although we think that Edelman's account captures an important subset of fiduciary law, we do not subscribe to his restricted view of fiduciary law as encompassing only voluntary types of fiduciaries and as excluding any statutory-based fiduciaries.

[68] Cf Andrew S Gold, 'The Loyalties of Fiduciary Law' in *Philosophical Foundations of Fiduciary Law* (n 41) at 176. But see Avihay Dorfman, 'On Trust and Transubstantiation' in *Philosophical Foundations of Fiduciary Law* (n 41) at 339, 341 (acknowledging the pluralism of trust law but insisting on its unified formal structure).

[69] Marriage is a particularly interesting case. Its strong identitarian dimension makes it closer to the office category, but the general availability of unilateral no-fault divorce implies that this dimension may not be as strong as with parenthood. Concern about asymmetrical vulnerability is also surely significant, but is again weaker, and the law is committed to the parties' equal authority: even in the most traditional couples, there is no issue of incapacity. This characterization seems to be reflected in modern marital property law and particularly the freedom of parties to execute premarital agreements limiting the sharing of property on termination. Here the law is typified by the combination of general mutability with a relatively rigorous unconscionability scrutiny and some limits on opt-outs (such as the impossibility of setting up temporary marriage).

[70] See respectively Elizabeth S Scott and Robert E Scott, 'Parents as Fiduciaries' (1995) 81 Va L Rev 2401; Dagan and Hannes (n 56).

[71] See Katharine T Bartlett, 'Rethinking Parenthood as an Exclusive Status: The Need for Legal Alternatives When the Premise of the Nuclear Family Has Failed' (1984) 70 Va L Rev 879, 887–90.

[72] See Barbara Bennett Woodhouse, '"Who Owns the Child?": Meyer and Pierce and the Child as Property' (1992) 33 Wm & Mary L Rev 995.

or unfitness.[73] The law has long discarded this conception, as inconsistent with modern views of parenthood, and as normatively unacceptable.[74] The conception is outdated because contemporary law recognizes not only biological parents, but also de facto parents not biologically-related to the child.[75] Even more importantly, the status-based conception of parenthood is normatively problematic, because it 'accords unwarranted legal protection to biological parents in ways that are both directly harmful and symbolically corrosive to the interests of their children.'[76]

Conceptualizing parents as fiduciaries offers a much more attractive model of the parent–child relationship than did traditional family law, and represents a typical instance of the fiduciary role as an office. This understanding of parenthood is grounded not in parents' rights, but rather in parents' *obligation* to serve the child's best interest.[77] It understands parenthood as a fiduciary category, by viewing parents as *entrusted*[78] with the duty to raise their children to adulthood and provide for their physical and psychological needs. Satisfactory performance of these tasks places substantial demands on the time, energy, and resources of parents. Parenthood shares many of the structural features of other types of fiduciary relationships: parents make an extensive range of decisions and perform many tasks that significantly affect the welfare and successful development of their children, and because of the complexity of their role, they require a considerable amount of discretion. But parents fulfil their obligations under conditions of information and control asymmetries and significant vulnerability, given the inability of children to protect and assert their own interests. This raises daunting concerns that the parents may be inclined to pursue their own potentially conflicting interests. Further, although individuals are assumed to have a choice about whether to become parents, children do not have a choice about undertaking this family relationship. In short, the parent–child relationship clearly falls outside the contract–type conception of fiduciaries.[79] Rather, it seems to epitomize Markovits' understanding of

[73] See Scott and Scott (n 70) at 2407.

[74] Notice that our analysis is limited to the *legal* understanding of parenthood. We do not deny that there is a social understanding of parenthood which is rooted in biology and is notably reflected in the rights of adopted children to learn the identity of their biological parents. Notice, however, that this is a much narrower understanding of a parent as an ancestor, which is focused on the child's right and does not entail—neither in law nor in our social norms—any authority of the biological parent.

[75] See Emily Buss, '"Parental" Rights' (2002) 88 Va L Rev 635, 637.

[76] Scott and Scott (n 70) at 2406.

[77] For our purposes we need not unpack the specific content of the child's interest. For an illuminating account of the main alternatives—self-determination and self-fulfilment—and the way they both avoid the seemingly unavoidable paradox insofar as children are concerned, see Joel Feinberg, 'The Child's Right to an Open Future' in William Aiken and Hugh LaFollette (eds), *Whose Child? Children's Rights, Parental Authority, and State Power* (Rowan and Littlefield, 1980) 124, 145.

[78] We deliberately use here the passive voice, so as not to imply that this trust relationship, which typifies (or at least should typify) parenthood, is necessarily dependent upon some positive act of authorization by the state or that children are the state's to allocate. The state is surely *not* analogous to the settlor of a trust; quite the contrary. Part of the point of analysing parenthood as a fiduciary relationship is that this conceptualization entails important *instructions to the state* as to how parenthood is to be (legitimately) regulated.

[79] There are many indicia for this difference, including the nature of benefits from parenthood, the type of sanctions from breach of parents' duty of loyalty, and the social—and often also legal—disapproval of attempts of parental withdrawal. But cf Margaret F. Brinig, 'Parents: Trusted but not

identitarian fiduciary relationships, bonds that are both broad in scope and have intrinsic value that extends beyond successful performance of caretaking tasks. Parenthood, in our taxonomy, is an office. The value of the relationship between the particular parent and specific child implies that parents are not fungible child-rearers;[80] their substitution can be accomplished only at considerable cost to the child's psychological health.[81]

The upshot is that, although the prominence of parental rights may seem to echo the status-based understanding of parenthood, contemporary law largely conforms to the conception of parenthood as an office. In contrast to traditional notions of parental rights, parental authority is allocated as a means of promoting the child's interests; indeed, 'fiduciary constraints are a necessary condition of [the legitimacy of] parental authority.'[82] To be sure, this allocation is usually governed by a process of self-identification at the child's birth, based on a willingness and capacity of biological or adoptive parents to undertake parental responsibilities. But where contests over parental identity and authority arise, often in cases involving unmarried biological fathers or de facto parents, legal protection is based on investment in and fulfilment of parental responsibilities. In this way, nontraditional (and non-biological) caregivers may be identified as additional or alternative parents.[83]

Properly understood then, parental rights are not based on a notion of entitlement, but are aimed—in line with the fiduciary understanding—at serving the child's interest in receiving good care from her parents. Parental rights are not a licence to engage in selfish behaviour, but a mechanism for aligning conflicting interests by rewarding good parenting and encouraging commitment and investment in children's welfare.[84] In short, parental rights function as a *quid pro quo*—constituting both incentive and reward for satisfactory parental performance. The legal deference to parents' judgement is premised on an assumption that the 'bonds between parents and children together with informal social norms … encourage parents to identify their interests with those of their children and to approach their performance as parents with a sense of moral obligation.'[85] On this view, good parenting can be expected to yield 'social approval and self-fulfillment', whereas deficient performance will result in 'guilt and social opprobrium'.[86]

Trustees Or (Foster) Parents as Fiduciaries' (2011) 91 BUL Rev 1231 (criticizing the fiduciary understanding of parenthood based on these distinctions from the contract type conception).

[80] As the text implies, our use of the term 'office' does not suggest the independence of offices from their various occupants (as is the case with respect to public offices, such as the President, but neither with parents nor with other types of fiduciary relationships, such as general partnerships). But cf Christopher Essert, 'The Office of Ownership' (2013) 63 U Toronto LJ 418, 430–5; Dennis Klimchuk, 'Equity and the Rule of Law' in Lisa Austin and Dennis Klimchuk (eds), *Private Law and the Rule of Law* (Oxford University Press, 2014) 247.

[81] See Scott and Scott (n 70) at 2402, 2415–20, 2431, 2445, 2452.

[82] Evan Fox-Decent, 'Fiduciary Authority and the Service Conception' in *Philosophical Foundations of Fiduciary Law* (n 41) at 363, 377.

[83] See Buss (n 75) at 650–54, 657–66; Scott and Scott (n 70), at 2434–35, 2456–62.

[84] See Scott and Scott (n 70) at 2404, 2440, 2463, 2476. Cf. Roderick M Hills, Jr, 'The Constitutional Rights of Private Governments' (2003) 78 NYU L Rev 144, 173–75, 203.

[85] Scott and Scott (n 70) at 2433.

[86] Ibid. It is furthermore premised on the significant effect of parents' satisfaction and enthusiasm for their role to their children's welfare. See ibid at 2430.

In this fiduciary regime, the state plays a limited but critically important role. The state has limited capacity to oversee parents' day-to-day childrearing (only few observers hold that children's welfare would be promoted by active intervention in parents' routine decisions).[87] Thus, potential conflicts of interest between parents and children are ameliorated largely through reliance on parents' psychological bonds with their children and on informal social norms. But monitoring arrangements play an important role in detecting and sanctioning serious defaults of parental obligations.[88] This realm of legally-imposed restrictions is limited in scope, but it is largely mandatory. This elaborate scheme of immutable regulation comfortably fits our characterization of parents-as-fiduciaries as a clear example of an office given the identitarian nature of parenthood and the profound vulnerability of children.[89] In fact, it seems to be the prominent example of an office, given that there are few—if any—other categories in which both of these features fully apply.

Even in the intact family setting, where bonding can be relied upon to do much of the work of promoting responsible parental behaviour, monitoring plays an important role. A series of preemptive rules—notably child labour laws and compulsory school attendance requirements—prescribe the boundaries of parental discretion to define their children's interests. Moreover, parents whose children are found to be abused or neglected are subject to formal state supervision until the deficient behaviour is remedied; their children may be removed from their custody and, if their default is judged to be irremediable, their parental rights can be terminated, followed by placement with substitute adoptive parents.[90]

Whereas state supervision of intact families is limited to preemptive rules and intervention for serious parental defaults, the need for oversight is more critical when parents do not live together. This is so, first, because self-interested behaviour by non-custodial parents is more prevalent and, second, because the potential for conflict between parents as joint fiduciaries is far greater when they separate (or have never lived together). Non-custodial parents may sometimes defect on obligations that they would have fulfilled before divorce, for example, because their children's significance to their identity has diminished or because the rewards of parenthood have diminished. Contact likely is less frequent, and, in some cases, accompanied by disputes with the former spouse over how best to promote children's interests. In order to address these difficulties the law provides an elaborate set of rules aimed at encouraging the continued fulfilment of parental obligations after divorce, either through shared custody or through continued authority and access for the non-custodial parent. Moreover, modern law sanctions uncooperative parents. Thus, to

[87] See Buss (n 75) at 647–49. Cf Martin Guggenheim, *What's Wrong with Children's Rights?* (Harvard University Press, 2005) Ch. 2.

[88] See Scott and Scott (n 70) at 2403–04, 2421, 2438–39, 2441, 2452, 2474–75.

[89] We do not claim, of course, that family law perfectly tracks the prescriptions of the conceptualization of parents as office-type fiduciaries. See Scott and Scott (n 70) at 2463–70. As with any interpretive account of the law, the gaps between the doctrine's implicit normative promise and its explicit details can, and indeed should, serve as the basis for (internal) critique and reform.

[90] See Scott and Scott (n 70) at 2238–39, 2242, 2252–53, 2255. See also ibid at 2447–48, 2453–54 (discussing the monitoring function of foster care plans).

assure that non-custodial parents fulfil their financial duty to their children, the law prescribes rules with increasingly tough sanctions for non-compliance with child support orders.[91]

Finally, not only are parents' core obligations largely immutable, they are also not fully assignable. To be sure, like other officeholders, parents can, and often do, outsource menial tasks and even delegate more substantial tasks and decisions, by putting the child in day care, hiring babysitters, and the like.[92] But beyond these limited forms of outsourcing, broader delegation of parental responsibilities to others may be quite consequential. Thus, a parent who leaves the child with a third party (such as a grandparent) for an extended period (years) could lose parental rights.[93] In general, the recognition of custodial rights in 'de facto parents' in recent years coheres with the substitution of the status-based conception of parental rights with an office-type fiduciary model, which grounds parental rights in parental responsibilities, while still understanding parenting in identitarian, rather than merely instrumental terms.

C. Financial Fiduciaries

Whereas parents present the ultimate identitarian category of fiduciary relationship and thus an obvious example for our category of an office, money managers are probably the ultimate instrumental fiduciaries, so we turn to the case of these financial fiduciaries, which we analyse as a contract type.

The instrumental nature of financial fiduciaries is straightforward. These fiduciaries—typically professional profit-making firms—manage (enormous amounts of) money: they are responsible for people's savings, pensions, and bequeathable fortunes. Indeed, in sharp contrast to the role of the parent-fiduciary in the child-beneficiary's life, the beneficiaries (and their benefactors, in appropriate cases) of these trustees find no intrinsic good in their relationship with their money managers. Rather, they resort to money managers as a means to an end: this contract type is instrumental to their autonomy because it allows them to enlist the superior skills, knowledge, and experience (and thus, arguably, judgement) of others for an important task that impacts significant aspects of their purely welfarist interests. Enabling such a delegation is autonomy-enhancing also because the alternative seems daunting given the resources—in time and expertise—that money management nowadays requires. The ability to safely delegate this task to others removes these burdens so that individuals can focus on intrinsically valuable projects.[94]

[91] See Scott and Scott (n 70) at 2246–52, 2455.

[92] Such delegations are properly subject to a negligence standard, which may entail liability when parents leave their children with a caretaker, who they have reason to know (or should know) poses a threat to the child or will be unable to provide adequate care. See, eg, *State v Goff*, 686 P.2d 1023 (Ore. 1984).

[93] See *Price v Howard*, 484 S.E.2d 528 (N.C. 1998). In this case, the court held that the presumption favouring the parent for custody did not apply, where the parent had voluntarily relinquished custody to a non-parent with whom the child had lived for a substantial period. See also *Blair v Ba*, 77 S.W. 3d 137 (Tenn. 2002).

[94] See Dagan and Hannes (n 56) at 91, 103–05, 118, 121.

If we were to pigeonhole financial fiduciaries in the innate status/open-ended contract binarism discussed in Part I, we would thus probably have opted for the latter alternative.[95] But this would lead to error. In fact, we believe that John Langbein erred on this basis when he advocated the substitution of a best interest rule for the traditional sole interest rule. Langbein correctly demonstrated that the sole interest standard and its attendant 'no further inquiry' rule gives way to a long list of exclusions and categoric exceptions. A transaction that is in the best interest of the beneficiary, but tainted by a benefit bestowed upon the trustee, is deemed acceptable where the trustee obtains the settlor's authorization, the beneficiary's informed consent, or the court's prior approval. Likewise, courts and legislatures have exempted classes of transactions that implicate the trustee's self-interest, granting special prerogatives to institutional trustees in the financial services industry, such as the authority to deposit trust funds in a financial institution affiliated with the trustee's intrafamilial transactions. Given the existing array of exclusions and exceptions, Langbein argued, a best interest rule that requires the trustee to prove the fairness of a given transaction would make trust law both more transparent and more clearly aimed at incentivizing transactions that best promote beneficiaries' interests.[96]

A financial fiduciaries law aimed at serving the welfare interests of beneficiaries properly responds to the parties' welfarist goals and the divergent consequences likely to arise in the different legal regimes given the distinct incentives they generate. Thus, it should indeed favourably carve out, as trust law does, exceptions to the sole interest rule to cover categories of cases in which optimizing beneficiaries' interests requires allowing fiduciaries some incidental benefits.[97] But by dismissing, indeed discarding, the normative core of financial fiduciary law—its signature principle of loyalty—Langbein's radical suggestion would have dismantled the cultural and social expectations that typify this contract type, which helpfully inform the parties' behaviour. As Melanie Leslie argues, stripping fiduciary duties of their moral content might dilute the stigma of money managers' opportunism. This unfortunate expressive consequence may, in turn, have detrimental implications on the material front as well, given the typical weakness of other means of guarding against abuse by financial fiduciaries (such as exit, monitoring, or market discipline).[98] In contrast, the unique development of the duty of loyalty in trust law subtly, if unintentionally, utilizes the gap between law's material effects and its expressive function.[99] Because financial fiduciaries law typically targets sophisticated professionals who have access

[95] Cf Stephen A Smith, 'The Deed, Not the Motive: Fiduciary Law Without Loyalty' at 213, in this volume.

[96] See John H Langbein, 'Questioning the Trust Law Duty of Loyalty: Sole Interest or Best Interest?' (2005) 114 Yale LJ 929.

[97] See Dagan and Hannes (n 56) at 101, 105, 109.

[98] See Melanie B Leslie, 'Trusting Trustees: Fiduciary Duties and the Limits of Default Rules' (2005) 94 Geo LJ 67, 90; Melanie B Leslie, 'In Defense of the No Further Inquiry Rule: A Response to Professor John Langbein' (2005) 47 Wm & Mary L Rev 541, 555–63. Needless to add that financial fiduciaries law also cannot rely on the intrinsic value of the fiduciary relationship which underlies the legal deference to parents' judgement.

[99] As in the case of parents, we do not claim that financial fiduciaries law perfectly achieves this task. One important pitfall relates to its traditional treatment of fiduciary pay as exogenous to the duty of loyalty. See Dagan and Hannes (n 56) at 118–21.

to ample legal advice, most doctrinal details are likely to be translated into incentives and to generate corresponding behavioural outcomes. But doctrinal details—unlike more fundamental legal concepts and institutions—rarely produce broad cultural consequences and, thus, rarely impact broader social norms. Accordingly, in entrenching the conception of the trustee as a person who is morally obligated to serve the beneficiary alone, trust law reinforces a socially popular perception of their role, and one that is instrumental in facilitating the safe delegation of welfarist interests to trustees.[100]

To function as a contract type financial fiduciary law must preserve this character so that the option it offers people remains distinctive and viable. But unlike offices, contract types are understood as a repertoire of *alternative* frameworks for voluntary arrangements available to people in pursuing their projects and ends of choice. This means, as noted in Section II, that contract types function best where they offer people more than one such framework for each major contracting activity. It also means that where no third-party negative externalities are at stake, their rules are by and large not immutable, but rather adjustable to the specific goals of the parties at hand. Both features typify the law of financial fiduciaries.

Thus, financial fiduciary law is one of two major frameworks our law offers for the task of managing money. When people resort to financial fiduciaries they expect them to follow the investment policy they would have adopted had they had the expertise to manage their own passive investments, hence trust law's prescription of diversification, which mimics what a prudent investor normally does with her own portfolio.[101] Corporate managers, by contrast, are expected to take a very different approach: they are required to stick to a single area of expertise and take on risky ventures consonant with the risk preferences of shareholders. This difference—as well as the availability of alternative means for securing loyalty in the corporate context (notably, the prospect of shareholder exit and shareholders' ability to replace the managerial team)—account for the difference between the relatively harsh duty of care of financial fiduciaries and the much more lenient duty to which corporate managers are subject.[102] So individuals seeking financial services can choose not only the contract type offered by financial fiduciary law, but also another contract type (the one offered by an investment in a corporation).[103] Having a real choice

[100] See Dagan and Hannes (n 56) at 106–07, 109–10. Another benefit to the unique structure of trust law, which might also be at risk under Langbein's proposed reform, is that conceptualizing deviations from the sole interest rule as exceptions serves as a reminder of the need to scrutinize the justifiability of these exceptions, an inquiry which is particularly important given the prospect of abuse. Ibid at 110–11.

[101] This rule is relatively new, to be sure, and by now controversial. Addressing this complex controversy is beyond the scope of this essay. For our purposes it is enough to say that insofar as it is problematic, its difficulties derive from the detrimental impact of the traditional way trustees (and trust advisers) are compensated. See Dagan and Hannes (n 56) at 113–14.

[102] See Dagan and Hannes (n 56) at 99, 108, 111–12.

[103] Adam Hofri-Winogradow has recently claimed that 'trust law and practice [tends to converge with] the law and practice of corporations.' See Adam Hofri-Winogradow, 'Contract, Trust and Corporation: From Contrast to Convergence' (unpublished manuscript). Insofar as this is indeed the trend, we find it—for the reason mentioned in the text—unfortunate.

between two distinct frameworks for the same activity is indeed one of the most important features that distinguish a contract type from an office.

Financial fiduciary law, again in line with its characterization as a contract type, by and large rejects immutability. Indeed, it is hard to see why any of its specific rules should be forced against the express preferences of the parties. After all, significant welfare interests of the beneficiaries are on the line, and while it is true that private parties suffer from cognitive-behavioural biases, limited willpower, and many other imperfections that may well justify stickiness, public officials are not necessarily immune from these either or, for that matter, other similar biases. Accordingly, financial fiduciaries law is comprised of a set of sticky default rules wrapped in two standards—the duty of loyalty and the duty of care—which can be similarly derogated, but not completely set aside. These standards serve, as noted, an expressive function, which is especially important in an environment that increasingly requires the carving-out of exceptions and exemptions. Opt outs are allowed, but are generally (although probably not sufficiently) scrutinized in order to guarantee that they reflect people's informed choice, notwithstanding the structural problems of information asymmetry and cognitive biases that typify even this type of fiduciary relationship and given the fact that a significant subset of the universe of these money managers' beneficiaries includes weak and unsophisticated individuals.[104]

Finally, financial fiduciaries can delegate the core of their tasks.[105] This possibility—which is now (as per the Uniform Prudent Investor Act) the default rule—is justified because, unlike parents, the task of financial fiduciaries is indeed instrumental, rather than identitarian. (This does not imply, to be sure, that we further endorse that rule's limitation of possible liability of such trustees to cases of negligent selection of the investment advisor. Quite the contrary: in order to ensure that they fully internalize the consequences of an inadequate delegation, these financial fiduciaries should also be liable if the delegation was to an entity or person who lacked the financial resources or insurance that could meet potential liability.[106])

V. Concluding Remarks

The status vs. contract divide is a core distinction in important sections of our private law, but its current understanding in binaric terms has facilitated its use as a foil and has thus undermined its conceptual and normative significance. In order to clarify normative debates and facilitate the conceptual contribution of Maine's seminal work, four, rather than merely two, ideal types are needed: innate status, office, contract type, and open-ended contract. Once the distinct meanings of these categories are clarified, we can see that in a liberal society most of our

[104] See Dagan and Hannes (n 56) at 115–18.
[105] See Uniform Prudent Investor Act §9 (1994).
[106] See Dagan and Hannes (n 56) at 116 n 137.

choices are between office and contract type. Focusing the analysis on *this* choice helps clarify its most important considerations, namely: the nature—identitarian or instrumental—of the relationships at hand and the significance and salience of asymmetrical vulnerability, as well as its major doctrinal implications: the question of immutability and the possibility of assignability. In this essay we used parents and financial fiduciaries as examples for office and contract type, but we believe that other classes of fiduciaries can also be helpfully analysed in similar terms.[107] We also hope that our new taxonomy will be proved beneficial for other segments of the law which have been hitherto subject to the constraining binarism of the conventional status to contract framework.

[107] A particularly interesting application arises in the context of ad hoc fiduciaries. This category of cases seems to come about in contexts of peculiar vulnerabilities or—and sometimes and—idiosyncratic identitarian relationships. In other words, in our taxonomy it stands for what can be termed as 'functional offices'.

3

Fiduciary Undertakings

*Matthew Harding**

I. Introduction

The field of fiduciary theory is in full bloom, a felicitous state of affairs for which the editors of this book deserve no small credit.[1] In that field are many starting points for inquiry. We might ask questions about the identity, character, and relation of the legal norms that are imposed on fiduciaries: 'no conflict', 'no profit', 'good faith', and so forth.[2] We might ask questions about the justification of fiduciary remedies: rescission, disgorgement, and compensation, to take three key examples. We might ask questions—the most intractable questions of fiduciary theory—about the circumstances in which people are recognized in law as fiduciaries. And we might ask questions about how such circumstances arise, ie, how people come to be situated such that the law recognizes them as fiduciaries. Of course, these questions are interrelated: for example, questions about the norms of fiduciary law are bound up with, and perhaps to a degree coextensive with, questions about fiduciary remedies.[3] But the field of fiduciary theory flowers brightest when academics not only seek to present expansive theories of fiduciary law, but also worry over seemingly narrower concerns. If nothing else, expansive theories can benefit from the detailed analysis that only targeted inquiry can deliver.[4]

* Melbourne Law School. I am grateful to Michael Bryan, Evan Fox-Decent, Rosemary Langford, Paul Miller, Jeannie Paterson, and Andrew Robertson for discussions and comments on this paper.

[1] See Andrew S Gold and Paul B Miller (eds), *Philosophical Foundations of Fiduciary Law* (Oxford University Press, 2014).

[2] As with most propositions in the field of fiduciary theory, the proposition that the norms of fiduciary law are imposed on fiduciaries is contested: see James Edelman, 'When Do Fiduciary Duties Arise?' (2010) 126 LQR 302; James Edelman, 'The Importance of the Fiduciary Undertaking' (2013) 7 J of Eq 128. I will return to Edelman's arguments below.

[3] Note, for example, Lionel Smith's recent work on the 'no profit' rule: 'Deterrence, Prophylaxis and Punishment in Fiduciary Obligations' (2013) 7 J of Eq 87 and 'Fiduciary Relationships: Ensuring the Loyal Exercise of Judgement on Behalf of Another' (2014) 130 LQR 608; 'Can We Be Obliged to Be Selfless?' in Andrew S Gold and Paul B Miller (eds), *Philosophical Foundations of Fiduciary Law* (Oxford University Press, 2014) 141.

[4] More generally, I think that Joshua Getzler is right to warn against 'theorizing which seeks to position the law around a constrained core of abstract principles, on the model of parsimonious modelling in microeconomics or moral philosophy': 'Ascribing and Limiting Fiduciary Obligations' in Andrew

Thus, in this chapter, I will have little to say about the content, character, and justification of the norms and remedies of fiduciary law. Instead, my focus will be on the circumstances in which the law recognizes people as fiduciaries, as well as the related question of how these circumstances arise. I am particularly interested in phenomena that have often been thought key to the identification of fiduciary relationships: fiduciary undertakings. My aim will be to develop a theoretical account of fiduciary undertakings. In Section II, I will offer a brief description of fiduciary undertakings. I will also argue that, while a fiduciary undertaking almost always figures in the explanation of why a person is recognized in law as a fiduciary, a fiduciary undertaking is neither a necessary nor a sufficient condition of this legal recognition. Section III will focus on the relation of fiduciary undertakings and contracts. I will argue that there are important lessons about fiduciary undertakings to be learned from debates between contractarians and anti-contractarians on the functions and conceptual basis of fiduciary law; I will also consider some legal questions raised by the use of contract terms to constitute, exclude, or limit fiduciary undertakings. Section IV will focus on the relation of fiduciary undertakings and the assumption and occupancy of social roles. I will argue that the law's tradition of characterizing certain relationship types as prima facie fiduciary acknowledges that the voluntary occupancy of certain social roles is a type of fiduciary undertaking; I will also consider questions about the scope of fiduciary undertakings that are raised by prima facie fiduciary relationships. Section V will conclude.

II. Fiduciary Undertakings: Necessary or Sufficient?

What are fiduciary undertakings? One part of the answer is to be found in the general character of undertakings; another is to be found in what judges and other authorities have said about the content of fiduciary undertakings. As to the general character of undertakings, one helpful starting point is the dictionary meaning of the noun 'undertaking' and the associated verb 'to undertake'. The *Oxford English Dictionary* shows that these words bear a range of meanings, from 'to take upon oneself', to 'promise or pledge', to 'be surety for', to 'accept the duty of attending to or looking after'.[5] These various meanings point to an important element of the general character of undertakings: a person who undertakes voluntarily commits herself to act in accordance with certain norms. This is true of core instances of undertaking, such as vows and promises, in which there is a commitment to some known and particularized norm. But it is also true of more diffuse forms of undertaking, like voluntarily occupying a social role or embarking on a course of conduct known to attract the operation of norms, whether or not those norms are known to

S Gold and Paul B Miller (eds), *Philosophical Foundations of Fiduciary Law* (Oxford University Press, 2014) 39 at 40. A sound general theory of fiduciary law is likely to be neither elegant nor simple.

[5] 'Undertaking' in *Oxford English Dictionary*, available at <http://www.oed.com>.

or particularized by the one making the commitment in question.[6] As to the content of fiduciary undertakings, a representative statement is found in the dissenting judgment of Mason J of the High Court of Australia in *Hospital Products Ltd v United States Surgical Corporation*. According to Mason J, a fiduciary undertaking is one 'to act for or on behalf of or in the interests of another person'.[7] Likewise, Cromwell J (for the Supreme Court of Canada) in *Galambos v Perez*: 'the fiduciary undertakes to act in the interests of the other party'.[8] Formulations like these point to the content of the norms attracted by a fiduciary undertaking: broadly speaking, these norms demand, at minimum, that fiduciaries serve the interests of others.

I now want to argue that a fiduciary undertaking is neither a necessary nor a sufficient condition of the law recognizing that a person is a fiduciary. That it is not a necessary condition is sometimes contradicted by judges and commentators. For example, in *Norberg v Wynrib*, McLachlin J of the Supreme Court of Canada asserted that 'fiduciary relationships ... are always dependent on the fiduciary's undertaking to act in the beneficiary's interests'.[9] Similarly, in his influential extra-judicial writings, James Edelman has stated that 'a fiduciary duty will not be imposed upon a person *without* an undertaking'.[10] One can see the appeal of these views: clearly the overwhelming majority of fiduciaries have undertaken to act in the interests of others. In most cases, there is a contract entailing or pointing to a fiduciary undertaking, or evidence of voluntary assumption of a social role requiring adherence to norms demanding service of others' interests. It is thus tempting to assert that an undertaking is a necessary condition for the imposition of fiduciary norms.[11]

I think that this temptation should be resisted, because there is at least one situation in which fiduciary norms are imposed absent an undertaking: where a parent is recognized as a fiduciary in relation to her child. In *M(K) v M(H)*, La Forest J of the Supreme Court of Canada declared that '[i]t is intuitively apparent that the relationship between parent and child is fiduciary in nature'.[12] Justice La Forest suggested that 'being a parent comprises a unilateral undertaking that is fiduciary in nature'.[13] But given the general character of undertakings, this seems difficult

[6] I will return to the topic of undertakings and the occupancy of social roles in Section IV.

[7] (1984) 156 CLR 1 at 96–97.

[8] [2009] 3 SCR 247 at [69]. See also Austen Scott, 'The Fiduciary Principle' (1949) 37 Cal L Rev 539 at 540; Paul Finn, *Fiduciary Obligations* (Law Book Co, 1977) at [467].

[9] [1992] 2 SCR 226 at 273.

[10] Edelman, 'The Importance of the Fiduciary Undertaking' (n 2) at 129 (emphasis in the original).

[11] A related point: in cases where the factual background includes a fiduciary undertaking, there seems no reason to doubt that the fiduciary undertaking operates as a source of normativity. However, as I will discuss below, this does not mean that other sources of normativity are absent, nor does it mean that a fiduciary undertaking operates as a source of fiduciary norms.

[12] [1992] 3 SCR 6, 61. For present purposes, I will bracket debates about whether parents are fiduciaries in relation to the personal, rather than economic, interests of their children; those debates belong to an inquiry into the content, character, and justification of the norms of fiduciary law, not to an inquiry into fiduciary undertakings. For a sense of the debate, contrast *M(K) v M(H)* and the decision of the Full Federal Court of Australia in *Paramasivam v Flynn* (1998) 160 ALR 203.

[13] Interestingly, immediately before stating this, La Forest J acknowledged that 'fiduciary obligations are imposed in some situations even in the absence of a unilateral undertaking by the fiduciary' ([1992] 3 SCR 6 at 63). Justice La Forest said nothing about the character of such situations, but

to accept. Recall that undertakings entail voluntary commitment to norms (in the case of fiduciary undertakings, norms demanding service of another's interests). Many parents do make a voluntary commitment to serve the interests of their children. Others, though, do not; for example, people who become parents unwillingly or unknowingly. Many such people, after they become parents (and, in the case of unknowing parents, after they discover that they are parents), voluntarily commit to the norms of parenthood; but sadly some do not. The parent who never wanted to be a parent and who never subsequently voluntarily commits herself to acting in the interests of her child cannot be plausibly said to have made a fiduciary undertaking.[14]

James Edelman argues that this is to misunderstand the way in which fiduciary undertakings are discerned.[15] For Edelman, an undertaking is not discerned with reference to the subjective beliefs or preferences of the putative fiduciary. It is, rather, a matter of 'objective manifestations of conduct';[16] namely, what 'would objectively be conveyed by what was said or done, having regard to the circumstances in which those statements and actions happened'.[17] On Edelman's view, the unwilling parent may have made a fiduciary undertaking where a reasonable observer would conclude from her actions that she had voluntarily committed herself to serving the interests of her child even if, subjectively, she had not. Edelman's argument may help to explain some cases of parental fiduciary obligation.[18] But it cannot explain why the law imposes fiduciary norms on the parent whose subjective unwillingness to act in the interests of her child is mirrored in objective manifestations of conduct: abandonment, neglect, or abuse. Moreover, Edelman assumes that it is appropriate to adopt a methodology drawn from contract interpretation in construing fiduciary undertakings. There might be a strong case for insisting on an objective methodology when interpreting texts,[19] but why should it be assumed without argument that these reasons apply also to interpreting conduct?

I wonder what he can have had in mind, given his view that becoming a parent constitutes a unilateral undertaking.

[14] Note Elizabeth S Scott and Robert E Scott, 'Parents as Fiduciaries' (1995) 81 Va L Rev 2401 at 2432 n 100, acknowledging that the assumption that parenthood is a voluntary choice is 'counterfactual in some instances', even if it holds true most of the time.

[15] Edelman, 'When Do Fiduciary Duties Arise?' (n 2) at 311–12.

[16] Ibid at 312.

[17] Ibid, quoting from *Ermogenous v Greek Orthodox Community of SA Inc* (2002) 209 CLR 95 at [25]. See also *Investors Compensation Scheme Ltd v West Bromwich Building Society* [1998] 1 WLR 896 at 912 per Lord Hoffmann: 'Interpretation is the ascertainment of the meaning which the document would convey to a reasonable person having all the background knowledge which would reasonably have been available to the parties in the situation in which they were at the time of the contract.'

[18] Although Edelman still bears the burden of showing how simply occupying a social role could serve as an objective manifestation of commitment to any particular norms: see further Andrew Robertson and Julia Wang, 'The Assumption of Responsibility' in Kit Barker, Ross Grantham, and Warren Swain (eds), *The Law of Misstatements: 50 Years on from Hedley Byrne v Heller* (Hart Publishing, 2015) 49. My own efforts to explain the relation of social roles and voluntary undertakings are found in Section IV below.

[19] For a defence of objective interpretation of constitutional, statutory, contractual, and other texts: *Byrnes v Kendle* (2011) 243 CLR 253 per Heydon and Crennan JJ.

Even if it could be shown that every parent makes a fiduciary undertaking in relation to her child, I think there is a further, more fundamental, reason to doubt that parents are deemed fiduciaries in law on that basis. Presumably, the law takes an interest in fiduciary undertakings because, by making such undertakings, people come to be subject to norms requiring that they serve the interests of others. But parents are subject to such norms whether they have voluntarily committed to abide by them or not. Fiduciary undertakings are thus, strictly speaking, superfluous in ascertaining whether parents are fiduciaries. Consider, for example, the legal duty of a parent to maintain her child. There are strong reasons to think that this duty is imposed on parents whether or not they have voluntarily committed to it;[20] even William Blackstone, who described becoming a parent as 'enter[ing] into a voluntary obligation', also acknowledged that a parent's legal duty to maintain her child 'is a principle of natural law; an obligation laid on [parents] by nature herself'.[21]

Blackstone's view also suggests that the voluntary commitment of a willing parent is not fundamental in explaining her subjection to moral norms demanding that she serve her child's interests. Such voluntary commitment is morally praiseworthy; it demonstrates that the parent understands and accepts the normative dimensions of her role.[22] But ultimately a parent owes moral duties to serve her child's interests simply because she is a parent; in other words, the moral duties of parents are not 'choice-dependent', to borrow a phrase from David Owens.[23] Indeed, given the profound vulnerability of children, the nature of the family as a social and economic institution, and human traditions and cultures, it is difficult to think of a social role in which moral duties are less likely to be a matter of choice. The insistence that the moral duties of parents are choice-dependent is, I suspect, rooted in the assumption that moral duties must always be choice-dependent, and there are good reasons to doubt this proposition.[24]

Having now shown that fiduciary undertakings are not a necessary condition of the law recognizing a person as a fiduciary, I now want to turn to the question whether they are a sufficient condition for such recognition. At first glance the proposition seems to suggest something strange; that I may become a fiduciary simply by promising to act in your interests even though I have no power or opportunity to do so, or that I may become a fiduciary by undertaking to carry out some discrete and mundane task that will serve your interests, like promising to water your plants while you are on holiday. There are some indications that circumstances like this might attract the interest of fiduciary law; for example, in *In re*

[20] See the learned discussion in the judgment of Baroness Hale in *R (Kehoe) v Secretary of State for Work and Pensions* [2006] 1 AC 42.

[21] *Commentaries*, Book 1, Chapter XVI, quoted in ibid at [50].

[22] To accept the normative dimensions of a role makes possible ways of succeeding morally that might not otherwise be available: see further Joseph Raz, *The Morality of Freedom* (Oxford University Press, 1986) at 353–57.

[23] See David Owens, *Shaping the Normative Landscape* (Oxford University Press, 2012) at 3–6.

[24] 'When I encounter the proverbial child drowning in the pond I must rescue the child regardless of my past choices. I may have done everything I could to avoid such encounters. I might have moved to the proverbial desert island where the child was then abandoned by a passing ship. Still I am obliged to rescue the child': ibid at 3.

Coomber; Coomber v Coomber, Fletcher-Moulton LJ talked of the fiduciary status of the 'errand boy who is bound to bring me back my change'.[25] But the dominant view is that a fiduciary undertaking, taken on its own, is not enough to engage the interest of fiduciary law.

This last proposition is supported by the considerable weight of authority identifying discretionary powers as important in explaining why the law recognizes a person as a fiduciary. Thus, in *Hospital Products*, Mason J spoke of an undertaking to serve the interests of another 'in the exercise of a power or discretion which will affect the interests of that other person in a legal or practical sense'.[26] In *Guerin v R*, in a widely-cited passage, Dickson J of the Supreme Court of Canada said: 'where … one party has an obligation to act for the benefit of another, and that obligation carries with it a discretionary power, the party thus empowered becomes a fiduciary'.[27] And leading academic works also point to discretionary powers as part of the factual backdrop against which the law will recognize a person as a fiduciary.[28] Now of course the fact that a person enjoys discretionary powers that may, when exercised, affect the interests of another is insufficient.[29] For example, the law does not always recognize as a fiduciary the donee of a power of appointment, even though such a person always enjoys a discretionary power to affect the interests of others.[30] Norms and discretionary powers must be combined in a certain way in relation to the putative fiduciary.

The precise nature of this combination is a large and difficult topic. For present purposes, I am content to make the following observations. To be recognized as a fiduciary, a person must be subject to norms demanding that she serve another's interests: such norms typically, but need not, apply in virtue of an undertaking. Moreover, these norms must constrain the exercise of discretionary powers. Such powers may be powers to affect the legal position of the person whose interests the power-holder is bound to serve but they may also be powers to affect a person's non-legal position (as seems to be the case in relation to a parent's powers over her child). Where a fiduciary undertaking is present, it may figure in the explanation of how the fiduciary came to enjoy the discretionary powers she enjoys. But the undertaking is not the normative source of the powers; the powers are instead presupposed

[25] [1911] 1 Ch 723 at 728. Note also Finn (n 8) at [467]: '[A fiduciary] is, *simply*, someone who undertakes to act for on behalf of another in some particular matter or matters' (emphasis added).

[26] (1984) 156 CLR 41 at 97.

[27] [1984] 2 SCR 335 at 384. See also *Frame v Smith* [1987] 2 SCR 99 at 136–38 per Wilson J.

[28] See, eg, Ernest J Weinrib, 'The Fiduciary Obligation' (1975) 25 U Tor LJ 1; JC Shepherd, *The Law of Fiduciaries* (Carswell, 1981); Deborah DeMott, 'Beyond Metaphor: An Analysis of Fiduciary Obligation' [1988] Duke LJ 879; Paul B Miller, 'A Theory of Fiduciary Liability' (2011) 56 McGill LJ 235.

[29] Note Frank H Easterbrook and Daniel R Fischel, 'Contract and Fiduciary Duty' (1993) 36 J L and Econ 425 at 436: 'Recent academic theories link the fiduciary relation to A's holding power over decisions important to B, and having discretion in the exercise of that power. Back to principals and agents! Agency is a necessary but not sufficient condition.'

[30] On the nature of powers of appointment: Lionel Smith, 'Understanding the Power' in William Swadling (ed), *The Quistclose Trust: Critical Essays* (Bloomsbury Publishing, 2004) 67; Geraint Thomas, *Thomas on Powers* (2nd ed, Oxford University Press, 2012) at 7–11.

by the fiduciary undertaking, which operates to constrain their exercise. In identifying the normative source of a fiduciary's discretionary powers, it is necessary in most cases to look to the voluntary action of persons other than the fiduciary (or the fiduciary acting in another capacity, as in the case of a declared trust), and in some cases it may be necessary to look to non-voluntary sources of authority (as in the case of the parent). The key point for present purposes is that the enjoyment of discretionary powers is a necessary condition of the law recognizing a person as fiduciary, but we must look beyond fiduciary undertakings to understand the sources of those powers.

III. Fiduciary Undertakings and Contracts

A. Functional and conceptual relations

One of the legacies of the law and economics movement in fiduciary theory is the notion that fiduciary law is functionally similar to contract law and that fiduciary relationships are functionally similar to contracts. The general idea is that fiduciary norms are best viewed, functionally, as specifying the terms the parties to a fiduciary relationship would have bargained for in a world of minimal transaction and enforcement costs.[31] Given this orientation to fiduciary law, it should be unsurprising that some contractarian economic analysis views fiduciary undertakings as functionally equivalent to contractual undertakings.[32] Recently, the law and economics approach has been supplemented by the more radical contractarianism of James Edelman.[33] Edelman argues that fiduciary law is contractarian in a conceptual sense. Not that Edelman thinks all fiduciary undertakings are contractual; he is careful to show that fiduciary undertakings might take the form of non-contractual but nonetheless voluntary assumptions of responsibility.[34] Rather, Edelman's thesis is that fiduciary norms are (non-hypothetical) implied terms of fiduciary undertakings, and that methods of contract interpretation are justifiably deployed in discerning such undertakings. For Edelman, where fiduciary undertakings are made by contract, fiduciary norms are implied contract terms and fiduciary and contract norms are conceptually equivalent. Where fiduciary undertakings are made other than by contract, fiduciary norms are closely analogous to implied contract terms.

Both contractarian approaches to fiduciary law may be challenged in several ways. For example, the functionalist contractarianism of economic analysis might be questioned on the basis that it neglects functions of fiduciary law that have nothing to do with private ordering but rather with the public policy of promoting and

[31] The locus classicus is Easterbrook and Fischel (n 29).

[32] This thinking is discernible, for instance, in John Langbein, 'The Contractarian Basis of the Law of Trusts' (1995) 105 Yale LJ 625 at 627: 'the deal between settlor and trustee is functionally indistinguishable from the modern third-party-beneficiary contract. Trusts are contracts.'

[33] Edelman, 'When Do Fiduciary Duties Arise?' (n 2); Edelman, 'The Importance of the Fiduciary Undertaking' (n 2).

[34] Edelman, 'When Do Fiduciary Duties Arise?' (n 2) at 306ff.

maintaining high standards of conduct in certain social and economic pursuits.[35] I have much sympathy with this, but will focus on developing an objection that bears primarily on Edelman's conceptual contractarianism. If successful, it will show that conceptual contractarianism about fiduciary law is unsound and that functionalist contractarianism is seriously incomplete.

The line of objection that I have in mind is pursued in two recent papers, one by Daniel Markovits, and the other by Stephen Galoob and Ethan Leib.[36] Markovits argues that there are important conceptual differences between contract norms and fiduciary norms; this is because parties to a contract and parties to a fiduciary relationship are placed in 'distinct deliberative postures' and contracts and fiduciary relationships are constituted according to 'distinct models of sharing'.[37] For Markovits, the model of sharing characteristic of a contract is one according to which the parties are entitled to be mutually self-interested and are not required to maintain deliberative regard for each other's interests as circumstances develop ex post in ways not provided for by contract.[38] In contrast, Markovits says, the model of sharing characteristic of a fiduciary relationship demands that the fiduciary eschew self-interest and exercise judgement and initiative in response to changing circumstances in order to serve her principal's interests.[39] Because of this, Markovits asserts, 'fiduciary relations and the obligations that they involve cannot inhabit a contractual form'.[40]

Similarly, Galoob and Leib argue that contractual norms and fiduciary norms have different structures. For Galoob and Leib, conformity to contractual norms does not necessarily entail any intentional action, whereas conformity to fiduciary norms invariably has an intentional element. Specifically, Galoob and Leib argue that conformity to contractual norms may be a matter of what they call 'accidental compliance', ie, unintentionally doing what one promised to do.[41] In contrast, they say, a fiduciary may conform to fiduciary norms only where she 'robustly attributes nonderivative significance to her beneficiary's interests'.[42]

What are the implications of these accounts for our understanding of fiduciary undertakings? They seem to suggest that fiduciary undertakings and contractual

[35] Perhaps the best-known proponent of the view that fiduciary law serves such public policy objectives is Paul Finn. See, eg, 'The Fiduciary Principle' in T G Youdan (ed), *Equity, Fiduciaries and Trusts* (University of Victoria, 1989) 1 at 27 ('[The fiduciary principle] originates, self-evidently, in public policy: in a view of desired social behaviour for the end this achieves. To maintain the integrity and utility of those relationships in which the (or a) role of one party is perceived to be the service of the interests of the other, it insists upon a fine loyalty in that service'); 'Fiduciary Reflections' (2014) 88 Aust LJ 127 at 142 ('[T]here is … more at issue than simply facilitating private ordering').

[36] Daniel Markovits, 'Sharing *Ex Ante* and Sharing *Ex Post*: The Non-Contractual Basis of Fiduciary Relations' in Andrew S Gold and Paul B Miller (eds), *Philosophical Foundations of Fiduciary Law* (Oxford University Press, 2014) 209; Stephen R Galoob and Ethan J Leib, 'Intentions, Compliance, and Fiduciary Obligations' (2014) 20 Leg Th 106.

[37] Markovits (n 36) at 210. [38] Ibid at 211–14. [39] Ibid at 214–18.

[40] Ibid at 210. [41] Galoob and Leib (n 36) at 108–15.

[42] Ibid at 115. As Galoob and Leib point out (at 129–31), in Australian fiduciary law, fiduciary norms are limited to proscriptive rules which do not demand intentional action of any sort: see *Breen v Williams* (1996) 186 CLR 71. Conceptual anti-contractarian arguments may therefore have less traction in relation to Australian law than they do in relation to the law of other jurisdictions.

undertakings are fundamentally conceptually and normatively distinct. However, in truth the arguments are perfectly consistent with the proposition that a person may make a fiduciary undertaking in contractual form. The key is in recalling the distinction between: (a) the conditions of the law recognizing a person as a fiduciary; and (b) the legal norms imposed on a person so recognized. A study of fiduciary undertakings is a (partial) study of (a), but conceptual anti-contractarians are interested in (b). To be sure, conceptual anti-contractarianism challenges Edelman's explanation of fiduciary undertakings, but this is only because, unusually, his account is at once an explanation of (a) and (b). Conceptual anti-contractarianism leaves unchallenged more mainstream views according to which the explanation of fiduciary undertakings is a separate matter from the explanation of the legal norms imposed on fiduciaries.

Indeed, conceptual anti-contractarian arguments help to clarify the implications of the fact that, in cases where fiduciary undertakings are made contractually, fiduciary undertakings are contractual. Thus, a contractual undertaking to serve another person's interests over time may be performed fully through the self-interested exercise of discretionary powers; as a matter of contract law, the most that might be demanded of the promisor is good faith performance, which is consistent with self-interested conduct even if it also entails regard for the interests of the counterparty to the degree necessary to ensure fidelity to the contract.[43] The fact that a fiduciary undertaking may be made in a given contract does not bear on what counts as sufficient performance of that undertaking as a matter of *contract* law. It instead means that non-performance of the undertaking is susceptible of analysis in more than one frame, as involving fiduciary breach as well as breach of contract.[44] Moreover, the promisor may be liable for fiduciary breach even in circumstances where she has fully performed her undertaking from the perspective of contract law, such as where she can show good faith performance but not adherence to higher fiduciary standards in the exercise of discretionary powers.[45] In these ways, as Mason J put it in *Hospital Products*, the contract 'provide[s] a foundation for the erection of a fiduciary relationship'.[46]

[43] See, eg, *Bhasin v Hrynew* [2014] 3 SCR 494 at [65] per Cromwell J (for the Court): 'Unlike fiduciary duties, good faith performance does not engage duties of loyalty to the other contracting party or a duty to put the interests of the other contracting party first'. And see also *Yam Seng Pte Ltd v International Trade Corporation Ltd* [2013] EWHC 111.

[44] Thus, in *Hospital Products*, the relevant non-performance generated claims for breach of contract and fiduciary breach. Only Mason J thought that it amounted to both; the majority of the Court thought that there was a breach of contract but no fiduciary breach because there was no relevant fiduciary undertaking in the contract: (1984) 156 CLR 1 at 41, 67–76 per Gibbs CJ, 117–19 per Wilson J, 119–25 per Deane J, 141–50 per Dawson J. Contrast Markovits' assertion that 'fiduciary relations squeeze out, rather than simply add to, the rights and duties associated with contractual good faith': (n 36) at 216 n 32.

[45] See further Richard Nolan and Matthew Conaglen, 'Good Faith: What Does It Mean for Fiduciaries, and What Does It Tell Us About Them?' in Elise Bant and Matthew Harding (eds), *Exploring Private Law* (Cambridge University Press, 2010) 318.

[46] (1984) 156 CLR 41 at 97.

B. Legal relations

If the debates between contractarians and anti-contractarians teach us anything, it is that undertakings to serve others' interests are fiduciary only in the sense that they may number among the reasons why the law recognizes a person as a fiduciary. The appellation 'fiduciary', when applied to such undertakings, points to this possibility and nothing more. With that in mind, I now want to consider the doctrinal relationship between fiduciary undertakings and contracts. This demands attention to the ways in which contract terms constitute, exclude, or limit fiduciary undertakings.[47] For analytical purposes, perhaps the most compelling cases are those in which contract terms expressly stipulate a fiduciary undertaking or the exclusion or limitation of such an undertaking. Two examples of such terms should help to illustrate. The first comes from *Australian Securities and Investments Commission v Citigroup Global Markets*.[48] There, the contract by which a client engaged an investment bank to advise it on a proposed corporate takeover provided that the bank was engaged 'as an independent contractor and not in any other capacity including as a fiduciary'.[49] The second term comes from *Noranda Australia Ltd v Lachlan Resources NL*, a case in which a joint venture agreement provided that the parties 'shall at all times act in relation to the joint venture in a bona fide manner to the intent that the relationship of the parties shall be fiduciary in nature'.[50]

The first and most important point to note is that the question of the meaning of contract terms is a matter of construction of the relevant contract.[51] The methodology is one according to which terms are to be ascertained, and their meaning worked out, applying the usual objective techniques of contractual construction.[52] Depending on the content and character of the contract, this exercise may deliver a range of results for the question whether the contract, by its terms, constitutes, excludes, or limits a fiduciary undertaking. The question may be determined by an express stipulation, whether purporting to exclude or limit a fiduciary undertaking (as in *Citigroup*) or to constitute such an undertaking (as in *Noranda*). However, an express stipulation may not be determinative if the overall meaning of the contract is clearly at odds with it. For example, an express stipulation purporting to opt out of a fiduciary undertaking might not be given effect if the balance of the contract

[47] A related question asks about ways in which contract terms purport either to make applicable or to exclude fiduciary norms such as 'no conflict', 'no profit', 'good faith', and so forth. I cannot explore this question fully here. For now, I simply make two points. First, in some cases a contract that purports to make applicable fiduciary norms may thereby manifest a fiduciary undertaking; in such a case fiduciary norms apply within the scope of the fiduciary undertaking but this is because they are imposed on the fiduciary by law, not by the contract. (See further D Gordon Smith, 'Contractually Adopted Fiduciary Duty' [2014] U Ill L Rev 1783.) And second, in some cases a contract that purports to exclude fiduciary norms may nonetheless entail a fiduciary undertaking; that said, where the exclusion of fiduciary norms is thoroughgoing this might necessitate the implication that the contract is inconsistent with any fiduciary undertaking.

[48] (2007) 160 FCR 35. [49] Ibid at [16]. [50] (1988) 14 NSWLR 1 at 13.

[51] In writing this paragraph I have been much assisted by Mark Leeming, 'The Scope of Fiduciary Obligations: How Contract Informs, but Does Not Determine, the Scope of Fiduciary Obligations' (2009) 3 J of Eq 1.

[52] See generally J W Carter, *The Construction of Commercial Contracts* (Hart Publishing, 2012).

makes clear that the putative fiduciary has undertaken to serve the interests of the other party in some matter for which the contract provides. Similarly, a broad, express stipulation purporting to opt in to a fiduciary undertaking might be interpreted as having a narrow scope if the contract as a whole makes clear that, in at least some of the matters for which it provides, the putative fiduciary is entitled to serve her own interests to the exclusion of those of the other party.[53] This, as it happens, was the case in *Noranda*.[54]

In cases where contracts do not contain express stipulations purporting to constitute, exclude or limit fiduciary undertakings, principles of contractual construction should be applied just as they are applied in cases where there are express stipulations. In some such cases a proper construction of the contract will reveal a fiduciary undertaking; in others, not. At times, judges have suggested that it is all but impossible in the absence of an express stipulation to construe a commercial contract as revealing a fiduciary undertaking.[55] It is true that a reasonable observer would not typically conclude that parties to such a contract intended to adopt norms requiring selfless service of the other's interests. That said, there is no reason of principle why a fiduciary undertaking might not, in exceptional cases, arise by implication from a commercial contract;[56] as Paul Finn has said, 'in commercial bargains struck at arms length between sophisticated parties with equal bargaining power, the need to make one part of their agreement fiduciary may be the only means reasonably available to them if they are to be able to enter into a detailed commercial arrangement the principal object of which is to promote their separate—and non-fiduciary—interests.'[57] Equally, of course, it should not be forgotten that an implied term may preclude a construction of the contract according to which it entails a fiduciary undertaking.[58]

That the relation of contract terms and fiduciary undertakings is first and foremost a question of contractual construction does not mean that contract law deals exhaustively with that relation. Consider the case where a contract excludes or limits a fiduciary undertaking in circumstances where the party who stands to benefit from the exclusion or limitation has undertaken to serve the interests of the other party during pre-contractual dealings. The case law shows that pre-contractual

[53] Thus, Mason J in *Hospital Products* (1984) 156 CLR 1 at 99: 'The fiduciary relationship, if it is to exist at all, must accommodate itself to the terms of the contract so that it is consistent with, and conforms to, them. The fiduciary relationship cannot be superimposed upon the contract in such a way as to alter the operation which the contract was intended to have according to its true construction.'

[54] (1988) 14 NSWLR 1 at 14–18.

[55] See, eg, *Hospital Products* (1984) 156 CLR 41 at 70 per Gibbs CJ, 118–19 per Wilson J and 149–50 per Dawson J; *Lac Minerals Ltd v International Corona Resources Ltd* [1989] 2 SCR 574 at 595–608 per Sopinka J; *John Alexander's Clubs Pty Ltd v White City Tennis Club Ltd* (2010) 241 CLR 1 at [92].

[56] Especially, it would seem, where the contract is of the 'relational' sort: see *Yam Seng Pte Ltd v International Trade Corporation Ltd* [2013] EWHC 111 at [142] per Leggatt J. I return to the question of relational contracts and fiduciary undertakings below.

[57] Finn, 'Fiduciary Reflections' (n 35) at 135–36. See also *Hospital Products* (1984) 156 CLR 41 at 99–100 per Mason J; A Mason, 'The Place of Equity and Equitable Remedies in the Contemporary Common Law World' (1994) 110 LQR 238 at 245 (describing fiduciary law as the 'spearhead of equity's incursions into the area of commerce').

[58] *Kelly v Cooper* [1993] AC 205.

fiduciary undertakings might be made where parties, while negotiating a contract that they expect will generate a fiduciary relationship between them, have begun to perform that anticipated contract.[59] Similarly, it has been said that, where a party discloses confidential information during pre-contractual negotiations, a fiduciary undertaking might be inferred from the fact of disclosure against the backdrop of known industry practice according to which receipt of information disclosed in confidence is conditioned by fiduciary expectations regarding the use of that information.[60] And where a party has begun to perform an advisory role she may thereby have made a fiduciary undertaking before a contract is entered into.[61]

In some cases of pre-contractual fiduciary undertakings, subsequent formation of the relevant contract is unlikely to fall within the scope of that undertaking. For example, this seems unlikely where a pre-contractual undertaking relates to the use of confidential information disclosed during negotiations. However, in other cases, such as those where parties have begun to perform an anticipated contract for fiduciary services of one kind or another, the pre-contractual fiduciary undertaking will almost certainly extend to the formation of the contract itself. And if the act of entering into a contract is within the scope of a pre-contractual fiduciary undertaking, then that act is—all else being equal—subject to the norms of fiduciary law. In other words, the performance of the act must be consistent with adherence to each of those norms and, if it is not, legal consequences may follow.[62]

One norm that seems to have direct application to such a case is the 'no conflict' rule according to which a fiduciary must not be in a position where there is a substantial possibility of conflict between her personal interest and the norms demanding service of her principal's interests that lie within the scope of her fiduciary undertaking.[63] Entering into a contract excluding or limiting a fiduciary undertaking, within the scope of a pre-contractual fiduciary undertaking, places the fiduciary in just such a conflict. If the fiduciary wishes to secure a self-interested exclusion or limitation in circumstances where her pre-contractual fiduciary undertaking demands that she serve her principal's interests when entering into the contract, she can do so only by making full disclosure of all materials facts prior to

[59] *United Dominions Corporation Limited v Brian Pty Limited* (1985) 157 CLR 1; *Chirnside v Fay* [2007] 1 NZLR 433. In the latter case, Blanchard and Tipping JJ of the Supreme Court of New Zealand doubted that a fiduciary undertaking was necessary in order for a party in the setting of pre-contractual negotiations to become subject to a norm demanding the service of the interests of the other party (at [81]–[82] and [85]). To the extent that these judges insisted that a fiduciary undertaking is not a necessary condition of the law recognizing a person as a fiduciary, I agree. However, I think that a fiduciary undertaking is invariably present where, before entering into a contract that they expect to generate a fiduciary relationship, parties begin to perform that contract; in those circumstances I think that the parties voluntarily assume responsibility to serve each other's interests.

[60] *Lac Minerals Ltd v International Corona Resources Ltd* [1989] 2 SCR 574 at 659–62 per La Forest J.

[61] See Simone Degeling and Jessica Hudson, 'Fiduciary Obligations, Financial Advisers and FOFA' (2014) 32 CSLJ 527.

[62] See PD Finn, 'Contract and the Fiduciary Principle' (1989) 12 UNSWLJ 76 at 92–6.

[63] See *Boardman v Phipps* [1967] 2 AC 46 at 123–4 per Lord Upjohn; *Canadian Aero Service Ltd v O'Malley* [1974] SCR 592 at 607–08 per Laskin J; *Chan v Zacharia* (1984) 154 CLR 178 at 198 per Deane J.

entering into the contract.[64] Such material facts presumably include facts about actions contrary to norms of fiduciary law that the fiduciary will be free to take due to the exclusion or limitation.[65] Absent such disclosure, the contract will have been formed in breach of the no conflict rule and the principal may have it set aside.[66] The contract, on a true construction, may well exclude or limit a fiduciary undertaking as desired by the fiduciary, but equity may nonetheless intervene to prevent the fiduciary from having the benefit of the bargain.[67]

A second type of case in which contract law proves inexhaustive on the relation of fiduciary undertakings and contracts is where a non-contractual fiduciary undertaking augments a contractual fiduciary undertaking. This possibility was alluded to by Dixon J of the High Court of Australia in *Birtchnell v Equity Trustees, Executors and Agency Company Limited*.[68] Speaking of circumstances where partners have, by contract, made fiduciary undertakings in relation to the matters provided for in that contract, Dixon J stated that '[t]he subject matter over which fiduciary obligations extend is determined by the character of the venture or undertaking for which the partnership exists, and this is to be ascertained, not merely from the express agreement of the parties, whether embodied in written instrument or not, but also from the course of dealing actually pursued by the firm.'[69] In other words, the full scope of the fiduciary undertakings of the partners is to be ascertained not only by looking to the terms of their contract, but also by considering non-contractual voluntary undertakings.

Cases where non-contractual fiduciary undertakings augment contractual fiduciary undertakings suggest that there is interesting work to be done exploring the distinctive contributions of fiduciary law to regulating relational contracts.[70] One such contribution is to be found in fiduciary law's role in controlling the exercise of discretionary powers in relational contracts.[71] This is important because parties to relational contracts often enjoy significant discretionary powers to affect each other's interests. Another equally important contribution is fiduciary law's willingness

[64] '[I]f an arrangement is to stand, whereby a particular transaction, which would otherwise come within a person's fiduciary duty, is to be exempted from it, there must be full and frank disclosure of all material facts': *New Zealand Netherlands Society 'Oranje' Incorporated v Kuys* [1973] 1 WLR 1126 at 1131–32 per Lord Wilberforce.

[65] See Joshua Getzler, '*ASIC v Citigroup*: Bankers Conflict of Interest and the Contractual Exclusion of Fiduciary Duties' (2007) 2 J of Eq 62 at 65–66.

[66] See, eg, *Maguire v Makaronis* (1997) 188 CLR 449.

[67] In the *Citigroup* case, even though the facts suggested that a pre-contractual fiduciary undertaking might have been present, the plaintiff did not press the point and so the effect of any such undertaking on the proper legal analysis of the facts was not considered: (2007) 160 FCR 35 at [306] and [333].

[68] (1929) 42 CLR 384. [69] Ibid at 407–08.

[70] There is, of course, disagreement on what constitutes a 'relational' contract: see, for example, the critical analysis in Melvin A Eisenberg, 'Relational Contracts' in Jack Beatson and Daniel Friedman (eds), *Good Faith and Fault in Contract Law* (Clarendon Press, 1997) 291. For present purposes, I need not take sides in those debates; it will suffice simply to point to those contracts that on anyone's view are 'relational' in a sociological sense, viz, long-term contracts establishing 'thick' relationships between their parties (such as distributorship agreements, franchise agreements, employment contracts, and the like).

[71] For an analysis of this contribution: Charles J Goetz and Robert E Scott, 'Principles of Relational Contracts' (1981) 67 Va L Rev 1089 at 1126–30.

to discern fiduciary undertakings in courses of dealing that are not provided for in relational contracts, but on which the parties may well embark as their relationship develops. Contract law's capacity to handle this aspect of the dynamism of relational contracts is limited, on account of its ex ante orientation.

IV. Fiduciary Undertakings and Social Roles

The occupancy of a social role can number among the reasons why the law recognizes a person as a fiduciary. This proposition is reflected in the recognition of certain types of relationship as fiduciary in a prima facie sense; in *Hospital Products*, Mason J provided a list of the best known such types of relationship, viz, trustee–beneficiary, solicitor–client, agent–principal, company director–company, partner–partner, and (perhaps more controversially) employee–employer.[72] In each of these categories of relationship, at least one party to the relationship occupies a social role—as trustee, or solicitor, or agent, etc—and the fact of this role-occupancy seems to be part of the explanation of why the law ascribes to the relationship a fiduciary character. But it remains unclear exactly why and how role-occupancy figures in that explanation.[73] Moreover, given that the law characterizes relationships such as trustee–beneficiary, solicitor–client, agent–principal, etc. as fiduciary only in a prima facie sense, there is work to be done understanding the questions that are thrown up by such characterization.[74] In what follows, I want to suggest that we may better understand these puzzles by approaching them with the notion of fiduciary undertakings in view. I will consider first the question why and how role-occupancy figures in the explanation of the law's ascription of prima facie fiduciary character to certain types of relationship, before considering questions about the scope of fiduciary undertakings that are raised by prima facie fiduciary relationships.

A. Role-occupancy and fiduciary relationship types

In order to understand why and how role-occupancy figures in the law's characterization of certain types of relationship as prima facie fiduciary, we should think more carefully about the nature and function of social roles. In an important article, Manfred Rehbinder describes a social role as a 'normative generalization' that is

[72] (1984) 156 CLR 41 at 96.

[73] See Miller (n 28) at 248–49. In comments on this chapter, Paul Miller challenged my assertion that these relationship types all entail the occupancy of a social role. I agree with Miller that in some of the relationship types, the relevant social role is (as in the case of agency) relatively poorly defined or overlaps with other, better defined, roles; nonetheless, I do think that in all cases where a relationship type is identified as prima facie fiduciary, a social role of some sort is picked out.

[74] In this regard, note *SEC v Chenery Corp*, 318 US 80 (1943) at 85–86 per Frankfurter J: 'to say that a man is a fiduciary only begins analysis; it gives direction to further inquiry. To whom is he a fiduciary? What obligations does he owe as a fiduciary? In what respect has he failed to discharge these obligations? And what are the consequences of his deviation from duty?'

'not sensed as actual behavior so much as a set of expectations about behavior'.[75] Rehbinder's language is a little opaque, but one plausible reading is that a social role is constituted by a sort of 'pre-packaged' set of norms and that it grounds expectations on the part of those who organize their affairs with reference to it. Understood in this way, we might say that social roles mediate between norms and the expectations of people whose practices engage with those norms in one way or another. Rehbinder suggests that this could be especially valuable in circumstances of complexity, where identification of and engagement with individual norms in an unmediated way might prove costly or difficult.[76] Among those who engage with norms are those whose conduct is guided and constrained by them. And so it follows from Rehbinder's account that a person who voluntarily occupies some social role may believe that she has thereby committed herself to abiding by the norms that constitute the role in question.

All of this has implications for fiduciary law. Earlier, I noted that, in prima facie fiduciary relationships, at least one party occupies a role an incident of which is a norm demanding the service of another's interests. In other words, in each of these relationship types, at least one party occupies a fiduciary role. Moreover, she typically occupies the fiduciary role voluntarily: serving as a trustee, a company director, or a partner is typically 'choice-dependent', to borrow again from David Owens.[77] Imagine a person occupying the role of trustee. Because of the mediating function of social roles, this person may believe that, simply by voluntarily occupying the role of trustee, she has committed herself to acting in accordance with norms that constitute that role. Given that one of those norms demands the service of another's interests, we may therefore say that the person who voluntarily occupies the role of trustee, believing that she is thereby committed to abide by role-constituting norms, makes a fiduciary undertaking. Thus, the fiduciary character of a relationship may flow from the fiduciary character of an undertaking, even if the

[75] Manfred Rehbinder, 'Status, Contract, and the Welfare State' (1971) 23 Stan L Rev 941 at 951. I learned of the existence of this article from the footnotes of Hanoch Dagan and Elizabeth S Scott's contribution to this volume, for which I am grateful to those two authors.

[76] Rehbinder (n 75) at 955: 'Contract law burdened man by forcing him to create for himself a legal position; the law of roles now allows him to choose among positions and behavioral standards, created and safeguarded by the state. As social life constantly increases in complexity, there is a growing need for more preformed and safeguarded roles.'

[77] See s 23 above. At this point it must be acknowledged that resulting and constructive trustees do not ordinarily occupy the role of trustee voluntarily. My sense is that when the relationship type 'trustee–beneficiary' is invoked in fiduciary law, judges typically have in mind express trustees, in which case we might plausibly assert that the relationship type is in fact more accurately described as 'express trustee–beneficiary'. If this is true, then of course it cannot be argued that resulting or constructive trustees are fiduciaries in the sense that, by voluntarily occupying the social role of trustee, they make a fiduciary undertaking. I am comfortable with this conclusion for two reasons. First, I think it is implausible to say that resulting or constructive trustees occupy a social role; rather, their trusteeship takes the form of susceptibility to highly specific individual norms that are not pre-packaged in the way characteristic of social roles: see further (in relation to constructive trustees) William Swadling, 'The Fiction of the Constructive Trust' (2011) 64 Curr LP 399. And secondly, I do not think that resulting or constructive trustees are typically fiduciaries, because they do not usually enjoy discretionary powers that, when exercised, will affect the interests of their beneficiaries.

subject matter of the undertaking is a social role and not the individual norms that are constitutive of the role.

For a social role to perform its mediating function successfully, those who organize their affairs with reference to the role must typically have some sense of its constitutive norms. Otherwise, the role will lose its normative traction as a source of expectations and basis for interpretation of behaviour. In the case of fiduciary roles, the burden of ensuring awareness of role-based norms is carried by different groups and institutions in different ways. For some fiduciary roles, much of that burden is discharged via the formal education and training of role-occupants. For example, solicitors typically assume that role after extensive education and training that exposes them in some detail to the normative contours of the role.[78] The work of role-maintenance may also be carried out by representative and regulatory bodies via codes of conduct or ethical standards.[79] Furthermore, a considerable portion of the burden is discharged by fiduciary law itself. Simply describing certain relationships as 'fiduciary' expresses the sense that the roles associated with those relationships entail norms demanding the service of another's interests. Imposing fiduciary norms such as 'no conflict' and 'no profit' on occupants of those roles serves by implication to reinforce the proposition that those roles demand selflessness.[80] And judges and others deploy more diffuse expressive strategies in helping to ensure that the occupants of different fiduciary roles understand the norms to which they are expected to adhere.[81]

In settings in which relevant practice communities are sufficiently aware of the normative constitution of fiduciary roles, it seems reasonable to infer that a person who voluntarily occupies such a role does so not only with a general belief that she is thereby committing herself to role-constituting norms, but also with a specific belief that those norms demand the service of others' interests.[82] But

[78] Although evidence suggests that solicitors may misunderstand those norms despite their education and training: Richard Moorhead and Victoria Hinchly, 'Professional Minimalism? The Ethical Consciousness of Commercial Lawyers' (2015) 42 J Law and Soc 387.

[79] Indeed, at times such sources of normative guidance are recognized in fiduciary law itself: see *Farrington v Rowe McBride and Partners* [1985] 1 NZLR 83 at 92 per Richardson J; *Hodgkinson v Simms* [1994] 3 SCR 377 at 412 per La Forest J; *Pilmer v Duke Group Limited (in liq)* (2001) 207 CLR 165 at [138]–[144] per Kirby J.

[80] I have written on this topic elsewhere: Matthew Harding, 'Disgorgement of Profit and Fiduciary Loyalty' in Simone Degeling and Jason Varuhas (eds), *Equitable Compensation and Disgorgement of Profit* (forthcoming 2016).

[81] See Edward B Rock, 'Saints and Sinners: How Does Delaware Corporate law Work?' (1997) 44 UCLA LR 1009; Gregory S Alexander, 'A Cognitive Theory of Fiduciary Relationships' (2000) 85 Corn LR 767.

[82] Indeed, in the case of at least some roles, it may be reasonable to infer that a voluntary role-occupant has a specific belief that she is thereby bound to abide by the norms of fiduciary law. Whether or not she has such a specific belief, the norms of fiduciary law may be described as terms of her voluntary undertaking: see further James Edelman, 'The Role of Status in the Law of Obligations' in Andrew S Gold and Paul B Miller (eds), *Philosophical Foundations of Fiduciary Law* (Oxford University Press 2014) 21. But this does not necessarily mean that those norms apply to the role-occupant because, or only because, she has undertaken them; they may still apply because they are imposed by law in light of her voluntary occupancy of a role in which she is required to act in another's interests, in which case her voluntary commitment to them is a welcome but legally superfluous matter.

the justification of the recognition of prima facie fiduciary relationships does not depend on the prevalence of belief that occupation of a role entails fiduciary strictures. It is enough that role-occupants typically assume their roles with a general belief that they are thereby committing themselves to role-constituting norms, whatever they happen to be.[83] Against the backdrop of this 'presumptive' legal landscape,[84] the voluntary occupant of a fiduciary role who claims not to have made a fiduciary undertaking bears the burden of demonstrating that her voluntary occupancy of the role does not entail such an undertaking. This brings me to my final topic: questions about the scope of fiduciary undertakings that are raised by prima facie fiduciary relationships.

B. Prima facie fiduciary relationships and questions of scope

Questions about the scope of fiduciary undertakings in prima facie fiduciary relationships can arise in one of two ways. First, it might be asked in respect of what matters the role-occupant has undertaken to act in the interests of another. In the case of some role-occupants, this question is answered by looking to the circumstances in which the role was assumed. For example, for trustees one may look to the terms of the relevant trust instrument. In some cases, it will be appropriate that attention be paid to the actual performance of the role. For example, in the case of partners, one might need to analyse the course of dealing pursued by the partners.[85] And a solicitor assumes her role when she is admitted to the practice of law, but the subject matter of her fiduciary undertaking is not usually known until she enters into discrete contracts with her clients for the provision of legal services.[86]

A second way in which questions of scope might arise in prima facie fiduciary relationships is in determining what effect is to be given to exclusion clauses. As Hanoch Dagan and Elizabeth Scott have pointed out, the extent to which parties may, by bespoke arrangement, vary role-constituting norms varies from role to role.[87] Dagan and Scott argue that fiduciary roles reflect this variation to such a degree that it is insufficiently precise to talk of the fiduciary 'role' in an undifferentiated way, and that instead we should organize analysis around more specific ideal types. Thus, a partner who assumes her role as partner pursuant to the terms of a partnership agreement against the backdrop of the general law may opt out of a fiduciary undertaking to a significant degree by specifying, in the partnership

[83] Similarly, it seems reasonable for fiduciary law to infer such a general belief where a person voluntarily acts as if she occupied a fiduciary role, such as where a person acts as a trustee or *agent de son tort*. See, eg, *Boardman v Phipps* [1967] 2 AC 41; *English v Dedham Vale Properties Ltd* [1978] 1 WLR 93. For a brilliant analysis of the former case as one in which the defendants acted as *agents de son tort*: Michael Bryan, '*Boardman v Phipps* (1967)' in Charles Mitchell and Paul Mitchell (eds), *Landmark Cases in Equity* (Hart Publishing, 2012) 581.

[84] See Miller (n 28) at 270–71.

[85] See *Aas v Benham* [1891] 2 Ch 244.

[86] *Hilton v Parker Booth and Eastman (a firm)* [2005] 1 WLR 567 at [28] per Lord Walker; *Strother v 3464920 Canada Inc* [2007] 2 SCR 177 at [133]–[134] per McLachlin CJ (dissenting in part).

[87] Dagan and Scott (n 75).

agreement, the ways in which she is entitled to act self-interestedly. In light of Dagan and Scott's analysis, partnership might be best described not as a fiduciary 'role' but rather as a fiduciary 'contract type', characterized by default terms that can be readily displaced.[88] In contrast, a company director subject to statutory fiduciary norms attached to a statutorily-defined role is not free to opt out of adherence to those norms except by declining the directorship; in this sense, directorship seems closer to the ideal type of fiduciary 'office', on Dagan and Scott's taxonomy, than it is to fiduciary 'contract type'.[89] Similarly, trusteeship seems more like a fiduciary 'office' than a fiduciary 'contract type', given that trustees may not opt out of fiduciary norms (elsewhere described as forming part of the 'irreducible core' of trusteeship).[90] Indeed, given the robustness with which the law prevents company directors and trustees from opting out of fiduciary undertakings, it seems almost misleading to characterize the relationships of company director–company and trustee–beneficiary as 'prima facie' fiduciary; it seems more accurate to say that they are fiduciary simpliciter.

To what extent should the occupant of a fiduciary role be permitted to opt out of her fiduciary undertaking? There are at least two competing policy objectives in play. First, in a legal order founded on liberal values, individuals should in general be free to set the normative terms on which they interact. This points in favour of permitting opt outs, so long as relevant legal and other requirements are satisfied. On the other hand, the mediating function of social roles depends on stability in the normative constitution of these roles; where this is lost, roles may lose their traction as normative resources and people may stop organizing their affairs with reference to them. Where fiduciary law too readily permits opt outs, there is a risk that fiduciary roles might cease to be comprehensible to those whose actions engage with them, and this might ultimately generate costs. Indeed, on one view those costs are best understood with reference to the very liberal values that seem to support unconstrained freedom to opt out. There are reasons to think that social roles can contribute to human autonomy by providing socially recognized options that may be the subject of autonomous choice;[91] thus, there are reasons to be sceptical about opt outs from a liberal point of view.[92] The variation in the extent to which fiduciary law permits occupants of fiduciary roles to opt out of role-constituting norms suggests that fiduciary law may apprehend the balance of these competing policy objectives differently in relation to different fiduciary roles.

[88] For a discussion of 'contract type', see ibid at 58–59.

[89] For a discussion of 'office', see ibid at 56–58.

[90] *Armitage v Nurse* [1998] Ch 241 at 253 per Millett LJ. Note also Finn, *Fiduciary Obligations* (n 8) at [11]–[14] describing directorship and trusteeship as 'fiduciary offices'.

[91] See generally Raz (n 22).

[92] This is not to say that such scepticism need extend to other opting out strategies, for example, the strategy of making a fiduciary undertaking but then seeking exemption from liability for breaches of the norms of fiduciary law within the scope of that undertaking, whether ex ante or ex post.

V. Conclusion

An understanding of fiduciary undertakings is critical to an understanding of fiduciary law, for the simple reason that such an undertaking is present in the overwhelming number of cases in which the law recognizes a person as a fiduciary. In any general project to theorize fiduciary law, then, theoretical work on fiduciary undertakings is bound to play a central role, and I hope that this chapter might represent a modest contribution to that theoretical work. But I want to conclude on a slightly different note. As I hope the chapter has shown, fiduciary undertakings, like all species of voluntary commitment, are a means by which we shape and direct our normative lives. Exactly how fiduciary undertakings perform this function depends on their relation to, and interaction with, other normative resources such as contracts and social roles, as well as the general normative landscape in which they figure. Thus I hope that this chapter might illuminate not only elements of fiduciary law but also aspects of that voluntary, creative engagement with norms on which social, cultural, and economic life, and ultimately human wellbeing, depends in so many ways.

PART II

CONTRACTUAL AND FIDUCIARY OBLIGATIONS

4

What if Fiduciary Obligations are like Contractual Ones?

*Gregory Klass**

Why does anyone care about the relationship between fiduciary obligations and contractual ones?

Fiduciary theorists pay more attention to the question than do contract theorists. The latter are more likely to talk about the relationship between contract law and tort law than about how contract law relates to the law of fiduciary obligations. This might be because tort law is more familiar and better understood. Or perhaps there are other reasons. In any case, this chapter takes it as given that claims that fiduciary obligations are like contractual ones are more about the purpose and principles of fiduciary law than about the law of contracts.

Anyone who argues that there is a deep similarity between fiduciary and contractual obligations faces a challenge: the two sorts of obligations are defined in very different ways. An obligation counts as contractual in virtue of how it comes into existence. Roughly speaking, a person acquires a contractual obligation by entering into an agreement for consideration. This simple formation rule applies across a wide range of transactions—anything from a corporate merger agreement to an agreement between family members. And it is neutral with respect to the content of the resulting obligations. Parties can, by and large, contract for whatever first-order obligations they wish, including fiduciary ones.[1]

A duty qualifies as a fiduciary obligation partly in virtue of the relationship between the obligor and the obligee and partly in virtue of its content. As Peter Birks observes, the word 'fiduciary' is anglicized Latin, meaning trustee-like. Fiduciary obligations are obligations that are similar to those of a trustee.

* Professor of Law, Georgetown University Law Center. This chapter benefited greatly from feedback from participants at the July 2015 UCL–Yale sponsored conference, Contract and Fiduciary Duty: Two Things or Just One? and at the November 2015 McGill sponsored conference, Contract, Status, and Fiduciary Law. I am also grateful for helpful feedback from, and conversations with, Donald Langevoort, Paul Miller, Prince Saprai, and Robert Thompson.

[1] Which is not to say that parties can contract for fiduciary remedies. Because this chapter focuses on possible similarities between contractual and fiduciary obligations, I largely ignore differences between the remedies that typically apply to each.

Contract, Status, and Fiduciary Law. First Edition. Paul B. Miller and Andrew S. Gold. Published 2016 by Oxford University Press.

> The truth is that 'fiduciary' is one of those words which means what it does, and what it does is to form a bridge from the express trust to other analogous situations … A fiduciary relationship is a relationship analogous to that between express trustee and beneficiary, and a fiduciary obligation is a trustee-like obligation exported by analogy.[2]

The relationships that generate fiduciary obligations share family resemblance.[3] Typically they involve an imbalance of power and a degree of trust. But not every relationship of that sort generates fiduciary obligations. And an obligation is a fiduciary one only if it has the right sort of content; notably, only if it requires of the fiduciary some degree of care and loyalty. The category of fiduciary obligations is defined at least as much by the obligations' content as by the relationships to which they attach.

Given the different ways the categories are defined, it is not surprising that there is some overlap between them. Some fiduciary relationships, such as that between an agent and a principal, originate in contractual arrangements. And entirely arms-length contracting parties might write fiduciary-like obligations into their agreement. From a purely analytic standpoint, the relationship between contractual obligations and fiduciary ones appears to be like that between organic produce and leafy greens. Membership in the first category turns on origins, membership in the second on structural features. Leafy greens can be organic, but need not be. Organic produce can include leafy greens, but also much else. The only analytic connection between the two is that both are ways of describing produce.

But law is not merely a matter of definition. Claims that fiduciary relationships are types of contracts or that fiduciary obligations are contractual in nature are not meant to state analytic truths. Nor are they claims that the law of fiduciary obligations should be subsumed into the law of contract. No one is arguing that because fiduciary obligations are contractual they should be subject to the consideration requirement, the Mailbox Rule, or *Hadley v. Baxendale*. What is being claimed is that there is some deep similarity or continuity between fiduciary obligations and contractual ones. 'Fiduciary obligations are contractual,' is best read as a metaphor. It is designed to prompt the listener to look for similarities or connections that she might not otherwise see.

This chapter examines three ways to unpack the metaphor. The first concerns the *content* of fiduciary obligations. The most plausible claim here is not that the content of fiduciary obligations is like that of contractual ones, but that the tools lawmakers apply to determine the content of fiduciary obligations should be the same ones they use to determine the content of contractual ones. The second possible claim concerns *causative events*. Fiduciary obligations and contractual obligations are both acquired obligations. They presuppose what Birks calls a 'causative event'. In contract law, the causative event is typically an agreement for consideration. In fiduciary law, the causative event is entering into the right sort of relationship. The

[2] Peter Birks, 'The Content of Fiduciary Obligation' (2000) 34 Israel L Rev 3, 8.

[3] See John Glover, 'The Identification of Fiduciaries' in Peter Birks (ed), *Privacy and Loyalty* (Clarendon Press, 1997) 269.

claim here is that there is a deep similarity between those causative events, one that illuminates the nature of fiduciary obligations. Third, much of contract law is made up of defaults, which parties have the ability to alter. Some fiduciary obligations are also defaults. Perhaps the *mutability* of fiduciary obligations reflects a deep similarity between the grounds of fiduciary and contractual obligations.

This chapter discusses each possible claim. My goal is not to provide a definitive resolution to any of them. By disaggregating them for separate consideration, I hope to cast some new light on each. The thrust of my argument, however, will be that any similarity between fiduciary obligations and contractual ones does not tell us much new about the former. The reason is that the grounds of contract law are more complex than is sometimes assumed. I conclude by identifying some reasons for caution when wielding the 'fiduciary obligations are contractual' metaphor.

I. Content

Is there anything that the content of contractual obligations tells us about the content of fiduciary ones? The best-known claim that there is can be found in the work of Frank Easterbrook and Daniel Fischel. Easterbrook and Fischel stake out a radical position: 'Fiduciary duties are not special duties; they have no moral footing; they are the same sort of obligations, derived and enforced in the same way, as other contractual undertakings.'[4] This section distinguishes several claims Easterbrook and Fischel make under this heading and discusses the grounds for each. I then describe and defend a minimalist contractualism about the content of fiduciary duties—one so minimal that it arguably does not deserve to be called 'contractualist'.

Analytic considerations already discussed suggest reasons to doubt that the content of contractual obligations can tell us anything about the content of fiduciary ones. A legal obligation is contractual not by virtue of its content, but by virtue of being generated in the right way. Contractual obligations are created by acts that satisfy the conditions of contractual validity, such as entering into an exchange agreement. They are, as philosophers say, content independent: the reason for recognizing the obligation does not turn on what the obligation requires.[5] Given that contract law says so little about the content of contractual obligations, why should we expect it to tell us anything about the content of fiduciary ones?

Of course, contract law is not entirely silent on the first-order obligations parties can contract for. Three generally applicable mandatory rules limit the performance obligations parties can put in their contracts. Courts will not enforce commitments that are against public policy, such as a promise to perform an illegal act; courts will not enforce terms that are unconscionable; and courts impose on all contracting

[4] Frank H Easterbrook and Daniel R Fischel, 'Contract and Fiduciary Duty' (1993) 36 J Law & Econ 425, 427.

[5] See, eg, Joseph Raz, 'Voluntary Obligations and Normative Powers (pt. 2)' (1972) 46 Proc Aristotelian Soc'y 79, 95–96 (Supp).

parties a mandatory duty of good faith.[6] But judicial interpretation and application of these rules suggest that they tell us little about fiduciary obligations. The public policy rule is a narrow one, emphasizing mostly third-party effects. Fiduciary obligations, on the contrary, look to be structured primarily for the benefit of the obligee. The unconscionability doctrine prohibits only the most extreme forms of advantage taking. It is a far cry from a fiduciary's positive duties of loyalty and care. Moreover, substantive unconscionability usually must be paired with some procedural defect to render a term unenforceable. Finally, as Daniel Markovits observes, the duty of good faith 'permits contracting parties to remain as self-interested within the contract relation as they were without it', requiring only that they 'limit their pursuit of their private interests according to the terms of their contractual settlement'.[7] Contract law demands from parties no more than the *minima moralia* of the marketplace, obligations that fall far short of the duties of loyalty and care that characterize fiduciary obligations.

If there is a connection between the contents of contractual and fiduciary obligations, it lies not in their substance but in the method of determining what those obligations are. This is one of Easterbrook and Fischel's claims. They call for 'filling gaps in fiduciary relations the same way courts fill gaps in other contracts. The subject matter may differ, but the objective and the process is identical'.[8] Call this the 'methodological continuity thesis'. No matter what the substantive differences between contractual and fiduciary obligations, lawmakers should use the same methods and procedures to determine their content.

Stated at this level of generality, the methodological continuity thesis is fairly weak. It is satisfied, for example, by the proposition that the content of both sorts of obligations should be that which a wise judge would decide—a claim that tells us almost nothing about the substance of either.

Easterbrook and Fischel fill in the methodological continuity thesis with a more robust theory of how lawmakers should determine the content of both types of obligations: hypothetical agreement. When a court must fill a gap in a contract, they argue, it should seek out terms the parties would have chosen if they had had the time and resources to reach agreement on the matter. For example, if the question in a contract case is whether a tenant had a duty to inform a lessor of an obscure term in a twenty-year-old lease when the tenant was laying the groundwork to invoke that term, the court should ask whether, if the parties had thought about the matter when negotiating the contract, they would have agreed to such a duty.[9] When a court seeks to determine the legal duties of a fiduciary, it should ask the same question. Given the practical problem that the fiduciary relationship

[6] The content of some contract types is governed by additional mandatory rules. Examples include usury laws, minimum wage laws, and consumer protection laws.

[7] Daniel Markovits, 'Sharing Ex Ante and Sharing Ex Post: The Non-Contractual Basis of Fiduciary Relations' in Andrew S Gold and Paul B Miller (eds), *Philosophical Foundations of Fiduciary Law* (Oxford University Press, 2014) 209, 213.

[8] Easterbrook and Fischel (n 4) at 429.

[9] The example comes from Judge Posner's opinion in *Market Street Associates Ltd. Partnership v Frey*, 941 F.2d 588 (7th Cir. 1991).

was aiming to solve—according to Easterbrook and Fischel, some form of agency problem—what duties would rational parties have agreed to assign to the fiduciary if they were given all the time and resources needed to think the problem through? I'll call this the 'hypothetical agreement method'.

There are two senses in which the hypothetical agreement method might be called 'contractual'. The first is the sense I've been discussing. According to Easterbrook and Fischel, it is the method that courts should use to determine the content of contractual obligations as well as fiduciary ones. The term 'contractual' seems especially appropriate in this respect, for the method feels especially natural when it comes to filling contractual gaps, where the parties have agreed on some terms but not others.

The hypothetical agreement method might also be called 'contractual' because a hypothetical agreement is like a hypothetical contract. In fact, the more common term in the literature is 'hypothetical contract'. But here care is required. Hypothetical agreements cannot do all the justificatory work that actual agreements or contracts do. Thinking about what parties *would* have agreed to is a way of identifying what terms can be expected to maximize their welfare. Self-interested, knowledgeable, and rational parties will agree to terms that they expect to maximize their respective gains from a transaction. The justificatory force of hypothetical consent lies not in the idea of consent, but in the welfare effects that it identifies. As Anthony Kronman observes:

> [O]nce we have concluded, for whatever reasons, that a rule is welfare-enhancing, the assertion that the parties to a hypothetical contract would voluntarily choose it adds nothing but rhetorical force to our conclusion; it is, so to speak, pure window-dressing. Hypothetical contract arguments are thus not really contractualist at all. They explain and justify their conclusion by an appeal to considerations of welfare alone.[10]

Easterbrook and Fischel's hypothetical agreement method is not so much a commitment to thinking of fiduciary obligations as contracts as it is a commitment to welfare economics.

Once we understand this, we can distinguish the hypothetical agreement method from a separate contractualist claim Easterbrook and Fischel make: that parties should have the power to modify their fiduciary obligations, or that '[a]ctual contracts always prevail over implied ones.'[11] The hypothetical agreement method does not ask what terms the actual parties to a transaction actually would have agreed to had they actually thought about the matter. It asks what terms perfectly rational and perfectly knowledgeable parties would have agreed to if granted all the time they needed to reach an accord. These imagined actors are given perfect knowledge, perfect rationality, and unlimited time in order to identify welfare-maximizing terms. It is not obvious that actual parties will arrive at the same result. On its own, the hypothetical agreement method does not entail that parties should have the ability to choose or alter their fiduciary obligations.

[10] Anthony T. Kronman, 'A Comment on Dean Clark' (1989) 89 Colum L Rev 1748, 1750.
[11] Easterbrook and Fischel (n 4) at 427.

One can get from hypothetical agreement to '[a]ctual contracts always prevail over implied ones', with either of two additional premises. The first is that parties are better positioned, by virtue of their knowledge and interests, to decide for themselves which terms best suit their needs than are courts, legislators, or regulators, who likely know less about the transaction at issue and do not have a stake in it. Alternatively, or in addition, one might argue that party choice is a separate and perhaps sufficient ground for enforcement. The first is a common premise of pro-market neoclassical economic analysis. The second is the defining claim of autonomy theories. Easterbrook and Fischel invoke both when they write that '[t]o say that express contracting is allowed is to say that the law is designed to promote the parties' own perception of their joint welfare.'[12]

I will say more about the value of party choice in fiduciary law in Sections II and III. For the moment, I simply observe that Easterbrook and Fischel need one of these two premises, or a third, to get from the hypothetical agreement method to their preference for party choice. But neither premise is uncontroversial. It might be that in some, if not all, fiduciary relationships we can expect lawmakers using the hypothetical agreement method to arrive at terms that create more value than those that the parties would choose. That might be so because parties are imperfectly rational, because parties have imperfect knowledge of the risks of the transaction, because parties have insufficient time and resources to weigh pertinent costs and benefits, or because one party is more sophisticated than the other or enjoys other bargaining advantages likely to produce an inefficient outcome. Alternatively, or in addition, it might be that the social interest in imposing one or another fiduciary obligation outweighs the value we attach to party choice. Sometimes the law imposes duties on persons that they don't want. We might worry about attaching too much weight to party choice especially where there is an imbalance of power or the opportunity for exploitation—common characteristics of fiduciary relationships. In short, one might accept Easterbrook and Fischel's narrower methodological claim about the value of hypothetical agreement without committing oneself to their more thoroughgoing contractualism about fiduciary obligations.

This is important because the hypothetical agreement method has real benefits. To ask what obligations fully informed and rational parties would have agreed to is to ask what obligations best serve the parties' interests. No matter what policies or purpose fiduciary obligations serve, they are clearly designed to protect beneficiaries' interests. And as Easterbrook and Fischel emphasize, changing one term in a transaction can have unintended adverse effects on other terms. Just as adding a warranty might result in an increase in the price of goods, increasing or decreasing the scope of a fiduciary's obligations might affect other aspects of her transaction with the beneficiary.

A beneficiary who does not value the new service or higher degree of loyalty at more than the cost of providing it is worse off, the opposite of a court's objective; if the beneficiary does

[12] Ibid at 429.

value the extra service at more than its cost, then the parties would have provided for this service by contract in a transaction-cost-free world.[13]

Because the hypothetical fully informed, perfectly rational negotiating parties take a holistic view of costs and benefits—trading off a cost here for a benefit there—the hypothetical agreement method should capture such negative welfare effects. Hypothetical agreement is a tool for thinking through the full range of effects a fiduciary obligation might have.

That is not to say that hypothetical agreement is or should be the sole method for determining the content, default or mandatory, of fiduciary obligations. First, it is not obvious that welfare economics captures all of the law's reasons for recognizing and enforcing fiduciary obligations. Second, the hypothetical agreement method provides less certainty than lawmakers might want. The most all-things-considered efficient mix of obligations often depends on empirical facts about which we know very little. These include parties' risk preferences, how much they know about the law and how much it affects their behaviour, and the power of reputational and other non-legal incentives. The absence of information about the values of these and other variables makes it easy to tell 'Just So' stories as to why a lawmaker's or theorist's preferred rule is the value-maximizing one.

Nonetheless, the hypothetical agreement method is helpful for identifying unintended costs that a proposed change in fiduciary obligations might bring. If one holds that fiduciary obligations are designed to protect or promote the welfare of beneficiaries, it is difficult to see why all of their welfare effects—intended and unintended—should not be considered when determining their content. The hypothetical agreement method does not commit a theorist to welfare economics or efficiency as the only goal when designing fiduciary obligations. But it provides an important check when doing so.

II. Causative Events

A second way in which fiduciary obligations might be like contractual ones is in their causative events—how one acquires the obligation. Because a contractual obligation comes from the obligor's voluntary agreement to it, the law of contracts is often treated as the paradigm of a private power-conferring law, and contracts as a form of private legislation. To the extent that fiduciary obligations are voluntarily acquired, one might think they too are chosen obligations, and that fiduciary law is, like the law of contracts, grounded in principles of autonomy or choice. A more complete account of contract law, however, suggests a more complicated picture.

There is no doubt that contract law gives private persons the ability to purposively undertake legal obligations when they wish.[14] Sophisticated parties are

[13] Ibid at 431.

[14] I discuss the themes in the following five paragraphs in greater detail in Gregory Klass, 'Three Pictures of Contract: Duty, Power and Compound Rule' (2008) 83 NYU L Rev 1726.

able to determine with precision when contractual obligations will attach, what the content of those obligations will be, how their agreement will be interpreted, who will enforce it, and the consequences of breach. And they can achieve those legal results by the simple mechanism of agreeing to them, which is to say, by expressing their shared intent to achieve those results. In such transactions, contract law operates as a private power-conferring law. It gives parties the ability to undertake new legal obligations when they wish.

That said, not all of contract law fits the model of private legislation. Contemporary contract law does not require that parties either intend or express an intention to undertake legal obligations.[15] 'Neither real nor apparent intention that a promise be legally binding is essential to the formation of a contract.'[16] Parties acquire contractual obligations simply by entering into exchange agreements, which are not distinctively legal acts. It is therefore possible for persons to acquire contractual obligations unwittingly. Corbin suggests the following example:

> There seems to be no serious doubt that a mutual agreement to trade a horse for a cow would be an enforceable contract, even though it is made by two ignorant persons who never heard of a legal relation and who do not know that society offers any kind of a remedy for the enforcement of such an agreement.[17]

The point is not that unexpected contractual obligations are common. It might be that the vast majority of contracting parties understand themselves to be entering into a legally binding agreement. But if so, that is an empirical fact, not a legal requirement. Contemporary contract law is designed to attach legal obligations not, or not only, because parties want them, but because they have entered into the right sort of relationship.

This feature of contract law suggests that it is designed to do more than confer on parties the power to undertake obligations when they wish. Contract law is also designed to impose legal duties on parties for reasons that have nothing to do with their intent *vel non* to acquire them. Contract theorists have suggested various reasons for such a duty-imposing function. These include the social interests in protecting a promisee's reliance, in supporting the practices of promise-making and promise-keeping, and in enforcing obligations of corrective justice that arise after a breach. Other evidence for contract law's duty-imposing function includes courts' openness to finding implied-in-fact contracts, the fact that a bare representation can generate an express warranty and default interpretive rules that are highly contextualist.

The causative events that generate contractual obligations are therefore various. Often those events can be characterized as acts of private lawmaking, in which parties

[15] There are exceptions. Among the complexities is the nominal rule in civil law countries and in Great Britain that '[i]n order to be bound by a contract a party must have an intention to be legally bound.' The Commission on European Contract Law, Ole Lando, and Hugh Beale, *Principles of European Contract Law* art. 2:101 cmt. B (Kluwer Law International, 1999). For a more detailed discussion, see Gregory Klass, 'Intent to Contract' (2009) 95 Va L Rev 1437.

[16] Restatement (Second) of Contracts § 21 (1981).

[17] Arthur Linton Corbin, *Corbin On Contracts* (West Publishing Company, 1st ed 1950) § 34 at 135.

intentionally undertake new legal obligations to one another. But the conditions of contractual validity do not require the expression of such an intent. In other transactions, the causative event is simply agreement to an exchange transaction.

This variety says something about the broader purposes of contract law. It suggests that with respect to the single duty to perform, contract law serves both a power-conferring and a duty-imposing function. I have called this the 'compound theory' of contract.[18] The compound theory maintains that contemporary contract law recognizes and enforces the single duty to perform for two very different reasons at once. It does so in order to give parties the power to purposively undertake new legal obligations to one another when they wish. And it does so in order to impose legal obligations on parties for reasons that do not involve party choice.

What about the causative events associated with fiduciary obligations? James Edelman has emphasized that most fiduciary relationships are based on the fiduciary's consent or agreement.[19] Edelman quotes with approval the Supreme Court of Canada's decision in *Norberg v Wynrib*:

> Although fiduciary relationships may properly be recognized in the absence of consent by the beneficiary—the consent of a child to his or her parents acting in a fiduciary capacity for the child's benefit is not required—they are more typically the product of the voluntary agreement of the parties that the beneficiary will cede to the fiduciary some power, *and are always dependent on the fiduciary's undertaking to act in the beneficiary's interests*.[20]

Fiduciary obligations are voluntary in the sense that one does not become a trustee, an executor, a guardian, a corporate director, a joint venturer, an agent, an attorney, a teacher or a priest by accident. One consents or agrees to the position. The resulting fiduciary obligations are therefore voluntary obligations in the sense that they are products of the fiduciary's voluntary acts. Does this suggest that fiduciary obligations are contractual in nature?

Edelman is probably wrong to claim that *all* fiduciary relationships originate in the fiduciary's consent or agreement. Courts have held, for example, that parents owe a fiduciary obligation to their children.[21] Although Edelman works hard to construe the role of parent as premised on a voluntary undertaking,[22] it is not obvious that this is the best reading of how a person acquires those obligations. More generally, because fiduciary obligations are identified as such by structural features of fiduciary relationships and by their content, there is no a priori reason why they might not sometimes attach to non-voluntary relationships.

That said, many fiduciary relationships are voluntary. Voluntary fiduciary relationships can be divided into two broad categories.

[18] Klass (n 14).

[19] James Edelman, 'When Do Fiduciary Duties Arise?' (2010) 126 LQR 302.

[20] Ibid at 313 (quoting *Norberg v Wynrib* [1992] 2 S.C.R. 226 at 273).

[21] See, eg, *M(K) v M(H)* [1992] 3 S.C.R. 6 (Australia). See also Elizabeth S Scott and Robert E Scott, 'Parents as Fiduciaries' (1995) 81 Va L Rev 2401.

[22] Edelman (n 19) at 311–12.

Some voluntary fiduciary relationships come into existence without the law's help. The relationships between teacher and student and between priest and parishioner, for example, are not in the first instance legal ones. They exist in and are defined by the social world in which we find ourselves, regardless of whether the law takes notice of them. The same can be said of some more discrete relationships that generate fiduciary obligations. A person who assumes management and control over trust property might become a trustee *de son tort*, whether she knows it or not.[23] Though these relationships are voluntary in the sense that the fiduciary voluntarily enters into them, there is no requirement or reason to expect that the fiduciary knows she is entering into a transaction that will alter her legal obligations in that way.

When the law attaches fiduciary obligations to such non-legal voluntary relationships, it looks to be serving a duty-imposing function, rather than a power-conferring one. Because the relationship can come into being without the law's help, we cannot be sure that the fiduciary knows, much less intends, the legal obligations that attach to it. The law of fiduciary obligations in these instances is designed to impose legal duties on fiduciaries not because they want or have undertaken those duties, but for other reasons.

And of course it is easy to imagine what those reasons might be. Fiduciary relationships are generally characterized by asymmetries of power, trust, and vulnerability. Fiduciaries typically enjoy discretionary powers or privileges, whose exercise can significantly affect the non-fiduciary's wellbeing. These powers and privileges often create the risk of opportunism, leaving the non-fiduciary especially vulnerable to the fiduciary's breach of trust. In such circumstances, the case for legal intervention to protect the non-fiduciary against neglect and opportunism is an easy one, and does not depend upon the fiduciary's intention to undertake the obligation.

If the fiduciary obligations that attach to such non-legal voluntary relationships are similar to contractual obligations, they are similar to contract law's duty imposing aspect—the fact that one can acquire contractual obligations unawares. The causative event in both cases is the choice to enter into a non-legal relationship of the right sort. The resulting obligations might be said to be voluntary in the sense that it could have been avoided. Yet the obligations have not been voluntarily undertaken in a more robust sense. There is no reason to expect that the obligor objectively intends, wants, or even expects the legal obligation. The law's reason for imposing the obligation cannot therefore be the obligor's intention to undertake it.

This similarity does not tell us much new about fiduciary obligations. Contract law's duty-imposing function is not distinctive, except in its pairing with contract law's power-conferring aspect. The duty-imposing side of contract law suggests comparisons to tort law or family law—other fields in which legal obligations are imposed are in order to protect vulnerable persons, to deter harmful behaviour, to compensate for wrongful losses, and so forth. A claim that fiduciary obligations are like the duty-imposing aspect of contract law does no theoretical work.

[23] See, eg, *King v Johnston,* 178 Cal. App. 4th 1488 (Ct. App. 2009)

Other fiduciary obligations attach to legally constituted relationships—relationships that cannot exist without the law's help. Examples of legally constituted fiduciary relationships include those between executor and legatees, between guardian and ward, between corporate director and shareholders, and between a licensed financial advisor and her clients. There are no executors outside the law of wills and probate, no guardians outside the law of guardianship, no corporate directors outside of the law of corporations, no licensed financial advisors outside of the regulatory framework they operate in. The relationships themselves are creatures of law. They are legally constituted. When a person knowingly becomes a fiduciary in such a relationship, she therefore understands herself to be assuming a new legal role[24] that involves new legal powers and obligations—though she may not understand what all those powers and obligations are. Unlike parents, priests, teachers, or borrowers, agreeing to enter into such a legal relationship is perforce agreeing to the legal role and everything that comes with it. If the fiduciary obligations that attach to extralegal voluntary relationships can be analogized to the duty-imposing side of contract law, perhaps the fiduciary obligations that attach to legally constituted voluntary relationships are more similar to the power-conferring aspect of contract law.

There is no question that the laws that establish the roles of executor, guardian, corporate, director, and licensed financial advisor are private power-conferring rules of a certain type. They confer on private persons, who satisfy certain conditions, the power to enter into a new legal role. A person becomes an executor, a guardian, a corporate director, or a licensed financial advisor by choice. In some instances the law requires that the choice be expressed in a formal legal act. To become an executor in the District of Columbia, a person named as such in a decedent's last will and testament must file a petition with the applicable court seeking an order naming her the executor for the estate.[25] To become the guardian of an adult, one must file a petition requesting assignment as such.[26] In other instances, no formal act is required, though the fiduciary must express her agreement to the new legal position or status. Thus to become a corporate director, one need express only an intent to undertake the position, usually in the form of an employment contract. In all these cases, however, the law grants the potential fiduciary the power to choose whether or not to accede to the new legal role, and it grants her the role based on the exercise of that choice.

I think the best available argument that the power to become a fiduciary of this sort is like the power-conferring aspect of contract law goes as follows: The legal role of fiduciary is just a bundle of Hohfeldian jural relations.[27] To be a fiduciary of

[24] Rather than 'new legal role', one might say 'new legal status'. I have chosen 'role' because 'status' is sometimes associated with legal situations that are not chosen, such as being a firstborn child. My use of 'role' encompasses both Hanoch Dagan and Elizabeth Scott's 'office' and their 'contract type' in their chapter, 'Reinterpreting the Status-Contract Divide: The Case of Fiduciaries' *infra* at 56–60.

[25] D.C. Code § 20–304(f)(6) (2012).

[26] Ibid § 21–2041 (2012).

[27] Wesley Newcomb Hohfeld, 'Some Fundamental Legal Conceptions as Applied in Judicial Reasoning' (1913) 23 Yale L J 16.

one type or another is to have a certain collection of legal duties, powers, privileges, immunities, and so forth. The new powers are often especially salient. But what makes the relationship a fiduciary one is that those powers come with certain obligations attached to their exercise. To say that someone is an executor is to say both that she has the legal powers to maintain and dispose of the estate's assets, and that she has the fiduciary obligations of care and loyalty in the exercise of those powers. To say that a person is a corporate director is to say both that she has the legal power to make certain executive decisions on behalf of the corporation, and that she has certain fiduciary obligations towards the shareholders. This way of understanding the role of a fiduciary suggests a deep similarity between legally constituted fiduciary relationships and many contracts. To purposively enter into a contract is also to knowingly effect a change to one's jural relations. Although the new obligation to perform is the most salient change, contracts often also come with new powers, privileges, immunities, and so forth. Both fiduciary law and contract law therefore give persons the power to purposively effect changes in their legal relations with others. Both enable private persons to alter their powers, privileges, immunities, and obligations. At least some fiduciary obligations are therefore best understood as the result of private legislative acts, comparable to contract law's power-conferring aspect.

The above argument relies on picturing the role of fiduciary as a bundle of jural relations. The bundle theory of property illustrates the power of that analytic approach. Decomposing an apparently simple and natural legal concept into its constituent parts can reveal otherwise hidden complexity and contingency, and suggest alternatives that might otherwise remain out of view.[28] But like other reductive projects, this mode of analysis can also have a levelling effect. It risks leaving important variables out of the equation.[29] Reducing fiduciary statuses to mere bundles of jural relations tells us something important about them. But it does not tell us everything.

In order to see why, consider a different analogy: to become a fiduciary in a legally constituted relationship is like acceding to a public office. Take the ability of the candidate who has received the most votes to become a member of Congress. Like other legal roles, to be a member of Congress is, from a one perspective, just to enjoy a special collection of legal powers, privileges, immunities, duties, and so forth. The most salient of these is the power to participate in the legislative process. But the office also comes with legal privileges and duties. The Speech and Debate Clause of the US Constitution, for example, gives members of Congress immunity from civil arrest while attending or travelling to and from a session of Congress.[30] The federal bribery statute makes it a crime for members of Congress and other public officials to receive anything of value in return for influence on their official

[28] See, eg, Thomas C Grey, 'The Disintegration of Property' (1980) 22 Nomos (Property) 69.

[29] For a similar point about bundle theories of property, see Thomas Merrill and Henry Smith, 'What Happened to Property in Law and Economics?' (2001) 111 Yale L J 357.

[30] U.S. Const., art. I, § 6(1); *Gravel v United States*, 408 U.S. 606, 614 (1972).

acts.[31] The power to become a member of Congress is the power to acquire a collection of new powers, duties, privileges, and immunities.

Like the fiduciary obligations of an executor, guardian, trustee, or corporate director, a Congressperson's duty to obey the bribery statute is in a sense voluntary. When taking the oath of office, she knows she is acceding to a new legal role. She might not be aware of every new power, privilege, immunity, or duty that comes with her new office. She might not know, for example, of her constitutional immunity from civil arrest under the Speech and Debate Clause. And she might not know that if she accepts a bribe, she will now be subject to criminal prosecution under the bribery statute. But her choice to assume the office, together with her generic awareness that it involves a new legal role, is enough to say that the new duties are voluntary ones. If she is later indicted under the bribery statute and complains that she is being held to too high a standard, one might reply, 'You knew, or should have known, or could have known, what you were getting into when you chose to take the oath of office.'

The example is relevant because there is an important difference between the power to become a member of Congress and the power to enter into a contract. The duties that the bribery statute imposes on members of Congress are voluntary in the sense that they are the knowable consequences of the decision to become a member of Congress. They are not, however, what we expect to motivate individuals to run for Congress. We do not expect people to seek to become members of Congress for the sake of the new legal duties they will thereby acquire.

Contractual obligations are different. Because contracts originate in exchange agreements, a person's reasons for entering into a contract are more closely tied to her resulting obligations. In a contractual exchange, one side undertakes an obligation as the price of the other side's return promise or performance. In the language of the Second Restatement, '[i]n the typical bargain, the consideration and the promise bear a reciprocal relation of motive or inducement: the consideration induces the making of the promise and the promise induces the furnishing of the consideration.'[32] A party who is engaged in exchanges of this sort does not merely expect the resulting duty to perform. She seeks it for instrumental reasons. Undertaking the duty to perform is essential to achieving her plans and projects, namely, receiving some promise or performance in return. Her new obligation allows her to accomplish what she could not otherwise. Contractual obligations are not merely expected, but specifically intended.

Both a member of Congress's legal duty not to accept a bribe and a contracting party's legal duty to perform result from the exercise of a legal power. The causative events are, in this respect, similar. But in other respects, the events are very different. We expect parties to enter into contracts for the sake of the new obligations they thereby acquire. We expect people to become members of Congress for the sake of the powers they thereby acquire, and not for the sake of the new duties. And these different expectations correspond to a difference in the law's reasons for imposing

[31] 18 U.S.C. § 201(b)(2).

[32] Restatement (Second) of Contracts § 71 cmt. b (1981).

the duty. When contract law functions as a power-conferring rule, the reason for recognizing the duty lies in the social interest in giving persons the ability to undertake new legal obligations when they wish. That reason presupposes that parties often enter into contracts seeking the resulting legal obligations. Because we do not expect people to enter public office for the sake of the new duties they thereby acquire, this cannot be the reason for imposing those duties. All this is a long way of explaining what was obvious from the start. The purpose of the federal bribery statute is not to give individuals the power, by becoming members of Congress, to acquire the duty not to accept bribes. It is to impose on members of Congress the duty not to accept bribes, whether they want that duty or not.

The question, then, is whether entering into a legally constituted voluntary fiduciary relationship is, with respect to the obligations that come with it, more like purposively entering into a contract or more like entering into a public office. There is considerable variety amongst fiduciary relationships, and there are probably at least as many reasons for becoming a fiduciary as there are types of fiduciaries. One person's reasons for serving as the legal guardian of her mentally incompetent sibling are likely to be very different from another's reasons for serving on a corporate board, and both of them might be different from a person's decision to serve as a licensed financial advisor. I believe that with respect to many legally constituted fiduciary relationships, however, there is a strong intuition that those entering into them do not typically do so for the sake of the legal obligations they thereby incur. Much more salient to, say, the position of an executor or that of a guardian are the legal powers the fiduciary acquires. The fundamental fiduciary obligations of loyalty and care ride atop those powers. The fiduciary's duty of loyalty is a duty to exercise those powers in the interests of the beneficiary; her duty of care is a duty to use a reasonable level of knowledge and expertise in exercising them. Fiduciary obligations are, in this sense dependent on fiduciary powers.[33] This conceptual ordering—which a bundle theory of fiduciary obligations does not capture—is often reflected in the reasons individuals choose to become fiduciaries. Although the fiduciary might know that by acquiring the new role she acquires those obligations, we do not expect her to undertake the role for the sake of the obligations.

This is not to say that fiduciary obligations are never salient. Especially when the fiduciary and beneficiary are engaged in an exchange of services for money, as are a financial advisor and her client, the scope of the fiduciary's duties of loyalty and care might be a key part of the deal. Here the fiduciary is being paid in part for performing her fiduciary obligations. Where this is so, the fiduciary's voluntary undertaking looks more like a contractual undertaking.

This suggests that the category of legally constituted voluntary fiduciary obligations is mixed. Entering into some relationships within the category is, with respect

[33] For a more thoroughgoing and ambitious account along these lines, see Paul B Miller, 'The Fiduciary Relationship' in Andrew S Gold and Paul B Miller (eds), *Philosophical Foundations of Fiduciary Law* (Oxford University Press, 2014) 63; Paul B Miller, 'A Theory of Fiduciary Liability' (2011) 56 McGill L J 235.

to the obligations one thereby acquires, more like becoming a member of Congress. Entering into others is, in that respect, more like entering into a contract.

The above analysis can be summarized using David Owens' fourfold classification of moral obligations, which divides up obligations according to whether and how they depend on the obligor's exercise of a prior choice.[34]

Obligations of the *null grade* in Owens' schema are choice independent. Owens suggests as an example the moral duty to help a child in distress. The obligation to assist simply exists, no matter what prior choices the obligor has made. Some fiduciary obligations—any that attach to being a parent—are of this null grade. Their causative events need not include a choice by the fiduciary. The reasons for imposing those obligations cannot depend upon choice.

A person incurs a *first grade* choice-dependent obligation as the result of her prior choice, but without regard to whether she knew she was incurring the obligation. By driving a car, for example, I incur a legal and moral obligation not to drive drunk, whether I know I am incurring it or not. Fiduciary obligations that attach to extra-legal voluntary relationships, such as those between a priest and parishioner, teacher and student, borrower and lender, are first grade choice-dependent. The existence of the obligation depends upon an exercise of choice, but not upon the chooser's knowledge of the legal obligations that she thereby incurs. Although the fiduciary obligation is choice-dependent, the law's reasons for imposing it do not appear related to that choice. Fiduciary obligations of this sort are comparable to contract law's duty-imposing function.

Obligations are *second grade* choice-dependent 'where someone's choice puts them under [the] obligation only when they make this choice in the knowledge that it might have the effect of putting them under this obligation.'[35] Owens suggests friendship as an example.

> Someone becomes my friend by spending time with me, by sharing various activities and experiences, by expressing interest and affection. And there are duties of friendship, things one is obligated to do for one's friends but not for other people. Still, one ignorant of the prevailing forms of friendship (perhaps newly arrived in this country and simply 'being friendly') could not be held to these expectations.[36]

The *third grade* of choice-dependence appears when a person not only must know that her choice will result in a new obligation, but must intend or appear to intend the obligation if she is to incur it. Obligations of this grade result from the exercise of normative powers. Promissory obligations are the example par excellence. A successful promisor undertakes a new obligation by virtue of her expression of an intent to do so.

My analysis of the fiduciary obligations that attach to legally constituted voluntary relationships can be restated as an argument that such obligations can be either second or third grade choice-dependent. Many such obligations are second degree

[34] The classification is introduced in David Owens, *Shaping the Normative Landscape* (Oxford University Press, 2012) 3–6.

[35] Ibid at 4. [36] Ibid.

choice-dependent. The fiduciary's *knowledge* that she will incur new legal obligations by assuming a new legal role might figure in the reasons for imposing them on her. They might, for example, remove an objection to imposing them.[37] But the law does not require that she intend to incur the obligations. Fiduciary obligations are third-degree choice dependent only when we expect fiduciaries to not merely expect, but also to intend, those duties, and when that intention is a reason for their legal recognition. Only fiduciary obligations of this type are comparable to the power-conferring aspect of contract law.

This section has focused on the different ways a fiduciary's choice figures in her acquisition of fiduciary obligations. The question is interesting because it tells us something about the sorts of reasons why the law might recognize those obligations. The relatively limited role of choice in the generation of many fiduciary obligations suggests that the law has other reasons for recognizing them.

III. Mutability

A third way fiduciary obligations might be like contractual ones lies in their mutability—the fact that some fiduciary obligations are defaults, which the parties can agree to alter. Although there are connections between an obligation's voluntariness and its mutability, the two are distinct design features. Whether an obligation is voluntary, in the sense I am using the term, turns on the types of acts that generate the obligation. Whether it is mutable turns on whether parties have the ability to alter the obligation that would otherwise attach to their acts.

This chapter does not address the positive question, whether or to what extent private parties can modify, or even extinguish, the fiduciary obligations that attach in virtue of their relationship. It is today clear that some fiduciary obligations are defaults. John Langbein has documented, for example, the default status of many obligations of gratuitous private trustees, which 'yield to the more particularized intentions that parties may choose to express or imply in their trust deal.'[38] Langbein's study, however, concerns only one type of fiduciary relationship.[39] More ambitious claims about the general mutability of fiduciary obligations need to be backed by similarly detailed studies of the law governing other members of the genus. Nor does Langbein fully explore the extent of parties' ability to modify a gratuitous private trustee's fiduciary obligations. Parties might have the power to alter some aspects of those obligations, yet there might remain an 'irreducible core'

[37] Joseph Raz distinguishes two ways that an actor's awareness of moral or legal consequences can figure into the justification of those consequences: 'positively as part of the reason for those consequences, or … negatively by removing an objection to them'. Joseph Raz, 'Promises in Morality and Law' (1982) 95 Harv L Rev 916, 929 (reviewing P S Atiyah, *Promises, Morals, and the Law* (Oxford University Press, 1981)).

[38] John H Langbein, 'The Contractarian Basis of the Law of Trusts' (1995) 105 Yale L J 625, 629.

[39] In fact, Langbein's study addresses only one form of trust. He excludes from his study commercial trusts, charitable trusts, resulting trusts, and constructive trusts. Ibid at 630–31.

of mandatory obligations they cannot avoid.[40] The extent to which the contemporary law of fiduciary obligations includes an irreducible core is another important question I do not address.

I am also not going to consider the normative question whether any given fiduciary obligations should be mandatory or alterable. Easterbrook and Fischel advance an argument for mutability based on the principles of welfare economics and an empirical claim about who can better assess which terms maximize party welfare. But pure welfare economics is hardly uncontroversial, especially outside of the context of corporate law, which is where Easterbrook and Fischel focus their analysis. And Easterbrook and Fischel's argument about the relative capacities of parties and lawmakers is an empirical claim, which might or might not be true and which might receive different answers in different contexts or for different sorts of fiduciary relationships. More generally, it is not obvious that the mutability question should get the same answer across the full range of fiduciary relationships. The reasons for empowering the parties to alter the fiduciary obligations of a corporate director or financial advisor might not apply to the fiduciary obligations of a guardian, trustee *de son tort,* or teacher. Whether a fiduciary's obligations should be mandatory, mutable, or some mix of the two is a design question to be answered on the basis of policy, purpose, and practical effects. Given the variety among fiduciary relationships, it would be odd if the answer were always the same.

This section instead addresses two related questions. The first is an interpretive-theoretical one. What does it mean that some fiduciary obligations are mutable? What can we infer about the law's reasons for recognizing a fiduciary obligation from the fact the obligation is only a default? The second, related question concerns legal design. What are the considerations that should go into setting default fiduciary obligations and determining what parties must do to contract around them?

The ability to purposively modify or opt out of fiduciary obligations is itself a legal power. If parties to a trust arrangement have the ability to structure it so as to exempt the trustee from the no-conflict rule, that is because the law of trusts gives them the power to do so. More precisely, it is because the rule permitting the exemption gives parties the ability to modify or extinguish the obligation by expressing their intention to do just that. Where fiduciary obligations are mutable, the law governing them confers on private parties the power to change those obligations. Default fiduciary obligations, together with the rules that say what parties must do to alter those obligations, are power-conferring laws.[41]

[40] See, eg, Alexander Trukhtanow, 'The Irreducible Core of Trust Obligations' (2007) 123 LQR 342; David Hayton, 'The Irreducible Core Content of Trusteeship' in A J Oakley (ed), *Trends in Contemporary Trust Law* (Oxford University Press, 1997) 47.

[41] The above paragraph skips over some considerations that are more important to an understanding of contract law than they are to a theory of fiduciary law. A default need not be power conferring. It is power conferring when it can be changed by virtue of an act that expresses an intention to effect a non-default legal state of affairs. It is not power conferring, or not only power conferring, if the default can be changed by acts that do not express a legal intent. Many contract defaults can be altered by non-juristic acts of the latter sort. In order to make an express warranty, for example, it 'is not necessary … that the seller use formal words, such as "warrant" or "guarantee", or that he have a specific intention to make a warranty'; U.C.C. § 2–313(2). It is enough to simply make a representation about the quality of the

It does not follow that the law imposing the fiduciary obligation in the first place is power conferring, or that it is designed solely to promote party choice. Consider the tort of negligence. By agreeing to an exculpatory clause, private parties can contract out of liability for negligently harming one another.[42] To agree to such a clause is to exercise a legal power. But it does not follow from the existence of that power that the primary purpose of the law of negligence is to promote party choice. In Owens' classification, the tort duty of care is at most grade one choice-dependent. Although it might result from a person's prior choice, say to operate a ski resort, the duty of care does not depend upon her knowledge that she was thereby acquiring the obligation, much less upon the expression of an intent to do so. The ability to contract out of negligence liability does not entail that negligence law is designed to confer the power to undertake a duty of care.

The point of the example is not that all fiduciary obligations are comparable to the law of negligence. I have argued that fiduciary obligations might be grade one, two or three choice-dependent. The point is simply that the power to alter an obligation does not entail that the obligation itself is the result of a power-conferring rule. Private parties' ability to modify a legal duty does not tell us everything we might want to know about the reasons for assigning it to them in the first place.

The same point applies to contracts. Without denying contract law's power-conferring aspect, a clear understanding of how contract defaults work illustrates ways that contract law, even when it gives parties the ability to choose, is often structured to recognize values other than party choice. A more complete understanding of this aspect of contract law illuminates what sorts of conclusions theorists can draw from the mutability of fiduciary obligations.

First, some basic concepts. Any mutable term, whether it belongs to contract law, fiduciary law, or some other area of law, is the product of two rules: a default rule and an altering rule. The default rule specifies the legal state of affairs absent the right legal actor's expression to the contrary. The associated altering rule specifies whose expression of what meaning in what form is sufficient, or necessary and sufficient, to change the default legal state of affairs. To take a simple example, section 2–314(1) of the Uniform Commercial Code establishes the implied warranty of merchantability: 'Unless excluded or modified … a warranty that the goods shall be merchantable is implied in a contract for their sale if the seller is a merchant with respect to goods of that kind.' This legal state of affairs is a default, for it applies only '[u]nless excluded or modified'. Section 2–316 contains associated altering rules, as it specifies several ways to exclude or modify the implied warranty. Section 2–316(3)(a), for example, provides that a seller's use of conventional phrases such

goods. Ibid § 2–313(1)(b). Similarly, 'an implied warranty can … be excluded or modified by course of dealing or course of performance or usage of trade.' Ibid § 2–316(3)(c). My sense is that there is not the same variety among the acts that can alter parties' fiduciary obligations. I believe that parties who act to alter their fiduciary obligations generally do so by expressing an intent to effect a legal change. But this is only an intuition. Further work on the law in this area would be interesting.

42 See Restatement (Second) of Contracts (1981) § 195.

as 'as is' or 'with all faults' suffices to exclude all implied warranties. And section 2–316(2) stipulates that when a seller does not use such phrases, 'to exclude or modify the implied warranty of merchantability or any part of it the language must mention merchantability and in case of a writing must be conspicuous.'

Contract defaults and altering rules are often designed to be choice promoting. So-called majoritarian defaults seek to capture the terms a majority, or at least plurality, of parties would choose. Majoritarian defaults promote party choice in several ways. First, they make it cheaper for parties to obtain the terms they want, as it costs less to remain silent than to speak. Second, when evidence is lacking, majoritarian defaults make it more likely that the court will impose the term that the parties actually wanted or expected. Third, majoritarian defaults are often easier for parties to anticipate, Family Feud style.

Non-majoritarian, information-forcing defaults, which are sometimes termed 'penalty defaults', can also be designed to promote party choice. When one party is more sophisticated than the other, setting the default against the sophisticated party's interests can give her a new reason to educate the other about relevant legal consequences—by expressly addressing them in order to contract around the default. Alternatively, or in addition, sharing that information can make it more likely that a court or third-party adjudicator will enforce the agreement that the parties intended. Information-forcing defaults can promote choice both by informing parties what they are choosing and by improving the accuracy of enforcement.

Contracts scholars have paid more attention to default rules than to the associated altering rules.[43] I have written a bit about altering rules, and Ian Ayres has recently devoted an article to their design.[44] Ayres identifies two variables in the design of altering rules relevant to promoting party choice: transaction costs and error costs.[45] Transaction costs are the costs to the parties of specifying a non-default term. Error costs occur when parties fail to understand the legal effects of their words and actions, or when courts fail to assign those words and actions their intended effect. Designing contract altering rules to maximize the parties' ability to get the terms they want requires minimizing, to the extent possible, both sorts of costs. Sometimes this involves a trade-off between the two. For example, formal requirements like the use of a writing or the inclusion of standard disclosures can reduce the chances of judicial or party error. But such requirements increase the costs of contracting around the default. Magic words like section 2–316's rule for 'as is' or 'with all faults' can reduce transaction costs. But when non-sophisticates do

[43] See, eg, Avery Weiner Katz, 'The Economics of Form and Substance in Contract Interpretation' (2004) 104 Colum L Rev 496, 503 (observing that on the question of 'how to interpret [parties'] efforts when they try [to overcome a default] ... the default rule literature has had little to say').

[44] Gregory Klass, 'Intent to Contract' (n 15) at 1461–75 (discussing the design of defaults and 'opt-out rules'), 1475–99 (applying the discussion of defaults and opt-out rules to analyse the conditions of contractual validity for four types of agreements); Ian Ayres, 'Regulating Opt-Out: An Economic Theory of Altering Rules' (2012) 121 Yale L J 2032. See also Brett McDonnell, 'Sticky Defaults and Altering Rules in Corporate Law' (2007) 60 SMU L Rev 383.

[45] See Ayres (n 44) at 2054–63.

not know the code, they can cause party error. Maximizing parties' ability to get the terms they want involves striking the right balance between these costs.

In short, there is no doubt but that contract default and altering rules can be designed to maximize the parties' ability to choose. Rules that include the above design elements—majoritarian or information-forcing defaults, altering rules designed to minimize both transaction and error costs—can be evidence that the law is designed to promote party choice, or that it functions as a power-conferring rule.

But default and altering rules can be designed to achieve other ends as well. They can do so in two ways: by changing the parties' incentives to pick one term or another and by using the law's expressive power.

A default establishes the legal state of affairs absent a relevant legal actor's contrary expression. Because parties have finite time, attention, and resources, they sometimes fail to opt-out of defaults even when, other things being equal, they would prefer a non-default legal state of affairs. As a result, defaults are generally sticky. A default's stickiness is largely a function of the altering rule associated with it—what it takes to opt-out of the default. As Ayres explains, '[t]he stickiness of a default derives from the relative difficulty of contracting around—particularly if the altering rules impede fully-informed contractors from contracting for certain non-default effects because of the costs of complying with the impeding altering rules.'[46] Consequently, the stickiness of a default is partly within lawmakers' control. Just as altering rules can be designed to promote choice by reducing the transaction costs of achieving a non-default term, they can alternatively be designed to impede party choice by increasing those costs. Writing requirements, prolix mandatory disclosures, magic words, and the like can all increase the cost of opting out of a default. Such altering rules impede departures from the default. Impeding altering rules can be used to impose something like a Pigouvian tax on attempts to achieve a non-default legal state of affairs.

Another way of putting this is that the choice between mandatory and default rules is not a binary one. There is a spectrum that runs from choice-promoting defaults and associated altering rules, which make it very easy to avoid a default, through to defaults with altering rules that make it more costly to avoid a default, and then on, at the far end of the spectrum, to mandatory rules that make it impossible to avoid a default.

This is important because sticky defaults can be used to advance social interests other than party choice. By setting the default at the socially preferred term, lawmakers can cause more contracts to include that term, while still giving sufficiently motivated parties the ability to opt out of it. As I have written elsewhere:

[46] Ibid at 2086. The stickiness of the default depends largely, but not entirely, on the altering rule. Defaults that do not correspond to the parties' expectations, for example, might stick because parties are less likely to know to contract around them, no matter what the altering rule. The same goes for a default against the interests of a non-sophisticated party, who is less likely to know that she should be contracting around it. Thus Ayres is not entirely correct when he writes that 'what makes a default sticky … has nothing to do with the content or desirability of the default itself.' Ibid.

Stickier defaults, and by implication costlier opt-outs … can mediate between the sometimes conflicting interests the law has in, on the one hand, granting parties the power to control the scope of their legal obligations and, on the other hand, imposing liability on parties because of extralegal wrongs they have committed, harms they have caused, or other considerations.[47]

Ayres, an economist, identifies only two reasons why lawmakers might want to make a default stick: 'to protect people inside (paternalism) or outside (externalities) the contract.'[48] A broader view of the non-choice-based reasons for imposing contractual obligations might include society's interests in enforcing the moral obligation to perform, in doing justice between the parties after breach, or in supporting the moral culture of making and keeping agreements. Impeding altering rules are tools that lawmakers can use to achieve those ends, while still giving sophisticated and sufficiently motivated parties the power to get the non-default terms they want.

A second way that a default can serve values other than party choice lies in law's expressive capacity. Because we live in a culture that expects laws to reflect collective values, contracting parties often read the default to signal a collective judgement about what sorts of terms or behaviours are moral, just, right, efficient, or otherwise socially preferred. This can be another cause of stickiness. Contract defaults stick not only when it is expensive to contract around them, but also when parties treat the legal default as a signal and use it to guide their choices and even to form their preferences. But the point here goes beyond incentives and stickiness. The default implied warranty of merchantability, for example, does more than give merchants a new reason to sell goods of passable quality. It says what we as a society believe the appropriate morals of the marketplace to be. The rule *caveat emptor* no longer expresses what we expect of sellers. The expressive dimension of defaults provides yet another avenue for advancing values beyond party choice.

In short, mutability does not entail that the default should either reflect the terms that the majority of parties want or be designed to elicit information to improve the quality of that choice. A default and the associated altering rule might be designed to serve goals that do not depend upon party choice, either because the default is likely to stick or because it expresses other social values.

What does this mean for the theory of fiduciary obligations? I argued in Section II that legally constituted fiduciary relationships are power-conferring laws in that they give parties the ability to choose whether to take on the role of a fiduciary. Default fiduciary obligations are power conferring in a different way: they give sophisticated and sufficiently motivated parties the ability to change their fiduciary obligations when they want. Insofar as fiduciary law builds in legal powers of this sort, it is similar to the power-conferring aspects of contract law.

But like the power to take on the role of the fiduciary, the fact that the parties have the power to alter their fiduciary obligations does not tell us everything we might want to know about the law's reasons for recognizing and enforcing those obligations in the first place, or even its reasons for permitting parties to modify

[47] Klass (n 15) at 1472. [48] Ayres (n 44) at 2084.

them. To answer those questions, we need to know more about the scope of the parties' power to alter their fiduciary obligations, about the law's reasons for picking a default obligation, and about what it takes for parties to contract around that default. It will be important to ask, for example, how sticky a default fiduciary obligation is, and whether it is sticky by accident or by design. One would also want to ask whether the default expresses a collective decision about the appropriate duties of a fiduciary, whether it is majoritarian, or whether it is simply a coordinating rule. Again, there is no reason to expect the same answer for every sort of fiduciary relationship, or for every fiduciary obligation. Neither the voluntary aspect of fiduciary obligations nor their mutability can be understood from 30,000 feet. Understanding the meaning of either requires closer examination.

IV. A Concluding Caution

There are several ways, then, in which fiduciary obligations are like contractual ones. Both are designed primarily to benefit parties to the relationship, making it important to ensure that their design takes into account both intended and unintended welfare effects. Asking which obligations fully informed rational parties would pick is, for both sorts of obligations, a way to check that. Both types of obligations are, by and large, voluntary obligations, in the sense that they come about only as the result of parties' voluntary acts—in the case of fiduciary obligations, entering into the right sort of relationship, in the case of contractual obligations, entering into an exchange agreement. Finally both sorts of obligations are sometimes mutable, giving private parties the power to alter the duties that attach to their relationship.

The question is whether these similarities tell us anything interesting about the law of fiduciary obligations. Contract law is often held up as the paradigm of a private power-conferring law. In fact, contract law serves a compound power-conferring and duty-imposing function. A more nuanced understanding of the design and functions of the law of contracts suggests that the structural similarities between fiduciary obligations and contractual ones tell us less about fiduciary law than we might hope. (The differences between fiduciary obligations and contractual ones might be more revealing.)

I would like to conclude by suggesting that not only are the similarities between fiduciary and contractual obligations uninformative, but too much emphasis on them risks importing into fiduciary law problematic aspects of the law of contracts. I am thinking here of the almost talismanic quality that, at least in the United States, appeals to consent play in the judicial interpretation and enforcement of contracts. Important and valuable though party choice is, the language of consent is too often used to obscure what is really going on between contracting parties. This can be seen, for example, in the governance of mass consumer contracts, which might put us on guard against attempts to understand fiduciary obligations on the model of contract law's power-conferring aspect.

As almost any cell phone owner or software user knows, consumers do not read or understand the contracts they agree to. Systematically collected empirical evidence backs this up.[49] Yet courts often take the consumer's bare act of consent signing a credit-card application, clicking an 'I Agree' radio button—as sufficient reason to enforce just about any term that the associated document contains. As many commentators have observed, such a rule effectively gives sophisticated drafters a *carte blanche* to include terms that are most favourable to the drafter. These include terms such as class action waivers and arbitration clauses that operate in practice to preclude recovery for breach and other wrongs.[50]

The results can be problematic for at least two reasons. First, emphasis on the formal act of consumer consent can distract from actual disparities between the parties' sophistication and power, and from the fairness and efficiency of the resulting terms. Our culture rightly valorizes freedom to contract and freedom of contract. It does not follow, however, that a consumer's bare act of consent to terms she has predictably neither read nor understood should license their enforcement, regardless of the terms' fairness or effect on consumer welfare. Yet much existing doctrine in the United States appears to do just that. When the only check on drafters is a consumer's bare act of assent, we should worry that consumers will suffer. Second, the widespread adoption in consumer contracts of drafters' preferred terms can result in the widespread deletion of rights that there is a social interest in maintaining. The contractual shifting of employment discrimination and other civil rights claims to private arbitration, for example, threatens to erode the development and effectiveness of those laws. The legal effect granted the bare act of consent also threatens broader social harms.

This too brief survey illustrates the potential costs of a certain type of contractualist thinking. A final lesson from contract law is to be on guard against placing too much weight on acts of consent when seeking to justify the content and enforcement of fiduciary obligations. Appeals to individual choice and consent are powerful forces in US legal culture, at times riding roughshod over other legal, moral, and policy arguments or principles. To characterize fiduciary obligations writ large as chosen obligations is to locate them within that rhetorical space. Doing so can lend credibility to private attempts to contract out of fiduciary obligations when our attitude should be more sceptical. And it can obscure other social interests that the law of fiduciary obligations serves.

[49] See, eg, Yannis Bakos, Florencia Marotta-Wurgler, David R Trossen, 'Does Anyone Read the Fine Print? Consumer Attention to Standard Form Contracts' (2014) 43(1) J Legal Stud 1; Omri Ben-Shahar and Carl E Schneider, *More Than You Wanted To Know: The Failure of Mandated Disclosure*, (Princeton University Press, 2014) Ch. 2.

[50] See J Maria Glover, 'Disappearing Claims and the Erosion of Substantive Law' (2015) 124 Yale L J 3052; Judith Resnik, 'Diffusing Disputes: The Public in the Private of Arbitration, the Private in Courts, and the Erasure of Rights' (2015) 124 Yale L J 2804; Margaret Jane Radin, *Boilerplate: The Fine Print, Vanishing Rights, and the Rule of Law* [Princeton University Press] 2013).

5

Contract, Consent, and Fiduciary Relationships

*Lionel D Smith**

I. Introduction

What is the relationship between contract and fiduciary obligations? In this chapter I aim to show that they are distinct juridical concepts. However, I will also explain what I understand to be the best understanding of the relationship between these two different concepts. They are distinct but overlapping. This is because fiduciary obligations arise when powers are held in a certain way. Such powers may come from a contract, which is why the concepts overlap; but they may come from another source, which is why the concepts are distinct.

This introduction lays out some groundwork. Section II explains why the concept of status is not relevant to the questions I am aiming to answer, at least according to my understanding of the concept of 'status'. Section III explains why contract and fiduciary duty are distinct, on any relevant view of the meaning of 'contract' (of which several will be explored). Section IV develops a positive account of the relationship between contract, consent, and fiduciary relationships.

A. Duties and relationships

My own view is that there are some duties that can properly be called fiduciary duties but that one of the features of this area of the law that has made it difficult to analyse is that there is more to a fiduciary relationship than a set of duties. Such a relationship also involves powers, including restrictions on the manner of exercise of those powers.[1]

* Sir William C Macdonald Professor of Law, Faculty of Law, McGill University. This research is part of a project on *Conflicts of Interest and Fiduciary Obligations,* funded by a Killam Research Fellowship during 2014–2016. I acknowledge with gratitude the support of the Killam Trustees. In addition to the seminar at McGill University at which all of the papers in this volume were presented, this paper was also presented at a seminar on 'Contract and Fiduciary Duty' at University College London on 9 July 2015. I am grateful to participants at both events for their helpful comments, and in particular to Stephen Smith even though he refuses to see reason.

[1] A full argument is in L Smith, 'Fiduciary Relationships: Ensuring the Loyal Exercise of Judgement on Behalf of Another' (2014) 130 LQR 608.

There are those who argue that fiduciary relationships are essentially contractual. They might think either that all fiduciary duties are contractual duties, or that all fiduciary relationships are contractual relationships.[2] Either way, I disagree. I will use the second formulation, in terms of relationships, but I think everything I say would also apply to the first formulation. I will call the position which I aim to disprove the 'contractarian position'.

B. Overlap and contradiction

What is the relationship between 'physician' and 'landscape artist'? They are definitely two concepts, or two intellectual categories; but the same person can be a physician *and* a landscape artist. Now consider 'freehold estate' and 'leasehold estate'. These are two distinct concepts or intellectual categories in a much stronger sense: they are mutually exclusive; the same estate cannot be freehold *and* leasehold.

Contractual and fiduciary relationships are two concepts in the first sense. They are distinct but not mutually exclusive. 'Contractual' as an adjective is, for most people, descriptive of the juridical source of a legal relationship. 'Contractual' in 'contractual relationship' means, at least for most people, that the relationship was created by a contract; or perhaps that it *is* a contract, and was created according to the rules for contract formation. 'Fiduciary' as an adjective is not so clear. Many people have expressed views on what it can mean, what it does mean, what it should mean. I suggest that when most people use it, they do not use it to make a claim about the juridical *source* of a relationship or duty; rather, to describe juridical *characteristics* of a relationship or duty. In this sense, it is not surprising that contractual and fiduciary relationships are not mutually exclusive, because they do not address or describe comparable incidents of relationships, in the way that freehold and leasehold describe comparable incidents of estates in land.

C. Generality and particularity

I also take it for granted that there is something in common among all fiduciary relationships, which is why we treat them as a juristic category. That may sound obvious but it is important to my argument. The reason is that any general claim can be disproved by a single counterexample.[3] Thus any claim that *all* fiduciary relationships have a shared characteristic (such as being contractual) can be disproved by a single counterexample, being an example of a fiduciary relationship

[2] Conversely, I am not (currently) aware of anyone who argues that all contractual duties are fiduciary duties, or that all contractual relationships are fiduciary relationships. cf D Markovits, 'Theories of the Common Law of Contracts' in the online Stanford Encyclopedia of Philosophy, <http://plato.stanford.edu>, 2.2, 'Contract as Fiduciary Obligation'. I disagree with Markovits, however, that the availability of gain-based remedies for breach of contract entails that the contractual relationship is fiduciary in nature (see L Smith, 'Disgorgement of the Profits of Breach of Contract: Property, Contract and 'Efficient Breach' (1994) 24 Can Business LJ 121).

[3] This is not a claim about law; it is a claim about reasoning.

that does not have that characteristic. The claim so disproved can be salvaged by disqualifying the counterexample; if that is not possible, the claim can only be salvaged by sacrificing its generality. Let me explain. To the claim 'all fiduciary relationships are contractual relationships', a potential counterexample is the case of the personal representative of a deceased person.[4] Once she assumes office, the personal representative owes fiduciary duties to the estate beneficiaries. It may well be the case that the personal representative has never met any of them, and it is quite possible for the personal representative to assume the office against the wishes of the beneficiaries. It is also possible that all of the beneficiaries lack contractual capacity. So it is clearly possible that the personal representative becomes a fiduciary towards the beneficiaries without contracting with them. Nor is it necessary that the personal representative have contracted with the deceased. Although such a case might be unusual, it is possible for someone who never met the deceased to become a personal representative (whether an executor or an administrator); and it is certainly possible for someone to become a personal representative who never made any agreement with the deceased to act in that capacity. Logically, this single case tends to show that the claim that 'all fiduciary relationships are contractual relationships' must be false.

There are two possible ways to disqualify the counterexample. One is to show that, at least according to some meaning of the word 'contractual', this relationship *is* contractual. I will devote some time below to rebutting that strategy. My point in this section is that the only other way out is to argue that the relationship between personal representative and estate beneficiary is not *really* a fiduciary one. If that were true, then the counterexample would be disqualified and the general claim could be salvaged.[5] But, one might think, in this case this is surely a hopeless position because the law is clear on this point; it would be difficult to argue that centuries of case law, and all the books on succession law, have got it wrong. The case of the personal representative is hardly a borderline case of a fiduciary relationship; it is considered by most persons to be at the core.

There is another version of this strategy, which is to argue that the general claim 'all fiduciary relationships are contractual relationships' was never meant to apply to personal representatives. They are in some special category, perhaps one called 'wills and estates'. But this amounts to an attempt to salvage the general claim by renouncing its generality, and it is only the general claim that I aim to address. If the claim 'all fiduciary relationships are contractual relationships' really means, 'all of the fiduciary relationships that I am interested in are contractual relationships', or, in other words, 'some fiduciary relationships are contractual relationships', then

[4] Here I do not aim to address this question as a matter of substance; we will return to it below. My goal here is only to show how a counter-example tends to falsify a general claim, and what responses might be relevant to the counter-example.

[5] Interpretive theories of law often lead their proponents to say that some part of the law, as widely understood, is misconceived. But where one is led to say that a very substantial part of the law, as widely understood, is misconceived, it tends to cease to qualify as an interpretive theory and to become rather an argument for law reform.

I might well agree with it, depending on how it is elaborated. The point is that in this version, it is not a general claim about all fiduciary relationships; it is a particular claim, and it is not obviously theoretically important or ambitious because it has abandoned generality. The person who holds this modest version actually agrees with me that it is false that 'all fiduciary relationships are contractual relationships'.[6]

II. Contract and Status

It is sometimes argued that the alternative to a contractual, or contractarian, view of fiduciary relationships is a status-based one. In this section I aim to explain why in my view the concept of 'status' is not relevant to the debate about whether fiduciary relationships are contractual. In the online *Oxford English Dictionary*, this is the second definition of 'status', identified as the legal connotation:

> a. *Law.* The fact or position of belonging to a group which is subject to certain legal rights or limitations; the legal classification corresponding to this; a person's legal condition with regard to freedom of movement or action, citizenship, the age of majority, etc. Also: an instance of this.[7]

In law, a status is traditionally a feature of one's legal personhood. What this means is that one carries it with one into all situations. Being a minor is a status that imposes certain limitations on capacity, which may be beneficial in the sense that a minor can escape many contractual liabilities. Being of unsound mind is also a status. Another status is being bankrupt: various duties and disabilities are imposed

[6] There is an example of this in a related context in J Langbein, 'The Contractarian Basis of the Law of Trusts' (1995) 105 Yale LJ 625. Langbein argued that express trusts are 'deals' or 'contracts' (627) but he had to address the clear counterexample of the case in which a person declares himself to be a trustee of property that he holds. Since a single person causes this trust (with its fiduciary relationship) to come into existence, it cannot be a deal or a contract. Langbein mentioned this issue near the beginning of his text (627–28), and returned to it in an appendix (672–75). He said that such trusts are used in three situations: they function as a kind of will-substitute, and end on the death of the settlor/trustee; they operate to save a failed gift; or, where they do operate as a trust during the life of the settlor/trustee, still they lead to a 'conventional three-party trust' (674) when the settlor dies. So he wanted to disqualify the counterexample: the first two situations he described as 'nontrusts' (672); the third as a 'way station[] to real [*sic*] third-party-trustee trusts' (672). But this strategy does not work, even if we agree with Langbein that in the first two categories the courts are allowing people to manipulate the law. The reason is that the third case (at least) is clearly a real trust, even if it is not a three-party trust. The observation that the trust may later have a different trustee does not help: it is the creation of the trust that falsifies the claim that all express trusts are deals. The fact that a caterpillar usually turns into a butterfly does not show that the caterpillar is not real. Since one counterexample disproves a general claim, Langbein has to admit that his thesis cannot apply to all express trusts (627, 672). His original ambitious claim that '[t]rusts are contracts' (627) is abandoned by the end of the article; he confines himself to express trusts (631) and then must leave aside not only self-declared trusts but also charitable trusts (631). By the end of the article, the claim becomes one that among express trusts, some have certain features in common with contracts. This is quite different from claiming broadly that trusts are contracts.

[7] <http://www.oed.com>. The *OED* goes on to give another legal sub-definition: 'b. *Law*. With reference to an organization, place, thing, etc.: legal standing or position (of a particular type); the official classification corresponding to this. Also: an instance of this.'

upon you, while on the other hand, none of your creditors can sue you, but must rather participate in the collective proceeding. Convicted criminals may lose not only their liberty, but in many jurisdictions their right to vote; this can be seen as a question of status, as can legal distinctions between citizens and non-citizens. Being a corporation is also a status that attaches to some persons and not to others, and that may lead to important differences in capacities, as well as rights, duties, and other jural relationships. Moreover, not all statuses are immutable: a corporation never becomes an individual, but a minor reaches the age of majority, a bankrupt can be discharged, a criminal can complete his sentence, and an immigrant may become a citizen. Importantly, in the traditional sense of the word, one cannot simultaneously hold two opposing statuses: one cannot be a minor and an adult, bankrupt and not bankrupt, a citizen and an immigrant, sane and insane.

This is exactly how Henry Maine used the word, even if he did not take account of all of the statuses known to the modern law; for him, status was part of the law of persons, in line with the conventional understanding that I outline above.[8] He argued that 'the movement of the progressive societies has hitherto been a movement *from Status to Contract*'.[9] By this he meant that modern law attaches many fewer constraints, than older legal systems did, to persons according to features of their personality. Roman law attached such constraints to slaves and even to free citizens who were 'in the power' of the *paterfamilias*. Legal constraints were attached to women by the common law, and other systems, until much more recently. Maine wanted to argue that the direction of progress has been that in modern law, people impose limits on themselves, by their own choice, using contract. He noted that such status-based legal limits as still exist (as in the case of minors and incapacitated persons) are there precisely because such persons are not fully able to operate in the contractual sphere.

Whatever the merits of Maine's thesis as a matter of legal or social history, he did not propose 'contract' and 'status' as mutually exclusive alternatives. A minor can make certain contracts, and so can a bankrupt and a corporation and an immigrant, even though all of these persons have a status that is different from an individual of the age of majority who is a citizen and not bankrupt.[10] It is a misunderstanding of Maine to read him as suggesting that whatever is not a creature of contract must be a creature of status, particularly when this is done in order to imply that

[8] H S Maine, *Ancient Law* (Oxford University Press, 1931) 140–1. [9] Ibid 141.

[10] For this reason I disagree with the project in H Dagan and E S Scott, 'Reinterpreting the Status-Contract Divide: The Case of Fiduciaries' in this volume, even though I agree with much of their analysis as to the misuse of the idea of status. They propose 'office' and 'contract type' as further refinements of the status–contract divide. In my view, there is no contract–status divide since the concepts are not opposed to one another. I also do not address the concept of 'office' in this chapter because it does not apply to all, but only to some, fiduciary relationships. An office is a set of juridical relationships that one holds, not personally, but in virtue of occupying a role that is impersonal in the sense that it may be surrendered to another. Trusteeship is an office, and so is a directorship of a legal person. However, agency (in the legal sense) is not an office, nor is the role of partner in a business partnership, nor are any of the innumerable ad hoc fiduciary relationships that may arise. The present chapter aims to identify features that inhere in *all* fiduciary relationships.

a non-contractarian approach is, for that reason alone, regressive or reactionary.[11] Like 'physician' and 'landscape artist', 'contract' and 'status' are different but not mutually exclusive. A better illustration for the logical relationship between 'status' and 'contract' would be the logical relationship between 'citizen' and 'marriage'.

What is more important is this. Starting from the conventional legal meaning of the word 'status', which is the meaning that Maine adopted, there is nothing in fiduciary law that can be said to arise from status, whether one accepts or rejects a contractual or contractarian view of fiduciary relationships. Being a fiduciary is not a status, and nor is being the beneficiary of a fiduciary relationship. In my view, this is demonstrated by the simple observation that the same person can owe fiduciary obligations to John, while being owed fiduciary obligations by Jane. The person does not have the *status* of 'fiduciary' or 'beneficiary'; rather, he is in two relationships with two different persons, both of which are fiduciary relationships, but in each of which he plays opposite roles. The juridical features that characterize fiduciary relationships arise from the *relationships*, not from anyone's status. They do not arise out of 'the fact or position of belonging to a group which is subject to certain legal rights or limitations'.[12]

Someone might say that being a fiduciary is a status, in the sense that one belongs to the group of 'fiduciaries'. But this is a definition of 'status' that tends to drain it of meaning. If we defined 'status' in this way, then every legal relationship would be, or arise from, a kind of status. Do we say that debtors owe money because they have the status of 'debtor', or vice versa? No; we aim instead to explain the source and incidents of the legal relationship known as a debt. It may be contractual or extracontractual by source, and it may have various features relating to quantum, limitations, enforcement, and so on. 'Status' only has an independent linguistic meaning if it identifies juridical features—all eight Hohfeldian relationships could be candidates, as could aspects of legal capacity—that can be explained precisely by a classification attached to one's personality, rather than by one's legally contingent relationships with others.

Finally, to attach status to relationships themselves, as opposed to attaching it to persons, brings in still another meaning of status. In fiduciary law, some relationships (like trustee-beneficiary) are automatically or presumptively fiduciary, but in the common law at least, any relationship can potentially be fiduciary in nature if it has the relevant features.[13] It is sometimes said that the relationships that are presumptively fiduciary are status-based relationships. This seems to address the status, not of persons, but of relationships. Whatever meaning one might attach to 'status', it would be difficult to give it a meaning in law that could be applied both to persons and to relationships between persons.[14] In other words, the 'status' of some relationships as presumptively fiduciary is not at all the same as the 'status' of

[11] This seems to be the implication of the discussion of Maine's argument in J Edelman, 'When Do Fiduciary Duties Arise?' (2010) 126 LQR 302, 302.

[12] *OED* (n 7).

[13] The debate about what those features are is ongoing; for my views, see Smith, note 1, and more briefly, Section III.F of this chapter.

[14] This explains my reservations in relation to P Miller, 'The Idea of Status in Fiduciary Law', in this volume.

persons. Although they may be related, the juridical features of legal relationships are not directly comparable to the juridical characteristics of persons.

For all these reasons, I do not further address the question of status. It is not that I think status is unimportant; rather, in my view it is not directly relevant to the debate about whether fiduciary relationships are contractual.

III. Contract, Agreement, Undertaking

There are a lot of debates about whether contracts should be understood as enforcing promises, or agreements, or as protecting reasonable reliance or expectations, or as something else.[15] It is not necessary to address any of this here. To address the question whether all fiduciary relationships are contractual relationships, however, it is necessary to give *some* meaning to the word 'contractual'. First, it is necessary to address and rebut an argument that is often made by contractarians but which does not actually seem to help them. After that, I will look at different possible meanings of 'contractual' that might be thought to apply to fiduciary relationships.

A. Prelude: the ability to modify obligations does not reveal their source

Many people supporting contractarian views have noted that fiduciary obligations can, at least to some extent, be modified by contract or argument. They argue that it follows from this that these obligations must themselves be creatures of contract, or agreement, or voluntary undertaking.[16] This argument is misconceived. The tort law duty of care does not arise by contract, agreement, or voluntary undertaking. It can, however, be modified or displaced by agreement. I can permit you to scratch the paint on my car, and then it will be lawful for you to do it; this does not prove that my rights in my car were created by an agreement, a contract, or an undertaking. Thus, the simple observation that an obligation can be modified by the parties to it does not tell us anything about the source of that obligation. And when most jurists call an obligation 'contractual', they are making a claim about the source of

[15] Stephen A Smith states that the view that contractual obligations are those that arise from promising is 'traditional and still orthodox': S Smith, *Contract Theory* (Oxford University Press, 2004) 56. He includes theories based on agreement within the category of promissory theories (54). He goes on to discuss reliance theories and transfer theories. See also RE Barnett, 'Contract Is Not Promise: Contract Is Consent' in G Klass, G Letsas, and P Saprai (eds), *Philosophical Foundations of Contract Law* (Oxford University Press, 2014) 42 and J Penner, 'Promises, Agreements and Contracts' in G Klass, G Letsas, and P Saprai (eds), *Philosophical Foundations of Contract Law* (Oxford University Press, 2014) 116 (contracts are agreements).

[16] FH Easterbrook and DR Fischel, 'Contract and Fiduciary Duty' (1993) 36 J of Law and Economics 425, 429–32; Edelman (n 11) 302–03. In fact, the core of the fiduciary relationship cannot be excluded without turning the relationship into another kind of relationship. See AB Laby, 'The Fiduciary Obligation as the Adoption of Ends' (2008) 56 Buffalo L Rev 99, 119–29. We will return to this below (Section III.F).

that obligation. Thus, the observation that an obligation can be modified by the parties to it does not tell us anything about whether the obligation is contractual.[17]

B. Contracts in the legal sense

If the contractarian claim were that every fiduciary relationship is created by a contract, in the technical legal meaning of the word 'contract', then it would be easy to disprove. Contracts require offer and acceptance. As we have seen, the executor or administrator contracts with no one in taking on that role. It is not possible to find a 'unilateral contract', in which one person makes an offer and the other person accepts by conduct; the reason is that the deceased person dies, and therefore loses legal personality and contractual capacity, before the accepting conduct.[18] Again, the person who, by unilateral declaration, makes himself a trustee of property for the benefit of someone else does not contract with anyone; a contract requires at least two parties. These are clearly fiduciary relationships and therefore it cannot be true that fiduciary relationships are always contractual.[19]

There are other reasons why it is clear that fiduciary relationships cannot all be contractual in the technical sense of that word. In the common law, a contract must be supported by consideration. Thus if a person acting gratuitously is held to owe fiduciary obligations, those obligations cannot be contractual in the strict sense.[20] And gratuitous action is indeed found in many relationships that are paradigmatically fiduciary. Trusteeship was, for centuries, presumptively gratuitous, and it still is in some common law jurisdictions; the same is true in some jurisdictions for corporate directors;[21] lawyers can act *pro bono*, and will still be fiduciaries; executors can and often do act gratuitously; and so on. Extended meanings of consideration can cover some situations, but this will not work for fiduciary relationships generally.[22] The consideration problem is acute in the case of *de facto* fiduciaries. One who unilaterally takes it upon himself to act as an executor, trustee, director, or agent, without

[17] In Section III.C, we will see that this is not always the case, but only because of an unusual meaning of 'contractual' adopted by some authors.

[18] A person might agree to act as executor before the testator's death, but (a) such acceptance is not binding and therefore is not contractual; (b) such acceptance before death is not necessary for a person to become an executor; (c) the only acceptance that is legally binding is that which occurs after death, and which therefore cannot be contractual. It is also relevant that an administrator (who acts in an intestacy) is appointed by the court and is a fiduciary.

[19] Other counterexamples would be the parent–child relationship, or that which obtains in Canada between the federal Crown and First Nations (and, in the US, between the federal government and First Nations in relationship to tribal property). Since some might dispute whether these are really fiduciary relationships, I do not rely on them here, although I think they support my case just as well.

[20] Consideration is not needed if the obligation is undertaken in a sealed deed, but it is clear that this is not necessary for a gratuitous fiduciary to be bound by fiduciary obligations.

[21] *Guinness plc v Saunders* [1990] 2 AC 663 (HL).

[22] Langbein (n 6, 632 n 31) finds consideration inasmuch as the trustee's promise induces the settlor to part with the trust property. Within the scope of his article, this argument does not work for those executors and administrators who have not agreed to act before death, nor for the self-declaration of trust (where anyway there is only one party). Outside of Langbein's context, this approach cannot work for gratuitous fiduciaries who do not receive property (such as gratuitous agents or lawyers who act *pro bono*).

ever being regularly appointed as such, will be fixed with fiduciary obligations.[23] No consideration, not even in the form of detrimental reliance, will be present in such a case.

The remedies available in fiduciary law also belie the claim that all fiduciary relationships are contractual relationships in the strict sense. A violation of the no-conflict rules allows the avoidance of juridical acts made in the exercise of fiduciary powers. This is not a remedy offered by the law of contractual obligations.[24] The law governing the disgorgement of profits by fiduciaries can best be understood as a primary obligation arising out of the fiduciary relationship, not as a remedy for breach of a duty.[25] Attempts to explain it as a deterrent sanction for wrongful conduct are unpersuasive for more than one reason.[26]

So we can leave aside the technical or orthodox sense of 'contractual' as clearly inapplicable to many fiduciary relationships.

C. Contracts in the law-and-economics sense

Perhaps the best-known statement of the contractarian position was by Easterbrook and Fischel, who argued that: 'Fiduciary duties are not special duties … they are the same sort of obligations, derived and enforced in the same way, as other contractual undertakings.'[27] Unfortunately, their argument is difficult to assess inasmuch as they were not clear as to what they understood 'contractual' to mean. We have already seen that according to the ordinary legal meaning of the word 'contractual', it is not the case that all fiduciary relationships are contractual relationships. Easterbrook and Fischel seem to have used a different meaning of 'contractual', and the challenge is to work out by inference what that meaning was. How, according to their view, are 'contractual undertakings' 'derived'?

[23] For executors, see *Gibson v Barton* (1875) LR 10 QB 329 (Div. Ct.), 338; for trustees, see *Dubai Aluminium Co. v Salaam* [2002] UKHL 48, [2003] 2 AC 366, [138]; for directors, see *Ultraframe (UK) Ltd. v Fielding* [2005] EWHC 1638, [1254]–[1257] (appeal as to costs dismissed, [2006] EWCA Civ 1660); for agents, A Nicol, 'Self-Appointed Agents: *English v. Dedham Vale Properties Ltd.*' (1978) 41 MLR 474.

[24] When contracts are annulled retroactively, it is not because of a breach of contract, but because of a failure to observe the rules for contract *formation.* For a fuller argument, see Smith (n 1).

[25] This is because the law does not care whether the fiduciary has breached any duty, or whether any loss was caused by the fiduciary's actions. A frequently cited statement of the law, by Lord Russell of Killowen in *Regal (Hastings) Ltd. v Gulliver* (1942) 1 All ER 378, [1967] 2 AC 134 (H.L.), 144–45, is as follows: 'The rule of equity which insists on those, who by use of a fiduciary position make a profit, being liable to account for that profit, in no way depends on fraud, or absence of bona fides; or upon such questions or considerations as whether the profit would or should otherwise have gone to the plaintiff, or whether the profiteer was under a duty to obtain the source of the profit for the plaintiff, or whether he took a risk or acted as he did for the benefit of the plaintiff, or whether the plaintiff has in fact been damaged or benefited by his action. The liability arises from the mere fact of a profit having, in the stated circumstances, been made.' For explanations of the no-profit rule as imposing a primary duty, see P Millett, 'Bribes and Secret Commissions Again' [2012] CLJ 583, 585; P Miller, 'Justifying Fiduciary Remedies' (2013) 63 UTLJ 570, 614–22; Smith (n 1) 628–31.

[26] L Smith, 'Deterrence, Prophylaxis and Punishment in Fiduciary Obligations' (2013) 7 J of Equity 87.

[27] Easterbrook and Fischel (n 16) 427.

At one point, they implied that a contractual relationship is one that both parties enter for gain.[28] If that were the definition, the argument would be self-defeating; we have seen in the previous section that there are very many relationships that are clearly fiduciary but which the fiduciary does not enter for gain.

If we assume that this was just a slip, what other meaning did they give to 'contractual'? They took the view that courts create the terms of contracts '… by prescribing the actions [*sic*; terms?] the parties themselves would have preferred if bargaining were cheap and all promises fully enforced.'[29] Thus, part of 'contract' consists of terms imposed by law. At the same time, they thought that parties to a contract *can* create and define their own terms, since they noted that '[a]ctual contracts always prevail over implied ones.'[30] On the orthodox view, a contractual obligation arises from a promise or agreement; contractual terms 'implied in law' do exist, but are exceptional and somewhat difficult to explain.[31] Easterbrook and Fischel, on the other hand, were willing to treat terms 'implied in law' as covering a great deal of ground, including all of fiduciary law.

According to Stephen Smith, a complete theory of contract has to answer two questions.[32] One is the 'analytic question', which is, 'what justifies calling an obligation "contractual"?' The other is the 'normative question', which is, 'what justifies enforcing contractual obligations?' Easterbrook and Fischel deploy an argument that courts aim for economic efficiency when they enforce—and create—contractual obligations. As Stephen Smith notes, such a theory aims to answer the normative question, not the analytical question.[33] Easterbrook and Fischel used the same kind of theory to argue about what makes good corporate law.[34] For economic analysts, the corporation is understood as a 'nexus of contracts'; but this can only be a metaphor from the perspective of the legal understanding of corporations as persons.[35] Presumably, Easterbrook and Fischel would use the same kind of theory if they were discussing what makes good tort law or good unjust enrichment law. The problem is that their theory does not say anything about where we find the line between, for example, tort law and contract law.

It thus seems difficult to evaluate the validity of Easterbrook and Fischel's claim about fiduciary duties being no different from 'other contractual undertakings' because they do not actually develop a theory or an argument as to what distinguishes contractual obligations from other obligations. Perhaps they felt no need

[28] Ibid 426: 'What do terms such as "duty of loyalty" mean? Because the process is contractual—because both principal and agent enter this understanding for gain—the details should be those that maximize that gain, which the contracting parties can divide.'

[29] Ibid 427. [30] Ibid.

[31] Smith (n 15) at 67–8, 307–14, arguing that terms implied by law pose difficulties, but not necessarily insurmountable ones, to all theories as to what obligations are properly called 'contractual'.

[32] Ibid 42–9. [33] Ibid 46–47.

[34] FR Easterbrook and DR Fischel, *The Economic Structure of Corporate Law* (Harvard University Press, 1991).

[35] Conversely, of course, the legal analysis of corporations as persons can only be a metaphor from the perspective of economics. Many misunderstandings have arisen as a result. A great deal of what may be called 'economic analysis of law' is actually economic analysis of the problems that the law is concerned with.

to, since their normative theory is one that they would wish to apply to all obligations. Again proceeding by inference, they seem to take the view that if a rule can be modified by agreement, the rule even in its unmodified form can be described as 'contractual'.[36] When I describe an obligation as 'contractual', I make a claim about the source of that obligation; Easterbrook and Fischel, it seems, only make the claim that the obligation (whatever its source) is capable of consensual modification. We have seen in an earlier section that almost every obligation or legal norm, whether it arises by operation of law, or by contract, or whether it is acquired by transfer from another, can be *modified* by agreement.[37] The fact that it can be modified by agreement is an important characteristic, but it does not tell us anything about the source of the unmodified obligation. It certainly does not tell us that it came from a contract, as that word is used in legal analysis. From the perspective of law and economics, it seems that the contrary is true: the fact that a norm can be *modified* by agreement means that we can discuss the norm, whether modified or not, as 'contractual'. This, by inference, is the position of Easterbrook and Fischel on what Stephen Smith calls the analytical question.

On this view, almost all private law obligations can be called contractual. In what I understand to be Easterbrook and Fischel's meaning of 'contractual', the tort law duty of care is a 'contractual' obligation, as is the obligation of a losing defendant to pay damages to the plaintiff as stipulated in the judgment of a court; both can be modified by agreement. The result seems to be that their argument claims much less than it seems to. In arguing that fiduciary duties are 'contractual', they did not argue that fiduciary duties arise by agreement or consent or promising. They did not even argue that fiduciary duties have a feature in common with, specifically, those obligations that arise by agreement or consent or promising. They only argued that fiduciary obligations have a feature (modifiability) in common with *other obligations;* their argument makes no special link between fiduciary obligations and *contractual* obligations, where 'contractual' means 'arising from a legal contract'.

When the non-legal and extraordinarily broad meaning that they attach to 'contractual' is unpacked in this way, then the very limited ambition of their claim that fiduciary obligations are contractual becomes clearer. It may be possible to agree with it, if one can do so while suspending agreement with their definition of 'contractual'. Their argument amounts only to saying that it is possible to modify

36 Similar, in my reading, is R Craswell, 'Contract Law: General Theories' in the online *Encyclopedia of Law and Economics*, <http://encyclo.findlaw.com>. Like Easterbrook and Fischel, Craswell presupposes that default rules (rules imposed by law, but which can be modified by agreement) can be called 'contractual' and are part of the law of contract; but he does not explain whether this means that tort duties are also 'contractual' (since they are imposed by law but can be modified by agreement), or, if not, how we are to distinguish 'contractual obligations' (whether imposed by law or arising by agreement) from other obligations that are not to be called 'contractual'. Indeed, some passages seem to imply that default rules are not contractual: in Section 14, Craswell writes, 'Any attempt to displace a default rule will normally have to satisfy (at a minimum) all the requirements of an enforceable contract.' This strongly suggests that the default rule itself is not properly called 'contractual'. Craswell's position on what Stephen Smith calls the analytical question is thus very difficult to discern.

37 Section III.A.

the contours of the legal incidents of a fiduciary relationship. Everyone agrees that the rules against acting in a conflict and against taking unauthorized profits can be varied, at least if the beneficiaries are fully capacitated. On the other hand, the core of the fiduciary relationship—roughly, the requirement to act in the interests of another—cannot be excluded without turning the relationship into another kind of relationship.[38]

Moreover, since they said that fiduciary obligations that have *not* been modified are default rules imposed by the law, Easterbrook and Fischel actually took a non-contractarian position, as many jurists would use the word 'contractarian'. This of course is somewhat paradoxical in the light of the title of their paper, but the paradox grows out of their usage of the word 'contractual'. If 'contractual' means 'arising from contract, agreement, or consent', then Easterbrook and Fischel's argument is that fiduciary obligations, since they are imposed by law, are not contractual.

Others have noted serious difficulties with the substance of Easterbrook and Fischel's argument.[39] In my view, even if one accepts their definition of the word 'contractual', their normative analysis is incomplete.[40] Moreover, even for the relationships that they do consider, their analysis is also unconvincing on its own terms.[41] For present purposes, however, the conclusion is simply that in relation to the question with which this chapter is concerned, their position is the same as mine: it is *not* the case that that all fiduciary obligations can be understood as arising voluntarily.

[38] See below, Section III.F.

[39] See the critiques in Laby (n 16) 110–19; P Miller, 'Justifying Fiduciary Duties' (2013) 58 McGill LJ 969, 982–83.

[40] Easterbrook and Fischel (n 16) refer to the list of fiduciary relationships that they consider (432–4) in assessing their account against other accounts as 'rudimentary' (434), and it is difficult to disagree. It does not include some important fiduciary relationships (such as executor–estate beneficiary) and it includes some relationships that are not (barring extraordinary facts) fiduciary relationships (such as lender–borrower). Their mention of the trustee–beneficiary relationship presupposes that the 'contract' is between the trustee and the beneficiary, unlike Langbein (n 6), who takes it to be between the settlor and the trustee (with the beneficiaries as non-parties who can enforce the trustee's obligations). While I disagree with both accounts, Langbein's understanding is more tenable, because speaking generally, the beneficiaries have no influence on the terms of the trust; indeed, a trust can be created without their awareness, and when they are lacking in contractual capacity.

[41] Their normative account claims that fiduciary obligations are imposed where (i) the beneficiary hires the special expertise of the fiduciary in relation to a complex role, and (ii) it is difficult for the beneficiary to monitor performance. But this does not match the law, even though they are purporting to give a theory of the existing law, and not a proposal for law reform. Their account would make many relationships fiduciary that are not (like corporate director–bondholder, professor–university, mechanic–client or baker–customer) and it does not explain why some relationships are fiduciary even though they do not have the identified characteristics (executors, trustees and agents with discretionary powers are always fiduciaries, although they may lack any identifiable expertise and indeed may have less than their beneficiaries, who, moreover, have wide rights to information allowing careful monitoring). The same problem of a lack of fit with the actual law bedevils other attempts to justify fiduciary obligations via purely economic analysis, such as R Cooter and B J Freedman, 'The Fiduciary Relationship: Its Economic Character and Legal Consequences' (1991) 66 NYU L Rev 1045 and R Sitkoff, 'An Economic Theory of Fiduciary Law' in A Gold and P Miller (eds), *Philosophical Foundations of Fiduciary Law* (Oxford University Press, 2014) 197.

D. Agreement

The contractarian claim might be better read as claiming that the obligations in fiduciary relationships have something important in common with contractual obligations, rather than being invariably created by contracts.[42] Most commentators take the view that the obligations existing in contractual relationships are, at least paradigmatically, voluntary obligations, in two different ways: they are undertaken voluntarily, and their content is created voluntarily. These characteristics seem to fit a promise theory of contract, but also a consent theory, an agreement theory, and even a transfer or a reliance theory. So one way to understand the contractarian position would be as holding that fiduciary obligations share these important characteristics with contractual obligations.

Before assessing this version of the contractarian thesis, it is important to note that it is more modest in its aspirations than the stricter version that was disproved earlier.[43] It is not a claim that fiduciary relationships *are* contractual, but only that they have important features in common with contractual relationships. This, if true, would still be important as shedding light on the justification of fiduciary obligations; but even if this version were accepted, its analogical nature would also place limits on what conclusions could be validly drawn from it.[44]

In my view, however, even the analogical version of the contractarian thesis is untenable. My suggestion was that the analogy with contractual obligations could be twofold: the analogical thesis is that fiduciary obligations are (i) undertaken by agreement, and (ii) their content is determined by agreement. On closer examination, neither claim is sustainable as a general claim. The first claim is addressed here; the claim about content, in the next section.

Not every acceptance can be understood as arising from agreement in the normal sense of the word. Take the simple case of a gift. It is possible, in the common law, to make a gift without consulting the donee; but the donee can always refuse the gift, when she finds out about it. Ultimately, a gift has to be accepted. It is not clear that it follows that a gift is a kind of agreement. The gift may be made on Day 1 (say by a unilateral deed of gift); the donee learns of it on Day 3. She may accept or reject; if she accepts, the gift is complete. But there never was a moment of agreement, in the normal sense of the word; there were two separate steps. Indeed, there was in a sense only one step, because the deed effects the conveyance on Day 1, so long as it is not rejected.[45]

[42] Sitkoff, ibid, specifies (197 n 3) that his argument presupposes agreement, not legal contracting. Langbein (n 6) says sometimes that (some) express trusts are 'contracts' (627), but more often that they are 'deals'.

[43] Section III.B.

[44] For example, Langbein (n 6, 664) uses contract doctrine (in the strict legal sense) to argue that settlors of express trusts should have enforcement rights by default (traditional trust law says the opposite). But not every agreement involves contracting; thus even if a relationship is based on an agreement, one cannot conclude that it should have the same characteristics as a contract in the strict sense.

[45] It was decided in *Standing v Bowring* (1885) 31 ChD 282 (C.A.) that agreement or acceptance or even knowledge are not needed for a gift to effect a transfer of property, subject to the donee's ability to repudiate when he or she learns of it. Where a gift is made by delivery, of course, the donee will usually be aware and will accept contemporaneously; but gifts can also be made without delivery, as by a deed.

It is true that in the civilian tradition, a gift is a bilateral contract. This is due to an understanding, dating to the post-classical period of Roman law, that every property transfer needs to be supported by a legal cause or justification.[46] But consider the case of a legacy, which is like a gift in some ways. A legacy is not understood to be contractual in the common law, nor in the civil law.[47] No one is required to accept a legacy; but even though it can be refused, nonetheless there is no need for an agreement in the normal sense of that word. After all, there need be no communication between testator and legatee while the former is alive; the legatee may only find out about the legacy after the testator's death. There is acceptance, but the time for agreement has passed. Unless contractarians propose to one-up the civilian view of gifts and to argue that even a legacy is a kind of agreement, it follows that the mere fact that one accepts something does not mean that one has made an agreement.

This directly addresses the case of the personal representative, who is always a fiduciary. He or she need not make any agreement with the deceased.[48] Again, one counterexample falsifies a general claim, and this is enough to falsify a claim that fiduciary relationships are always justified by agreement.[49]

Perhaps even stronger is the case of the unilateral declaration of trust. It is not possible to make an agreement with oneself, but it is possible to make oneself into a trustee of property that one holds, thus creating a fiduciary relationship between oneself and the beneficiaries. This counterexample is also enough to falsify the modified contractarian thesis.[50]

[46] In classical Roman law, rather as in the common law, a gift was understood simply as a transfer of property, or some other unilateral act; it did not require a contractual framework. Under Constantine (3rd–4th century CE), the law moved towards seeing gift as a unified category; under Justinian (6th century CE), it became a kind of contract. See R Zimmermann, *The Law of Obligations: Roman Foundations of the Civilian Tradition* (Juta & Co., 1990) 479–95. The modern civilian understanding of the contract is that while it usually creates obligations, this is not necessarily so; it can alternatively, or additionally, have the function of transferring rights (see for example the Civil Code of Québec, art. 1433).

[47] For the civilian, the will is the legal cause that supports the transfer.

[48] Of course he or she *may make* an agreement with the deceased while the latter is alive, but this clearly is not necessary as a general proposition. Langbein (n 6, 637) argues that the executor does fit a contractarian model, because the role must be accepted voluntarily. But as we have seen, acceptance is not the same as agreement. Arguments based on the unilateral undertaking of the fiduciary (and not on agreement) are addressed in the next section. Langbein also suggests (ibid 675) that the court takes the place of the deceased and the executor makes an agreement with the court. This seems quite untenable: on the one hand, the court cannot agree *on behalf of* someone who no longer exists; on the other hand, the court does not make an agreement on its own behalf. Just as it will enforce a legacy, should the legatee accept it, the court merely enforces the testator's choice of executor, should the executor accept the role.

In the case of an intestacy, the court appoints the administrator, who applies to act and, again, must accept to act. It would be equally strange to construe this as an agreement between the court and the administrator. Whether it is the appointment of an executor or an administrator, or the resolution of a lawsuit in tort or breach of contract, the court does not make agreements with the parties before it; acting as an organ of the State, it administers and applies the law.

[49] I agree with Markovits: '… the contractarian approach to fiduciary law commits not so much error as partial truth.' D Markovits, 'Sharing Ex Ante and Sharing Ex Post' in A Gold and P Miller (eds), *Philosophical Foundations of Fiduciary Law* (Oxford University Press, 2014) 209, 219.

[50] See also n 19. The parent–child relationship also occasions reflection on the idea of agreement. It is a role that must be accepted, in the sense that a parent can always withdraw from the custodial

The case of the corporate director is also, in my view, inconsistent with the agreement thesis (and *a fortiori* with the strict contract thesis). Assume that A is elected to be a director of B Corp by shareholders C, D, E, and F. Their voting is consensual and voluntary. A does not have to accept when he is elected, but he does. That is also voluntary. So it is voluntary on all sides, but does A make an agreement with anyone? In my view, he has not made an agreement with the corporation, nor with any of the shareholders. He gets his powers, duties, and rights from the statute, and possibly from the corporate constitution; he does not get them due to any agreement.[51] In this, he is like an elected politician.

E. Undertaking

One reaction to this is to desist from looking even for an agreement, and to say instead that fiduciary obligations are based on an undertaking. This view has been proposed by Edelman.[52] An undertaking can be unilateral, so on this view it is not necessary to look for an agreement. This addresses the concerns raised in the previous section. This 'undertaking' view might not be correctly described as 'contractarian', because the undertaking idea is more about unilateral actions than about agreements.[53] But it shares with contractarian views an attempt to link fiduciary obligations to consent, through the claim that the *content* of those obligations is not imposed by law, but is shaped by a voluntary act that has juridical effect. That is because this is an argument about the justification for fiduciary obligations: it asserts that such obligations are justified precisely because they were voluntarily undertaken.[54] Obviously that argument can only work to the extent that it is true that fiduciary obligations are voluntarily undertaken obligations; in other words, to the extent that in each case, the content of the obligations corresponds to the undertaking that was given.

In my view, this claim is not tenable as a general proposition. Take the case of the director, A, which has just been discussed. It may be perfectly accurate, as a matter of ordinary language, to say that A has undertaken to be a director of B Corp. But

parental role, if necessary by surrendering the child to the care of the State. This will not affect an obligation of support, but it will end the fiduciary relationship, which depends on parental authority: *Louie v Lastman (No. 1)* (2002) 61 OR (3d) 449, 217 DLR (4th) 257 (C.A.). When the State is in the role of parent, it assumes the fiduciary role: *K.L.B. v British Columbia* [2003] 2 SCR 403, 230 DLR (4th) 513. But even though one can relinquish the role of parent, so that it follows that (in a sense) one must accept it, it would be very strange to say that one takes it on by agreement. With whom would one agree?

[51] Of course he *may make* an agreement with any or all of them, but that is beside the point. No agreement is needed for a person to become a director.

[52] Edelman (n 11). I agree that in *some* situations, undertakings are important in constituting fiduciary relationships. We will return to this in Section III.F. Here we are evaluating whether Edelman's thesis can be a general one.

[53] Although Edelman himself invokes Maine's move from 'status to contract': ibid 302.

[54] Without this element, the argument would be trivial. If it only said that people cannot be forced into fiduciary relationships, it might be true (although there are cases that might disprove it) but if it did not go on to say that the undertaking is what gives content to the fiduciary obligations, it would say very little, and would not be what people usually mean by a theory of fiduciary obligations.

the legal incidents of the fiduciary relationship that he enters are not shaped by the content of the particular undertaking that A made. They come from the governing statute, and possibly from case law and the particular corporate constitution. The undertaking has no explanatory or justificatory role in relation to the content of the obligations.[55]

I would argue that this is also true in respect of fiduciary relationships that are governed by case law, like agency, executorship, and trusteeship of an express trust. No one is forced into any of these roles, so we might say that people undertake them. But the undertaking theory claims more; it claims that the juridical elements of the fiduciary relationship are created by and referable to the undertaking given. The natural implication would be that it would be possible to create a whole range of fiduciary relationships, just as it is possible to create a whole range of contractual relationships. Of course, some elements of the fiduciary relationship (notably, the rule against unauthorized profits and the rule against exercising fiduciary powers while in a conflict) can be adjusted in advance. But the default package is fixed, which makes it very difficult to see how it can have been created individually by the individual undertaking given by each individual fiduciary. And the package applies even to the fiduciary who is wholly innocent of what he is letting himself in for. Assume that John finds out, after the testator's death, that the testator named John as his executor. John agrees to act; he will be a fiduciary, regardless of how little he knows about fiduciary obligations.

Edelman's response to this is to say that the undertaking must be objectively interpreted, as with a contractual promise.[56] But in order to make this work, he must take the idea of objective interpretation to extraordinary lengths.[57] Again, contracts are infinitely variable despite the objective principle; why are the legal incidents of fiduciary relationships so uniform? Moreover, his approach seems unable to explain the boundaries of fiduciary obligations. Assume that Mary is moving away on short notice. If her friend John agrees to sell Mary's car and put the proceeds in Mary's bank account, he is an agent, and then a trustee of the proceeds, with the full panoply of fiduciary obligations in both roles. If he agrees to repair

[55] The same is true in respect of the relationships mentioned in n 19. Indeed, Edelman apparently concedes that his theory cannot be a general one; it cannot explain cases where the fiduciary's powers are derived from statute: J Edelman, 'The Role of Status in the Law of Obligations' in A Gold and P Miller (eds), *Philosophical Foundations of Fiduciary Law* (Oxford University Press, 2014) 21, 23.

[56] Edelman (n 11) 312–25.

[57] In my view, the analysis of Stephen Smith, 'The Deed, Not the Motive: Fiduciary Law Without Loyalty', in this volume, also suffers from this defect. Stephen Smith also makes the same error as M Conaglen, *Fiduciary Loyalty: Protecting the Due Performance of Non-Fiduciary Duties* (Hart Publishing, 2010), in seeing fiduciary obligations as justified by the aim of increasing the likelihood of performance of objectively defined non-fiduciary duties (or a 'mandate' in Stephen Smith's somewhat civilian terminology). The fundamental problem with this approach is that it contemplates that a fiduciary can act lawfully even if he is seeking to harm his beneficiary, so long as (whether intentionally or not) he fulfils his objectively defined non-fiduciary duties. This is squarely inconsistent with *Eclairs Group Ltd v JKX Oil & Gas plc* [2015] UKSC 71, [15] and the long line of cases cited there. This approach also makes it impossible to produce a workable definition of conflict of interest (see Smith (n 1) 623 note 62), and it contemplates that the law imposes deterrent sanctions (in the form of profit-stripping) on people who have not done anything wrong (see Smith (n 1) 627; Smith (n 26)).

her leaky roof while she is away, and she leaves him a key to the house, he is not a fiduciary. Is his undertaking, objectively interpreted, really so different?

Edelman even argues that the obligations of a person who becomes a parent, involuntarily, towards the child, can be seen as created by an undertaking that they make towards the child.[58] This seems almost fantastic. Imagine a country in which everyone over 18 is required to perform mandatory military service. Would it be helpful to say that the military service obligation arises because of the undertaking that each person gives? To say that by remaining in the jurisdiction, each person has manifested conduct which, objectively interpreted, reveals an individual undertaking to perform military service? Edelman is required to take the idea of objective interpretation so far that it seems clear that he is really addressing legal incidents that are imposed, at least defeasibly, by the law.

It is true of most fiduciary relationships that *being in* the relationship is consensual, either in the strong sense that one enters it voluntarily, or at least in the weak sense that one can leave it if one wishes.[59] It does not follow from this that the juridical features of the relationship are consensual in the sense of being shaped by the consent of the particular parties.[60] Now someone might take a still wider meaning of 'contractual' or 'consensual' than we have seen yet. This person might say that if being in a relationship is voluntary or consensual, then all obligations and other incidents that the law attaches to the relationship are rightly called 'consensual' or 'contractual'. This approach to terminology would mean that all of the obligations the law attaches to being married would be 'contractual'; and it would allow the same label to be attached to the incidents of fiduciary relationships, in every case or almost every case.[61] Such a wide usage of these words, however, seems very far from their normal meaning, and in any event makes only a very unambitious claim about fiduciary law.[62]

[58] Ibid 312.

[59] Even the parent–child relationship is covered by the weaker sense. The relationship between the State and some or all of its citizens, however, may not be covered by either sense.

[60] Examples of obligations arising from marriage also show this structure. One enters the relationship consensually; it does not at all follow that the obligations arising from the relationship are shaped by the individual agreements or undertakings that the parties give: Markovits (n 48) 220–22; Smith (n 1) 613.

[61] Even on this approach to the meaning of 'contractual', some fiduciary relationships might be impossible to call contractual: see n 58. Those relationships are capable of explanation under my own approach, which is discussed in the next section.

[62] Since it does not make a claim about the source or justification of fiduciary obligations, and rather only seems to say that fiduciary relationships—at least, those that are entered into voluntarily—are entered into voluntarily.

One factor that may explain some attempts to defend contractarian theories of fiduciary law is the undeniable consideration that not everyone owes fiduciary obligations or is in a fiduciary relationship. Many of the duties imposed by law (say in tort or in criminal law) are owed, more or less, by everyone. Conversely a duty which is non-general, and which therefore owes something to the particular situation of the particular parties, may seem to call for a contractual or consent-based analysis. This instinct is, however, misplaced for fiduciary relationships, just as much as it is for obligations arising from marriage, for those that arise where a person voluntarily declares bankruptcy, and so on.

F. Consent and fiduciary relationships

Up to this point, my purpose has been to show that none of contract, agreement, or consent can usefully serve as a general theory for the justification of fiduciary obligations. In other words, the contractarian thesis (in its different forms) cannot explain *all* of fiduciary law. In this section, I change gears and explore the ways in which consent and contract *are* relevant to the juridical incidents of fiduciary relationships.

Early on I referred to physicians and landscape artists: two concepts, but two concepts that can overlap. It is clear that a fiduciary relationship can be created by a contract. It is also clear that in such a case, the legal incidents of the relationship can be moulded by a contract, which might be the same contract that created the relationship, or another contract. It is also the case that the legal incidents of the relationship can be altered by consent that is not effected in a contractual form. If a trustee acquires an unauthorized profit, and all the beneficiaries, being fully informed and of full legal capacity, consent to the profit, then the profit can be retained.[63]

But I have aimed to demonstrate that the juridical content that the relationship has by default is not *shaped* by consent or agreement or undertaking. It arises by operation of law when the relationship of the parties has certain characteristics. Moreover, not every juridical element of the relationship is freely modifiable inasmuch as if some elements are not present, the relationship will not be fiduciary. If we are dealing with contracting parties (which of course we are not, in many fiduciary relationships), this is the sense in which they do not have absolute freedom: it is the law that decides whether the relationship is fiduciary; if it is, certain things follow; some but not all of them are subject to modification.

Is there a way to make sense of all this in a way that provides a *general* account of all fiduciary relationships, while at the same time making room for such aspects as are subject to modification by consent? I hold what might be called an interpretive theory of fiduciary relationships.[64] When one person holds powers over another, the question is *how* the first person holds them. Does he hold them as assets, like money in his pocket? This is how contracting parties generally hold their rights, and it is how most non-contractual rights are held too. Or, does he hold them in a managerial capacity, for and on behalf of another person? Answering these questions requires the interpretation of the power, including the circumstances of its grant. This is what makes this approach a general one: these questions can be asked of powers that have been granted by contract, or some other voluntary act, but also of powers that have been conferred by a statute, or by the common law, or by the Constitution.[65]

[63] No consideration or contractual structure (offer and acceptance) is required: J Payne, 'Consent' in P Birks and A Pretto (eds), *Breach of Trust* (Hart Publishing, 2002) 297.

[64] Smith (n 1). My aim is also to produce an account of the law that is interpretive in the sense used in n 5 above. My account is thus interpretive in two different senses: it aims to interpret and respect the existing law; and, it operates via the interpretation of the relationship between the parties.

[65] In the case of ad hoc fiduciary relationships arising voluntarily, the interpretative exercise may be greatly aided, or settled, by the presence of an undertaking to act on behalf of another. In this sense,

A crucial feature of this account is the central place that it gives to the *quality* or *capacity* in which powers (or other juridical prerogatives) are held. Capacity, in this sense, is a transversal concept: it cuts across the sources of legal powers, since those sources may be contractual or not, and this is why contractarian accounts cannot be fully general.[66] Capacity cuts across other legal categories as well, notably the fundamental distinction between private law and public law; and this is why fiduciary law does not belong exclusively to either.

If the result of the interpretative exercise is the conclusion that the powers are held managerially, the relationship is fiduciary.[67] This means, first, that the powers must be exercised in what the fiduciary believes are the best interests of the beneficiary. This is the core of the fiduciary relationship. Secondly, as a protection for this core, the powers may not be exercised when the fiduciary is in a conflict. If they are, the exercise is voidable. The reason is that in a conflict situation, even a good faith fiduciary may be unable to be sure that he or she is acting for the right reasons: that is, acting in line with the core requirement of the relationship. It is possible for this *protection* of the core of the relationship to be given up by fully informed and fully capacitated beneficiaries, since in general people can do what they want with their rights; the beneficiaries, of course, do not generally hold their rights in a fiduciary capacity. Thirdly, the no-profit rule arises as a natural consequence of the characterization of the relationship. Since the fiduciary holds powers for and on behalf of the beneficiary, any profit or other advantage which he extracts is also held for and on behalf of the beneficiary. It is so held as a primary right of the beneficiary, not as a remedy for wrongdoing; that is why the law is not concerned with arguments about loss, harm, or other counterfactuals. Again, this can be waived by fully informed and fully capacitated beneficiaries, since the right belongs to them and is held for their own benefit.

The core is not modifiable. This is not because the law in this area rejects freedom of contract. It is because the law, and not the parties, defines certain legal relationships. It is quite common for commercial parties to write contracts which state that the relationship between them is not a partnership. This is because they do not want to worry about making each other liable for torts or contracts, which partners can do. These no-partnership clauses determine nothing. The question is whether the relationship between the parties fits the law's definition of a partnership. The parties can freely decide whether or not to be in a partnership, but they cannot decide what a partnership is. Fiduciary relationships are exactly like that.[68]

undertakings can be crucial in some contexts, even though they cannot provide a general account of fiduciary relationships.

[66] I am not here referring to legal capacity in the sense of one's ability to act in law; that is, in the sense that leads us to say that a minor lacks full legal capacity. This is why I said 'quality or capacity'; the focus is on the way in which the powers are held.

[67] In what are often called per se fiduciary relationships, the interpretative exercise has already been effected for the relevant categories of relationships.

[68] Although they are not like that for exactly the same reason. In the partnership context, it is mainly because of a concern for the position of third parties that the law does not allow the parties to define what is a partnership. The text immediately below explores why there is a similar restriction in the fiduciary context. For other examples of mandatory legal characterization of relationships, see Smith (n 1) 614.

Langbein qualified his contractarian view about trusts by recognizing that there are some features of trust law that are mandatory. One of these is that a trust must benefit the beneficiaries; trust terms inconsistent with this principle risk being treated as void. When he tried to provide an explanation for this, that could be squared with his understanding of trusts as implementing a 'deal' between the settlor and the trustee, he said that where a settlor retains control (presumably in the unusual case of a revocable trust), he can react to changing circumstances; but where he does not, he cannot.[69] The implication seems to be that since the settlor cannot react to changes in circumstances, his original intention does not need to be respected. It is not clear that this is an explanation of the rule that he was trying to explain; it is merely a description. But the mystery that Langbein was trying to solve is revealed to be an illusion if we put aside saying that a trust is a 'deal', and say rather more traditionally that it is a relationship in which trustees hold property for the benefit of the beneficiaries.[70] People can do what they like with their property, and can make all kinds of deals. But if they choose to create a trust, they are choosing a legal relationship that has characteristics. One of them is that the trustees hold the property for the benefit of the beneficiaries. Charities apart, the beneficiaries must generally be people, because the trustees must owe their obligations, regarding the benefit of the property, to someone. Anyone who does not wish to attract that characteristic should choose some other structure.[71]

Indeed, in the second part of his article, Langbein explains other mandatory rules (such as core fiduciary duties, and requirements of information disclosure to beneficiaries) in exactly this way:

> Trust terms that would excuse bad faith, or dispense with fiduciary obligation, or conceal the trust from its beneficiaries would make the trust obligation illusory, effectively allowing the trustee to loot the trust. Because, however, the settlor has named the beneficiary and not the trustee as the ostensible beneficiary of the trust, the inference is ordinarily compelling that the settlor did not intend to displace the beneficiary and substitute the trustee as beneficiary.[72]

This is similar to what I am saying about fiduciary relationships. Contractarians do not need to fear every mandatory rule. Sometimes mandatory rules are definitional. What Langbein is saying here is that the words 'trustee' and 'beneficiary'

[69] J Langbein, 'Mandatory Rules in the Law of Trusts' (2004) 98 Northwestern U L Rev 1105, 1110–11. See also the later essay J Langbein, 'Burn the Rembrandt? Trust Law's Limits on the Settlor's Power to Direct Investments' (2010) 90 BU L Rev 375.

[70] DJ Hayton, P Matthews, and C Mitchell, *Underhill and Hayton: Law Relating to Trusts and Trustees* (17th edn, LexisNexis/Butterworths, 2007) art 1.1(1).

[71] Langbein says (n 64, 1110) that it is a 'puzzle' that a settlor cannot create a trust obliging the trustee to destroy a work of art, when it could be destroyed (subject to public law restrictions, I would add) by the owner (or presumably via contract). But this does not seem puzzling when we recall that such a trust would be a non-charitable purpose trust and so invalid. The art-destruction trust could possibly be created in some jurisdictions that permit non-charitable purpose trusts.

[72] Ibid 1126–27. See also Sitkoff (n 41) 205–06, who makes a similar argument. Thus, if we go back to burning the Rembrandt, the trust is presumably supposed to benefit beneficiaries who are persons, unless it is a charitable trust; on either hypothesis, the direction to destroy the painting is simply repugnant to the principal aim of the trust.

have legal meanings; if a trust instrument is internally inconsistent in naming a person as beneficiary but not treating them as the beneficiary (or in naming a person as trustee but treating them as a beneficiary or an owner), it is not a violation of personal liberty to conclude that some meaning must be given to the instrument as a whole. And in such a case, the most obvious interpretation may well be that the beneficiary should benefit, and terms inconsistent with that should be ignored.[73]

The same can be said of fiduciary relationships. Many are created in bilateral agreements, and in those situations, the parties are not obliged to create them if they don't want to. But while they can craft their relationship as they wish, it is the law, and not the parties, that decides what relationship has been created. If one party holds powers not for his own benefit but for the benefit of the other, no one should be too surprised if the law requires that first person to exercise the power in what he perceives to be the best interests of the other. But the reason that contractarian theories do not work generally in fiduciary law is that the crucial interpretive exercise is the same, regardless of the source of the powers. People don't usually acquire powers unless they accept to do so, and this is why it is usually the case that a fiduciary has in some sense agreed, accepted, or undertaken to act. But the question whether there is a fiduciary relationship is not answered by construing the agreement, acceptance, or undertaking; it is answered simply by construing the powers, that may have come from an agreement but may also have come from a statute or from the common law.

Every estate of a deceased person (whether there is a will or not) needs someone to administer it. If a person becomes incapacitated, it will be usual for a court to name someone to look after their property and their medical care. These are situations where the fiduciary can accept to act, or not, but has no role to play in shaping the powers, duties, and other incidents of the fiduciary relationship. The role is offered to her, and she can take it or leave it. The reason the role is a fiduciary one is that it is clear that the powers that go with it are held in a managerial capacity, to allow the one who holds them to look after the affairs of other persons. And the same is true even in fiduciary relationships that do involve an agreement or a contract. Consider express trusts, where the trustee is not the settlor. There may be variations in all sorts of details, such as the terms of a trust and the trustee's right to compensation. But the core fiduciary structure will always be there, because it does not depend on the terms of the particular trust. It depends on the trustee's holding powers for the benefit of others.

Thus, what is true across all fiduciary relationships is this: what makes the relationship fiduciary is the way in which the powers, wherever they came from, are held.

[73] Depending on all the circumstances, another interpretation might be that the trustee is actually the owner; or that the trustee must follow the instructions of the settlor. The latter would be one kind of 'sham' trust.

IV. Conclusion

Contract and fiduciary duty are two distinct concepts. They are related in many ways. Some (but not all) fiduciary relationships are created by a contract. In some (but not all) relationships, it may be crucial to construe a contract (or an undertaking) in order to decide whether the relationship is fiduciary. In some (but not all) fiduciary relationships (whether created by contract or not), the default juridical incidents of the relationship may be modified by contract or agreement.

But speaking generally, across *all* fiduciary relationships, what makes a relationship fiduciary is the manner in which one party holds powers that may affect the other. The characterization of the relationship depends on the interpretation of those powers. And those powers can have any of a range of juridical sources: statute, common law, or agreement. That is why it is a mistake to think that fiduciary relationships are always contractual relationships.

6

Fiduciary Law as Equity's Child

*Irit Samet**

I. Introduction

In this chapter, I argue that the fiduciary doctrine is a successful brainchild of the Courts of Equity, and that it should be preserved as a distinct bundle of legal rights and duties. The most powerful modern challenge to this view is the argument that fiduciary law is in fact a species of contract law since, on a correct analysis, the fiduciary duty of loyalty is nothing but a default term in agency-type contracts. The chapter analyses this view as a type of 'fusion' project, ie, as another strand in the ambitious endeavour to unify Equity and Common Law. The contractarian fusion project in the context of fiduciaries, it is argued here, works on two levels: conceptual—'how fiduciary law is to be understood', and practical—how the law of fiduciaries should be (re)formulated if it is to reflect its correct classification as a branch of contract law. But the project is misguided on both levels. The contractarian analysis of fiduciary relationships in terms of contract law matches neither the present law, nor the popular conception of typical fiduciary relationships, and stands in opposition to widely-shared public policy considerations. A closer analysis would also reveal that it is an expression of a specific perception of the role of State, and not a neutral analytic exercise, as its proponents try to present it.

Equity's picture of the law of fiduciaries as *sui generis*, with its own terminology, rules, and remedies is doing a far better job than its contractarian-fusion counterpart. I will attempt to show how the equitable doctrine reflects the fact that fiduciary law is designed to achieve a purpose that is materially different from that of contract law. In marking out a distinct legal zone in which fiduciaries must operate, Equity uses its distinct features to create an environment where fiduciary relationships, and the confidence and trust they assume, can flourish. A contractarian interpretation of the fiduciary position, I argue, will be devastating for this environment. But without this protective wrap the whole scheme of fiduciary relationships is in danger of withering

* Reader in Private Law, King's College, London. I am grateful to participants in the UNSW Private Law Reading Group and in the UCL–Yale workshop on 'Fiduciary Law and Contract Law: One or Two Things?' and, in particular, to Andrew Gold for their helpful comments. All the remaining mistakes are mine.

Contract, Status, and Fiduciary Law. First Edition. Paul B. Miller and Andrew S. Gold. Published 2016 by Oxford University Press.

away. The chapter runs as follows. First, I present the traditional understanding of the law of fiduciaries as developed in Equity. I then delineate the suggestion that the law of fiduciaries should be (re)united with the law of contract, and point out the way in which it exemplifies the advantages of a fusion project. In Section C, I argue that reconceptualization in terms of contract would undermine the necessary conditions for a market environment in which fiduciary relationships can flourish, and that this would have a dangerous effect of frustrating people's expectations from the law. In Section D, I attempt to show how the equitable features of the fiduciary doctrine (its unique terminology and paternalistic approach to *ex ante* opt-out) are conducive to managing the complicated position of people on whose advice and management skills we rely.

A. In equity

Fiduciary duties, many believe, elude precise definition. Broadly speaking, the fiduciary is a (legal) person who is in a position to exercise power over another ('principal') and is under an obligation to do so for the exclusive benefit of the principal. Historically, '[t]he courts [of Equity] have tended to impose fiduciary duties where one party has a continuing authority or power over another, which is hard to monitor and control, and which exposes the entrusting party to a special vulnerability.'[1] For our purpose I use a most helpful definition offered by Paul Miller: in a fiduciary relationship, he says, 'one party (the fiduciary) exercises discretionary power over the significant practical interests of another (the beneficiary)'.[2] The range of situations in which fiduciaries possess power to act for the benefit of principals spans from the intimate—like guardianship, or doctor–patient—to the anonymous, as in pension fund managers vis-à-vis millions of savers. But the power which the fiduciary has over the principal is always rooted in the way in which the fiduciary 'stands in substitution' for the principal for some critical aspect of the latter's enterprise.

When we look at the core examples of fiduciary relationships in light of this definition, it becomes clear that they share a common basic structural feature, viz, sharp inequality that stems from the vulnerability and dependency of the principal upon the fiduciary. In response to the power transfer and the asymmetry it creates between the parties, the Courts of Equity developed a *de novo* legal mechanism for regulating their relationship, which departs from the general framework of contract law in some crucial points. First and foremost, the fiduciary is expected to exhibit a rare mode of action: selflessness. The Courts of Equity famously labelled this requirement the 'duty of loyalty', so that loyalty has been widely recognized as the essential mark of the dutiful fiduciary.[3] The question what, if anything, the

[1] Joshua Getzler, 'Ascribing and Limiting Fiduciary Obligations: Understanding the Operation of Consent' in A S Gold and P B Miller (eds), *Philosophical Foundations of Fiduciary Law* (Oxford University Press, 2014) 43.

[2] Paul Miller, 'Justifying Fiduciary Duties' (2013) 58 McGill LJ 235, 262.

[3] See Millett LJ in *Bristol and West Building Society v Mothew* Ch 1 [1998] (CA) at 18. In this chapter I therefore leave out other duties of fiduciaries like the duty of care or investment, and concentrate on the 'no conflict' rule.

duty of loyalty really requires of the fiduciary is a thorny one. But for our purposes here I will adopt, without further argument, Lionel Smith's view that the duty of loyalty has highly specific content, namely, 'to exercise judgement in what the fiduciary perceives to be the best interests of the beneficiary'.[4] This is, of course, a lot to expect of anyone. If we want to ensure that fiduciaries act only to promote their principal's interests, the first thing we must do is prevent them from acting in their own interests; because, as Justices Gaudron and McHugh of the High Court of Australia quipped: 'Duty and self-interest, like God and Mammon, make inconsistent calls on the faithful'.[5]

And thus, the most important concrete expression of the overarching obligation to be loyal to your principal is the 'no conflict' rule, according to which fiduciaries must not act where a conflict between their interests and the interests of their principal *may* arise.[6] Only if they ask the principal for specific permission, are fiduciaries allowed to make a decision which could advance their own affairs. The 'no conflict' rule is enforced strictly, with no concession for a sincere mistake about the potential for personal gain. And the disgorgement remedy that is offered upon its infringement sends a very strong message to actors who contemplate the promotion of their own interests while acting *qua* fiduciaries.[7] The response to breaches of fiduciary duty is so dramatic, that Hardwicke LC once remarked that 'to compel trustees to make up a deficiency, not owing to their wilful default, is the harshest demand that can be made in a court of equity.'[8]

Any attempt to provide a coherent analysis of fiduciary duties in terms of 'loyalty' must take into account the danger that it may lead the reader to make the 'mistaken assumption that all fiduciaries owe the same duties in all circumstances. This is not the case.'[9] In the case of relationships which seem to feature the fiduciary–principal structure ('fact-based') as well as for parties in established categories of fiduciary duties ('status-based'), 'the facts and circumstances must be carefully examined to see whether in fact a purported agent … is in a fiduciary relationship … [The] relationship must [then] be examined to see what duties are thereby imposed on the agent, to see what is the scope and ambit of the duties.'[10] The fiduciary label, it must be remembered, covers a large span of relationships, and as you would expect, the fiduciary duties which are implied by these human interactions are not uniform; different fiduciary relationships give rise to differing measures of control over the fiduciary's freedom of action. In the famous words of Frankfurter J 'To say a man is a fiduciary only begins the analysis'.[11] This flexibility in the application of the

[4] Lionel Smith, 'Fiduciary Relationships: Ensuring The Loyal Exercise Of Judgment On Behalf Of Another' (2014) 130 LQR 148, and analysis in Section 2(i).

[5] *Breen v Williams* (1996) 186 CLR 71 at 108.

[6] *Keech v Sandford* (1726) Sel Cas Ch (HL) 62 (Chancery).

[7] *Boardman v Phipps* [1967] 2 AC 46 (HL).

[8] *Jackson v Jackson* (1737) 26 ER 324, at 325.

[9] *Henderson v Merrett Syndicates* [1995] 2 AC 145 at 206 A–D, per Lord Browne-Wilkinson.

[10] *Boardman v Phipps* [1966] UKHL 2, at 127, per Lord Upjohn.

[11] *SEC v Chenery Corporation*, 318 US 80 at 85 (1942). See also Lord Mustill in *re Goldcorp Exchange Ltd (in receivership)* [1995] 1 AC 74 (PC), at 98.

doctrine is a source of great strength, but it has led many to lose sight of the unifying basis of the fiduciary doctrine. From here, the road is short to the (mistaken) view that the existence and boundaries of the fiduciary duty is wholly dependent on the way in which the parties chose to design their relationship; or, that, to make the law of obligations more coherent, it *should* be so dependent. In the next section I will present one such attempt to reconceptualize the fiduciary duty as a derivative of the parties' will *tout court*. In the following sections, I will show why this attempt is misguided and harmful.

B. Fusion: fiduciary duties as species of contractual obligations

Outside the USA, most people who write about fiduciary doctrine, while they may hotly debate the details, share an underlying assumption: the set of duties and remedies which come under the heading of 'fiduciary law' is a *sui generis* legal framework devised by Equity as a reaction to the distinct features of the fiduciary position. This tenet has been challenged by the American-based Law & Economics movement which put forward a rival 'contractarian' interpretation of this area of law according to which fiduciary duties are no more than a species of contractual obligations: 'fiduciary duties are not special duties; they have no moral footing; they are the same sort of obligations, derived and enforced in the same way, as other contractual undertakings'.[12] In contrast to the traditional jurisprudence which focuses on the power relations between fiduciary and principal, the contractarians highlight the voluntary transfer of power which stands at the basis of (at least) a lot of the core cases, ie, on the agreement that starts off many of the fiduciary relationships around us.

According to this 'contractarian' picture of the law of fiduciaries, the courts, in their wisdom, realized that a certain fairly popular constellation gives rise to conditions in which one party to a relationship can exploit the other's weakness to generate profit for herself, while reducing the overall efficiency of their common enterprise. Economists have long been discussing the implications of this 'agency problem'. What was colourfully named 'duty of loyalty' is therefore the law's answer to the challenge to 'design a body of law applicable to agency relationships that minimizes agency costs while preserving the benefits of agency'.[13] This is a pretty successful solution to the agency problem, as the strictly enforced 'no conflict' rule and the disgorgement remedy for breaching it deter potential abusers. And so, legal economists argue, it is reasonable to believe that parties to agency-like relationships would have adopted the fiduciary mechanism, had they invested time in looking for a solution to the moral hazard that is embedded in their prospective relationship.[14]

[12] Frank H Easterbrook and Daniel R Fischel, 'Contract and Fiduciary Duty' (1993) 36 JL & Econ 425, 427. Other *loci classici* are John H Langbein, 'The Contractarian Basis of the Law of Trusts' (1995) 105 Yale LJ 625; Henry N Butler and Larry E Ribstein, 'Opting out of Fiduciary Duties: A Response to the Anti-Contractarians' (1990) 1 65 Wash L Rev 1, 1.

[13] Robert Sitkoff, 'An Economic Theory of Fiduciary Law' in A S Gold and P B Miller (eds), *Philosophical Foundations of Fiduciary Law* (Oxford University Press, 2014) 200.

[14] This empirical presumption is itself highly contentious. As Conaglen points out, the fiduciary duty is so onerous, that it is actually 'quite unclear how fiduciaries would react if their principals were openly

Now, since the law should aim to lower transaction costs by setting up those conditions which parties who negotiate at arms-length would have adopted of their own accord (had they invested the resources to negotiate them), it rightly introduced the duty of loyalty as a special *default* provision, ie, a contract term that is included automatically in agency-like agreements unless the parties agree otherwise.[15] On this understanding, the constraints set by fiduciary law are analogous to various other control-mechanisms which were gradually put in place as our understanding of the dynamics between contracting parties developed. Thus, contracts entered into in the context of insurance, consumer transactions, and real-estate, all raise concerns lest one party may tie the other party to an obligation he did not really choose to assume. The lawmaker offered solutions to this problem, sometimes in the form of implied terms that are far stickier than the fiduciary duty (as in the case of insurance contracts). This, however, never prevented us from thinking about these relationships as basically contractual. The fiduciary relationship is no different—we are dealing with parties to a contract unto which the law grafted some default terms. And so, 'we can only understand when fiduciary duties arise if we conceive of them as obligations based upon manifestations of a voluntary undertaking to another'.[16] Like other contractual obligations they are merely a manifestation of the parties' will, albeit one which is expressed by way of omission to act.

Much of the discussion of fiduciary law, both in case law and in academia, is therefore out-of-focus. The unusually strict and heavily litigated 'no conflict' rules have indeed drawn much attention, say the contractarians, but this should not obscure the fact that they are no more than 'base case' provisions:

> The critical point to understand under the contract theory is that fiduciary duties are not distinct from the contract but are simply one of many drafting alternatives … [I]t is irrelevant that the terms invented by courts, like suits manufactured for potential consumers, are not the product of a bargaining process and may even be contrary to what particular parties would want. If the parties can choose the terms by either accepting them or contracting around them, the result of this choice is a contract.[17]

The orthodox discourse of fiduciary law invests so much energy in questions like 'who is a fiduciary' and 'how, and to whom, should the disgorgement remedy apply', that it tended to neglect a crucial point: fiduciary relationships mostly start off with a voluntary undertaking to assume such duties.[18] And this voluntary element is the key for a successful account of fiduciary law.

to ask them to be bound by fiduciary obligations' (Matthew Conaglen, *Fiduciary Loyalty: Protecting the Due Performance of Non-Fiduciary Duties* (Hart Publishing, 2010) 217).

[15] A close but different version, that of James Edelman, sees the fiduciary duties as implied terms, which are grafted onto the agreement 'by the standard principles of construction and implication' based on the parties' reasonable expectations (James Edelman, 'When Do Fiduciary Duties Arise?' (2010) 126 Law Quarterly Review 302, 316).

[16] Ibid at 302.

[17] Butler and Ribstein, 'Opting out of Fiduciary Duties: A Response to the Anti-Contractarians' (n 12) 29.

[18] Edelman, 'When Do Fiduciary Duties Arise?' (n 15) 310–13.

A major analytical gain of the contractarian analysis, if correct, is the (re)unification of two overlapping areas of law, viz, fiduciary and contract. The fiduciary doctrine, so the argument goes, is portrayed as essentially different only due to an historical accident: the separation of Equity and Law. Like other fusion projects, contractarianism calls on us to take a fresh look and examine the substance of the fiduciary duty in detachment from its institutional history.[19] Once we do so, we will discover that there is nothing in the fiduciary duty that cannot be accounted for in terms of contract law. Understanding the fiduciary relationship as a subspecies of contract law opens the way to an informed application of the insights and analytical framework of contract law. Fusion of contract and fiduciary law would thus lead to a more coherent jurisprudence of agreement-based relationships. For once we (re)situate the fiduciary relationship in the landscape of contract law the courts will (hopefully) focus on the voluntary obligation that stands at their basis, as they do with any other contract. This would lead not only to analytical coherence, but also to a better analysis of the cases at hand as the courts would pay attention to hitherto neglected aspects of the relationship.

Proponents of various fusion projects also emphasize the severe problems in terms of horizontal justice which result (in their view) from the application of Equity's doctrines to some cases and Common Law doctrines to other cases, which are not sufficiently different to merit a dissimilar treatment. Contractarians in the fiduciary context can make a claim in this direction as well. Reconceptualizing the law of fiduciaries as a branch of contract law, so the argument would go, should put an end to the inefficient and unjust special treatment which is currently meted out to principals, in comparison with many other vulnerable parties to 'ordinary' contracts. The present (perceived) need to pay so much attention to the question whether a certain relationship is fiduciary or merely contractual, is born out of the striking differences that hang on this classification. The unfortunate result is that parties to essentially similar relationships are bound by very different legal regimes, because the one is classified as 'contract' and the other as 'fiduciary'.[20] In a truly fused law of fiduciaries, many of the differences between principals and other vulnerable parties will disappear. Understanding that the former is just a sub-class of the latter will drive the courts to focus on the undertaking at the basis of the engagement, so that less would hang on the classification of a certain relationship as 'fiduciary' (see more on these differences in Sections D.1 and D.2 below).

Removing the label, and flavour, 'Equity' from fiduciary law would thus serve to promote two fundamental legal virtues: analytical coherence and horizontal justice. In the area of fiduciary doctrine we thus find one of the most sophisticated versions of the wider fusion challenge to Equity. As even while they do not use the language of 'fusion', the contractarians are bent on ridding the fiduciary doctrine of its equitable

[19] See for example, Andrew Burrows, 'We Do This at Common Law but That in Equity' (2002) 22 Oxford Journal of Legal Studies 1; Sarah Worthington, *Equity* (2nd edn, Oxford University Press, 2006); Douglas Laycock, 'The Triumph of Equity' (1993) 56 Law and Contemporary Problems 53.

[20] See examples of such different treatment to (seemingly) similar cases in Lionel Smith's chapter in this volume.

nature. John Langbein for example, includes fiduciary duties in his larger 'trust as contract' project and says that 'despite decades of pulpit-thumping rhetoric about the sanctity of fiduciary obligations, fiduciary duties in trust law are unambiguously contractarian. The rules of fiduciary law mean to capture the likely understanding of the parties to the trust deal'.[21] And thus, although no contractarian (that I have read) explicitly places his/her argument in the context of the fusion debate, it is a perspective which adds to the appeal of this position by revealing its contribution to both fairness and legality. From the other direction, if it is successful, the contractarian project would lend substantial support to the fusionists' efforts to undermine the independent status of Equity, as fiduciary law is surely one of the latter's most cherished doctrines.

In spite of some judicial endorsement of the contractarian interpretation, contractarians struggle to explain away all those instances of fiduciary relationships that clearly fall out of their framework as they do not take root in an agreement between two people, or are totally voluntary (so that no consideration is paid).[22] Most notable, fiduciary duties can arise out of relationships that are not contractarian in nature, like trusts operated by law, or non-contractual agency. They can also precede the contract as prospective partners embark upon the conduct of the partnership business or venture before finalizing the terms of the partnership agreement.[23] In response, the contractarians may argue that the agreement-based fiduciary relationship is what Max Weber called an 'ideal type', ie, a concept that does not respond to all the characteristics of the phenomenon, but does aim to capture its core essence in a way that facilitates a successful analysis.[24] For, at the end of the day, the very large majority of fiduciary relationships are indeed agreement-based, and the fact that the loyalty duty is stretched to cover atypical relationships (in that respect) attests to the effectiveness of the fiduciary mechanism. This expansion, so the argument would go, should not divert our attention from the core case of an agreement-based relationship. But even if the contractarians can successfully account for types of fiduciary relationship that do not agree with their theory, at the end of the day, the property of 'having been initiated by a contract' is incidental to fiduciary relationships. Taking the contract-based cases as an ideal type therefore results in a skewed analysis of this legal institution.

The extent to which the gap between the contractarian understanding of fiduciary relationships as contractual and the positive law is at all damaging for this fusion project is partly dependent on the nature of the contractarian project. In

[21] John Langbein, 'The Contractarian Basis of the Law of Trusts' (1995) 105 Yale Law Journal 629.

[22] For endorsing cases, see for example *Hospital Products Ltd v United States Surgical Corporation* (1984) 156 CLR 41 (AHC) 97; *Henderson v Merrett Syndicates* [1995] 2 AC 145 (HL) at 206 A–D; *Jordan v Duff & Phelps*, 815 F.2d 429 (7th Cir. 1987).

[23] Many other examples are scattered all over Lionel Smith's chapter in this volume. See also Harding's chapter in this volume in which he argues that 'fiduciary undertaking, understood as a voluntary commitment to a norm or norms demanding service of another's interests, is neither a necessary nor a sufficient condition of the law recognising that a person is a fiduciary'.

[24] Max Weber, *Economy and Society: An Outline of Interpretive Sociology* (University of California Press, 1978) 19–22.

many bold statements of the argument (eg, 'fiduciary duties are not distinct from the contract but are simply one of many drafting alternatives'; 'fiduciary duties are not special duties'[25]), it is presented as an analytical argument, ie, as one which aims to *explain* fiduciary relations as merely contractual arrangements, and the law of fiduciaries as a response to the unusually high transaction costs of specification and monitoring in this type of contract. In other contexts, however, economic lawyers openly advance a reformist agenda. And if this is the case here as well (in spite of the misleading presentation), then, inasmuch as the present fiduciary law does not match their analysis, their project can be read as a call to change it, so as to (re)integrate fiduciary law with contract law. It is this normative sense of contractarianism, namely, that fiduciary relationships *should* reflect the principles of contract law, which I want to focus on.

The contractarian interpretation indeed aims to introduce analytical clarity into the legal discourse on fiduciaries. But their program goes well beyond the lofty mission of correcting a muddled legal classification. If accepted, the reclassification of fiduciary law as a branch of contract law would have some crucial practical ramifications. I now turn to discuss the ways in which the contractarian understanding of the fiduciary duty would change the practice of fiduciary relationships, and the damaging effect which these changes would have on this vital legal institution. There are, I think, four main aspects of traditional fiduciary law that will undergo a profound change if this fusion project goes ahead:[26]

a. *Language*: The terminology in which the fiduciary relationship was traditionally set (mainly of loyalty and selflessness) would have to be abandoned, or reinterpreted as legal terms of art.
b. *The Road In*: Perhaps the most dramatic change would take place on the way into the relationship: those parties who are willing to invest the time and resources to devise their own answer to the 'agency puzzle' should be allowed to do so.
c. *The Way Out*: The way to wind up an existing relationship would also have to change, as at the moment you cannot leave a fiduciary relationship in a similar manner to the way you terminate a contract.
d. *Remedies*: The generous remedies both in measure (profit-stripping) and in kind (proprietary) will have to be realigned with what is available for aggrieved parties to an unfulfilled contract.

In the next sections I will argue that, in contrast with the contractarian argument, Equity was right to mark out the fiduciary relationship as essentially different from

[25] Butler and Ribstein, 'Opting out of Fiduciary Duties: A Response to the Anti-Contractarians' (n 12) 29; Easterbrook and Fischel, 'Contract and Fiduciary Duty' (n 12) 427.

[26] Some contractarians, like Langbein, also include in their project a diminution of the fiduciary duty itself—from having to pursue the 'sole' interest of the principal, to a requirement to pursue only his 'best' interest. I have argued elsewhere against this move (Irit Samet, 'Guarding the Fiduciary's Conscience—A Justification of a Stringent Profit-stripping Rule' (2008) 28 Oxford Journal of Legal Studies 763), but it is not an integral part of a contractarian-fusion project. The crucial point is that the fiduciary duty is a default rule; its precise content is a separate question.

contract, and as a *sui generis* equitable doctrine. Focusing on the first two markers ('The Road In' and 'Language') I will argue that the equitable perception of fiduciary law offers a (much) better response to the challenges at the basis of this relationship. A fusion reform would not turn this valuable institution into a more just one, nor render its jurisprudence more coherent. In this case, therefore, the price of maintaining a dualist system of Equity and Common Law is worth paying.

C. Separation: fiduciary relationships are *sui generis*

Non-contractarians readily admit that the 'observations that fiduciary duties commonly arise from consent are entirely valid'.[27] Moreover, even among those who oppose fusion, '[t]here is no doubt that the contract governing the relationship between the parties is very important. It can affect the scope of the obligation of loyalty'.[28] These propositions, however, do not entail the contractarian conclusion that fiduciary law can and should be understood as a species of contract law. Agreement-based obligations and fiduciary duties indeed interact but they remain, conceptually and practically, separate elements of the relationship between the parties (on how they interrelate see pp 163–65 below). This, I wish to argue, is because, in fiduciary law, Equity sets out to achieve a different *purpose* from that which is served by contract law.

It is not easy, and maybe impossible, to provide a concise account of the goals of contract law. This is because, as Peter Benson notes, 'the world of contract theory presents itself as a multiplicity of mutually exclusive approaches with their own distinctive contents and presuppositions', and each approach comes with its own idea about the aims of, and justification for, State enforcement of contractual promises.[29] However, the two prominent approaches within the liberal conception (viz, 'contracts as promises' and efficiency-based theories), while deeply divergent with regards to other matters, seem to agree that a contract is a form of cooperation that is achieved by each party working to promote his or her own ends. Thus, for those who believe that '[c]ontracts … are tools for realizing individual self-determination by means of voluntarily entering legally binding agreements', contract law is an arena where 'basically competent, adult persons, different and unequal in every empirical aspect, meet each other as … equal in dignity, equal in their basic rights and abilities, and equal in their entitlement to make use of their rights by entering mutually binding agreements.'[30] And even while in other areas of private law they may well reject the maximization of overall efficiency as an extraneous goal

[27] Getzler, 'Ascribing and Limiting Fiduciary Obligations: Understanding the Operation of Consent' (n 1) 40. 'Commonly', but not in all cases.

[28] Lionel Smith and Remus Valsan, 'The Loyalty of Lawyers: A Comment on 3464920 *Canada Inc. v. Strother*' (2008) 87 Canadian Bar Review 247, 267.

[29] Peter Benson, 'Contract' in Dennis Patterson (ed), *A Companion to Philosophy of Law and Legal Theory* (2nd edn, Wiley-Blackwell, 2010) 29; see also Alan Schwartz and Robert Scott, 'Contract Theory and the Limits of Contract Law' (2003) 113 Yale Law Journal 543, Introduction.

[30] Thomas Gutmann, 'Some Preliminary Remarks On A Liberal Theory Of Contract' (2013) 76 Law And Contemporary Problems 39, 39 and 41.

that does not, and should not, determine the law, 'in the field of contract law … [normative and positivist] objections [to efficiency considerations] are substantially diminished'.[31] This, says Avery Katz, is because 'much of contract law has been developed with the goal of facilitating exchange between business firms or commercial professionals' and it thus lends itself easily to efficiency concerns. Charles Fried shares this observation: '[t]he convergence of [law-and-economics analysis and the contract as promise project] is particularly salient [in] the design of institutions that facilitate the coordination, through agreements, of the energies of otherwise independent persons'.[32]

It seems therefore that we can identify a camps-crossing consensus that in the contract framework 'the parties [are] free to be self-interested within their contracts—as self-interested as they were without them, subject only to honoring the terms of their agreements'.[33] Consequently, the basic position from which the rights and duties of parties to contract are determined is *ex ante*. As Fried explains:

> [T]hat both the Kantian ethics of respect and the economic analysis of law concern themselves with general rules and proceed ex ante (i.e., before the parties know how a particular undertaking will work out) explains why the two methods arrive at similar, if not identical conclusions.[34]

Looking forward from the moment the parties assumed a mutual commitment, a contractual promisor is thus obliged 'to go only the distance, and only along the path, that the contract to which she and her collaborator agreed specifies'; '[d]escribing a relationship as a contract both assumes and legitimates the adoption of a purely self-interested preference function by both parties'.[35]

Creating a space in which people can meet, communicate and form cooperative unions which will enable each of them to pursue their goals is a worthy enterprise. But in designing the law of fiduciaries, Equity had a very different purpose. The duty of loyalty is designed to construct a space where affiliations in which a party who occupies a position of power *shuns* the advancement of his or her self-interest can flourish. The fiduciary relationship requires a special space because, given human nature, it is (almost) universally the case that decisions taken in conditions of conflict of interests are in danger of being biased in favour of the decision-maker. In order to create an environment in which people are happy to entrust their affairs unto the hands of another who vows to handle them for the

[31] Avery Katz, 'Economic Foundations of Contract Law' in Gregory Klass, George Letsas, and Prince Saprai (eds), *Philosophical Foundations of Contract Law* (Oxford University Press, 2014) 175.

[32] Charles Fried, 'The Ambitions of Contract as Promise' in Gregory Klass, George Letsas, and Prince Saprai (eds), *Philosophical Foundations of Contract Law* (Oxford University Press, 2014) 23.

[33] Daniel Markovits, 'Good Faith as Contract's Core Value' in Gregory Klass, George Letsas, and Prince Saprai (eds), *Philosophical Foundations of Contract Law* (Oxford University Press, 2014) 278.

[34] Fried, 'The Ambitions of Contract as Promise' (n 32) 23.

[35] Quotes from Markovits, 'Good Faith as Contract's Core Value' in *Philosophical Foundations of Contract Law'* (n 33) 283; Margaret M Blair and Lynn A Stout, 'Trust, Trustworthiness, and the Behavioral Foundations of Corporate Law' (2001) 149 U Penn L Rev 1735, 1784.

entrustor's own good, Equity redefines the relationship between the parties as revolving around an exceptional duty of loyalty.

The complete relinquishment of the entrustee's self-regard which this duty implies, expresses the fact that selflessness is the constitutive virtue which defines, animates and justifies the fiduciary relationship. As McLachlan J remarked in the Supreme Court of Canada: 'The foundation and ambit of the fiduciary obligation are conceptually distinct from the foundation and ambit of contract and tort … The fiduciary relationship has trust, not self-interest at its core'.[36] In carving fiduciary relationships out of the ordinary cohort of agreement-based associations, Equity acknowledged that the element of selflessness is definitive of these relationships, and at the same time it renders them fragile—an island of other-regarding attitude in a rough sea of self-interest pursuit. Nurturing and cultivating this kind of interpersonal reliance requires an imposition of a specialized legal regime but this has costs—what they are, and whether it is worth it are questions which defenders of Equity's position on fiduciary law have to grapple with. Below I show what is the prize to be won for preserving Equity's defences of this special kind of relationship. And as the prize is substantive it is, I think, worth the modest sacrifice in terms of horizontal justice and respect for people's preferences which keeping Equity and Common Law distinct in this context demands.

1. *What classifying a relationship as fiduciary can do for us and the case of financial fiduciaries*

It has been shown, convincingly in my view, that some classic fiduciary relationships cannot be properly understood without a commitment to selflessness. In cases of guardians, lawyers, or doctors, an ability to negotiate a legitimate regard for the fiduciary's own interest would change the legal nature of the relationship in such a profound way that it would no longer correspond with the popular perception of the commitment at their basis.[37] The argument about these types of relationship is that there is a *conceptual* mismatch between the framework of contracts and the nature of these relationships. But in this section I want to make an anti-fusion argument that applies also to relationships that, while they are treated as 'fiduciary' by the law, can also lie quite comfortably within a contractual framework without losing their conceptual coherence. The argument against reinterpreting this type of relationship as merely contractual is therefore more challenging to the anti-fusion camp, and must run on different lines than the analytical argument made in the context of guardians and doctors. A prominent example of an affiliation that could, coherently, be interpreted as purely contractual is the impersonal relationship that we have with those people who manage our savings, pensions or property, and/or

[36] *Norberg v Wynrib* [1992] 2 SCR 226 at 272.

[37] See Daniel Markovits, 'Sharing *ex ante* and Sharing *ex-post*: The Non-Contractual Basis of Fiduciary Relations' in AS Gold and PB Miller (eds), *Philosophical Foundations of Fiduciary Law* (Oxford University Press, 2014) 223; Smith and Valsan, 'The Loyalty of Lawyers: A Comment on 3464920 Canada Inc. v. Strother' (n 28).

advise us in relation to these matters (the 'financial fiduciary'). I therefore examine this interesting case after I make a more general argument in favour of maintaining the equitable doctrine for all relationships in which, to requote Miller, 'one party (the fiduciary) exercises discretionary power over the significant practical interests of another'.

In Equity, we saw, once you have taken it upon yourself to handle other people's affairs for their own benefit, or advise them in a way that assumes high levels of trust and confidence, you sign up for a whole package of fiduciary duties; your relationship acquires a new dimension of commitment that is expressed in a specialized language and implies substantial limitations on your freedom of action. A full-blown contractarian interpretation will change all that.[38] The contractarians present the reclassification of the fiduciary duty as motivated by a value-neutral analysis of the nature of the relationship: observing it through a lens unclouded by sentimental attachment to legal history reveals the duty of loyalty to be just 'one of many drafting alternatives' available to the parties.[39] But this claim for neutrality, I will argue, is false. Whether to reconceptualize fiduciary law as contract or not is a political decision, not an analytical exercise.

If we take seriously the ample evidence for the law's ability to 'shape behavior [not only] through simple reward and punishment … [but also through] its ability to use indirect, subtle, and sophisticated techniques [which] shape … normative commitments', we will see that, in devising a specialized regime for fiduciary relationships, the courts of Equity took a stance in favour of State support for this social institution.[40] In marking out the fiduciary relationship as a special sector—with its own language and rules, Equity helped to create a friendly environment for relationships that are based on a commitment to promote someone else's self-interest. Here is how. Fiduciaries, like all of us, take their cue from the law when evaluating their actions: given 'the diverse nature of society, the law is perhaps a particularly powerful source for shaping and sustaining moral norms, because … [it] is a common denominator for all citizens'.[41] The message sent through the way in which a legal norm is formulated and presented is therefore extremely important as it has a profound effect on the way people evaluate their and others' behaviour.

This expressive function of the law has deep ramifications for the context of fiduciaries: if the law were indeed to communicate to fiduciaries that their position is not materially different from that of 'ordinary' parties to a contract, it would be missing a great opportunity to help spread and reinforce the view that there is something *deeply wrong* in using the fiduciary position to push forward your own interests. When the law requires something as extraordinary as selflessness (because

38 Hanoch Dagan and Sharon Hannes, 'Managing Our Money' in AS Gold and PB Miller (eds), *Philosophical Foundations of Fiduciary Law* (Oxford University Press, 2014) 115–18.

39 Butler and Ribstein, 'Opting out of Fiduciary Duties: A Response to the Anti-Contractarians' (n 12) 29.

40 Kenworthey Bilz and Janice Nadler, 'Law, Psychology, and Morality' in H Ross Brian (ed), *Psychology of Learning and Motivation*, vol 50 (Academic Press, 2009) 104.

41 Ibid at 108.

this is by far the best way to ensure that the legal duty to manage other people's affairs for their own benefit is fulfilled) it needs to send a very clear message that something unusual is happening in these relationships. The pursuit of self-interest is nowadays so widely legitimized (and often praised as 'individualism'), that selflessness has become a rare and fragile virtue, one that is hardly known in any other field of law.[42] It is easy therefore, almost natural, for fiduciaries to slide back unto a default state of mind of self-regard; especially so if in their social circle or 'industry' fiduciary disloyalty is not considered as particularly shameful (no worse, say, than breaching a contract).

A contractarian reformulation of the fiduciary duty would rob the party on whose management or advice the other party relies of the recognition, so forcefully inculcated by Equity, that by agreeing to be a fiduciary they embark on a relationship of a unique nature. The perception that she occupies a distinct locus entrenches in the fiduciary the sense that her duty towards the principal is like no other in private law—a duty which requires virtues that are hardly ever expected in legal relationships. This self-understanding is vital to the prosperity of fiduciary relationships. Given the difficulty of monitoring the fiduciary's actions, and the high chance of a quick profit, the fiduciary relationship is heavily reliant on the fiduciary's inner resolve to abstain from breaching her duty (I expand on this point in Section D.1 below). The 'fiduciary relationship' is a social institution that, much more so than contract, depends for its success on people's general inclination to do what they think is morally right, ie, to follow their conscience. The expectation that they do so is not naive. In contrast with the *homo economicus* we meet in books, a vast body of empirical research shows that *real* people tend to adopt pro-social attitudes (like generosity, compassion, and a sense of distributive justice) when dealing with strangers, even when this implies a setback to their interests.[43] This predisposition to do the right thing, and the expectation that others will do the same (aka 'trust'), are at the basis of people's willingness to enter into, and the ongoing success of, fiduciary relationships.[44]

That said, plenty of research also shows that when a *lot* is at stake—an opportunity for a large profit or a risk of incurring a serious loss—people are likely to revert to self-serving behaviour.[45] And so, as Lynn Stout notes, 'if we want to promote conscientious behavior, we need to give conscience breathing room to work ... experimental gaming suggests that if we want people to be good, it is important not

[42] On the uniqueness of the altruism which Equity demands of the fiduciary see Peter Birks, 'The Content of Fiduciary Obligation' (2000) 34 Israel L J 3, 17–22.

[43] See, for example, David Sally, 'Conversation and Cooperation in Social Dilemmas: A Meta-Analysis of Experiments from 1958 to 1992' (1995) 7 Rationality & Society 58, esp 62–73. The paper summarizes over 100 studies for this period.

[44] For empirical research on the widespread expectation and confidence that others will act in an unselfish way, see Colin Camerer and Richard H Thaler, 'Anomalies: Ultimatums, Dictators and Manners' (1995) 9 The Journal of Economic Perspectives 209; Martin A Nowak, Karen M Page, and Karl Sigmund, 'Fairness versus Reason in the Ultimatum Game' (2000) 289 Science 1773.

[45] Sally, 'Conversation and Cooperation in Social Dilemmas: A Meta-Analysis of Experiments from 1958 to 1992' 75.

to tempt them too much to be bad'.[46] The position of the fiduciary is one where the choice to renounce your self-interest will often cost you dear, at least in terms of opportunity loss. Given the slim chances of being caught in action, how can we trust fiduciaries to renounce their self-interest and show the pro-social behaviour which the duty of loyalty requires? How, in other words, do we create the 'breathing room' that is necessary for their conscience to dissuade them from exploiting their position even when external incentives are too weak to do so? One way of encouraging people to remain on (or adopt) an unselfish track is to create the right 'social context', viz, the 'players' perceptions of what others expect and need, how others are likely to behave, and what others' relationships are to themselves'.[47] Ample research shows that 'social context is such a powerful determinant of conscientious behavior that it can trigger near-universal prosociality in some games, and near-universal selfishness in others.'[48] In particular, the tendency to cooperate in a 'social dilemma' (a behaviour which, recall, reduces your private benefit) increases significantly if the task is considered cooperative, and decreases considerably if it is perceived as competitive.[49]

In crafting the fiduciary duty as a specialized regime, Equity creates a social context in which players understand themselves as participating in a collaboration, rather than a contest; it fashions a space in which what could be seen as a competitive venture is perceived as an opportunity for altruistic behaviour. The move from contract to fiduciary is an example of a '[re]framing [of] both economic and social conditions' which encourages a powerful player to make a psychological commitment to act pro-socially, and promote the principal's interests, even at the expense of her own good.[50] The huge potential of legal cues to influence people's perception of the moral reality is here used by Equity to send an unambiguous message as to the right (self-abnegation) and wrong (self-regard) in the fiduciary relationship. If, however, people come to internalize the contractarian view of the fiduciary duty as just one more 'drafting alternative' for their contract, the opportunity to send this message would be lost. The breathing room that is necessary to keep people on the right side, even in circumstances of great temptation, would be destroyed. Entrustees would remain in the same self-centred groove that is typical of our *modus operandi* in the market. This would have a deep effect on the way they acted and felt as fiduciaries: they would negotiate an opt out from the 'default' fiduciary duties whenever they were in a position to pressure the potential principal. Keeping their own good at the back (if not the front) of their mind, they would seek ad-hoc

[46] Lynn A Stout, 'Killing Conscience: The Unintended Behavioral Consequences of "Pay for Performance"' (2014) 39 Journal of Corporation Law 525, 546–47.

[47] Blair and Stout, 'Trust, Trustworthiness, and the Behavioral Foundations of Corporate Law' (n 35) 1768.

[48] Stout, 'Killing Conscience: The Unintended Behavioral Consequences of 'Pay for Performance' (n 47) 542; Sally, 'Conversation and Cooperation in Social Dilemmas: A Meta-Analysis of Experiments from 1958 to 1992'(n 44) 62.

[49] Blair and Stout, 'Trust, Trustworthiness, and the Behavioral Foundations of Corporate Law' (n 35)1768, and sources cited there.

[50] Ibid at 1785.

authorization whenever an opportunity to serve themselves cropped up (if a general exclusion were impossible); and when examining the question whether a situation they confronted might give rise to a conflict of interests, they are perhaps more likely to give a wrong answer if they were in a 'me first' gear. And given the great difficulty of detecting breaches of fiduciary duty, many principals would stand to lose.

This is hardly the attitude that underlies a flourishing culture of fiduciary relationships. Increased numbers of violations, and constant assaults against the essence of the fiduciary duty in the form of pressure on principals to negotiate an opt-out, will undermine the vitality of this type of legal relationship. Changing the self-understanding of people in fiduciary positions will thus have a profound effect on the vigour of this social institution.[51] This would be a great loss for potential principals, as well as for would-be fiduciaries—inasmuch as the fiduciary position is an opportunity for people to exercise personal and civic virtue.[52] For those who believe that a 'main purpose of fiduciary law ought to be to enable people to form, maintain and develop relationships characterized by a cycle of trust and trustworthiness, relationships that are both instrumentally and intrinsically valuable', deserting Equity's specialized regime would thus undermine the foundations of this venerable institution.[53] Indeed, contractarians may think that cultivating a friendly environment for trust-based relationships is not the business of the State. According to this view, the State, through the law, should give effect to people's preferences—here, to be or not to be a fiduciary. But the law should not, on this view, subvert different preferences by imposing the duty of loyalty in certain situations just in order to support this or that social institution.[54]

If this is indeed the basis of the contractarian argument, then, whatever may be its merits, it turns out to be a substantive rather than analytical claim. That is to say, the way the legal economists present their project as a mere reclassification—which implies indeed changes in the law, but is otherwise politically-neutral—is misleading. Given the profound changes in the practice of entering into, and the running of, fiduciary relationships that the contractarian project envisages, the real argument between the contractarians and Equity is a political/ideological one: can the State force on some parties a legal regime they did not choose in order to foster a kind of trust-based relationship that cannot thrive otherwise? The extent to which

[51] See also Tamar Frankel, 'Fiduciary Duties as Default Rules' (1995) 74 Or L Rev 1209, 1211: '[I]n terms of both psychological fact and organization of the law, a name is important and reclassification can be treacherous'.

[52] On the fiduciary position as an opportunity for virtuous actions, see Irit Samet, 'Fiduciary Loyalty as Kantian Virtue' in AS Gold and PB Miller (eds), *Philosophical Foundations of Fiduciary Law* (Oxford University Press, 2014).

[53] Matthew Harding, 'Trust and Fiduciary Law' (2012) 33 Oxford Journal of Legal Studies 81, 96; and Joshua Getzler, '"As If" Accountability and Counterfactual Trust' (2011) 91 Boston U L Rev 973, 973. Moreover, as Harding explains there, the fiduciary duty facilitates the growth of trust, and hence of non-instrumental value, even where the relationship did not start off as a trust-based relationship (pp 97–99).

[54] In Section IV.2 below, I argue that Equity is much more respectful of people's preferences in the context of fiduciaries than its enemies are willing to admit.

the State should direct interaction between its citizens is, of course, a question that lies well beyond the boundaries of this chapter. But I hope to have made a case for the proposition that Equity's interpretation of the fiduciary position as a distinct legal institution helps to create an environment in which these trust-based relationships can flourish, and that if you believe the State should work to support them, you should be anti-fusionist on this occasion.

Yet, even if you doubt whether it is indeed the State's business to promote this type of social good, there is another reason why you can (and should) still be in favour of a law that is (at least) perceived as friendly to this type of relationship. Here is why: if the legal system were to refuse to lend the fiduciary relationship the special support it requires in order to thrive, public trust in the system as a whole could be eroded. This is because people expect the legal system to follow their deeply-entrenched moral convictions.[55] Typical fiduciary affiliations, like trustee–beneficiary, doctor–patient, and guardian–ward are deeply rooted in civil society.[56] Moreover, like marriage, even the most personal of the fiduciary relationships has a strong legal aspect, and people (I think) are conscious of this fact. If so, they are likely to expect that the law of fiduciaries would reflect the high value of these relationships by facilitating, protecting, and even encouraging their formation. But this expectation would be deeply frustrated by a contractarian analysis of fiduciary relationships. The view that these relationships are yet another kind of contract does not correspond at all to the public perception of the fiduciary position as the foundation of a venerable social institution that is based on selflessness. Such tension between the public perception of the moral underpinnings of a situation and the law's response to it is very unhealthy for civic society. Deep gaps between the public's view of what the law *should* look like and the shape it *actually* takes have been shown to be destructive of public trust in the legal system as a whole.[57] Adopting the contractarian project will thus have a negative externality (ie, a detrimental effect that goes beyond the present or potential principals and fiduciaries) that must be taken into account even by those who believe that the law should have a very limited role in supporting social institutions that express the citizens' perception of the good.

The argument around the classification of financial fiduciaries is a concrete, and most topical, expression of the abstract considerations we have just discussed. The sophistication of the current investment markets makes everyone who has some wealth to manage (including a pension fund), and no wish (or capacity) to invest his spare time in doing so, dependent on financial fiduciaries. And so, these professionals, like lawyers and doctors, have become a part of many people's lives. The

[55] Empirical evidence for the existence of such expectation is ample. See for instance, Tom R Tyler, *Why People Obey the Law* (Princeton University Press, 2006), Chapter 5; Paul H Robinson and John M Darley, *Justice, Liability, and Blame: Community Views and the Criminal Law* (Westview Press, 1995).

[56] As shown by Tamar Frankel, *Fiduciary Law* (Oxford University Press, 2011) Chapter 2.

[57] As plenty of research shows, see for instance, Jonathan Jackson, 'Why Do People Comply with The Law? Legitimacy and the Influence of Legal Institutions' (2012) 52 British J Criminology 1051; Janice Nadler, 'Flouting the Law' (2005) 83 Texas L Rev 1399.

fiduciary duty was once described by Sir Anthony Mason as 'the spearhead of equity's incursion into the area of commerce';[58] and nowhere is this incursion deeper than in the case of financial fiduciaries.[59] The contractarian argument, which seeks to view the fiduciary duty as a contractual obligation, indeed cuts more ice in this case than in that of doctors or guardians. For in the context of finance, the relationship between entrustor/advisee and entrustee/advisor typically features relatively sophisticated parties whose relationship is devoid of personal attachment. This makes it possible, at least analytically, to think of the relationship as just another type of commercial affiliation in which both parties can *legitimately* eye the bottom line. The bundle of rights and duties which these parties sign up for (so the argument goes), merits no specialized categorization; it is just another species of contract. However, I want to argue that reclassification of the relationship between the financial fiduciary and her client as contractual would have deep negative effects and should therefore not be attempted (even if the new understanding would be conceptually coherent).

Fiduciary principles can feature in the regulation of financial intermediaries in many ways.[60] When relationships between a financial intermediary and client are found to be fiduciary, this, no doubt, has profound ramifications for the way the intermediary manages her business.[61] According to the contractarians, practical matters of such kind are the only consequences of reclassifying the fiduciary position as that of a party to a contract so as to allow parties to choose whether the manager/advisor will assume a duty of loyalty or not. But we know that this is not true. The question whether the relationship between client and financial intermediary pertains, by definition, to a *sui generis* equitable class, or is subsumed under the common law category of contract has profound ramifications for the intermediary's self-perception, the extent to which she internalizes the requirement of selflessness, and (hence) to the willingness of the client to trust her, as well as to the level of public trust in the industry as whole. A decision to accept or reject fusion in this area of law is therefore a conclusion in a political debate about the extent to which the State should buttress public trust in this crucial industry, not an analytical exercise in legal categorization. It is a decision about the legitimacy of the expectation that

[58] Anthony Mason, 'The Place of Equity and Equitable Remedies in the Contemporary Common Law World' (1994) 110 LQR 238, at 245.

[59] The question whether 'financial advisor' is an 'office' which attracts fiduciary duties is a thorny one. For a positive answer in the UK, see Article 19 I of the Markets in Financial Services Directive 2004/39/EC; in the USA, see Brian Luster and Steven Abernathy, 'Does Obama's Endorsement Of A Fiduciary Standard Change The Wall St. Status Quo?' *Forbes*, 10 March 2015, <http://www.forbes.com/sites/brianluster/2015/03/10/does-obamas-endorsement-of-a-fiduciary-standard-change-the-wall-st-status-quo-2/>.

[60] For taxonomy and examples of the relationships between investors and financial fiduciaries, see Pamela F Hanrahan, 'Fiduciary Duty and the Market: Private Law and the Public Good' available at <http://papers.ssrn.com/sol3/paperscfm?abstract_id=1184443> 6–12.

[61] See, for example, in the context of investment banks: Andrew Tuch, 'Investment Banks As Fiduciaries: Implications For Conflicts of Interest' (2005) 29 Melb U L Rev 478, and the decision of the Australian Federal Court in *Australian Securities and Investments Commission v Citigroup Global Markets Australia Pty Ltd* (No 4) (2007) 160 FCR 35.

those who manage our money, or on whose financial advice we rely, should perceive their position as implying a special commitment to selflessness to the people who trust them, and about the role of the State in creating an environment where such a commitment is widespread, respected, and supported. The devastating financial crisis of 2008, and the ensuing colossal loss of trust in the financial system and its agents, drove many people to think afresh about these questions.

Interestingly, it is with respect to the category of financial advisors and investment managers—where we are most likely to find the sophisticated actors whose plea for liberty to choose their own way the contractarians are so keen to address—that we find a resounding call for regulatory enforcement of fiduciary duties. The starting point of such calls is the observation that:

> [p]oor culture in financial services firms (including investment banks, brokers, financial advisers and investment managers) has been implicated in the Global Financial Crisis (GFC) and the events that have followed; and failure by these firms to put their clients' interests at the ethical centre of their endeavours is often identified as the core cultural deficit.[62]

And things have not got much better since then. Many believe that the current informational asymmetries, misaligned incentives, and artificially elongated chains of intermediation still create a dangerous rift between the financial sector and the 'real economy'. Moreover, the financial institutions' response to the post-crisis regulatory surge did not do much to restore trust, as it consisted mainly of 'doing things right—ie, technical compliance with whatever legal rules existed at the time—rather than doing the right thing'.[63] The regulators, on their part, prioritized enforcement over prevention, which in turn tended to push financial institutions into a defensive posture.[64] The utility of *ex ante* regulation of this sector has anyway decreased as a result of 'increasing complexity in financial flows … eroded institutional cultures, and confounded traditional regulatory frameworks'.[65]

One medicine that is thought by many to be at least worth a shot is the imposition of mandatory fiduciary duties on financial advisers. This, so the thought goes, would be a good way of rebuilding the 'ethical core' of the industry, and thus of restoring people's trust in the financial system in the post-crisis era.[66] The fiduciary framework is thought to break away from '[t]he traditional tools for supervising counterparties

[62] Pamela F Hanrahan, 'The Fiduciary Idea in Financial Services Law' in J O'Brien and G Gilligan (eds), *Integrity, Risk and Accountability in Capital Markets: Regulating Culture* (Bloomsbury Publishing, 2014), 203, and see sources cited there.

[63] D Sarro and E Waitzer, 'Fiduciary Society Unleashed: The Road Ahead for the Financial Sector' (2014) 69 Business Lawyer 1081, 1084, the authors give numerous examples at pp1085–88.

[64] Ibid at1089, 1100–13.

[65] Ibid at 1083.

[66] A lot has been written on the meltdown of trust in the financial industry and its agents. For instance, 'The 2014 Makovsky Wall Street Reputation Study', <http://www.makovsky.com/insights/blogs/word-on-the-street/28-insights/blogs/word-on-the-street/641-wall-street-reputation-study-2014> in which 81% of financial firms reported that the financial crisis still had major impact on stakeholders' perception, and a staggering 77% said that industry risk was the same or more than in 2007; See also The Institute for the Fiduciary Standard, 'Wall Street to Try to Win Back Investor Trust', <http://wwwthefiduciaryinstituteorg/2013/11/06/wall-street-to-try-to-win-back-investor-trust/> and sources cited there.

available through the law of contract, [which] cannot guarantee the effective delivery of specialized services'.[67] For a healthy market of financial services '[i]ndividuals ... need to trust that the specialists they rely upon will keep their best interests at heart. Fiduciary law aims to promote this trust'.[68] A great advantage of the fiduciary doctrine in this context is that due to its equitable nature it can resist the danger of 'creative compliance' which afflicts targeted, *ex ante* rule-based regulation.[69] For the fiduciary doctrine is conceived as 'difficult to define and inherently flexible ... [and as forming] the background to other more definite duties, allowing the courts to intervene where the interests of justice require it'.[70] In that respect, '[f]iduciary law is like the rest of equity, but more so.'[71] By using morally-infused language instead of setting a long list of technical rules, the equitable duty is much better at creating a social context in which the law's addressees are motivated to comply with the law's spirit, rather than to look for ways to bypass it by sticking to its letter. If collapse of trust stands at the root of the crisis, then designing a space where other-regarding behaviour is encouraged and nurtured looks to many like a good part of the solution.

In the next section I continue to explore the ramifications of the contractarian fusion project for the law which applies to fiduciaries, and the conditions in which they operate. But moving away from the conceptual reframing to the concrete amendments that are implied by the contractarian project, I will focus on two issues: the terminology of fiduciary law and the ways in which the parties can opt out of the fiduciary regime.

D. Two features of equitable fiduciary law and why we should preserve them

1. *Language*

It is agreed by everyone that the most imminent threat to the principal is undetected exploitation of the fiduciary's position with the purpose of enriching the fiduciary at his expense. As you would expect of economic lawyers, the contractarians highlight the structure of external incentives which underlies the fiduciary doctrine. They rightly point out the way in which the disgorgement remedy dissuades fiduciaries from using their inherent advantage to subvert the goal of the agreement.[72] The law of fiduciaries,

[67] Sarro and Waitzer, 'Fiduciary Society Unleashed: The Road Ahead for the Financial Sector' (n 64) 1090.

[68] Ibid.

[69] On the dangers of 'creative compliance' with clear ex ante rules see, for instance, Doreen McBarnet and Christopher Whelan, 'The Elusive Spirit of the Law: Formalism and the Struggle for Legal Control' (1991) 54 MLR 848; John Braithwaite, 'Rules and Principles: A Theory of Legal Certainty' (2002) 27 Austl J Leg Phil 47.

[70] Law Commission 215, Fiduciary Duties of Investment Intermediaries—A Consultation Paper, 2013), sec.14.62.

[71] Henry Smith, 'Why Fiduciary Law is Equitable' in AS Gold and PB Miller (eds), *Philosophical Foundations of Fiduciary Law* (Oxford University Press, 2014) 272.

[72] Robert D Cooter and Bradley J Freedman, 'The Fiduciary Relationship: Its Economic Character and Legal Consequences' (1991) 66 NYU L Rev 1045, 1053–57; Samet, 'Guarding the Fiduciary's Conscience—A Justification of a Stringent Profit-stripping Rule' (n 26) 769–70 and sources cited there.

they say, is using the safe trick of creating a strong disincentive to breach even where close monitoring is impracticable, by introducing harsh punishment for those who do get caught. But, as is typical of economic lawyers, they completely neglect the role of *internal* incentives in the battle against fiduciary disloyalty.[73] Their blindness to the way in which the law can, and must, enlist the inner motivation to do what is right is particularly unfortunate in the context of fiduciary law. For fear of punishment cannot do the work of deterring fiduciaries from abusing their position all on its own. Empirical studies show that the effect of deterrence-inducing mechanisms on misbehaviour is weak, and may even be negative.[74] To the war on disloyalty, we must also enlist the fiduciary's moral sensitivities, viz, her sense of guilt and shame which can strengthen her ability to resist the temptation inherent in her position. And this is exactly what Equity is doing when it uses the ethically-loaded terminology of 'loyalty' to describe the fiduciary duty. By casting the basic legal duty of the fiduciary in terms of 'loyalty', Equity aims to recalibrate the fiduciary's inner compass in a direction that is very different from the standard of honesty that is normally expected in private law.[75]

This reading of the concept of 'fiduciary loyalty' as invoking the ethical sense of the term is in a stark contrast with the contractarians' position. Their answer to the question, 'What do terms such as "duty of loyalty" mean?' makes no reference to the ordinary meaning of the word 'loyalty', and ignores its ethical implications: '[b]ecause the process is contractual—because both principal and agent enter this understanding for gain—the details should be those that maximize that gain, which the contracting parties can divide'.[76] And most strikingly: 'The duty of loyalty must be understood as the law's attempt to create an incentive structure in which the fiduciary's self-interest directs her to act in the best interest of the beneficiary'—any ethical resonance is banished in favour of 'self-interest'.[77] The contractarian interpretation of 'loyalty' follows Oliver Wendell Holmes' path of law, in which phraseology 'drawn from morals ... [means] something different in law from what it means in morals'.[78] This, I have argued in this chapter, is a very different path from that trodden by Equity. Below, I summarize an argument I make elsewhere to the effect that if we sterilize the notion of 'loyalty' and treat it as a legal term of art, we will miss out on the ingenuity of Equity in utilizing the ethical

[73] On the way legal economists neglect the internal drive to do good (ie, 'conscience'), see Lynn A Stout, *Cultivating Conscience: How Good Laws Make Good People* (Princeton University Press, 2011) Chapter 2.

[74] See sources in Bilz and Nadler, 'Law, Psychology, and Morality' (n 40) 113.

[75] See my Samet, 'Fiduciary Loyalty as Kantian Virtue' (n 52). The text above is a summary.

[76] Easterbrook and Fischel, 'Contract and Fiduciary Duty' (n 12) 426. For a sceptical view of the usefulness of loyalty in the thick sense in the context of fiduciaries, see also Peter Birks who finds the concept of loyalty to be 'less than useful [for it] fails to hit the nail on the head' (Birks, 'The Content of Fiduciary Obligation' (n 42) 2).

[77] Cooter and Freedman, 'The Fiduciary Relationship: Its Economic Character and Legal Consequences' (n 72) 1074.

[78] OW Holmes and JC Williams, *The Path of the Law and The Common Law* (Kaplan Publishing, 2009) 8. See Chapter 1 Section 3.3.

implications to encourage compliance. Its failure to embrace these ethical implications is a most unfortunate aspect of the fusion project.

The term 'loyalty' is widely understood to connote a deep sense of selfless devotion.[79] On the basis of this sentiment, a *virtue* of loyalty can develop.[80] By 'virtue' I mean a stable *disposition*, which the virtuous cultivates because she *knows* that people who are so disposed, tend to do the right thing. The virtuous can develop the desired quality of mind by training their emotions to work in tandem with what virtue requires.[81] And thus, when Equity sets 'loyalty' as the centrepiece of the fiduciary's role, it is urging the fiduciary to cultivate a disposition towards loyalty, that is, a state of mind in which her *emotions* reflect an *understanding* that her fiduciary status requires selfless action. Heeding Equity's advice on this matter will greatly assist the fiduciary to do her job properly. This is because fiduciaries are at constant risk of being torn between *desire* to serve their own good, and *reason* which tells them that their duty is to act in a selfless manner. Such inner strife is tiring, and victory is anything but assured. The fiduciary can do with any help. By pressing fiduciaries to be loyal, Equity recruits the potential of the emotive part (here, via sense of loyalty) to rearrange the order of priorities within the conative part of the psyche. It advises the fiduciary not to rely solely on the consciousness of duty to keep her on the right course, as the temptations she is likely to face along her journey as a fiduciary will be hard to resist; developing and nurturing a sense of loyalty towards her principal, a feeling that 'I just cannot do that to him', will help her to fight off the strong urge to act for her own good.

True, the adoption of dispositions cannot be enforced. But the function of law is not limited to the issuance of enforceable directives. The law can influence social norms in many different ways. As expressive theories of law remind us, a significant part of its value lies in the 'statements' made by the law.[82] The real importance of such laws is the long-run effect of the message they send out about the impropriety of certain behaviour and the change they inculcate in social norms and the social meaning of action. In tapping the common understanding of 'loyalty', equity encapsulates a social norm about the disposition appropriate to fiduciaries. It may

[79] It is, of course, a complex emotion with dark, as well as heart-warming instances, see examples in RE Ewin, 'Loyalty and Virtues' (1992) 42 Philosophical Quarterly 403; Marcia Baron, *The Moral Status of Loyalty* (Kendall/Hunt Publishing Company, 1984).

[80] Some writers, like Simon Keller (Simon Keller, *The Limits of Loyalty* (Cambridge University Press, 2007)) and James Penner who endorses his view (James Penner, 'Is Loyalty a Virtue, and Even if it is, Does it Really Help Explain Fiduciary Liability?' in AS Gold and PB Miller (eds), *Philosophical Foundations of Fiduciary Law* (Oxford University Press, 2014)) do not think that loyalty is a virtue (at least not a 'positive' one, that is,with an independent content). But Penner is using a different concept of virtue from mine, and he relies on Keller's highly minimalist definition of loyalty. For a rich positive sense of loyalty, see, for instance, George P Fletcher, *Loyalty: An Essay on the Morality of Relationships* (Oxford University Press, 1993) Chapters 2–4.

[81] Aristotle, *The Ethics of Aristotle: the Nicomachean Ethics* (Rev edn, Penguin, 1976) 1102a13–1103a3, 1104b4–9.

[82] Cass Sunstein, 'On the Expressive Function of Law' (1996) 144 U Penn L Rev 2021, 2032; for a full presentation of the expressivist theory of law, see Elizabeth S Anderson and Richard H Pildes, 'Expressive Theories of Law: A General Restatement' (2000) 148 U Penn L Rev 1503. Obvious examples are laws that forbid littering.

also seek to realign a 'culture' that spread in certain classes of fiduciaries with widespread social expectations from them; such could be the case of financial fiduciaries, whose perception about their position as self-serving is strongly out of kilter with the expectations of many of those who entrust unto them the management of their financial affairs. And though the recommendation to cultivate a sense of loyalty cannot be enforced, its presence is still important as an 'expression of social value … [which is] possibly, the most important function of the courts'.[83] The contractarian suggestion that the moral language used by Equity to describe the fiduciary duty should be emptied of extra-legal connotations is therefore harmful. And since, as Lynn Stout shows, overlooking the potential of internal incentives to promote compliance is part and parcel of the law and economics outlook as a whole, the terminological change is not incidental to the contractarian interpretation of fiduciary law. Adopting their view would necessarily lead to a dwindling of the rich ethical meaning that imbues the terminology of loyalty. When this happens, we will be missing another crucial piece of the defence against fiduciary disloyalty.

2. *The road into the relationship*

In this section I wish to examine the implication of the contractarian project for the point of entry into the fiduciary relationship. In Equity, the fiduciary duty starts off life as a double-layered commitment: (1) a contract (or other legal source) which tells the fiduciary what she needs to do for the principal (make sure he gets a decent education/build a South-American modern art collection/try to cure his cancer etc), and (2) a fiduciary duty of loyalty which tells her how to do it, namely, selflessly. These elements are linked but fundamentally separate, expressing the view that 'the essence of a fiduciary relationship is that it creates obligations of a different character from those deriving from the contract itself'.[84] According to the contractarian interpretation, by contrast, the point of entry into a fiduciary relationship has a single layer, which consists of an agreement that includes a duty to avoid conflicts of interest (either explicitly or by way of a default rule). The duty of loyalty is not a separate element of the obligation, but an additional term in the contract, which the parties to agency-like relationships are free to discard.

As a matter of description (at least with regards to Anglo-Australian law), 'it is simply not the case that fiduciary duties can be contracted around in the same way as can other forms of civil obligation'.[85] And in US law, 'there are … some *mandatory rules* in fiduciary law that cannot be overridden by agreement' like the prohibition on trustees to act in bad faith or unfairly. And consequently, Easterbrook and Fischel's assertion that 'all rules [of fiduciary law] are freely variable by contract in advance' is erroneous.[86] But even if Conaglen and Sitkoff's depiction of the present

[83] Robert Cooter, 'Expressive Law And Economics' (1998) 27 Journal of Legal Studies 585, 585–86.
[84] Lord Mustill in *re Goldcorp Exchange Ltd (in receivership)* (n 11) at 98.
[85] Conaglen, *Fiduciary Loyalty: Protecting the Due Performance of Non-Fiduciary Duties* (n 14) at 219. See Chapter 8 Section I in his book for a comprehensive review of the authorities on this point.
[86] Sitkoff, 'An Economic Theory of Fiduciary Law' (n 13) 204–05; Mark Leeming, 'The Scope of Fiduciary Obligations: How Contract Informs, But Does Not Determine, the Scope of Fiduciary Obligations' (2009) Journal of Equity 181–83.

law as reflecting Equity's point of view is right, I argue that an anti-fusion position still owes an answer to the *normative* version of the contractarian challenge; that is, we need to explain why we must not change the law so as to allow sophisticated parties to choose, *ex ante*, to reject the law's solution to a problem they face. For in doing that we will be treating the parties like all other *sui juris* parties to agreements who are free to design their own answers to the challenges raised by their envisaged cooperation. Above, I pointed out the negative effects that such change would have on the fiduciary's self-perception and hence on the vitality of the fiduciary relationship. Here I want to argue further that, given the special conditions of fiduciary relationships, the equitable model which offers the possibility of concrete authorization and some exceptional opt outs often offers a *better* protection of the parties' liberty.

As 'legally enforceable standard-form provisions that reduce transaction costs', fiduciary duties, say the contractarians, are but one option that is open to parties who are about to embark on an agency-like relationship:

> In selecting between fiduciary duties and alternative constraints, the parties consider both the costs and benefits of fiduciary duties, and at the margin trade off fiduciary duties for other constraints ... But the parties also may conclude that the costs of fiduciary duties outweigh their gap-filling benefits ... [in such cases] the court ... should not apply fiduciary duties if the parties have opted out of them.[87]

The value which the opting out option instantiates is therefore respect for the parties' choice to solve the agency problem in a different way from that suggested by the State (namely, the requirement of complete abstinence from entering a situation in which a conflict of interest may arise). Principally, they may negotiate an exclusion of the duty of loyalty in return for a lower price for the fiduciary's services—a price which takes into account the risk that she will make sub-optimal decisions that are tainted by conflict of interest. As a free choice of autonomous agents, it deserves respect. For economic lawyers, fulfilling the parties' preferences will also lead to an increase in overall efficiency (at least in the right market conditions). In Equity, in contrast, once the parties shape their relationship in a certain way that Equity deems as fiduciary, an imposition of loyalty duty ensues like the day follows the night (with some carefully crafted exceptions—see below).[88] But is Equity's approach really less respectful of the parties' freedom to choose what is good for them?

The first thing to remember is that Equity allows the parties to consensually remove the duty of loyalty with regards to *concrete* conflicts of interests.[89] The fiduciary can disclose her interest(s) in any specific move she contemplates and ask the

[87] Butler and Ribstein, 'Opting out of Fiduciary Duties: A Response to the Anti-Contractarians' (n 12) 29–30.

[88] See Lionel Smith's chapter in the volume.

[89] This has been the case at least since the beginning of the nineteenth century (see Conaglen, *Fiduciary Loyalty: Protecting the Due Performance of Non-Fiduciary Duties* (n 14) Chapter 8 n 10 for many early authorities on this point).

principal to authorize her decision in spite of the (possible) conflict. The principal can, of course, affix a price tag to such authorization, the quantum of which would be far more reflective of the risk he is taking than any 'global' price he can name at the outset of the relationship. In that respect, the principal is not like the ordinary party to a contract who is expected to set a price for future eventualities. For the gap between what the principal knows at the point of entry and what he knows down the road is far greater than is typical in the contractual setting. After all, the fiduciary relationship is built on the assumption that at the moment of inception the parties *cannot tell* which decisions the fiduciary will have to make. This is why the terms which define the fiduciary's prescriptive obligations are open-ended, and the discretion she has to exercise is typically quite strong. The information gap thus created between the parties—the *raison d'être* of the duty of loyalty—normally deepens as the fiduciary makes more and more moves on behalf of the principal.

But then the idea that the principal can make an informed decision about the price, which properly reflects the risk that the fiduciary will make biased decisions on his behalf, is highly dubious. As Whincop asks (without supplying a satisfactory answer) 'how can one establish specificity in the context of a protean concept?'[90] Sure enough, Equity's mechanism of ad-hoc authorization is not perfect in that respect. The uncertainty at the outset cuts both ways: there will be occasions when specific authorization cannot be obtained, and the fiduciary would incur opportunity costs that *she* could not have priced into the *ex ante* agreement (so the fiduciary's salary cannot fully embed her losses from giving up opportunities that require operation in conditions of conflict of interest). But, as Joseph Stiglitz once remarked '[i]t is simply impossible to pay for trust every time it is required'.[91] The way in which Equity allows parties to negotiate local exclusions is therefore *more* respectful of the parties' preferences, as it takes into account the fact that preferences in regards to open-ended obligations cannot be properly formed while the obligations are largely inchoate. Once an actual occasion for a conflict of interest arises, so that the principal can really calculate the risk, and name his price, Equity will give full effect to the parties' preferences with regards to the duty of loyalty.

The need to ask for specific authorizations surely has a cost. For sophisticated parties that cost can possibly be reduced by a crafty packaging of a certain *type* of decisions that involve specific conflicts of interests so that *ex ante* disclosure and concession can cover bigger clusters of decisions. But either way, the decrease in the liberty of those parties who could have somehow calculated the value of an *ex ante* waiver is a price worth paying for what a 'general frown' over such waivers communicates; namely, that fiduciary-type relationships should be governed by a principle of loyalty, and unless specific circumstances militate against it, fiduciaries should orient themselves in a different manner to the one they are accustomed to in other legal relationships: selflessness instead of self-regard. The constraints at the

[90] Michael Whincop, 'Of Fault and Default: Contractarianism as a Theory of Anglo-Australian Corporate Law' (1997) 21 Melb U L Rev 187, 203.

[91] Joseph E Stiglitz, 'In No One We Trust' *New York Times* (New York, 22 December 2013).

'in' stage thus join other elements in the fiduciary package in sending a strong message to people who are in, or about to assume, a fiduciary position: this is a special zone, with distinctive obligations and dangerous pitfalls. Beware. In this way, the law helps to create the right conditions for fiduciaries to fulfil their duties and for fiduciary relationships to flourish as an option for handling one's affairs.

It must also be noted that Equity has always taken very seriously the agreement which launches the fiduciary relationship (when one exists, of course). It is generally accepted that '[t]he nature of the contractual relationship can help determine the scope and intensity' of the fiduciary duties.[92] True, '[t]he fact that a fiduciary relationship is expressly disclaimed is not decisive', but the parties' preferences as to the nature of their relationship dictate to a large extent the shape that it will take.[93] The relationship between the contract and the duty of loyalty according to Equity is helpfully described by Smith and Valsan in the following way: 'The contract indicates what it is that the … fiduciary must do on behalf of the [principal] … The fiduciary obligation indicates *how* the [fiduciary] must do it: decisions must be made loyally'.[94] Thus, the Australian High Court explains in *Maguire v Makaronis* that 'to say that the appellants stood as fiduciaries to the respondents calls for the ascertainment of the particular obligations owed to the respondents and consideration of what acts and omissions amount to failure to discharge those obligations'.[95] The parties' preferences as to the scope and goals of their cooperation are thus highly respected by the equitable doctrine of fiduciaries. But once the parties have chosen a form of affiliation that exhibits the power relations that give rise to a serious agency problem, they will have to accept *ex-ante* the protective umbrella of the duty of loyalty. They would only be able to close it once the principal knows for sure what type of rain is likely to come down on him (and calculate how wet he is willing to get in order to allow the fiduciary to benefit from a specific move).

Equity is also highly sensitive to the market conditions in which different actors operate, and the different expectations that are borne as a result. Its flexibility in that respect is nicely summarised by Fletcher Moulton LJ's statement in In *re Coomber*:

> Fiduciary relations are of many different types … in some minds there arises the idea that … every kind of fiduciary relation justifies every kind of interference. Of course that is absurd … There is no class of case in which one ought more carefully to bear in mind the facts of the case … than cases which relate to fiduciary and confidential relations and the action of the Court with regard to them.[96]

And so, even while the Courts of Equity are reputed to have shown '[u]ncompromising rigidity… when petitioned to undermine the rule of undivided

[92] Getzler, 'Ascribing and Limiting Fiduciary Obligations: Understanding the Operation of Consent' (n 1) 47. See also Smith and Valsan, 'The Loyalty of Lawyers: A Comment on 3464920 Canada Inc. v. Strother' (n 28) 267.

[93] Leeming, 'The Scope of Fiduciary Obligations: How Contract Informs, But Does Not Determine, the Scope of Fiduciary Obligations' (n 86) 10.

[94] Smith and Valsan, 'The Loyalty of Lawyers: A Comment on 3464920 Canada Inc. v. Strother' (n 28) 268.

[95] *Maguire v Makaronis* (1997) 188 CLR 449 at 464.

[96] [1911] 1 Ch 723 at 728–29.

loyalty by the "disintegrating erosion" of particular exceptions', we do see willingness to give ground when fully fledged fiduciary duties will undermine a socially valued practice.[97] Accordingly, in *Kelly v Cooper*, Lord Brown-Wilkinson stated that '[i]t is not possible to say that all agents owe the same duties to their principals: it is always necessary to have regard to the express or implied terms of the contract'.[98] About the case at hand, he held that an estate agent was entitled to act for other principals selling competing properties and to keep confidential the information obtained from each of those principals. The Privy Council thought very sensibly that the principal must have appreciated that the nature of an estate agent's business is 'to act for numerous principals' since residential estate agents and similar professions 'must be free to act for several competing principals; otherwise, they will be unable to perform their function'.[99]

Thus, as is appropriate for an equitable doctrine, the fiduciary duty is flexible enough to be rolled off when the custom and market conditions of a specific industry so require. But this does not mean that the contract between the parties is the sole determinant of the fiduciary duty in each case. As Lord Walker explained in *Hilton v Barker Booth* (a case of a lawyer who placed himself in a conflict of duties to disclose information about the client on the one hand and to act for his best interests on the other hand):

> [T]he content of the contractual duty of full disclosure [is] rooted in the fiduciary relationship between solicitor and client ... [And] [s]ince he may not prefer one duty to another, he must perform both as best as he can. This may involve performing one duty to the letter of the obligation, and paying compensation for his failure to perform the other.[100]

In *Rossetti Marketing* the Court of Appeal restated the general principle that a commercial agent occupies a fiduciary position and owes a 'single-minded duty of loyalty' to her principal. The estate agent remains an exception.[101] The case of commercial agency shows how the equitable doctrine has sufficient internal resources to adjust the intensity and breadth of the fiduciary duty to the nature of the relationship envisaged by the parties, and to the business environment in which they operate. Another measure of flexibility is Equity's willingness to look beyond the agreement and take the parties' actions as implying either a reduction or elevation of the fiduciary duties.[102] When we add the option to exclude the duty of loyalty in concrete situations, we get a picture of an equitable doctrine that pays deep respect

[97] *Meinhard v Salmon*, 164 N.E. 545 (N.Y. 1928) (N.Y.S.C.) (Cardozo J) 546.

[98] *Kelly v Cooper* [1993] AC 205 (PC) at 214. [99] Ibid at 205.

[100] *Hilton v Barker Booth and Eastwood* [2005] UKHL 8 (UKSC), at 42, 44. In a unanimous decision, the SC underlined *Moody v Cox* [1917] 2 Ch 71 which forbade conflict of duties as a breach of duty of loyalty, as good law.

[101] *Rossetti Marketing Ltd v Diamond Sofa Company Ltd* [2012] EWCA Civ 1021 (CA), at 24. See also AHC in *Australian Securities and Investments Commission v Citigroup Global Markets Australia Pty Ltd* (No 4) (2007) 160 FCR 35.

[102] See Leeming, 'The Scope of Fiduciary Obligations: How Contract Informs, But Does Not Determine, the Scope of Fiduciary Obligations' (n 86) 14–16 and sources cited there.

to the parties' specific needs and wishes, albeit within a more restrictive framework that reflects the deep differences between contractual and fiduciary relationships.

The contractarians cannot therefore argue that if we want to pay the parties' preference its due respect we must reinterpret the fiduciary duty as a default contractual term. For there is a serious sense in which the equitable regime of [*ex post* authorisation + exceptional *ex ante* opt-outs] is *more* respectful of whatever *informed* choices the parties can make. Moreover, in the end, it is up to every society to decide whether private arrangements are to be sanctified even where that may lead to increasing abuse and endanger the whole institution of fiduciary relationships, or accept a compulsory legal regime that may not have room for some genuine preferences. As Butler and Ribstein conclude: 'While the question is ultimately one of policy, the fundamentally contractual nature of fiduciary duties means that they should be subject to the same presumption in favor of private ordering that applies to other contracts'.[103] Being contractarians, they believe that the conceptual point they make (namely, that fiduciaries are best understood in terms of the common law of contracts) lays extra weight on the pro *ex ante* opt-out side of the scale. Yet, as we saw, their insistence that fiduciary and contract relationships have a similar 'nature' is false. Their analysis of the duty of loyalty in terms of default terms is in line with neither the present law, nor the popular conception of typical fiduciary relationships, nor with widely-shared public policy considerations. Whether we wish to embrace the contractarian project is ultimately a question of whether we are willing to harness the legal system to protect the integrity of fiduciary relationships, and accept that in some cases genuine and informed preferences will not be respected, or, at least, not in the most efficient way.

Conclusion

In this chapter I endeavoured to show why an ambitious proposal to fuse one of Equity's most distinctive doctrines with a neighbouring Common Law doctrine should be abandoned. In spite of some gains that are typical of such fusion projects, in terms of horizontal justice and analytical coherence, the price that we would have to pay for transforming the equitable duty of loyalty into an ordinary contractual obligation would be too high in a number of ways. For in spite of a superficial resemblance, the equitable doctrine of fiduciaries does not match the law of contract in either purpose or practice. We saw how according to both deontological autonomy-based and teleological efficiency-based accounts, the goal of contract law is to create a space where free people can legitimately use each other in order to promote their personal advantage. This space is indeed highly valuable as it allows efficient cooperation between individuals to take place even if they are complete strangers, and facilitates autonomy-enhancing activity. But fiduciary law is designed to promote a

[103] Butler and Ribstein, 'Opting out of Fiduciary Duties: A Response to the Anti-Contractarians' (n 12) 32.

different good. In fiduciary law, I argued, Equity aims to create an area free of self-regard—an area which is necessary in order to protect the integrity of this special type of highly-valuable relationship. The distinctively equitable features of the fiduciary doctrine—the use of standards, the morally-infused language, and the flexibility in application—are essential for attaining this goal. Together, we saw, these features work to establish a social context in which people in fiduciary positions are motivated to act in a pro-social manner in spite of the great temptation to act selfishly, with the result that the relationship is built upon the strong foundations of trust and confidence that it requires. A contractual self-understanding of their role as fiduciaries, while it would leave more room for individual preferences as to the nature of the affiliation, would undermine this social context, and with it the stable basis of the relationship.

I reached the conclusion that the real debate with the contractarians does boil down to a conceptual argument about the correct analysis of the law, but rather amounts to a political controversy about the role of the State in facilitating and buttressing social goods such as fiduciary relationships. And though this is surely not the place to conduct such political debate, I pointed out some other considerations which must be taken into account when making up your mind about it. First, a negative externality in the form of the damage to the credibility of the legal system arises whenever a serious gap opens between what people believe the law should do and what it actually does. Given the centrality of fiduciary relationships to the fabric of the community, a deep dissatisfaction is likely to develop about the very little that a contractarian-style law would actually do to support them.

We also saw that in terms of respecting the parties' preferences, the equitable doctrine is actually doing a better job than the suggested contractarian regime. This is because the open-ended nature of the fiduciary relationship makes it very hard to reach an informed decision about the price of a general opt-out favoured by the contractarians. Equity, in contrast, allows for authorization to sidestep the duty of loyalty only in concrete situations where the principal's preferences are much more likely to be genuine and well-informed. Equity, as we would expect, is also flexible enough to allow general opt-out where the nature of the industry really calls for such exceptions. These considerations, I hope, offer further support to my claim that in the context of fiduciary law the project of fusion should be deserted, so that Equity and Common Law are left as distinct bodies of law that regulate different aspects of these highly valuable relationships.

7

Formal Elements of Contract and Fiduciary Law

*Emily L Sherwin**

I. Introduction

A central dilemma of private law is how to reconcile general rules with particular justice. Determinate general rules,[1] consistently applied by courts in adjudication of disputes, allow private actors to coordinate their actions and minimize errors of judgement. At the same time, determinate rules are almost always overinclusive: in some of the cases to which they apply the results they prescribe are wrong, all things considered. If the rule is well designed, most actors will do better over the long run by following the rule than they would by exercising their best judgement case-by-case. Some might outperform the rule, but not all will judge correctly whether they fall into this category—all actors, including mistaken actors, believe that whatever their best judgement recommends is best. It follows that the rule will be most effective if all actors understand that it will be enforced in all cases that fall within its terms. Yet, in some of those cases enforcement will not be just: judges will be asked to enforce a rule that ought not apply to the case before the court.

I propose that contract law and fiduciary law have responded to this dilemma in different ways. Contract law, with its history in the dual systems of law and equity, has resources that allow courts to announce determinate, seemingly absolute, rules but make exceptions at the enforcement stage when the outcome of the rules seems

* Frank B. Ingersoll Professor of Law, Cornell Law School. I am grateful for comments by Kevin Clermont, Michael Dorf, Robert Hillman, Andrei Marmor, Paul Miller, and participants in the Cornell Law School Summer Workshop, the Yale Center for the Study of Private Law/University College London Symposium on Contract and Fiduciary Duty, the Workshop on Philosophy of Private Law at Cornell Law School, and the Contract, Status, and Fiduciary Law Symposium at McGill University.

[1] Legal rules span a continuum running from highly determinate rules ('drive on the right') to vague standards ('use reasonable care'). I use the term 'rules' for all points along this continuum, but most of my discussion pertains to rules that are sufficiently determinate that a competent speaker will know whether they apply and what they require in most cases. For useful discussions of the types and functions of rules, see Frederick Schauer, *Playing By the Rules: A Philosophical Examination of Rule-Based Decision-Making in Law and Life* (Clarendon Press, 1991) 1–121; Isaac Ehrlich and Richard A Posner, 'An Economic Analysis of Legal Rulemaking' (1974) 3 J Legal Stud 257; Louis Kaplow, 'Rules vs. Standards: An Economic Analysis' (1992) 42 Duke L J 557.

particularly harsh. Fiduciary law, a product of the equity system, is somewhat less effective in concealing the bottom line. Thus, at least in elaborating the core duty of loyalty to the interests of beneficiaries, courts have developed a relatively straightforward combination of broad standards of behaviour and concrete prophylactic rules, backed by strict rules of enforcement.

The discussion that follows is primarily descriptive. I do not judge which formal pattern is superior, and I make only tentative suggestions about properties of fields of law that conduce to one pattern or the other. I suspect that, as with much private law, history has played a large part in shaping formal features of the law.

II. The Problem of Rules

Before turning to particular fields of law, it may be useful to describe the principal formal dilemma of law—the problem of general rules and particular outcomes. Rules of private law are general by nature because they must govern an unspecified set of future cases. General rules are often, although not always, stated in relatively determinate form. Particularly in areas of law that serve as the background for privately created arrangements, determinacy has a number of advantages.[2] One is that determinate rules can control errors of human judgement: a clear and well-designed default rule can avoid mistakes in the content of private obligations that result from systematically biased or inexpert assessment by the parties. Another advantage of determinate rules is to coordinate the actions of parties with disparate interests and no way of reading each other's minds.[3] Determinate rules place recognizable limits on the creation and enforcement of private arrangements. In doing so, they define when and to what extent transactions will be supported by law and allow the parties to plan with confidence.

The drawback of determinate rules is that even a very good rule is likely to be imperfect in its application to particular cases. Any rule stated in concrete, general terms will sometimes lead to outcomes that are mistaken when judged against the underlying objectives of the rule or against ordinary understandings of fairness. A rule that is imperfect in application may nevertheless be a good rule if it prevents more errors—including errors that result from the parties' inability to coordinate their actions through reliable agreements—than it causes by occasional misapplication to cases. Yet, even when the rules are optimal in form and content, courts will come under pressure to depart from them in recalcitrant cases. In other words, they will come under pressure to do equity in the Aristotelian sense of correcting general laws when their bluntness leads to error.[4]

[2] For a utilitarian defence of enabling rules for private ordering, see John Rawls, 'Two Concepts of Rules' (1955) 64 Phil Rev 3, 24–28.

[3] For discussion of coordination and other benefits of determinate rules, see Joseph Raz, *The Morality of Freedom* (Oxford University Press, 1986) 49–50; Schauer (n 1), at 149–55; 'Gerald J Postema, Coordination and Convention at the Foundations of Law' (1982) 11 J Legal Stud 165, 172–86.

[4] Aristotle, *Nicomachean Ethics* 1138b25 (Terence Irwin trans, Hackett Publishing, 1985) ('And this is the nature of what is decent—rectification of law in so far as the universality of law makes it deficient').

One way to characterize the difficulty posed by determinate rules is that they provide a blueprint for advantage-taking. If the law defines a distinct set of conduct rules or conditions for valid obligations, a clever opportunist may seek advantage in ways that, while not technically prohibited, are nevertheless unfair. Henry Smith suggests that the primary function of various substantive and remedial doctrines derived from the equity side of legal history, including both equitable excuses from contract obligation and the law governing fiduciary duty, is to prevent this type of opportunism. Equitable standards of performance and equitable discretion in granting remedies allow courts to review particular transactions after the fact and to adjust the outcomes of rules if they detect signs of overreaching.[5]

Smith's point about opportunism is persuasive, but it misses other dimensions of the problem of determinate rules. As Smith recognizes,[6] one difficulty with Aristotelian equity is that superimposing standards of equitable discretion on a relatively determinate set of legal rules for private ordering can undermine the coordination benefits of the rules. If parties anticipate equitable adjustments in particular cases, transactions become unreliable and responsibilities become unpredictable. Smith responds that for this reason, post-hoc equitable adjustments should be limited to cases of opportunism: if equitable adjustments to rules are confined to opportunism, little or no harm is done to the coordination benefits the rules provide for parties acting in good faith. Opportunists, in contrast, know who they are and so can protect themselves against liability and ensure the reliability of their transactions by behaving better.

Limiting equity to cases that present indicia of opportunism, however, leaves several aspects of the problem of rules unresolved. One difficulty is that opportunism is an inexact standard. There will be cases of borderline opportunism, in which parties may not recognize that what they are doing is a form of overreaching they ought to avoid and judges assessing transactions retrospectively may mistake luck for opportunism. Given these uncertainties, the possibility that courts might, after the fact, impose an additional set of limitations on enforcement of transactions or grounds for liability dilutes the general assurance of legal reliability on which the practice of private ordering depends.

More importantly, the moral pressure that strict enforcement of determinate rules places on judges is not limited to cases of likely opportunism: it also arises whenever determinate rules lead to outcomes that are out of line with the rules' purposes or otherwise unjust to the parties. Determinate rules for private ordering presumably are designed to support mutually beneficial transactions. Yet, even the best-designed rules will yield some transactions that fall significantly short of this ideal, simply because the rules are blunt. From the perspective of someone

[5] See, eg, Henry E Smith, 'Why Fiduciary Law Is Equitable' in Andrew S Gold and Paul B Miller (eds), *Philosophical Foundations of Fiduciary Law* (Oxford University Press, 2014) 261; Yuval Feldman and Henry E Smith, 'Behavioral Equity' (2014) 170 J of Institutional and Theoretical Economics 137; Henry E Smith, 'Equity as Second-Order Law: The Problem of Opportunism', available at <http://papers.ssrn.com/sol3/papers.cfm?abstract_id=2617413> (15 January 2015).

[6] See, eg, Smith, 'Why Fiduciary Law Is Equitable' (n 5) at 270, 278.

designing an ideal legal system, this should not matter: if consistent application of determinate rules will produce coordination benefits that outweigh the errors the rules produce in particular cases, then judges should follow the rules as written. From the judge's perspective, however, this argument will not be persuasive. The judge may understand that over the long run, the legal system will function best if all judges follow the rules in all cases; but the judge will also know that determinate rules are imperfect and sometimes produce erroneous results. If evidence before the judge indicates that the present case is one in which the outcome of the rule is wrong, the judge will conclude that she ought not follow the rule.

The judge may well be wrong about this. Judges are, of course, capable of error. Moreover, for psychological reasons, they are particularly likely to err when a rule appears to dictate a bad result. Judges consider one case at a time, and the human situations of the parties immediately before them are likely to be more salient than the potential long-term effects of an exception to a rule. Consequently, they are likely to underestimate the loss of error control and coordination that will follow from exceptions they and others make to the rules.[7]

Thus, the problem of determinate rules is not limited to opportunism. Imagine a society in which most or all parties intend to do what is right—to avoid harming others, to perform their obligations honestly, and not to overreach. Imagine also that the rules that govern this society are well designed in the sense that if both actors and judges follow them regularly, the sum of outcomes over time will be better, measured by the purposes of the rules, than they would be if judges responded to private interactions case-by-case. Even under these ideal circumstances, rules will sometimes misfire and judges will sometimes conclude that, all things considered, the purposes of the rules will be best served by refusing to enforce the rules. In some of these cases the judge will be correct; in others the judge will be incorrect because the judge has misjudged the long-term effects of non-enforcement. Yet, whether or not the judge's conclusion is correct, enforcing the rules will seem immoral and possibly irrational to the judge (if rationality is taken to mean responsiveness to one's perceived current reasons for action).[8] If the judge follows his or her sense of equity and makes an exception, the result will be some decrease in the effectiveness

[7] See Jeffrey J Rachlinski, 'Bottom-Up and Top-Down Decisionmaking' (2006) 73 U Chi Rev 933, 942–43 (discussing the effects of affect and availability biases in judicial decisionmaking); Frederick Schauer, 'Do Cases Make Bad Law?' (2006) 73 U Chi L Rev 883, 895 (observing that judges, as rule-makers, are subject to the availability bias). See, generally, Daniel Kahneman, Paul Slovic, and Amos Tversky (eds), *Judgment Under Uncertainty: Heuristics and Biases* (Cambridge University Press, 1982) 163; Thomas Gilovich, Dale Griffin, and Daniel Kahneman (eds), *Heuristics & Biases: The Psychology of Intuitive Judgment* (Cambridge University Press, 2002); Scott Plous, *The Psychology of Judgment and Decision Making* (Temple University Press, 1993).

[8] It may be possible to interpret practical rationality in a diachronic sense, so that it is rational for an agent to act on prior intentions to follow a plan or adopt a rule without reconsidering one's intention at the time of action. See generally Michael E Bratman, *Intentions, Plans, and Practical Reason* (Harvard University Press, 1987) (proposing an intention-based theory of temporally extended rationality); Scott J Shapiro, *Legality* (Harvard University Press, 2011) (extending a similar theory to law). Epistemic rationality, however, is generally understood as a requirement for formation of current beliefs, in response to current grounds for belief. Thus, an epistemically rational judge will believe that she ought not follow the rule.

of the governing rules, as rules. In a given case, the effect may be small; overall, it may be significant.

This is a dilemma for all of law, and especially for branches of law that are designed to support private ordering of economic affairs. The most promising way out of the dilemma is to somehow shelter the coordination benefits of determinate rules from the effects of equitable adjustments to rules in particular cases. I will propose that contract law has accomplished this in various ways and that, for the most part, the law governing fiduciary duties of loyalty has not. The reasons for this difference are partly historical and partly due to the different ways in which legal rules operate in these two areas of private ordering.

III. Contracts

My discussion of contract law focuses on rules governing enforceability of agreements. The primary function of these rules is to provide assurance of official support for the practice of contractual exchange. Rules of contract formation tell potential parties what actions are needed to create an obligation. Rules governing relief from obligation inform them that certain negotiating strategies such as intentional misrepresentation will render the obligation avoidable; that certain defects, such as a mutual mistake in assumption, will excuse performance of the obligation; and, by implication, that other strategies or defects will not affect the obligation. Most importantly, the basic rules of contract law reassure that if parties follow the steps outlined in the rules of contract formation and avoid the conditions that give rise to an excuse, the courts will provide a remedy in case of breach. Specifically, the disappointed promisee will be entitled to a remedy equal to the value of the promisee's bargain, in the form of either performance in kind or damages measured by the value of performance. Determinacy is an important feature of these foundational contract rules because clear, concrete rules allow private actors to plan around the prospect of an enforceable agreement.

For the reasons outlined in the preceding section, determinate rules of contract law will also result in enforcement of some bargains that are inefficient or unfair. The promisee may have overreached in some way that does not meet standard definitions of fraud or mistake. Alternatively, the agreement may produce significantly unequal outcomes for the parties for reasons that do not involve opportunism by the winner but nevertheless engage sympathy for the loser. Assuming that the justification for judicial enforcement of contract obligations is to support exchanges that leave both parties better off, enforcement of the bargain in both types of case will appear to be a mistake. It will also appear unfair to the promisor.

The intricate set of rules governing enforcement of contracts tells a different story. Although the basic rules guarantee promisors the benefits of their bargain, in kind or in dollars, courts may deny specific enforcement of contracts when one party misread the written agreement, the mistaken party was particularly vulnerable to mistake, and the other party may have suspected, but kept quiet about, the mistake.[9] They may deny specific enforcement when, with no suggestion of overreaching by the promisee, the passage of time and changes in the promisor's circumstances have made performance very difficult.[10] They may deny injunctive protection against interference with a contract if they judge that the plaintiff acted inequitably toward the defendant in acquiring the contract.[11] They may also grant relief when one party has relied on a precontractual promise or a promise made without consideration.[12] Decisions of this kind have their origins in the courts of equity before law and equity were procedurally merged; they also exemplify Aristotle's conception of equity as correction of errors that result from the generality of rules. The effect is that, despite the importance of coordination and assurance in contract law, the conditions for contract enforcement are not highly determinate in application.

Of course, remedial decisions have precedential value, and the comparatively indistinct excuses they recognize are part of the body of contract law. In fact, however, indeterminate exceptions to contract enforcement may not interfere substantially with the basic message the legal system sends to parties: that contracts are legally binding in the absence of fraud or mutual mistake. The reason is that indeterminate remedial defences are relatively obscure. Traditionally, at least, they affect only equitable remedies for contract enforcement and leave damage remedies intact.[13] The availability of damages might seem to cancel the effect of the equitable defence. In theory, damages replicate the value of performance, and so leave the promisee in the same position it would have occupied if the contract had been performed. In practice, however, there are limitations on the damage remedy,

[9] For example, in *Panco v Rogers*, an elderly man signed an agreement for sale of his home for a price that was less than half what he thought he would receive. The buyer practiced no detectable fraud, but the court refused to order a conveyance and instead limited the buyer's remedy to damages. 87 A.2d 770 (N.J. Ch. Div. 1952).

[10] For example, in *Patel v Ali*, the promisor agreed to sell her interest in her home to the promisor. Without fault by either party, the closing was delayed. In the interim, the promisor developed cancer, lost a leg, and had two babies, and her husband was sentenced to prison. The court refused to order the promisor to convey the home. [1984] 1 Ch 283.

[11] For example, in *Carmen v Fox Film Corp.*, Carmen entered into an employment contract with Fox while still a minor in New York. Upon reaching majority, she repudiated the Fox contract and entered another contract on better terms. Fox threatened Carmen's new employer and Carmen sued. The court held that, although Fox was liable to Carmen for damages for interference, it would not enjoin Fox from interfering. 269 F. 928 (2d Cir. 1920).

[12] For example, in *Hoffman v Red Owl Stores*, Hoffman took a number of costly steps at Red Owl's request during franchise negotiations that eventually broke down. The court held that, although the parties never entered a contract, Hoffman could recover damages for expenses incurred in reliance on Red Owl's representations that a deal would soon be struck. 133 N.W.2d 267 (Wis. 1965). Promissory estoppel, the doctrine applied in this case, can be seen as a response to the underinclusiveness of determined rules for contract formation, rather than the overinclusiveness of rules of enforcement.

[13] For an extensive treatment of equitable defences to contract enforcement, see Edward Yorio, *Contract Enforcement: Specific Performance and Injunctions* (Little, Brown, 1989) 101–26. In all three of the cases described above, the court denied only injunctive relief. In *Carmen v Fox Film Corp* (n 11), Carmen went on to recover damages. In both *Panco v Rogers* and *Patel v Ali*, the court made clear that rescission was not available; therefore the promisor remained liable for damages. 87 A.2d at 773; [1984] 1 Ch at 288.

including the jury's prerogative to incorporate equitable considerations into the measure of damages, that may make damages an inferior option.[14]

Thus, although the contract remains technically valid and enforceable, the effect of an indeterminate remedial defence is often to render the contract practically unenforceable. To understand this, however, parties must be familiar not only with the defence in question but also with the defects in the damage remedy. Lawyers who regularly give transactional advice should have a working knowledge of remedial doctrine and equitable defences. Yet, remedial rules, particularly those that are equitable in origin, are diverse, vague, and contextual, making it difficult to specify at the time of transacting whether and how they may come into play. Consequently, when the contract is made, parties are more likely to focus on the relatively concrete set of rules that tells them that their contract will be enforced.

The consequence is that, through the largely unseen workings of remedial defences, contract law may be able to achieve both the coordination benefits of determinate rules defining binding contracts and the more fine-tuned outcomes that remedial defences make possible. It can be fair and efficient in particular cases and also provide assurance that contracts that meet the more determinate and more widely known requirements of contract law will be backed by the courts.

The reassuring message that contracts are enforced involves a certain type of systemic dissembling, and it will sometimes break down. Modern legal realism about doctrinal distinctions has also tended to cause the legal and equitable sides of contract law to converge. Still, contract law traditionally has, and probably still does, broadcast a fairly strong message that if you enter a contract the law will require you to perform your part, while at the same time engaging in leniency case by case.

The idea of a dual legal system, one part guiding conduct and the other guiding adjudication of particular disputes, dates at least to Bentham.[15] Bentham, of course, approached law from a strictly utilitarian perspective. He believed that as a general matter, the principle of utility required a set of laws that would provide security of expectations for private actors. Accordingly, he proposed that laws regulating private conduct should be embodied in a clear and comprehensive code. Substantively, the code would follow utilitarian principles; formally, however, it would be determinate, simple, comprehensive, and publicly accessible.[16]

At the same time, however, Bentham was committed to direct utilitarian analysis in adjudication of disputes: the task of the judge was to apply the principle of utility

[14] Normally when a plaintiff seeks an injunction there are already defects in the damage remedy, such as values that cannot easily be measured in money. There are also certainty requirements and limits on consequential damages that make damages less than fully compensatory. And, as noted in the text, standards for review of jury verdicts give juries considerable discretion over the amount of any award.

[15] My discussion of Bentham relies on Gerald Postema's excellent work on Bentham's views on law. Gerald G Postema, 'Bentham and the Common Law Tradition' (1989). Postema's discussion of Bentham draws on and reconciles many of Bentham's writings, including, among others, *Of Laws in General* (HLA Hart ed, Athlone Press, 1970); *An Introduction to the Principles of Morals and Legislation* (JH Burns and HLA Hart eds, Athlone Press, 1970); and *Constitutional Code* (J Rosen and JH Burns eds, Clarendon Press, 1983).

[16] Postema (n 9) at 403–08.

directly to the facts of each case and determine what outcome would maximize utility for the parties involved. Thus, in Bentham's ideal legal system, the code that governed conduct would not directly govern adjudication. It might serve as a guide to the demands of utility, and as evidence of the parties' expectations, but it would not dictate the results of particular cases. Decisions would be public, to ensure that judicial discretion was subject to the constraining effects of moral disapproval. They would not, however, serve as precedents for future decision-making. Each decision would reflect a fully particularistic balance of utilities, based solely on the facts before the judge. Any effects that the decision might have on future adjudication would not enter into the judge's deliberation.[17]

For various reasons, well described by Gerald Postema, who has written at length on Bentham's design for law, a legal system of the type Bentham described is not likely to be workable. It is unrealistic to ask the public to disregard the public outcome of decisions adjudicating the rights of particular parties. The public may also be uncomfortable about disparate resolutions of seemingly similar cases, with no effort made to announce rules of decision that might explain the results.[18] Yet the motivation is understandable: ideally, a legal system should combine clarity about rights and obligations with a fine-grained response to particular cases.

Some years ago, Meir Dan-Cohen considered the structurally similar possibility of 'acoustic separation' of conduct rules and decision rules in criminal law.[19] Dan-Cohen proposed that rules of criminal law serve two functions: to regulate conduct and to guide judges in applying the law after the fact. In criminal law, the conduct component of rules typically is geared to general deterrence, while the decision component may incorporate leniency for particular defendants. Normally, these objectives must be accommodated within a single rule; but Dan-Cohen observed that, in a various criminal law contexts, legal rules and the procedural framework in which they operate have the effect of directing one version of the rules to actors and another to adjudicators.[20] For example, the law may combine a rule of conduct with a defence or set of defences that either are too vague or too variable in application to be understood by ordinary actors.[21] The result is a condition of 'partial acoustic separation', in which actors receive one message and adjudicators receive another, somewhat different, message about the content of the law.[22] The plan is not deliberate, as Bentham's was; it results without direction from the form of the rules and the nature of their audiences. Dan-Cohen had mixed feelings about this

[17] Ibid. Postema explains that Bentham's design for law was a reaction to the common law, which he viewed as arbitrary and unjust, as well as incapable of securing expectations. Case-by-case interpretation of immemorial custom leads to an unacceptable level of uncertainty. To control uncertainty, courts turn to the doctrine of *stare decisis*, which replaces uncertainty with inflexibility, and so creates pressure to deviate from the rules in order to reconcile the law with social needs and social change. At this point, the judge's discretion is complete and uncontrollable: the judge can either follow the rule or depart from the rule, and cite good reason for either choice. See ibid at 279–86 (describing what Postema calls the 'paradox of inflexibility').

[18] Ibid at 453–59.

[19] Meir Dan-Cohen, 'Conduct Rules and Decision Rules: On Acoustic Separation in Criminal Law' (1984) 97 Harv L Rev 625.

[20] Ibid at 630–34. [21] Ibid at 639–41. [22] Ibid at 631.

phenomenon, but identified a number of instances in which it seemed to be in play in the criminal law.

A similar naturally occurring division between conduct rules and decision rules can be traced in contract law, where it serves to resolve, in part, contract law's particular version of the problem of rules. Contracting parties need assurance that their agreements will be legally enforced. Assurance, in turn, requires clarity about the creation of contract obligations and the conditions under which courts will enforce them. Doctrines that allow courts to recognize additional, less well-defined excuses in particular cases will muddy the message of enforcement unless they are mainly confined to the audience of decision-makers.

It seems plausible, however, that there is a significant degree of acoustic separation in contract law, isolating the general rule of enforcement from the more particular remedial defences that courts often recognize. Remedies themselves are at the fringe of lay understandings of law. The distinctions between legal and equitable remedies, and the limitations that make damage remedies an incomplete means of enforcement, are complex and unlikely to be widely understood, at least at the time of agreement when determinate rules perform their coordinating function. To the extent that lawyers understand the remedial consequences of a breach, they are unlikely to specify the full range of possibilities until after a breach, when decisional questions have taken on practical importance.

Of course there is no hermetic division between conduct rules and decision rules in contract law. Morever, the degree of acoustic separation between rules of conduct and rules of decision has decreased over time as traditional distinctions between legal and equitable defences have become less prominent in legal decision-making and indeterminate standards such as unconscionability have been introduced to the primary law.[23] Yet, at least some discrepancies between rules and remedies continue to exist, and continue to go largely unnoticed.

To the extent that acoustic separation in contract law persists, the dual character of the legal system is not public, as it was in Bentham's plan. Instead, it results in a form of deception, in that private actors are given an inaccurate message about the extent to which courts will enforce contracts. Of course, there is no deliberate duplicity involved: confusion about remedies is an accidental by-product of history, which happens to accommodate systemic objectives that would otherwise conflict. And, if my description is correct, the benefits are significant: remedial confusion promotes coordination without requiring courts to maintain an inflexible posture in hard cases.

[23] See, eg, U.C.C. § 2–302 (unconscionability); Restatement (Second) of Contracts § 153(a) (enlarging definitions of mistake), § 161(b) (enlarging definitions of fraud), § 208 (unconscionability) (1981).

IV. Fiduciary Arrangements

The law governing fiduciary relations not only serves different objectives, but follows a different formal pattern. In the context of fiduciary relations, providing clear assurance of legal backing for a private arrangement is not the primary concern. Planning is certainly important in many fiduciary contexts: parties must assess the need to delegate control of assets and the risks they take by entering into a fiduciary relationship, either as a fiduciary or as a beneficiary. Yet, the basic problem of enforcement—the understanding that whatever they agree to will be enforced by the courts—is addressed by contract law. Thus, rather than enabling the parties to transact, the focus of fiduciary law is on defining the implied duties of those who accept or find themselves in fiduciary positions and deterring fiduciaries from violating those duties.[24]

The duty that most prominently defines fiduciary responsibility and distinguishes it from contractual obligation is the duty of loyalty to the interests of the beneficiary of the fiduciary relationship. Accordingly, my focus here is on loyalty and not on the more diverse and contractual duty of care. Nor do I address the special problems affecting the duties of corporate fiduciaries: my discussion is confined to the loyalty standards traditionally applied in the area of estates and trusts.

Initially, the duty of loyalty imposed on trustees takes the form of a very broad standard. In Benjamin Cardozo's words, the standard is not just 'honesty', but 'honor the most sensitive'[25]—a phrase with no meaning that we all nevertheless understand in a general way. In the area of estate and trust law, the standard of loyalty is then fortified with highly determinate rules forbidding specific types of misconduct. Most notably, trustees are strictly prohibited from transacting with a trust on their own account.[26] In applying this rule, courts typically say that the good faith of the trustee and the reasonableness of the transaction are irrelevant: once a prohibited transaction is shown, there is no further inquiry into the circumstances of or justifications for the particular breach.[27] The objective of this rule is to deter the trustee, not only from favouring its own interests over those of the beneficiaries but also from engaging in transactions in which it could prefer its own interests. Strong deterrence is necessary because even a well-meaning fiduciary may be subtly

[24] To some extent, contract law does this also—for example, by imposing a duty of good faith in performance of obligations. See generally Restatement (Second) of Contracts § 205 (1981); see also Robert A Hillman, *Principles of Contract Law* (West, 2004) 259 (treating the duty of good faith as primarily a matter of contract interpretation). This function of contract law, however, is subsidiary to the enabling role that law plays in supporting private agreements with the threat of enforcement.

[25] *Meinhard v Salmon*, 164 N.E. 545, 546 (N.Y. 1928). *Meinhard* is not a trust case, but is widely cited in decisions imposing sanctions on trustees who self-deal.

[26] See generally IIA Austin Wakeman Scott and William Franklin Fratcher (eds), *Scott on Trusts* § 170.1–170.25 (4th ed, Little, Brown, 1987) (detailing the rule and its many specific variants).

[27] See generally IIA *Scott on Trusts* (n 26) § 170.2, 170.25. Corporate fiduciaries are subject to more lenient rules that allow the fiduciary to prove that the transaction was fair. See, eg, 1 ALI, *Principles of Corporate Governance: Analysis and Recommendations* (American Law Institute, 2008) § 502b.

affected by self-interest, and also because the beneficiary of the relationship typically is not in a position to monitor the fiduciary's behaviour.[28]

If I am correct that the primary objective of rules governing the fiduciary duty of loyalty is to deter breach rather than to coordinate the understandings of parties to a transaction, it makes sense to state the duty initially in the form of an indeterminate standard of behaviour such as 'honor the most sensitive'. A vague standard of liability will encourages risk-averse fiduciaries to resolve doubts in a maximally cautious way and avoid behaviour that could possibly be interpreted as disloyal. A more precise definition would pose the danger of opportunism in the interstices of rules. Once this relatively indeterminate general standard is in place, however, additional, determinate prohibitions such as the rule against self-dealing serve to amplify deterrence by banning specific behaviour.

John Langbein has criticized the more determinate components of the duty of loyalty applied to trustees, in particular the strict prohibition on self-dealing and the no-further-inquiry rule.[29] Langbein argues that these rules over-deter: in some cases, a transaction in which the trustee has an interest is the best available means of advancing the interests of the beneficiaries. In Langbein's view, courts that insist without exception that trustees must act in the *sole* interest of their beneficiaries may sacrifice the *best* interests of the beneficiaries in the process. Langbein attributes the strict preventative rule followed by courts to procedural and fact-finding deficiencies that are no longer present in modern courts. His solution is to presume misbehaviour in cases of self-dealing, but to allow the trustee to establish that the particular transaction was reasonable and served the interests of the beneficiaries. In other words, he would introduce an element of post-hoc equity to the rules.

Others have defended the prevailing rules, citing the subtle pressures that interest places on the fiduciary and the difficulty of monitoring fiduciaries who are not subject to market control. Both problems, they suggest, are best handled by a strict prohibition against self-dealing without informed consent from beneficiaries or judicial approval in advance.[30] So far, the law does not appear to have moved significantly in Langbein's direction. Instead, courts continue to cite and apply strict rules against self-dealing and to reject arguments for contextual exceptions.[31]

[28] See, eg, Paul B Miller, 'The Fiduciary Relationship' in *Philosophical Foundations of Fiduciary Law* (n 5) at 63 (proposing a 'fiduciary powers' approach to fiduciary law, which focuses on the authority exercised by fiduciaries); Smith, 'Why Fiduciary Law is Equitable' (n 5) at 12 (identifying inherent vulnerability and difficulty of monitoring as distinguishing features of fiduciary relationships).

[29] John H Langbein, 'Questioning the Trust Law Duty of Loyalty: Sole Interest or Best Interest?' (2005) 114 Yale LJ 929. See also Gregory S Alexander, 'A Cognitive Theory of Fiduciary Relationships' (2000) 85 Cornell L Rev 767 (suggesting that courts tend to judge fiduciaries according to relational 'schemas' rather than hard facts).

[30] See, Melanie B Leslie, 'In Defense of the No Further Inquiry Rule: A Response to Professor John Langbein' (2005) 47 Wm and Mary L Rev 541; Robert H Sitkoff, 'Trust Law, Corporate Law, and Capital Market Efficiency' (2003) 28 J Corp L 565, 572–3. See also Restatement (Third) of Trusts § 78 cmt b (2007) (citing the following remark in Daniel Gilbert, 'I'm OK, You're Biased' *The New York Times* (New York, 16 April 2006), Section 4, p 12: '[b]ecause the brain cannot see itself fooling itself, the only reliable method for avoiding bias is to avoid the situations that produce it').

[31] See Restatement (Third) of Trusts (n 30) § 78(2) & cmt c (stating a strict rule against self-dealing, subject only to exceptions in 'discrete circumstances' enumerated in comments).

With some relatively minor exceptions, acoustic separation between determinate rules of conduct and less determinate remedial exceptions appears to be absent in the law governing self-dealing by trustees.[32] Strict rules against unauthorized self-dealing are backed by some of the most powerful remedies courts possess.[33] For example, a fiduciary who participates in a losing transaction must restore the value of the initial trust fund. If the fiduciary profits from the transaction, it must disgorge all gains. If the fiduciary exchanged products of the tainted transaction for other assets, the court will use historically equitable tracing remedies to complete the disgorgement by capturing appreciation. In each case, the remedial rule is designed to impose maximum liability, without exception, in every case of breach of duty.

As a result, the message the law gives to the parties and the message it gives to courts in this area of law is the same: the fiduciary must live up to the duty of loyalty. Particulars are relevant only insofar as they enhance the background standard of loyalty; they do not affect either the prohibition against self-dealing or the remedial consequences of the prohibition. It follows that the type of leniency Langbein recommends could not be accomplished quietly, through the use of relatively obscure conduits for judicial discretion. Instead, the introduction of greater case-by-case leniency would require a straightforward revision of the standard of loyalty governing trustees, adopted without the type of protective cover that would preserve the deterrent effect of current rules.

The close correspondence between stated rules of conduct and remedies in the case of trustee self-dealing raises the question why this area of law has failed to develop a separate set of more lenient, acoustically separate decision rules. One possible answer is that the attraction of leniency in the application of determinate rules is less compelling in this context than it is in contract law and other fields. Courts may still feel the pull to extend equity to hapless fiduciaries who are unaware of the rules. There are cases—probably many cases—in which unskilled parties assume fiduciary duties in the context of estates and family trusts with no clear understanding of the rules against self-dealing.[34] Yet, by definition, the fiduciary has a personal interest in the outcome of a transaction that should be guided by the

[32] There is at least one way in which courts may make allowances in a fiduciary's favour in compelling cases: the effect of a disgorgement remedy may be tempered by apportionment of gross profits between the fiduciary and the beneficiaries claiming breach of duty. American courts traditionally have been reluctant to make significant allowances for the defendant's efforts and expenditures in obtaining illicit profits, but are willing to apportion profits in some circumstances. See generally Restatement (Third) of Restitution and Unjust Enrichment § 51 (2011). The standards courts apply in measuring this type of allowance are sufficiently murky to create a limited form of acoustic separation at the remedial stage.

[33] See generally, Restatement (Third) of Restitution and Unjust Enrichment (n 26) § 51(4), 53(3), 55; III Scott on Trusts (n 32) § 197–213.

A debated question is whether, in the case of an otherwise authorized sale of trust property by a self-dealing trustee, the trustee's liability should be measured as of the date of the sale or the date of judgment. Under the second of these measures, the trustee is held liable for all appreciation the beneficiaries might have received if the property had not been sold at all, even though they would not have realized this amount in the ordinary course. See Matter of Rothko, 372 N.E.2d 291 (N.Y. 1977).

[34] Leslie proposes that the rules should be softened for nonprofessional trustees. Leslie (n 30) at 582–83 (suggesting also that appellate decisions have moved in this direction).

interests of the beneficiaries. Amateur trustees are just as susceptible to the influence of self-interest as professional trustees and their activities are equally, if not more, isolated from view. Moreover, even when a self-dealing fiduciary engages sympathy, the fiduciary is not typically the victim of overreaching or external misfortune of the type seen in contract cases. Instead, the fiduciary is a victim of his or her own folly and ignorance of the rules. Accordingly, equity in the Aristotelian sense may be a relatively minor concern.

Perhaps the best explanation why fiduciary law has not developed a system of acoustic separation to cover hard cases is simply that there is no readily available mechanism for separate transmission of law to actors and decision-makers. Both the rules governing fiduciary duty and the remedies courts use to enforce fiduciary duty have their origins in equity, so the historical division between law and equity provides no cover for variations in rules. Further, unlike remedies for contract enforcement, remedies for breach of the fiduciary duty of loyalty do not vary in their effect on the defendant: all are geared toward elimination of any profit the fiduciary may have realized from a breach. Choice of remedy, therefore, is not a natural vehicle for acoustic separation.

Nevertheless, there may sometimes be pressures for Aristotelian equity in fiduciary law. Consider *Will of Gleeson*, a decision of the Illinois Court of Appeals that illustrates the stringency of the rule against self-dealing.[35] Mrs. Gleeson named Colbrook, the tenant of her 160-acre farm, as executor of her will and trustee of a testamentary trust for her three children (two daughters and a son who was described in the opinion as incompetent). Reading between the lines, Colbrook appears to have accepted these responsibilities out of a sense of duty to Mrs. Gleeson and her family.

Mrs. Gleeson died on 14 February 1952. On 1 March, while estate proceedings were pending, Colbrook renewed his own farm lease for an additional year, as permitted by the terms of the lease. He and a partner continued to farm the land until March 1953, when he leased it to another party. The trust beneficiaries filed an objection to Colbrook's accounts as trustee, seeking disgorgement of Colbrook's share of the farm profits for 1953. Colbrook defended on the ground that (1) the 1952 farming season began just fourteen days after Mrs. Gleeson's death; (2) replacement farm tenants were not readily available; (3) Colbrook acted openly and discussed the lease renewal with the two competent trust beneficiaries; (4) Colbrook voluntarily raised his own rent for 1952 from \$6 to \$10 per acre; and (5) Colbrook and his partner had sown wheat the previous fall and would lose their harvest if they gave up the lease. The appellate court required Colbrook to disgorge his farming profits, citing the rule against self-dealing and the accompanying rule of no-further-inquiry into the circumstances or outcome of the transaction. '[T]he good faith and honesty of the petitioner or the fact that the trust sustained no loss on account of his dealings therewith … can avail petitioner nothing so far as a justification of the course he chose to take …'[36]

[35] 124 N.E.2d 624 (Ill. App. 1955).

[36] Ibid at 627. The court pointed out that there was no evidence that Colbrook had tried to obtain a new tenant in 1952, and that if he wanted to continue the lease, he could have declined to act as

In *Will of Gleeson*, the defendant, Colbrook, was unquestionably guilty of self-dealing. He also had an interest in the outcome: he wanted to realize the value of the wheat he had sown the previous fall. Yet he was also an amateur trustee, who appears to have accepted his fiduciary position as a favour to Mrs. Gleeson and her family and had probably never heard of the rule against self-dealing. He seemed honest; he seemed to be trying to maximize the trust income in the year following Mrs. Gleeson's death. And in fact, continuing the lease was probably the best plan for the farm.

The problem in this case is not a problem of over-deterrence: an amateur who does not know the rules will not be deterred by them. The problem is that Colbrook intended no wrong, and may in fact have done what was best, all-things-considered. At least, this is how the case appeared to the trial judge, who, after hearing Colbrook's story, rejected the beneficiaries' claim to his farm profits during the period of the lease. The court that imposed sanctions on Colbrook was the appellate court, working from a paper record of the trial. It may be that imposing the sanction was in fact the best response, given the loss of deterrence that a lenient precedent, especially at the appellate level, might have on the deterrent value of the rules. Yet for a trial court that observes the parties and concludes that the defendant has done no wrong, imposing sanctions will be difficult.

My guess is that in many cases of this type, trial judges will respond, as quietly as possible, with leniency that contradicts the stated rule. They may cheat a bit in their findings of fact, or they may omit facts from their official description of the case. Yet the legal system provides them no support for leniency of this type, as it does in contract cases. To do equity, judges must break the rules of law and legal decision-making.

V. Conclusion

The object of this essay has been to point out a difference in the way contract law and fiduciary law respond to the dilemma inherent in legal rules. To guide conduct effectively and allow private actors to coordinate their actions, legal rules must be general, determinate, and not subject to unlimited ad hoc revision at the point of application. In particular cases, judges are under moral and psychological pressure to make exceptions that can undermine the long-term coordination effect of rules. Contract law has evolved in a way that tends to create an acoustic division between general rules defining contractual obligations and remedial rules governing enforcement of obligations, and thus provides judges with a degree of cover at the point of application. Loyalty requirements for fiduciaries, especially as applied to trustees, do not provide similar protection. Judges who make exceptions to the rules must

executor and trustee. *Will of Gleeson* is now more than sixty years old, but the rule it states is still regularly cited and applied. See Restatement (Third) of Trusts (n 26), § 78, cmt b (2007).

either do so openly or design their own methods of circumventing the rules, without help from the law.

Prescriptively, very little follows from these observations. It is difficult to generalize about what characteristics of an area of law make strategies that rely on acoustic separation, selective transmission of conduct rules, and decision rules particularly useful. The need for determinate rules probably is stronger when the primary objective of a body of law is to enable private agreement than when the primary objective is to deter undesirable conduct. The appeal of hidden leniency is strongest when the grounds for leniency take the form of excuses rather than justifications for conduct: when a determinate rule forbids justified conduct, the solution is not equity but a change in the law.[37] Beyond this, however, the dilemma of general, determinate rules is present in all areas of law.

In any event, acoustic separation is not a state of affairs that can be engineered in the interest of more effective administration of law. The conditions that allow for a compromise between rules and leniency in contract law are accidental by-products of a long history in which law and equity once operated separately on the same subject matter. Any deliberate attempt to create conditions of this type would raise serious questions about the integrity of law.

[37] Thanks to Andrei Marmor for this observation.

PART III

LOYALTY AND MORALITY ACROSS CONTRACT, FIDUCIARY, AND TORT LAW

8

Accommodating Loyalty

*Andrew S Gold**

I. Introduction

Two puzzles have emerged in the recent literature on fiduciary law. First, how should we think about loyalty? And second, in what sense should the law take account of loyalty? There is no consensus answer to the first question, and that is unlikely to change.[1] This, in turn, has implications for the second question—for the contested content of loyalty means the law will inevitably diverge from extra-legal understandings of what loyalty requires. Moreover, these differences between types of loyalty can matter a great deal.

Imagine that George is a guardian for his mother, who is in a permanent coma. In making health care decisions on her behalf, what will loyalty require of him? Let's assume hypothetically that, in this jurisdiction, George's legal obligation of loyalty will require him to act in her best interests in the absence of contrary instructions from a court.[2] Suppose that for George, however, what it really means to be loyal is to act according to what she would have wanted. The differences between these two types of loyalty would matter a great deal to the loyal fiduciary.

* Professor, DePaul University College of Law. I wish to thank Stephen Bainbridge, John Coates, Erin Delaney, Evan Fox-Decent, Avihay Dorfman, Stephen Galoob, John Gardner, Joshua Getzler, John Goldberg, Vicki Jackson, Tonja Jacobi, Lyman Johnson, Simon Keller, Ethan Leib, Christian List, David Luban, Paul Miller, Arden Rowell, Matthew Sag, Irit Samet, Nadav Shoked, Joseph Singer, Rob Sitkoff, Gordon Smith, Henry Smith, Victor Tadros, Deborah Tuerkheimer, Laura Valentini, and Julian Velasco for helpful comments on the ideas in this paper. I am also grateful to participants in the Harvard Law School Faculty Workshop, the Harvard Private Law Workshop, the Obligations Discussion Group at Oxford University, the McGill Conference on Contract, Status, and Fiduciary Law, the Fiduciary Law Workshop at BYU Law School, and a faculty workshop at the Notre Dame Law School. Any errors are my own.

[1] Granted, if we define loyalty in a very thin sense—as, for example, the notion that a person should take the side of the person or thing to whom she is loyal—we may approach a rough consensus. But once we seek a more specific sense of what it means to 'take the side' of another, conceptions of loyalty rapidly diverge.

[2] The precise requirements for guardian decision-making vary by jurisdiction, and may incorporate consideration of the express desires and personal values of the ward. See Lawrence A Frolik and Linda S Whitton, 'The UPC Substituted Judgment/Best Interest Standard for Guardian Decision Making: A Proposal for Reform' (2012) 45 U Mich J L Reform 739, 742–47.

Alternatively, imagine that Jack, an agent for Jill, takes his loyalty obligations very seriously. He feels loyal to Jill both as his principal and as his friend, and outside the law he understands true loyalty to mean that he must act in her best interests. Agency law, however, indicates that he must comply with Jill's instructions, even if those instructions are not going to benefit Jill. From the law's perspective, loyalty is constrained by a duty of obedience.[3] Although many loyalty-based relations allow or even encourage paternalistic conduct by the loyal party, agency law takes a different path.

These are examples of how legal conceptions of loyalty and extra-legal conceptions can diverge. There are many other contexts in which gaps between law and extra-legal loyalty arise, just as there are many types of loyalty. Some see loyalty in terms of a subjective intent to benefit another, while others see loyalty as a bar on conflicts of interest; some see loyalty as calling for white lies in certain contexts, while others think loyalty always requires honesty; some see loyalty in terms of obedience to instructions, while others think loyalty permits and even calls for paternalism. Are such divergences cause for concern? In some cases, yes. The reasons why, however, are not always the reasons that scholars assume, and the potential responses depend substantially on which reasons are at stake.

The debate over how law and morality relate is well-trodden ground.[4] Substantially less has been said about the connection, if any, between law and other normative systems. This chapter will focus on an important type of extra-legal obligation, and it is an obligation that is only contingently moral: loyalty. Often, loyalty is one of the more powerful influences in our lives. Loyalty to family or to close friends can be a vital part of our self-understanding, and loyalty obligations are taken seriously in a wide range of contexts. Yet the relation between law and extra-legal loyalty has received limited attention. It is worthwhile to consider how law and loyalty fit together—and how they ought to fit together.[5]

While descriptive concerns will arise, this chapter will ultimately concentrate on the normative questions of whether and how law should address questions of

[3] It should be noted that, while an agent's duty of loyalty may be distinguished from an agent's duty of obedience, compliance with a principal's instructions is intertwined with legal understandings of loyalty. See Deborah A DeMott, 'The Fiduciary Character of Agency and the Interpretation of Instructions' in Andrew S Gold and Paul B Miller (eds), *Philosophical Foundations of Fiduciary Law* (Oxford University Press, 2014) 321 (noting that the agent's 'fiduciary duty to the principal furnishes a benchmark for interpretation' of the principal's instructions).

[4] Often, what is at issue is a conceptual claim about law. See, eg, HLA Hart, *The Concept of Law* (3rd edn, Oxford University Press, 2012) 185–212; Ronald Dworkin, *Law's Empire* (Harvard University Press, 1986); Jules Coleman, 'Negative and Positive Positivism' (1982) 11 J Leg Stud. 139; Joseph Raz, 'Authority, Law, and Morality' in *Ethics in the Public Domain* (Oxford University Press, 1994) 210. In other cases, the claim is normative. See Jeremy Waldron, 'Normative (or Ethical) Positivism' in Jules Coleman (ed), *Hart's Postscript* (Oxford University Press, 2001) 411 (describing a normative version of positivism).

[5] On some accounts, loyalty is foundational for morality, suggesting a close tie between the two subjects. See Simon Keller, *The Limits of Loyalty* (Cambridge University Press, 2007) 182 ('Royce, in *The Philosophy of Loyalty*, and Fletcher, in *Loyalty*, both set out to show that loyalty is the foundation of good moral thinking, and they both defend accounts of morality that are built around the notion of loyalty').

loyalty. In particular, it will consider whether the law's take on loyalty should reflect loyalty practices outside the law. Legal understandings of loyalty often look very different from extra-legal understandings, and in a variety of distinctive ways. Does this divergence call for reform, so that the law better reflects extra-legal conceptions of loyal behaviour? Not necessarily. While there are those who believe that complying with a loyalty obligation is moral, or that being a loyal person is virtuous, it is not hard to find examples of undesirable loyalty. In some cases, loyalty can even be noxious.

Instead of reflecting extra-legal loyalty based on ties to morality, I will argue that the law should accommodate loyalty. Under an accommodationist approach, law should make room for the extra-legal practices of loyal agents—it should give people space to pursue loyalty as they understand it. Section II of this chapter will first consider the possibility that law should reflect extra-legal loyalty based on the moral nature of loyal conduct as such. This possibility will be rejected, given potential divergences between loyalty and morality, and given practical difficulties related to enforcement. Section III will introduce the idea of accommodationism as an alternative. This section will also assess the challenges in applying an accommodationist approach to a practice like loyalty. Despite these challenges, it concludes that there are good reasons to accommodate extra-legal loyalty. Section IV will consider several means by which law can accommodate loyalty. Section V will then conclude.

II. The Reflective Approach to Law and Loyalty

Arguably, when legal relationships implicate extra-legal loyalty obligations, courts should make sure that legal doctrine matches these obligations.[6] On one account, this conclusion is based on the morality of loyal behaviour. For example, it might be claimed that a corporate director's duty of loyalty to her shareholders should reflect the robust sense of loyalty that exists outside the law, given the moral significance of loyal conduct. From this perspective, if the law enforces a lesser standard of behaviour, this would not show adequate respect for the genuine moral obligations the director owes. In other words, this is an application of the view that law should enforce interpersonal morality—a view known as the reflective approach.[7]

The reflective approach raises a fundamental question about the nature of loyalty, for in order to assess this perspective, we need to assess the moral status of loyal behaviour. This, unfortunately, is not a simple task. Certain scholars find

[6] An alternative view might suggest that there should be some relationship between the two types of loyalty, even if not perfect correspondence. Cf Stephen R Galoob and Ethan J Leib, 'Intentions, Compliance, and Fiduciary Obligations' (2014) 20 Legal Theory 106, 108 (suggesting, in the fiduciary context, that '[o]ur analysis supposes that there is and should be a connection between the institutional and noninstitutional versions of certain normative concepts').

[7] See Seana Valentine Shiffrin, 'The Divergence of Contract and Promise' (2007) 120 Harv L Rev 708, 713 ('Reflective approaches take interpersonal morality as a template for legal rules, sometimes implicitly').

something morally desirable about extra-legal loyalty. Others, however, are adamantly opposed to the idea that loyalty is moral, and question its status as a virtue. The value of loyalty is contested, and it is by no means obvious that loyal behaviour is desirable for its own sake.

It is quite reasonable to think that some loyalty obligations have a moral underpinning. Morality may call for someone to act loyally to her friend, particularly where the friend has reasonably relied on her presumed loyalty.[8] And, while there is some controversy over the ability to contractually enter into a loyalty obligation, contracts arguably provide a context in which morality requires compliance with loyalty obligations.[9] Promises might also ground a morally significant loyalty obligation, depending on one's theory of loyalty. For example, there may be cases in which an individual promises to be loyal, thus creating a moral duty to be loyal in light of that promise. Accordingly, even if loyalty lacks a moral basis as a general matter, in specific contexts loyalty can take on a moral dimension—loyalty and morality are at least sometimes linked.

We can also recognize this feature in fiduciary settings. Suppose that a given extra-legal conception of fiduciary loyalty calls for a fiduciary to act in the best interests of her beneficiary. This loyalty norm will impact the expectations of fiduciaries and beneficiaries in predictable ways. We can easily imagine cases in which a fiduciary has undertaken to act in the best interests of a vulnerable party when exercising discretion over her assets, and in which the vulnerable party has also accepted that undertaking and relied on it in planning her affairs. Morally speaking, the fiduciary will have an obligation to act loyally, in light of the structure of the relationship, the fiduciary's choice to be loyal, and the other party's reliance. Loyalty will be what morality calls for.

Still, it is highly problematic to claim that the law should adopt the same content as extra-legal loyalty based on its alleged moral status. A sceptic might object that law should not be in the business of making people act morally. But even if we accept the premise that law ought to enforce interpersonal morality it would not follow that law should enforce loyalty duties as such, and that is because loyalty isn't always moral. Loyalty may even be pernicious, and perfectly recognizable examples of loyalty are unacceptable from a moral perspective. The loyal Nazi is not a contradiction in terms.[10] Nor is the loyal thief: the common idea of 'honour among

[8] For helpful discussion of the obligations of friendship, see David Owens, *Shaping the Normative Landscape* (Oxford University Press, 2012) 96–117; Ethan J Leib, 'Friends as Fiduciaries' (2009) 86 Wash U L Rev 665.

[9] For accounts that are sceptical of the ability to enter into a contractually grounded loyalty obligation, see Daniel Markovits, 'Sharing *Ex Ante* and Sharing *Ex Post*: The Non-Contractual Basis of Fiduciary Relations' in Andrew S Gold and Paul B Miller (eds), *Philosophical Foundations of Fiduciary Law* (Oxford University Press, 2014) 209, 216–18; Stephen R Galoob and Ethan J Leib, 'Intentions, Compliance, and Fiduciary Obligations' (2014) 20 Legal Theory 106; D Gordon Smith, 'Contractually Adopted Fiduciary Duty' (2014) U Ill L Rev 1783.

[10] See Irit Samet, 'Fiduciary Loyalty as Kantian Virtue' in Andrew S Gold and Paul B Miller (eds), *Philosophical Foundations of Fiduciary Law* (Oxford University Press, 2014) 125, 128 ('The "Loyal Nazi" makes perfect sense, and the "disloyal Nazi" (say the party member who betrays the party's principles for a bribe) lacks exactly the kind of admirable trait that we try to capture with the notion of loyalty'); Keller (n 5) at 22 (noting that 'there could be a loyal Nazi').

thieves' can readily incorporate loyalty within a criminal enterprise. It is hard to argue in favour of a legal system that would support and enforce these applications of loyalty.

Indeed, even if we avoid the egregious cases in which understandings of loyalty call for terrible behaviour, we may find loyalty and morality occupy separate spheres. As Harry Frankfurt notes: '[t]here is nothing distinctively moral, for instance, about such ideals as being steadfastly loyal to a family tradition'.[11] Being loyal to a family tradition may certainly be valuable and important to us, and as Frankfurt emphasizes, this pursuit may have commanding authority in our lives. It may still seem strange to say that we are morally bound to be loyal to a family tradition, even if it is appealing in certain respects, and even if it means a lot to us.

One could respond by reshaping loyalty in procrustean fashion, so that its requirements precisely fit a given view on what morality requires.[12] While that is an option, the resulting picture of loyalty would be dramatically different from common-sense understandings of what loyalty is. In ordinary usage, it is perfectly coherent to speak of a conflict between what loyalty requires and what morality requires.[13] If a person asks in response to a white lie, 'Why did he lie to her?' it would be perfectly coherent for someone to respond: 'It was wrong to lie, but he did it because he was being loyal to his friend.' Reshaping loyalty into morality not only removes the interesting questions raised by legally enforced loyalty, it distorts loyalty as it is usually recognized.

One might argue that the law should require a particular extra-legal understanding of loyalty because that form of loyalty is a virtue. For example, consider Irit Samet's recent virtue-based account of fiduciary loyalty. As she suggests, there are thin and thick conceptions of loyalty. On a thin account, 'the duty of loyalty … instructs fiduciaries to take the principal's good as the sole end of their actions.'[14] In contrast, when loyalty is understood in its thick sense, loyalty 'implies a specific emotional and intellectual orientation towards one's principals'.[15] It is 'an attitude in which selfless action comes easily, and exploitation of weaknesses is unthinkable'.[16] She contends that equity adopts the thick conception, and that the thick conception can be virtuous.[17]

[11] See Harry G Frankfurt, 'The Importance of What We Care About' in *The Importance of What We Care About* (Cambridge University Press, 1998) 80, 81.

[12] See Keller (n 5) at 192 (describing a view in which true loyalty involves giving something its moral due).

[13] See Samet (n 10) at 127–28 ('If we describe loyalty by reference to 'what is due' we restrict the range of its objects to worthwhile ones. But this, unfortunately, does not work.'). It is, however, entirely possible that specific conceptions of loyalty will have their content delimited by moral obligations. Cf Thomas Scanlon, *What We Owe to Each Other* (Harvard University Press, 1998) 164–66 (describing duties of friendship that are sensitive to the demands of right and wrong).

[14] See Samet (n10) at 126. [15] See ibid at 139. [16] Ibid at 140.

[17] Note that this claim may be valid even if particular instances of loyal behaviour lead to bad outcomes. See ibid at 128 ('Like sincerity, integrity, and (arguably) courage, loyalty is the kind of virtue which does not guarantee the moral quality of actions that are informed by it'). See also Alasdair McIntyre, 'The Nature of the Virtues' in Roger Crisp and Michael Slote (eds), *Virtue Ethics* (Oxford University Press, 1997) 118 ('It is in the character of a virtue that in order that it be effective in producing the internal goods which are the rewards of the virtues it should be exercised without regard to consequences').

This chapter will not take a position on the possibility of loyalty as a virtue, but it bears noting that the claim is contested. James Penner argues that loyalty is a 'minor vice, like indiscriminateness', rather than a form of virtuous behaviour.[18] On his account, loyalty is instead a negative virtue.[19] Loyalty does not have a positive value from this perspective, but there is a vice involved in cases of disloyalty. Special relationships give rise to opportunities for wrongs that wouldn't otherwise exist, and Penner suggests that the knowing commission of such wrongs is disloyal.[20] Likewise, Simon Keller also contends that loyalty is not a virtue; it is not the kind of character trait, he claims, that one would want one's child to have.[21] On Keller's view, a child with loyal tendencies will be at risk of the various types of undesirable loyalty that pose moral concerns.[22]

Still, perhaps the virtue claim will be more compelling if we adopt a conception of loyalty that has the features Samet describes. She is well aware that loyalty has multiple meanings, and argues that equity has adopted a particular meaning—the one given by the thick sense of loyalty. That is to say, she understands equity to be adopting a sense of loyalty that incorporates a certain intellectual and also emotional orientation towards one's principal. Granted, the descriptive claim here is debatable, as the legal doctrine can be read quite differently. One prominent reading of fiduciary loyalty sees loyalty in terms of anti-conflicts rules, and this could express a very thin view of what loyalty is. Moreover, Samet suggests that the 'common understanding of loyalty' is the one equity has adopted,[23] yet common understandings of loyalty often permit or encourage white lies. A lie-permitting loyalty is very different from the Kantian perspective Samet supports.[24]

Assume nonetheless that Samet's descriptive claims are accurate—there remains a substantial practical difficulty. Given the premise that a thick sense of loyalty is called for by the law, we still face challenges in enforcing such loyalty. Epistemic concerns are one problem: in many cases, it may be impossible for a fiduciary to ever be sure that she has complied with the applicable standard of conduct.[25] In addition, the subjective aim of advancing another's best interests is very hard to police.[26] Courts are in no position to peer into the fiduciary's mind, hoping to

[18] See JE Penner, 'Is Loyalty a Virtue, and Even if it is, Does it Really Help Explain Fiduciary Liability?' in Andrew S Gold and Paul B Miller (eds), *Philosophical Foundations of Fiduciary Law* (Oxford University Press, 2014) 159, 163.

[19] The classic account of a negative virtue is in Joseph Raz's analysis of the rule of law. See Joseph Raz, 'The Rule of Law and Its Virtue' in *The Authority of Law* (Oxford University Press, 1979) 210, 224.

[20] See Penner (n 18) at 166.

[21] See Keller (n 5) at 156–58.

[22] One might argue that loyalty is part of the morally virtuous life, in combination with the whole package of virtues. I am grateful to John Finnis for emphasizing this point. This possibility, however, may exacerbate the problems of legal enforcement described below. While it is difficult in many contexts for law to enforce a given virtuous type of loyalty, the challenge is substantially greater if loyalty's merit is linked to the presence of other concurrently existing virtues.

[23] See Samet (n 10) at 130.

[24] See Lionel Smith, 'The Motive Not the Deed' in Joshua Getzler (ed), *Rationalizing Property, Equity, and Trusts: Essays in Honour of William Burn* (Oxford University Press, 2003) 53, 81 (suggesting that a white lie 'can be an act of loyal deceit').

[25] See Lionel Smith, 'Can We Be Obliged to Be Selfless?' in Andrew S Gold and Paul B Miller (eds), *Philosophical Foundations of Fiduciary Law* (Oxford University Press, 2014) 141, 150.

[26] See Samet (n 10) at 130.

discern what actually motivated the fiduciary, or which factors truly influenced her deliberations. Loyalty, if understood in the subjective terms that Samet adopts, will be remarkably hard to oversee. And this isn't just a matter of the fiduciary's intent. Samet's account calls for emotional attachment; emotions are not only hard to mandate, they may be impossible for individuals to control.[27]

Indeed, forced loyalty often does not feel like loyalty at all.[28] If loyalty is understood in a very thin sense—such as a prohibition on conflicts of interest—then enforcement is not particularly troubling. But when loyalty is connected with emotional attachment, forced loyalty is potentially counterproductive (and for some types of loyalty, forced loyalty is conceptually impossible). There may be a self-defeating quality to legal enforcement in such cases.[29] Samet is aware of the enforcement concern, and accordingly she emphasizes the expressive components of fiduciary law.[30] Unfortunately, this too is problematic. Part of what the law expresses in fiduciary cases is that legal duties are mandatory where they apply (whether or not enforced), and that notion is in tension with the way emotions work in practice. While Samet indicates that courts invoke the thick sense of loyalty as an expressive recommendation, fiduciary duties are not described by courts as recommendations, even in cases where direct enforcement is lacking.[31] Courts describe loyalty in terms of a legal command.

Furthermore, there is great difficulty in predicting how a thick sense of loyalty will affect behaviour in concrete, real-world cases. Samet emphasizes 'the honest fiduciary, for whom the relationship with the principal is an occasion for morally worthy activity'.[32] Yet this may build in artificial constraints on the emotional attachments experienced by actual loyal agents. Suppose we accept that a focus on the principal's good should be the sole end of a fiduciary's actions, and also that the fiduciary should form an emotional attachment that supports the pursuit of that end. What if the principal's good would be advanced by a breach of contract with a third party?[33] What if the principal would be better off if she were misled by

[27] See John Deigh, 'All Kinds of Guilt' in his *Emotions, Values, and the Law* (Oxford University Press, 2008) 159, 167 ('This illustrates, then, how failure to maintain the emotional commitment, to satisfy the requirements of fidelity and loyalty, can be involuntary. To satisfy the requirements, one must have certain feelings and not have others, and whether one has the former or is free of the latter is typically not within one's power').

[28] See Avihay Dorfman, 'On Trust and Transubstantiation: Mitigating the Excesses of Ownership' in Andrew S Gold and Paul B Miller (eds), *Philosophical Foundations of Fiduciary Law* (Oxford University Press, 2014) 339, 347 ('For, just like norms of politeness, legal enforcement of sincere loyalty is contradictory, since compelled loyalty is not loyalty properly so called').

[29] See John Gardner, 'What Is Tort Law For? Part 1: The Place of Corrective Justice' (2011) 30 Law & Phil 1, 20–21 (noting that a legal norm might be directly or indirectly self-defeating).

[30] See Samet (n 10) at 130 ('By drawing on the common understanding of loyalty equity sends a powerful message about the disposition appropriate to fiduciaries').

[31] See Julian Velasco, 'The Role of Aspiration in Corporate Fiduciary Duties' (2012) 54 Wm & Mary L Rev. 519 (indicating that unenforced fiduciary standards of conduct are nonetheless legal duties).

[32] See Samet (n 10) 131.

[33] Cf. Shiffrin (n 7) at 729 n 41 (discussing the question whether 'corporate law require[s] those with a fiduciary duty of care or loyalty to shareholders to pursue an efficient breach if it would clearly enhance share value').

the fiduciary? Whatever our views on these cases, these are probably not the kind of outcomes associated with the ideal of the 'honest fiduciary'. Emotional attachments, if formed, may lead in unpredicted directions, and the law cannot reliably constrain such outcomes.

Other virtue-based accounts are unlikely to fare better, and for similar practical reasons. We therefore have cause to hesitate over loyalty mandates, at least if our aim is to incorporate moral concepts into legal doctrine. Loyalty obligations are only contingently moral, and loyalty's connection to moral virtue is debated. In addition, supposing that we can customize loyalty to fit an ideal type, the law is not well positioned to enforce those forms of loyalty that are most plausibly virtuous. Even if it would be a good idea in the abstract to enforce extra-legal loyalty, many of its morally desirable instantiations are very difficult for the legal system to monitor, let alone mandate.

III. The Accommodationist Approach

There is another possibility, however. Instead of adopting the reflective approach, perhaps the law should instead accommodate extra-legal understandings of loyalty. This view is much more promising. In order to see what such a view would look like in fiduciary contexts, however, it will help if we first consider its application in a more standard setting—that is, where legal practices and moral practices overlap. Contract law provides a well-known example, and this is where the accommodationist idea has been elaborated most clearly. I will then turn to fiduciary loyalty in the following section.

Seana Shiffrin helpfully sets forth the accommodationist approach in her recent work on contract theory.[34] As she divides theories of private law, there are three basic approaches. The first, the reflective approach described above, suggests that the law should mirror the requirements of interpersonal morality—it 'takes interpersonal morality as a template for legal rules.'[35] The second, a separatist approach, suggests that the law should be viewed as an independent sphere from morality.[36] The two realms should be kept apart, either for normative, political reasons, or because the law has different goals from interpersonal morality. In Shiffrin's view, both of these approaches have elements of truth, but she does not endorse them. As an alternative, she suggests a third, intermediate way—the *accommodationist* approach.

On the accommodationist view, 'even if enforcing interpersonal morality is not the proper direct aim of the law, the requirements of interpersonal morality may appropriately influence legal content and legal justifications to make adequate room for the development and expression of moral agency.'[37] As she argues:

[34] Ibid. [35] Ibid at 713. [36] Ibid. [37] Ibid at 715.

[W]hen a legal practice is pervasive and involves simultaneous participation in a moral relationship or practice, the content and normative justification for the legal practice must be acceptable to a reasonable moral agent with a coherent, stable, and unified personality.[38]

Based on this premise, Shiffrin offers three principles that should regulate the relation between legal and moral norms. First, 'what legal rules directly require agents to do or refrain from doing should not, as a general matter, be inconsistent with leading a life of at least minimal moral virtue.'[39] Second, 'the law and its rationale should be transparent and accessible to the moral agent.'[40] Acceptance of the law's rationale by the moral agent 'should be compatible with her developing and maintaining moral virtue.'[41] Third, and finally, 'the culture and practices facilitated by law should be compatible with a culture that supports morally virtuous character.'[42]

A. The contract setting

As Shiffrin notes, contracts present a clear example of a legal practice that simultaneously involves a moral practice. Contract law presents itself as involving enforceable promises,[43] and it is reasonable to think that many contracting parties see themselves as engaged in an act of promising. Promises, in turn, create moral obligations independent of their legal effect.

Quite possibly, contract law and promissory morality could converge; contract law might parallel morality. On Shiffrin's view:

Contract law would run parallel to morality if contract law rendered the same assessments of permissibility and impermissibility as the moral perspective, except that it would replace moral permissibility with legal permissibility and it would use its distinctive tools and techniques to express those judgments.[44]

But contract law does not always parallel morality in this way.[45]

To be sure, areas of divergence will not always be a concern. Where there are distinctively legal grounds of justification, Shiffrin suggests divergence may even be appropriate.[46] So, for example, she suggests that '[t]he reluctance to order specific performance could be justified on familiar, distinctively law-regarding grounds,

[38] Ibid at 717. [39] Ibid at 718. [40] Ibid. [41] Ibid. [42] Ibid at 719.

[43] See Restatement (Second) of Contracts § 1 (defining a contract as a promise or set of promises).

[44] See Shiffrin (n 7) at 722.

[45] The extent of divergence is a matter of debate. Shiffrin identifies a variety of areas in which contract law diverges from promissory morality, including: the prevalence of the expectation remedy in place of specific performance; the rarity of punitive damages; the duty to mitigate; and the consideration doctrine. See ibid at 722–27. But see Charles Fried, 'The Convergence of Contract and Promise' (2007) 120 Harv L Rev Forum 1 (questioning whether there is divergence in several areas); Andrew S Gold, 'Consideration and the Morality of Promising' in Jason W Neyers and others (eds), *Exploring Contract Law* (Hart Publishing, 2009) (questioning whether there is divergence with respect to the consideration doctrine).

[46] See Shiffrin (n 7) at 733 (as Shiffrin describes such an argument, it involves 'a moral argument whose range is specifically tailored to the special, normatively salient properties of law and its appropriate content and shape').

such as the difficulty and expense of ordering and supervising performance by a reluctant party and, in some cases, the unseemly and disproportionate domineering nature of such state-enforced orders on individuals.'[47] The accommodationist approach is thus context-sensitive, and takes into account the law's rationale for a divergence between law and moral principles. This may mean that a divergence between law and morality is appropriate, or even desirable under the right circumstances.

In other cases, however, distinctively legal grounds of justification are simply not available. One of Shiffrin's suggestions is the doctrine of efficient breach. She argues that, to the extent the law condones or facilitates efficient breaches of contract, it is adopting a view on the keeping of promises that is inconsistent with moral principles. In such contexts, the law is not forcing people to act immorally—they do not have to breach—but on her view it is adopting a rationale for contract law that diverges from the moral practice of promising.[48] Whether or not promissory morality diverges from contract law in the way she suggests is a matter of debate,[49] and I will not take a position on that question here. Regardless of one's position on the specifics of promissory morality, the upshot of Shiffrin's argument should be evident: where legal practices involve simultaneous participation in moral practices, as in contract law, there is cause for the law to accommodate the understandings of moral agents.

B. The fiduciary setting

For structural reasons, this accommodationist approach is highly suggestive in the fiduciary setting.[50] Just as contracts simultaneously engage moral agents in overlapping legal and moral obligations, so too fiduciary relationships simultaneously engage them in overlapping legal and extra-legal loyalty obligations.[51] For example,

[47] Ibid.

[48] See ibid at 730–33. But cf Michael G Pratt, 'Contract: Not Promise' (2008) 35 Fla St U L Rev 801.

[49] See, eg, Steven Shavell, 'Why Breach of Contract May Not Be Immoral Given the Incompleteness of Contracts' (2009) 107 Mich L Rev 1569 (arguing, based on contractual incompleteness, that breach may often be seen as moral); Jody S Kraus, 'The Correspondence of Contract and Promise' (2009) 109 Colum L Rev 1603, 1610 (arguing that 'most of the contract doctrines to which correspondence critics object in fact respect promissory morality, either by refusing to enforce promises intended not to be legally enforceable or by enforcing the corresponding moral rights and duties to which breach of promise gives rise'); Daniel Markovits and Alan Schwartz, 'The Myth of Efficient Breach: New Defenses of the Expectation Interest' (2011) 97 Va L Rev 1939 (suggesting that sellers 'make promises in the alternative: to provide goods or services to a buyer or to make a monetary transfer to him in lieu of those goods or services. Accordingly, a promisor who voluntarily implements the transfer rather than the action terms does not breach her contract but performs it …').

[50] For prior references to Shiffrin's accommodationist argument as it relates to fiduciary law, see Galoob and Leib (n 9) at 108 n 7; Andrew S Gold, 'The Loyalties of Fiduciary Law' in Andrew S Gold and Paul B Miller (eds), *Philosophical Foundations of Fiduciary Law* (Oxford University Press, 2014) 176, 179 n 12; Andrew S Gold, 'The New Concept of Loyalty in Corporate Law' (2009) 43 UC Davis L Rev 457, 503 n 208. Cf Dorfman (n 28), at 347 n 35 (allowing for the possibility that the moral foundations of trust law could be associated with the ethics of trust or loyalty even if the law does not compel compliance).

[51] Note that this overlap may be present outside of fiduciary contexts, and also that a legal accommodation of loyalty may show up in settings beyond fiduciary law. Evidentiary privileges raise an

a guardian will not just have legal cause to be loyal to his ward; extra-legal loyalty is also triggered, often quite powerfully. A director will not just have legal cause to be loyal to her corporation or its shareholders; extra-legal loyalty is once again a central concern. In addition, fiduciary law frequently represents itself as involving loyalty, with courts repeatedly referencing loyalty duties. Indeed, it is hard to think of a law-based fiduciary relationship that does not implicate both legal and extra-legal loyalty to a beneficiary.

The difficulty is that loyalty obligations as such are not obligations of morality (or at least not necessarily so).[52] The framework Shiffrin applies to contract law is frequently inapplicable to fiduciary law because loyalty obligations are often distinct from moral obligations.[53] It is this divergence that makes the accommodation problem especially interesting. There are various normative systems with which the law might concern itself, loyalty being just one example.[54] Honour systems have also been linked to private law.[55] But loyalty is the rare case in which an apparently non-moral set of norms is pervasive in the law, at the surface level of legal concepts.[56] Fiduciary law presents a structure analogous to the one in contract law, but with loyalty duties instead of promissory duties at stake—and the difference is a difference in kind.

Notice that, if we take loyalty and morality as distinctive concerns, the proper application of accommodationism is substantially more complex. It is not at all clear to what extent we should want the law to make room for the expression of loyal agency. We could readily think that the law should not make room for the loyalty experienced by members of an organized crime family. We might be sceptical

interesting example of potential accommodation for extra-legal loyalty obligations. I thank Martha Minow and Erin Delaney for noting this possibility.

[52] This is not to deny that many legal fiduciary relationships involve simultaneous engagement in moral practices. It seems quite plausible to say they do. But the law draws on loyalty, and that is a distinctive normative feature of these relationships.

[53] As some readers have noted, there are also important questions concerning the effect of promises that on their terms require morally unacceptable conduct. On some accounts, such promises create a type of obligation. See Margaret Gilbert, 'Three Dogmas About Promising' in Hanoch Sheinman (ed), *Promises and Agreements: Philosophical Essays* (Oxford University Press, 2011) 80. If wicked promises do create obligations, however, such obligations would seem to conflict with all things considered moral responsibilities.

[54] Interestingly, loyalty obligations are not the only potentially non-moral obligations with which fiduciary law may be concerned, at least from a historical perspective. See Michele Graziadei, 'Virtue and Utility: Fiduciary Law in Civil Law and Common Law Jurisdictions' in Andrew S Gold and Paul B Miller (eds), *Philosophical Foundations of Fiduciary Law* (Oxford University Press, 2014) 287, 288 ('Fiduciary obligations spring initially from non-commercial relationships that reflect an economy of honour'). See also *Meinhard v Salmon*, 249 N.Y. 458, 463–64 (Ct. App. 1928) (describing a fiduciary's obligations in terms of a 'punctilio of honour the most sensitive'); Gold (n 50) at 493 ('Acting honorably towards another is a particular way in which the nonbetrayal aspect of loyalty is expressed'). While loyalty and honour may overlap, these are distinctive concerns.

[55] See Nathan B Oman, 'The Honor of Private Law' (2011) 80 Fordham L Rev 31.

[56] John Gardner is correct in suggesting that legal systems may concern themselves with multiple virtues. See John Gardner, 'The Virtue of Justice and the Character of Law' in his *Law as a Leap of Faith* (Oxford University Press, 2012) 238, 240. Yet we do not ordinarily see these other virtues at the level of legal doctrine in the way that loyalty is evident in fiduciary law.

of making allowances for corporate directors who feel loyalty toward each other when they should be focusing on loyalty to shareholders. These are not minor concerns: such loyal behaviour can be quite damaging. On the other hand, there are a variety of reasons to think accommodation is desirable, at least in some form. I will turn to these reasons next.

1. Individual-centred arguments

The potential rift between loyalty and morality does not in itself rule out accommodation as a legitimate path. There are strong arguments for accommodation that do not implicate the type of relationship between law and morality that subsists in contract law. These arguments are less prominent in private law theory—as they focus on public law settings—but it is well worth turning to them here. Accommodation in these contexts often involves allowances for conduct that is not morally compelling, and in some circumstances even enables conduct that is morally doubtful. For example, in a book chapter on egalitarianism, Shiffrin notes: 'On the common justification, accommodation practices protect people from having to make wrenching, difficult choices between comparably weighty, central values.'[57] Such difficult choices may merit accommodation even if the commitments at issue are, from another's perspective, erroneous. In some cases, loyalty may also involve these types of choices, particularly where loyalty involves close family members. Accommodation of these loyalties makes sense for the same reasons it does in other settings of closely held personal values.

Indeed, loyalty often plays a central role in our self-understanding.[58] As Samet notes, 'Loyalty tends to attach to relationships which form part of our identity. In close relationship[s] of that type, the distinction between actions that serve "me," actions that serve "you," and those that serve "us" is not always well defined.'[59] Indeed, loyalty may be integral to the pursuit of our ground projects—those projects that give meaning to our lives.[60] Not all relationships implicate this type of

[57] Seana Valentine Shiffrin, 'Egalitarianism, Choice-Sensitivity, and Accommodation' in R Jay Wallace, Philip Pettit, Samuel Scheffler, and Michael Smith (eds), *Reason and Value: Themes from the Moral Philosophy of Joseph Raz* (Oxford University Press, 2004) 270, 288.

[58] See A John Simmons, *Justification and Legitimacy: Essays on Rights and Obligations* (Cambridge University Press, 2001) 80 ('Alasdair MacIntyre has argued ... that "the rational justification of my political duties, obligations, and loyalties is that, were I to divest myself of them by ignoring or flouting them, I should be divesting myself of a part of myself, I should be losing a crucial part of my identity"') (quoting Alasdair MacIntyre, 'Philosophy and Politics' in JL Capps (ed), *Philosophy and Human Enterprise* (United States Military Academy Class of 1951 Lecture Series 1982–83) at 58).

[59] See Samet (n 10) at 127. See also Josiah Royce, 'The Philosophy of Loyalty' in John J McDermott (ed), *The Basic Writings of Josiah Royce* (Fordham University Press, 2005) 855, 863 (suggesting that loyalty 'tends to unify life, to give it centre, fixity, stability').

[60] As Bernard Williams has explained, a person 'may be identified with his actions as flowing from projects and attitudes which in some cases he takes seriously at the deepest level, as what his life is about'. See JJC Smart and Bernard Williams, *Utilitarianism: For and Against* (Cambridge University Press, 1973) 116. See also Bernard Williams, 'Persons, Character and Morality' in *Moral Luck* (Cambridge University Press, 1981) 1, 13. While the primary concern here is with the ground projects of the loyal party, it should be noted that loyalty may also be concerned with the ground projects of the beneficiary. See Paul B Miller and Andrew S Gold, 'Fiduciary Governance' (2015) 57 Wm & Mary L Rev 513, 561.

loyalty, and even deeply felt loyalty obligations may fail to implicate our identity or our most basic ground projects.[61] It is nonetheless reasonable to expect that some relationships will involve feelings of loyalty that are tied up with our sense of self or our most meaningful pursuits.

Context will matter, but given the above possibilities, a divergence between loyalty and the law can create significant burdens for loyal agents. Not everyone is strongly affected by feelings of loyalty, but it is safe to assume that those who are so affected represent a large portion of most populations. Likewise, relationships that trigger loyalty are frequent, with loyalty built into friendships and family relationships that are common to almost everyone. Individuals who do not experience loyalty to any real degree may well exist, but they are a rare breed.

Thus far, our focus has been on particularly strong forms of extra-legal loyalty. The scope for accommodation of extra-legal loyalty can extend further to include settings of less significant yet personally valuable decision making. Cases involving deeply felt commitments or central values are not the only contexts in which accommodation may be appropriate: '[a]ccommodation permits people some aspects of their lives in which they do not have to police themselves and others so hard or so comprehensively.'[62] As Shiffrin suggests:

> At least in the American context, I suspect … that the areas of decision around which there should be some accommodation would include decisions relating to personal relationships and their place within one's life … decisions relating to the development and exercise of significant, individuating virtues—such as charity, compassion, mercy, honesty, integrity; and decisions relating to one's body and one's physical appearance.[63]

These decisions, or at least some of them, need not implicate moral deliberation. Decisions relating to one's physical appearance, for example, are only contingently moral decisions. Such decisions may nonetheless deserve accommodation, and loyalty obligations may be implicated in this way as well; indeed, choices 'relating to personal relationships and their place within one's life' classically implicate loyalty.[64]

Granted, accommodation often involves freedom of speech and religion. These concerns may seem far afield from the present context, and fiduciary law settings will not always intersect with fundamental values. In some cases, as with differing

[61] See Keller (n 5) at 14 (noting that '[p]eople cannot lose their deep and passionate loyalties without changing, but they can do so without changing into other people').

[62] See Shiffrin (n 57) at 293. See also ibid at 296 ('having the space to make even trivial choices purely on the basis of the small, specific reasons that trivial options provide seems like an important component of being an individual who exercises sovereignty over her environment').

[63] Ibid at 296. An additional concern may involve the felt experience of autonomy. See Seana Valentine Shiffrin, 'Paternalism, Unconscionability Doctrine, and Accommodation' (2000) 29 Phil and Public Affairs 205, 239 (indicating that accommodation 'may be necessary to retain spheres of activity in which agents can act autonomously and reap the goods associated both with acting freely and with the feeling that one acts freely').

[64] Moreover, there may even be cases in which immoral decisions merit accommodation for reasons of toleration. See Seana Valentine Shiffrin, *Speech Matters: On Lying, Morality, and the Law* (Princeton University Press, 2014). We sometimes accommodate conduct that manifests weakness. As Shiffrin suggests, 'accommodating such flaws through forbearance is a way publicly to manifest compassion and understanding for one another's shortcomings.' See ibid at 163.

views on health care decisions by a close family member, the meaning of loyalty is contested and reflects deeply felt commitments. In other cases, variations in the content of loyalty may be less likely to upset a fiduciary's sense of identity or personal values. On some occasions, loyalty holds great meaning, while at other times it does not. The important thing is that we can anticipate cases in which deeply felt commitments are involved. Likewise, we can anticipate cases in which accommodation of extra-legal loyalty will be appropriate even where the interests at stake are smaller.

The reasons to accommodate extra-legal loyalty will vary from one relationship to another. That said, they include the possibility that loyalty will engage deeply felt commitments, central to a fiduciary's identity (as may arise in guardianship cases involving close family members); the possibility that loyalty-based decision making will involve choices as to personal relationships and their place in a fiduciary's life (as may arise in the context of partnerships); the possibility that even questionable types of loyalty may deserve a degree of toleration (as may arise in relationships where a given type of loyalty is undesirable but exerts great psychological force for loyal agents). Of course, even where there are genuine reasons for accommodation, they may be outweighed in a given setting.[65] For present purposes, the point is that such reasons exist.

2. *Systemic arguments*

Arguments for accommodation may also draw on the risk of broader, systemic effects that can result from a divergence between law and extra-legal loyalty.[66] These broader effects may take varying forms. For example, it might be that gaps between law and extra-legal loyalty will impact the ways in which individuals view their loyalty obligations, with implications for their tendency to comply with legal commands. Or, it might be that there are consequences that have a more localized aspect. Perhaps divergence between law and extra-legal loyalty will impact trust within fiduciary relationships, with the effect that these relationships do not function as well as they might. Alternatively, information costs may be increased when the law selects a loyalty standard that does not match a pre-existing extra-legal conception. Several of these possibilities will be discussed below.

Granting that loyalty is not necessarily moral, we can still draw on an analogy to moral norms. Where legally recognized duties diverge from extra-legal moral understandings, this can decrease compliance with the law's commands.[67] A similar

[65] Reasons not to accommodate may take more than one form. One important example is when the interests of the beneficiary outweigh the interests of the fiduciary. A concern with accommodation for loyal fiduciaries should not obscure the expectations of beneficiaries. Another category involves types of loyalty that advance undesirable ends. Consider, for example, the loyalties that can be implicated in a case like *Evans v Abney*, 396 U.S. 435 (1970) (involving a testamentary trust with racially discriminatory provisions). I thank Joseph Singer for noting the *Evans v Abney* example.

[66] Cf Shiffrin (n 7) at 714 (indicating the significance that a culture of promising has for a just social system).

[67] See Paul Robinson and John Darley, 'The Utility of Desert' (1997) 91 Nw U L Rev 453 (discussing this possibility in the criminal law setting); Janice Nadler, 'Flouting the Law' (2005) 83 Tex L Rev

divergence with respect to loyalty could bring about comparable effects. Whether non-compliance eventuates is an empirical question, and the empirical data where moral norms are at issue is not necessarily helpful in predicting outcomes for loyalty norms. It might be that legal systems lose moral credibility when they step too far away from conventional moral norms, but not when they give us novel accounts of loyalty. Even so, the structure, content, and emotional attachment involved with loyalty obligations suggest that we should at least take seriously compliance-related risk.[68]

The risk of non-obedience may also have particular relevance at the more fine-grained level of fiduciary relationships. Suppose that a divergence between law and extra-legal loyalty norms does result in less compliance with fiduciary loyalty obligations. When a fiduciary breaches legally mandated loyalty obligations, this violation can quite predictably cause beneficiaries to distrust the fiduciary. If such breaches are widespread, the resulting lack of trust could significantly impact the successful functioning of the relationship at issue.[69] For example, in the public corporations context, trust is thought to play a crucial role in corporate success.[70] Admittedly, the policy analysis in this sphere is intricate: trust takes different forms, and we need to be cautious in seeking to increase trust in case we overshoot the mark.[71] If shareholders overtrust directors, for example, this can also lead to undesirable outcomes.[72] Nonetheless, it is plausible to think that noncompliance—and the effects noncompliance can have on beneficiaries' trust of fiduciaries—is a consideration that matters for the efficacy and health of fiduciary relationships.[73]

There are also additional bases for accommodating extra-legal loyalty norms, at least if that accommodation takes a certain form. While loyalty norms are not

1399 (indicating that the perceived legitimacy of a law or legal outcome can influence compliance with unrelated laws). See also Robert Cooter, 'Expressive Law and Economics' (1998) 27 J Legal Stud 585, 596 (suggesting that 'law breeds respect by tracking morality').

68 That some individuals understand loyalty obligations to be examples of moral obligations is further cause to consider the compliance effects of legal doctrine that diverges from widely held understandings of interpersonal morality. Even if people are mistaken in thinking that loyalty is moral, the perceived moral status of loyalty can have significance for their behaviour.

69 Note that there are also other functions of loyalty worth considering here. See Albert O Hirschman, *Exit, Voice, and Loyalty: Responses to Decline in Firms, Organizations, and States* (Harvard University Press, 1970) 81 (describing a context in which 'loyalty is at its most functional when it looks most irrational, when loyalty means strong attachment to an organization that does not seem to warrant such attachment because it is so much like another one that is also available').

70 See Jonathan R Macey, *Corporate Governance: Promises Kept, Promises Made* (Princeton University Press, 2008) 40–42; Margaret M Blair and Lynn A Stout, 'Trust, Trustworthiness, and the Behavioral Foundations of Corporate Law' (2001) 149 U Pa L Rev 1735.

71 For example, trust may take either a cognitive or an affective form. See Frank B Cross, 'Law and Trust' (2005) 93 Geo LJ 1457, 1464–68.

72 See Claire A Hill and Erin Ann O'Hara, 'A Cognitive Theory of Trust' (2006) 84 Wash U L Rev 1717, 1785–86.

73 In addition, there may be cases where concerns about trust are tied to values other than efficiency. See Matthew Harding, 'Trust and Fiduciary Law' (2013) 33 Oxford J Leg Stud 81, 96 (suggesting that 'a main purpose of fiduciary law ought to be to enable people to form, maintain and develop relationships characterized by a cycle of trust and trustworthiness, relationships that are both instrumentally and intrinsically valuable').

moral norms as such, they share key structural features with moral norms. Like many norms of interpersonal morality, loyalty norms commonly have a bilateral structure. Loyalty is in many cases owed by one individual to another individual, with a characteristic relation between rights, duties, wrongs, and remedies.[74] People often have a well-developed understanding of what loyalty requires of them that is just as intuitive as their sense of moral obligation. And, furthermore, individuals' commitment to loyalty is commonly felt with a similar forcefulness. These features suggest an information cost basis for legal doctrine to converge with at least some extra-legal loyalty norms.

As Thomas Merrill and Henry Smith note, simple and accessible moral norms may substantially cut down on information costs for both courts and regulated parties.[75] Tort law provides a good example. As Smith has developed, the morality in tort law has a modular structure.[76] It limits the categories of information that bear on decision making by both courts and regulated parties. Accordingly, '[t]he information cost theory dovetails with deontological theories of torts for the simple reason that legal norms that draw on widespread moral norms are easier to communicate.'[77] The modular structures prevalent in conventional interpersonal morality thus cut down dramatically on the information that must be assessed in determining liability. These features are shared by loyalty duties. Indeed, it is entirely possible that loyalty provides these benefits while being simpler to figure out than the results of a complete moral analysis of duties.[78] In some cases, loyalty may be less sensitive to context than morality.

Legal doctrine that converges with extra-legal loyalty norms may thus have significant information cost advantages. This is not to say that fiduciary law always resembles this picture, or that it needs to in order to obtain a type of simplicity. Whether or not they track extra-legal norms of loyalty, the anti-conflict rules are quite simple, and quite easily communicated: don't have conflicts of interest, and don't have conflicts of duties. In many settings, however, fiduciary loyalty obligations are appropriately more nuanced, taking into account novel contexts in which one party may be misusing discretionary authority over the assets and person of another. In these settings, opportunism risks can justify more flexible fiduciary standards that operate on a case-by-case basis.[79] The difficulty is in knowing what

[74] Loyalty does not always have these features outside the law. See Simon Keller, *The Limits of Loyalty* (Cambridge University Press, 2007) 22 (describing brand loyalty and other types of loyalty that are not directed at individuals). Nor, for that matter, does fiduciary law always have these features. See Miller and Gold (n 60) (describing fiduciary duties of loyalty where loyalty requires advancement of an abstract purpose).

[75] See Thomas W Merrill and Henry E Smith, 'The Morality of Property' (2007) 48 Wm & Mary L Rev 1849, 1850 ('For property to serve as an in rem coordination device, the morality upon which it rests must be simple and accessible to all members of the community').

[76] See Henry E Smith, 'Modularity and Morality in the Law of Torts' (2011) 4 J Tort L 1, 17.

[77] See ibid at 29.

[78] Cf ibid at 30 n 134 ('I do not rule out that for information cost reasons, the message of tort law might diverge from that of the best moral theory, because it is easier to communicate').

[79] See Henry E Smith, 'Why Fiduciary Law Is Equitable' in Andrew S Gold and Paul B Miller (eds), *Philosophical Foundations of Fiduciary Law* (Oxford University Press, 2014) 261, 273 (noting that 'fiduciary law is vague and open-ended around the edges').

content should fill in those standards, and extra-legal understandings of loyalty offer a ready to use, accessible answer to this question.[80]

In fact, efforts to accommodate extra-legal loyalty may converge with a hypothetical bargain approach to fiduciary obligations.[81] On a leading view, fiduciary loyalty is to be figured out by determining what the parties to a fiduciary relationship would have bargained for in a world of zero transaction costs.[82] If courts focus on the particular parties, the information costs imposed by this calculation can be quite high. Even if courts focus on a majoritarian perspective, the analysis can still be complex.[83] If we assume that most parties would take information costs into account, however, then it is quite possible they would select terms that roughly parallel salient extra-legal norms of loyalty. And in that case the sermonic language in many fiduciary opinions may serve a functional purpose—it signals the type of extra-legal loyalty at issue.[84]

3. *Summary*

Each of the above possibilities suggests reasons why accommodating extra-legal loyalty norms may be valuable. In some cases, the reasons have to do with burdens placed on individual loyal agents; in other cases, the reasons are more concerned with the systemic effects of divergence between law and extra-legal loyalty. As with morality, divergence between law and extra-legal loyalty can occur in several ways. It may be that there is a direct conflict: the law may simply mandate a form of loyalty that contradicts the requirements of an extra-legal form of loyalty. In other cases, the law's rationale may send messages about what loyalty requires that are inconsistent with a loyal agent's extra-legal understanding of loyalty. Or, alternatively, the law may set forth doctrines that undermine a culture of loyal behaviour, by creating cynicism about loyalty or by developing habits among the regulated parties that are inconsistent with existing views on what loyalty requires. The next section will consider examples of divergence between law and extra-legal loyalty.

[80] Note also that concerns with information costs may dovetail with concerns about trust in fiduciary relationships. Cf Curtis Bridgeman, 'Contracts as Plans' (2009) U Ill L Rev 341, 378 ('The threat of legal enforcement of contracts can create trust in someone where it may not have existed, or been strong enough, before. But trusting someone is not enough unless one has confidence that the person understands his legal responsibilities').

[81] I thank Rob Sitkoff for suggesting this possibility.

[82] See Frank Easterbrook and Daniel Fischel, 'Contract and Fiduciary Duty' (1993) 36 J L & Econ 425.

[83] This is well-recognized by proponents of the approach. See ibid at 445 ('Creating hypothetical contracts is difficult. Judges have less information than the parties').

[84] Cf Gregory Alexander, 'A Cognitive Theory of Fiduciary Relationships' (2000) 85 Cornell L Rev 767, 777 (hypothesizing that fiduciary roles implicate a cognitive schema, such that the moralizing language of fiduciary law is linked to the behaviour of judges).

C. Examples of divergence

The possibility of divergence between legal loyalty and extra-legal loyalty may seem abstract. The current section sets forth plausible cases of divergence between the loyalty recognized in fiduciary law and the loyalty recognized extra-legally. These examples suggest several distinct ways in which legal loyalty may conflict with extra-legal loyalty; they also indicate the potential weight of the burden on loyal agents. The examples are by no means exhaustive, but they will hopefully show the broad significance of the issue for legal policy. In some cases, there may be distinctively legal grounds for divergence, or it may be counter-productive to address the divide. In other cases, however, divergence may be a legitimate ground for accommodation.

1. Best interests versus preferences

The guardian–ward relationship presents the divergence issue starkly. Imagine a case in which a guardian is fiduciary for an individual who is now in a permanent coma. On one legal approach, guardians are supposed to act in the best interests of their ward.[85] This means that, in reaching decisions on health care for the ward, the guardian should seek to advance the ward's best interests, even if the ward would have preferred another health care choice. On another legal approach, the guardian should look toward the apparent wishes of the ward.[86] What would she have wanted? This means that health care choices might not be in the ward's best interests as the guardian understands them, but legal loyalty could require these choices nonetheless. These two standards both draw on commonly held understandings of loyalty but they can pull in different directions.[87]

In such cases, the guardian is frequently a close family member of the ward, and cares deeply about being loyal to her. This is not a weakly felt loyalty, such as we might see with a friendly acquaintance or a new colleague. This is a profound loyalty. Suppose that there is a conflict between the ward's extra-legal sense of loyalty and the law's understanding. For example, imagine George, who wants most of all to follow his mother's perceived health care wishes, yet is mandated by law to seek her best interests instead (or vice versa).[88] Moreover, such choices may not be

[85] Lawrence A Frolik, 'Is A Guardian the Alter Ego of the Ward?' (2007) 37 Stetson L Rev 53, 66 (describing the role of a best interests standard in property management settings).

[86] See ibid at 59–60 (describing the development of this approach).

[87] As noted in the introduction, another variant may arise under agency law. A paternalistic agent may feel that true loyalty calls for advancing her principal's best interests, or for doing what she thinks her principal really wants, rather than performing according to instructions as the law requires. On the importance of following instructions under agency law, see Deborah A DeMott, 'The Fiduciary Character of Agency and the Interpretation of Instructions' in Andrew S Gold and Paul B Miller (eds), *Philosophical Foundations of Fiduciary Law* (Oxford University Press, 2014) 321. Likewise, the sole interest rule in trust law may be in tension with an extra-legal understanding that a beneficiary's best interests should be the loyal party's core concern.

[88] Irit Samet suggests that the guardian's wish may be an expression of love rather than loyalty. I agree that love is crucial here, but I think loyalty may nonetheless be implicated in a powerful fashion in these cases. It bears noting, however, that in some of these cases commitments grounded in something other than loyalty may also call for accommodation. I thank Dick Fallon and Simon Keller for indicating this possibility.

easily avoided: the significance of a divergence between legal loyalty and extra-legal loyalty is increased by the reality that guardians may not feel comfortable allowing someone else to serve in this role.

2. Loyalty to multiple beneficiaries

Corporate law also provides important examples. Directors classically owe loyalty to their shareholders as a matter of law. For a variety of reasons, directors are likely to also feel loyalty to the corporation's employees. Directors often work with employees for years, and, in some cases, these employees may be understood to be part of 'the corporation' to which the directors owe loyalty. In addition, if the directors are constituency directors, they are likely to feel loyalty to the parties responsible for their election to the board. In some cases, extra-legal loyalties are problematic, as when structural bias causes directors to feel loyalty toward their fellow board members. In other contexts, there is substantial debate whether director loyalty to non-shareholders is a desirable thing. Whether such loyalty is beneficial or not, however, it can clearly conflict with legal doctrine that describes fiduciary loyalty as isolated to the shareholder class.

Notice also that, in certain cases, legal doctrines on director loyalty could limit this concern while substituting a different one. A prominent example arises where courts adopt a truncated vision of fiduciary loyalty. Significantly, in some jurisdictions judges have concluded that loyalty only encompasses a rule against conflicts of interest and conflicts of duties.[89] This doctrine could decrease the risk that directors will think they owe loyalties to one party when the law tells them they owe loyalties to another party—but it may pose another challenge. Should corporate directors grow accustomed to purely conflict-based understandings of loyalty, it is very possible this understanding will spill over into their other loyalty practices. Directors might de-emphasize the affirmative devotion that is characteristic of much extra-legal loyalty,[90] and the culture that grounds loyal behaviour might then be weakened. Of course, whether this actually occurs is an empirical question, but if it does, this could offer another case for accommodation.[91]

[89] For discussion of this reading and its history, see Smith (n 25), at 144–45 (describing judicial understandings in Australia).

[90] This is, however, a matter of conjecture. The ways in which legal doctrine affects social norms are complex, and further empirical work is required in the loyalty setting. On law and its impact on social norms, see, eg, Richard H McAdams, 'The Origin, Regulation, and Development of Norms' (1997) 96 Mich L Rev 338; Richard H McAdams, *The Expressive Powers of Law: Theories and Limits* (Harvard University Press, 2015) 150–51. Likewise, there is an important question whether a legal doctrine's perspective on morality will be internalized. See Kenworthey Bilz and Janice Nadler, 'Law, Psychology & Morality' in D Medin and others (eds), *Moral Cognition and Decision Making: The Psychology of Learning and Motivation* (Academic Press, 2009) 101. Similar questions may arise with respect to the internalization of loyalty norms.

[91] A further possibility is that law may indicate that loyalty should come to an end at a certain point, when a thicker, extra-legal sense of loyalty will continue to hold sway. For discussion of this possibility, see Simon Keller, 'Fiduciary Duties and Moral Blackmail' (ms on file with author). See also Samet (n 10) at 127 (noting that 'the fiduciary is generally free to leave her post').

3. *Contradictory loyalty*

For some loyal agents, a legal loyalty obligation may create substantial burdens not just in particular contexts, but across the board. Consider the recent 'shaping account' of fiduciary loyalty developed by Stephen Galoob and Ethan Leib. Galoob and Leib contend that it is not possible to accidentally be loyal (a point which distinguishes promises and contracts, as one can accidentally keep promises or perform contracts). On their view, fiduciary loyalty has three elements:

> A fiduciary acts loyally toward a beneficiary only if (1) the beneficiary's interests matter to the fiduciary's deliberation; (2) these interests matter *solely* because they are the interests of the beneficiary rather than for some other reason; and (3) the fiduciary is disposed to revise her deliberations based on changes to the beneficiary's interests.[92]

Suppose that the law subjects fiduciaries to this type of loyalty obligation. This possibility would raise significant concerns for a legal system that seeks to limit the burdens placed on loyal agents.

Under the standard view of legal obedience, citizens should obey the law because it is the law.[93] This obedience may be understood extra-legally as a matter of loyalty, and it often is. It would put an incredible burden on such loyal parties if they are simultaneously expected to comply with the law on the basis that it is the law, and also expected to be loyal fiduciaries under the shaping account. The loyal individual is supposed to take the beneficiary's interests into account because the law says so, but the shaping account of loyalty tells us that the beneficiary's interests must be taken into account solely because they are the beneficiary's interests. In following the law because the law says so, the loyal individual will be taking the beneficiary's interests into account for the wrong reasons. In order to avoid this bind, one might object to the standard view of legal obedience.[94] That said, even if legal authority does not call for following the law because the law says so, many think that it does.[95] If the law were to adopt the shaping account, many loyal agents would thus face an impossible challenge.[96]

[92] Galoob and Leib (6) at 117 (emphasis added).

[93] See Scott Hershovitz, 'The Authority of Law' in Andrei Marmor (ed), *Routledge Companion to Philosophy of Law* (Routledge, 2012) 65, 66–67.

[94] Cf ibid 66–70 (rejecting the standard view, while recognizing that it is widely held). For a leading example of the standard view, see Joseph Raz, 'The Duty to Obey' in *Ethics in the Public Domain* (Oxford University Press, 1994) 343 (suggesting that, if one followed a law for reasons of its justice, 'in acting for these reasons one would not be obeying the law, one would not be conforming because that is what the law requires'). See also Andrei Marmor, *Philosophy of Law* (Princeton University Press, 2011) 61 ('Whenever the law imposes an obligation or requires you to do something, it conveys a dual message: You *ought* to do it, and you ought to do it *because the law says so*'). How often citizens are motivated by the standard view is a matter of some debate. See Frederick Schauer, *The Force of Law* (Harvard University Press, 2015) 43–74 (discussing this question).

[95] For helpful analysis of this perspective in the private law setting, see Stephen A Smith, 'The Normativity of Private Law' (2011) 31 Oxford J Leg Stud 215.

[96] I write in hypothetical terms here because, at least in my view, the law has yet to adopt the shaping account. It should also be noted that similar concerns may arise for extensions of the shaping account in other settings. Cf Ethan J Leib and Stephen R Galoob, 'Fiduciary Political Theory: A Critique' (2016) 125 Yale L J 1820.

IV. The Variability Challenge

The above illustrations suggest that divergences can occur, and that they can be significant. This raises the question of how we should respond. Interpersonal morality is often a matter of consensus within a given community, even if it is debated on the margins.[97] If loyalty practices showed a similar level of agreement, accommodation could be a much simpler task. But instead, loyalty is multifaceted. As Justice James Edelman notes: 'In law as in life, loyalty cannot be understood without knowing the performance in relation to which loyalty is required.'[98] In fact, the problem may be worse than that, as a given performance may not narrow things down. Loyalty, on many accounts, is highly variable in its aims, origins, emotional attachments, and potential moral constraints.

Indeed, different types of loyalty may implicate very different perspectives on what a loyal party should try to do. Consider the split between agency-type loyalty and trust-type loyalty. A loyal agent's primary concern is to act consistently with the instructions of her principal. A loyal trustee's primary concern is often to act in the best interests of her beneficiaries, irrespective of their contrary instructions. Both types of conduct qualify as a type of loyalty but they are hardly the same kind of behaviour. In the first case, paternalism is unacceptable; in the second case, it is par for the course. Or, consider the potential divide between loyalty as affirmative devotion and loyalty as being true. Showing affirmative devotion to someone may, on some accounts, call for a white lie. Being true to that person, on the other hand, will consist precisely in the loyal party's refusal to lie.

What this means is that we cannot readily point to an extra-legal loyalty norm that law should accommodate by converging on that norm's content. Whichever loyalty norm is chosen, there will likely be divergence from another significant loyalty norm. It might be argued that particular loyalty norms fit particular relationships—which is true to a degree—but for any given relationship there will often be notable variations in the types of loyalty that loyal agents consider apt. Moreover, it will often be unhelpful to reduce divergent loyalty norms to their common features; efforts to find common features typically result in extremely thin conceptions of loyalty.[99] If a legally adopted loyalty obligation is to have real substance to it, it will inevitably diverge from important extra-legal loyalty conceptions.

[97] Note that Shiffrin's argument for accommodating promissory morality focuses on areas in which she contends that morality has uncontroversial content. See Shiffrin (n 7) at 720–21. As she recognizes, there are areas in which the significance of promising raises disputes.

[98] See James Edelman, 'The Role of Status in the Law of Obligations: Common Callings, Implied Terms, and Lessons for Fiduciary Duties' in Andrew S Gold and Paul B Miller (eds), *Philosophical Foundations of Fiduciary Law* (Oxford University Press, 2014) 21, 22. See also Samet (n 10) at 126 ('Loyalty, like love and jealousy, can take different shapes, and stretch over a wide range of emotional states, according to the type of relationship in which it is anchored'); Keller (n 5) at 21 ('There are many different ways of being loyal; a particular loyalty may involve any of several kinds of motive, so long as they have a certain basic structure, and it may involve any of several quite different ways of acting').

[99] For discussion of this possibility, see Gold (n 50) at 190–93.

The remainder of this Section will consider several means to accommodate loyalty, given this backdrop. The answer is not to mandate a unified approach to loyalty, as this will inevitably diverge in substantial ways from extra-legal conceptions. In this context, accommodation will require some form of choice for loyal agents. Mechanisms that permit such choice, however, can take a number of forms.

A. Contractual modifications

A basic mechanism for accommodation of extra-legal loyalty is to allow for contractual modifications. In some circumstances, this may allow for loyalties that have qualitatively different content from conventional legal defaults, or this may allow for loyalties that are owed to distinctive groups of beneficiaries. Alternatively, contractual modifications may work with existing loyalty content, but narrow its scope or otherwise limit its application. Not all fiduciary relationships are a good fit for this approach to accommodation. For example, relationships in which the beneficiary is involuntarily part of the relationship and incompetent to waive his or her rights—for example, parent–child relationships—are not apt for contractual modification. In many other cases, however, contracts provide room for loyal agents to pursue types of loyalty that might otherwise diverge from legal mandates.

Interestingly, there may also be contexts in which accommodation points away from contractual freedom. Some argue that fiduciary loyalty is incapable of being produced by contractual means.[100] This should not be surprising—the loyalty of friends cannot be mandated by a bargain,[101] and other types of loyalty may have similar features. In contrast to this view, a contract-focused legal doctrine may implicitly express the understanding that fiduciary loyalty is contractual at its core,[102] and some courts appear to hold this perspective. In addition, courts have explicitly recognized contract-created fiduciary duties.[103] Tacitly or otherwise, these approaches express a particular view on the type of loyalty embedded in fiduciary law. A legal regime that takes fiduciary loyalty as contractual, however, is inconsistent with a particular extra-legal understanding, one in which loyalty cannot be produced by agreement. Unsurprisingly, contractual modifications are not well suited to accommodate this type of loyalty.

[100] See *supra* n 9.

[101] See David Owens, *Shaping the Normative Landscape* (Oxford University Press, 2012) 106 (noting that 'one cannot take on obligations of *friendship* simply by communicating the intention to do so'); Joseph Raz, 'Respect for Law' in his *The Authority of Law: Essays on Law and Morality* (Oxford University Press, 1979) 257 ('The friendship itself, involving an intricate web of reciprocal dispositions and attitudes, cannot be created by an act of commitment. It has to grow, develop, and cement over time').

[102] Note, however, that the ability to contractually modify fiduciary obligations does not necessarily mean that the underlying fiduciary duties stem from contracts. See Markovits (n 9) at 219–20 ('But the fact that parties possess a formal power to abandon or vary certain rules that elaborate a fiduciary's duties of loyalty and care, or even that they may sometimes be free to choose from a menu of alternative constructions of these duties, does not render fiduciary obligation contractual').

[103] See *Gerber v Enterprise Products Holdings LLC*, 67 A.3d 400 (Del. 2013).

That being said, other conceptions of loyalty are easily reconciled with contractual origins. The point of the present chapter is to bring to the surface the existence of different extra-legal conceptions of loyalty and to assess how the law should take these conceptions into account (if at all). Accommodationism is relevant to the debate over contractual modifications regardless of the reader's perspective on the contractual origination of fiduciary obligations. In some cases, the importance of accommodation will provide added support for contractual freedom, given that it allows parties to opt into customized loyalty types that match their understandings of loyalty. In other cases, it may suggest the importance of immutable loyalty as a component of particular fiduciary relationships.[104]

B. Non-enforcement

Another mechanism—non-enforcement—is exemplified by the Business Judgment Rule in corporate law. Under the Business Judgment Rule, courts will refuse to second guess directors' substantive business decisions, barring conflicts of interest, corporate waste, or egregious failures of process.[105] This doctrine has been justified in a variety of ways. Justifications include: a focus on the proper balance between authority and accountability;[106] the difficulty in otherwise addressing hindsight bias;[107] questions of judicial expertise in the business setting;[108] problems of radical uncertainty;[109] and incentives for desirable director risk-taking.[110] Accommodation offers another justification.

Consider instances in which extra-legal understandings implicate the recipients of a fiduciary's loyalty. Notice that the Business Judgment Rule enables directors to act to advance various employee and community interests, as well as the public interest more broadly understood.[111] In each instance, these decisions may benefit the corporation and its shareholders in the long term (charity, for example, creates

[104] Concern with effects on a culture that supports loyalty obligations may be particularly relevant here. Cf Melanie B Leslie, 'Trusting Trustees: Fiduciary Duties and the Limits of Default Rules' (2005) 94 Geo LJ 67, 88–94 (discussing the effect on social norms resulting from contractual modifications to trust law fiduciary duties).

[105] The Business Judgment Rule is often described as: 'a presumption that in making a business decision, the board acted on an informed basis, in good faith, and in the honest belief that the action taken was in the best interests of the company'. *Aronson v Lewis*, 473 A.2d 805, 812 (Del. 1984).

[106] Stephen M Bainbridge, 'The Business Judgment Rule as Abstention Doctrine' (2004) 57 Vand L Rev 83.

[107] Jeffrey J Rachlinski, 'A Positive Psychological Theory of Judging in Hindsight' (1998) 65 U Chi L Rev 571, 621.

[108] See, eg, *Dodge v Ford Motor Co.*, 170 N.W. 668, 684 (Mich. 1919) (refusing to intervene in a decision regarding the expansion of a business, and noting '[t]he judges are not business experts').

[109] Andrew S Gold, 'A Decision Theory Approach to the Business Judgment Rule: Reflections on *Disney*, Good Faith, and Judicial Uncertainty' (2007) 66 Md L Rev 398.

[110] William T Allen and others, 'Realigning the Standard of Review of Director Due Care with Delaware Public Policy: A Critique of *Van Gorkom* and Its Progeny as a Standard of Review Problem' (2002) 96 Nw U L Rev. 449, 455.

[111] See Einer Elhauge, 'Sacrificing Corporate Profits in the Public Interest' (2005) 80 NYU L Rev 733, 770.

good publicity). Often, directors aim to help the corporation and its shareholders through such decisions. In some of these cases, the relevant conduct may instead be motivated by a director's self-interest. But in other cases, these socially-focused types of business decisions may reflect extra-legal conceptions of loyalty that diverge from a legally adopted shareholder primacy norm. The wide range of behaviour that is effectively left unmonitored by the courts enables directors to act pursuant to extra-legal loyalties that diverge from a legally endorsed standard of conduct.[112]

C. Vagueness and ambiguity

Another possibility addresses standards of conduct themselves.[113] Indeterminacy in the content or direction of fiduciary loyalty means that fiduciary actors will often need to interpret their obligations. Where a range of interpretations is reasonable, and that range coincides with a set of extra-legal conceptions, this will enable fiduciaries to select the type of loyalty that corresponds to their subjective understanding of loyalty, or perhaps, to their local community's extra-legal understanding of loyalty. So long as the range of reasonable interpretations is suitably broad, divergence between legal and extra-legal loyalty will be decreased.

More precise specification of duties may also crowd out intrinsic motivations to comply, at least under some circumstances.[114] If this pattern applies to fiduciary loyalty, then a legal effort to precisely mandate a given type of extra-legal loyalty might dissipate intrinsic motivations to comply, with concomitant effects on a fiduciary's performance. Vagueness could then have advantages not only because it can be interpreted consistently with a broad range of loyalty conceptions, but also because it may increase the likelihood that what is motivating fiduciaries to follow a given fiduciary mandate is at least in part their sense of extra-legal loyalty.[115]

There may also be a more subtle benefit to this approach. In some cases, there may be value in legal vagueness because that vagueness will induce moral deliberation.[116]

[112] Emily Sherwin's work suggests another ex post option—courts may quietly provide equity on a case-by-case basis in those circumstances where it would seem particularly harsh to enforce strict rules. Cf Emily Sherwin, 'Formal Elements of Contract and Fiduciary Law' at pp 180–81 in this book. There is also an additional possibility: the law might provide that no legal duty of loyalty is owed, in the process giving loyal actors additional space to act loyally according to a subjective or local understanding.

[113] Note that the effect of a fiduciary standard of conduct may be quite significant even if a doctrine like the Business Judgment Rule limits its actual enforcement. See Douglas G Baird and M Todd Henderson, 'Other People's Money' (2008) 60 Stan L Rev 1309, 1323 (noting that many directors 'want to do what they are supposed to do').

[114] For a discussion of the literature on crowding out and an application to equity more generally, see Yuval Feldman and Henry E Smith, 'Behavioral Equity' (2014) 170 J Inst & Theor Econ 137.

[115] We should also recognize that rules and standards have various other costs and benefits separate and apart from those features linked to a fiduciary's understanding of loyalty. See, eg, Louis Kaplow, 'Rules versus Standards: An Economic Analysis' (1992) 42 Duke LJ 557.

[116] See Seana Valentine Shiffrin, 'Inducing Moral Deliberation: On the Occasional Virtues of Fog' (2010) 123 Harv L Rev 1214. See also Gold (n 50) at 193 (noting that loyalty could have similar features). As Shiffrin also notes, accommodation may enhance freedom 'by facilitating certain sorts of purer deliberation that themselves represent a kind of valuable freedom'. See Shiffrin (n 57) at 289.

Parties will take the time to figure out what morality calls for. Vagueness with respect to loyalty, however, may also induce deliberation on what loyalty requires. This is not necessarily the same thing as moral deliberation although we can anticipate overlap—but given the role that loyalty plays in our lives, this type of deliberation may be quite valuable in its own right. When courts adopt vaguely defined loyalty duties, they may not only be making room for clear-cut extra-legal loyalty conceptions, they may also be making room for the deliberation by which individuals ascertain what their extra-legal loyalty obligations are.[117]

D. A menu approach

A further way to address accommodation concerns is to provide a menu.[118] Suppose, for example, that one believes that extra-legal loyalty is only satisfied in those cases where the loyal party acts in the best interests of the party to whom she is loyal. Not all fiduciary relationships may reflect this idea of loyalty but the law can offer categories of relationship that do so. Under this approach, no particular conception of loyalty wins out, but various conceptions are represented in the law. Differing loyalty conceptions are thus accommodated, at least for those individuals who are able to opt into a fiduciary relationship that matches their extra-legal understanding of loyalty.

This approach dovetails with arguments for structural pluralism. In private law settings, structural pluralism suggests that broad fields like property, contracts, or torts should not be understood in terms of one single regulative principle.[119] On this view, there are multiple institutions within these fields, each with their own regulative principle. In turn, the range of choices offered by these institutions has been justified on autonomy grounds. As elaborated by Hanoch Dagan, the benefit of this variation is that it allows parties to have an adequate range of options among which to choose: the variety of choices in social forms helps individuals to be part authors of their own lives.[120]

These same insights are applicable to fiduciary law. As Dagan and Sharon Hannes note: 'fiduciary law could encompass, as structural pluralism prescribes, a number of distinct private law institutions.'[121] Whether or not particular choices are always

[117] That said, vagueness and ambiguity can also provide opportunities for misuse of fiduciary powers. Cf Tamar Frankel, 'Watering Down Fiduciary Duties' in Andrew S Gold and Paul B Miller (eds), *Philosophical Foundations of Fiduciary Law* (Oxford University Press, 2014) 242, 254–55 (describing problems raised by the transformation of one fiduciary regime into another).

[118] In fiduciary law, menu strategies are particularly prominent in corporate settings. See, eg, Ian Ayres, 'Menus Matter' (2006) 73 U Chi L Rev 3, 4–6 (discussing menus with respect to corporate law default rules).

[119] See Hanoch Dagan, 'Pluralism and Perfectionism in Private Law' (2012) 112 Colum L Rev 1409.

[120] See ibid at 1421–25. On the linkage between a range of choices and autonomy, see Joseph Raz, *The Morality of Freedom* (Oxford University Press, 1986) 372–77. For the connection between autonomy and self-authorship, see ibid at 204 ('An autonomous person is part author of his own life').

[121] See Hanoch Dagan and Sharon Hannes, 'Managing Our Money: The Law of Financial Fiduciaries as a Private Law Institution' in Andrew S Gold and Paul B Miller (eds), *Philosophical Foundations of Fiduciary Law* (Oxford University Press, 2014) 91, 97.

the best option along a given metric, the availability of each choice is itself significant, as the selection among options plays a constitutive role in an autonomous life. An accommodationist approach focuses on the importance of extra-legal obligations in the lives of fiduciaries, rather than the availability of choices as such, but it points to a similar policy prescription. A range of options gives loyal agents an increased ability to select a relationship corresponding to their own views on loyalty.

E. Implications

There are, then, multiple mechanisms for accommodating extra-legal loyalty. This reality means we can now recognize an additional difficulty in accommodating loyalty. While a variety of perspectives can support accommodation of loyal agents whose extra-legal conception of loyalty differs from a given legal conception, the particular mechanisms for accommodation are not all going to match well with each perspective. One might anticipate an incompletely theorized agreement on the law's treatment of loyalty,[122] but there is cause to think that the policy prescriptions that flow from each distinctive ground for accommodation will be inconsistent.

For example, suppose that accommodation is justified on an information cost basis. As Robert Sitkoff has emphasized, information cost concerns can help justify the mandatory core of fiduciary obligations.[123] The strength of this justification will depend on context, including whether the fiduciary relationships at issue involve entities that are required to file with the state.[124] That said, the information cost benefits Sitkoff identifies—benefits that flow from clearly demarcated lines between relationship-types—will diminish if fiduciary loyalty is subject to substantial contractual modifications, and likewise if fiduciary loyalty is overly vague.[125] The same basic point may apply in this context. In contrast, a menu approach could work well if information costs are our primary concern, especially if the boundaries between menu choices are clear.

If we instead justify accommodation on the basis that loyalty is often tied closely to our central commitments, or our ground projects, then we will be particularly concerned with those settings in which loyalty has these features. In that case, contractual modifications may be an especially important mechanism, as they allow highly individualized loyalty obligations for those individuals with an idiosyncratic but deeply felt sense of loyalty. On the other hand, this justification might be relationship-sensitive. Fiduciary relationships such as guardianships that frequently implicate deeply felt commitments might be more apt for accommodation

[122] See Cass Sunstein, 'Incompletely Theorized Agreements' (1995) 108 Harv L Rev 1733.

[123] See Robert Sitkoff, 'An Economic Theory of Fiduciary Law' in Andrew S. Gold and Paul B. Miller (eds), *Philosophical Foundations of Fiduciary Law* (Oxford University Press, 2014) 197, 204–06.

[124] See ibid at 206.

[125] On the connection between vague standards that induce moral deliberation and high information costs, see Smith (n 76) at 30 n 134.

than fiduciary relationships that commonly involve a more detached interaction between fiduciary and beneficiary.

Likewise, there are important differences between a non-enforcement strategy and a vagueness strategy. The Business Judgment Rule may facilitate tacit violations of a legal conception of loyalty, in the name of an extra-legal conception. Where non-enforcement is the chosen strategy, accommodation may mean that the law effectively ignores a legal breach. That mode of accommodation can impact fiduciary behaviour differently from alternative approaches, and it may have sizable expressive effects. Yet vagueness has its own well-recognized costs that may be avoided by a non-enforcement alternative. In addition to information costs, increased litigation and decision costs are real possibilities under a vagueness approach.

In each case, prior value commitments and empirical assumptions may suggest that one or another approach to accommodation is preferable. Our reasons for accommodating may allow for consensus on the idea that fiduciaries should have some sort of space to be loyal from an extra-legal perspective. Yet, depending on why we support accommodation, we may find that the law should accommodate in very different ways.

V. Conclusion

There are multiple reasons for the law to incorporate extra-legal conceptions of loyalty. For example, such loyalty norms may lower information costs, or they may mirror a hypothetical bargain among contracting parties. Recently, however, it has been suggested that the law should incorporate extra-legal loyalty because of what it means to be loyal—loyalty is thought desirable because of its links to interpersonal morality. Unfortunately, it does not make sense to legally mandate loyalty duties based on their general moral status, or based on loyalty's part in a virtuous life. Loyalty frequently diverges from morality, and in some cases loyalty may be quite pernicious. It is, moreover, quite impractical to enforce those types of loyalty that are most plausibly virtuous.

Even so, loyalty can play an important constitutive role in an individual's life, and in many cases it implicates deeply felt commitments. This chapter suggests that, rather than seek to reflect extra-legal loyalty based on its morality, the law should instead aim to accommodate loyal agents—it should create space for individuals to act in accord with their extra-legal understandings of what loyalty requires. Just as there is cause to accommodate moral agents whose contracts simultaneously implicate promissory morality, there is cause to accommodate loyal agents whose fiduciary relationships simultaneously implicate extra-legal loyalty. The reasons for accommodation must be different—loyalty is not co-extensive with morality—but these reasons nonetheless exist.

Yet accommodating loyal agents calls for distinctive measures. The content of loyalty obligations is usually thought to vary across contexts, relationships, and communities. Making room for moral agents often means watching out for a divergence between legal duties and moral duties. Making room for loyal agents, by contrast, will often mean providing a menu of legal options, or allowing space for contractual modifications of legal relationships, or limiting the role for judicial enforcement. In other words, accommodation here means variance. What type of accommodation is appropriate, however, will depend on our reasons for accommodating.

9

The Deed, Not the Motive

Fiduciary Law Without Loyalty

*Stephen A Smith**

It is widely assumed that a concern for loyalty lies at the heart of fiduciary law: '[T]he distinguishing obligation of a fiduciary', Lord Millet wrote, 'is the obligation of loyalty'.[1] Against this view, this chapter argues that not only is loyalty not a central concern of fiduciary law; it is not a concern at all. Nor should it be. What matters in fiduciary relationships is that fiduciaries fulfil their mandates[2] (eg, executing a trust, promoting the principal's business, providing legal services). Whether that task is performed loyally is not, and should not be, the law's concern. Indeed, in most fiduciary relationships the issue of loyalty cannot even arise because in most cases impossible for fiduciaries to act loyally—or disloyally—even if they were inclined to do so. I further argue that the unimportance of loyalty in fiduciary relationships has four implications for the broader understanding of fiduciary law: (1) the no-conflict rule is a prophylactic duty; (2) the no-profit rule is part of the no-conflict rule; (3) disgorgement of profits is a remedy for breach of the no-conflict duty; and (4) fiduciary law is in most cases part of contract law, broadly understood.[3]

* I am grateful to Evan Fox-Decent, Andrew Gold, Paul Miller, and Lionel Smith for their comments on earlier versions of this chapter. The title was inspired by Lionel Smith's essay, 'The Motive Not the Deed' in Joshua Getzler, *Rationalizing Property, Equity and Trusts: Essays in Honour of Edward Burn* (Oxford University Press, 2003) 53.

[1] *Bristol & West Building Society v Mothew* [1998] Ch 1, 18. See also Lionel Smith, 'Fiduciary Relationships: Ensuring the Loyal Exercise of Judgement on Behalf of Another' (2014) 130 LQR 608 ('Although they may disagree about many things in relation to fiduciary obligations, courts and commentators agree that the law of fiduciary obligations is about ensuring loyalty': 609); Paul Miller, 'Justifying Fiduciary Remedies' (2013) 63 UTLJ 570 ('[I]t is not seriously disputed that fiduciary relationships give rise to a duty of loyalty': 585); Graham Virgo, *The Principles of Equity and Trusts* (Oxford University Press, 2012) ('The key obligation of a fiduciary is one of loyalty': 480); and Arden LJ in *Item Software (UK) Ltd v Fassihi* [2004] EWCA Civ 1244 (the duty of loyalty is 'the fundamental duty to which a director is subject': [41]). A dissenting view is James Penner, 'Is Loyalty a Virtue, and Even If It Is, Does It Really Help Explain Fiduciary Liability?' in Andrew Gold and Paul Miller (eds), *Philosophical Foundations of Fiduciary Law* (Oxford University Press, 2014) 159.

[2] Throughout this chapter, 'mandate' is a synonym for what Matthew Conaglen describes as the fiduciary's 'non-fiduciary duties': Matthew Conaglen, *Fiduciary Loyalty: Protecting the Due Performance of Non-Fiduciary Duties* (Hart Publishing, 2010) 32–58.

[3] With the possible exception of (3), these conclusions are not novel. My critique of the role of loyalty was inspired by James Penner (n 1), while my endorsement, with qualifications, of the contractual

I. Fiduciary Law Does Not Care About Loyalty

Loyalty is a complex concept. But on any plausible account, it has two features that are fatal to loyalty-based explanations of fiduciary law.[4] The first is that ascriptions of loyal behaviour always have a temporal element: there is no such thing as instant loyalty. To act loyally—or disloyally—towards another person[5] you must already have a meaningful relationship—a 'history' of some kind—with that person.[6] Helping someone whom you have just met—for example helping a stranger to cross the street—is commendable, but it is not an instance of loyalty. This temporality explains why allegations of disloyalty are most commonly made in long-term relationships and why they are rarely, if ever, made in the context of casual encounters.

As we will see in a moment, the impossibility of acting loyally or disloyally towards others—unless you are already in a meaningful relationship with them—is a problem for loyalty-based accounts of fiduciary law regardless of how 'meaningful' is defined. However, it may be helpful to mention that the key element appears to be a notion of commitment. Questions of loyalty arise when individuals have committed themselves to others. Consistent with loyalty's temporal aspect, the relevant commitment must itself have a temporal element: commitments that make loyalty possible typically involve identifying in some way with another person, and are usually understood in terms of a particular and on-going role, for example, friend, lover, or supporter. Importantly, simply making a promise or undertaking towards another person does not, standing alone, give rise to the kind of relationship in which loyalty becomes possible. The duty to keep a promise arises at the instant a promise is made and may arise in full force between strangers. Indeed, explicit promises are relatively rare between persons who have close relationships and, when they are made in such relationships, they are typically a sign that the relationship

view of fiduciary duties draws heavily on James Edelman, 'When Do Fiduciary Duties Arise?' (2010) 126 LQR 302. My conclusion that the no-conflict rule is a prophylactic duty and that the no-profit rule is a part of the no-conflict rule has been defended by many, but most ably and exhaustively by Conaglen (n 2).

[4] My account of loyalty draws on the work of Simon Keller, *The Limits of Loyalty* (Cambridge University Press, 2007); Penner (n 1); Joseph Raz, *The Morality of Freedom* (Oxford University Press, 1986) 353–57); and Matthew Harding, 'Disgorgement of Profit and Fiduciary Loyalty' in Simone Degeling and Jason Varuhas (eds), *Equitable Compensation and Disgorgement of Profit* (Bloomsbury Academic, forthcoming). However, as the account is meant to describe the ordinary understanding of loyalty, its veracity rests ultimately on its congruence with that understanding.

[5] Throughout this chapter, my focus is loyalty *towards other individuals,* but it is no doubt possible to be loyal towards families, teams, and other groups. It may also be possible to be loyal towards non-persons, for example, towards causes, countries, or roles, though it is arguable that in such cases the actual object of loyalty remains a person or persons. The argument that follows does not turn on whether or not it is possible to be loyal towards things other than humans.

[6] See Penner (n 1) 162–64.

is not as close as it appears.[7] Promises are typically employed between individuals who cannot count upon—and so are unwilling to rely upon—one another's loyalty. Thus, even where a promise is fulfilled because of a felt moral obligation—and therefore because of an implicit recognition of a promisee's moral worth—we do not describe its performance as an instance of loyalty. It is only where a promisor is already committed to a promisee that promise-breaking can qualify as an instance of disloyalty. Like giving money to a stranger, keeping a promise made to a stranger may be commendable, but it is not an instance of loyalty.

The temporality of loyalty is fatal to loyalty-based explanations of fiduciary law because fiduciary relationships may arise—and do arise in full force—between parties who have no prior relationship. To be sure, some fiduciaries have meaningful relationships with their beneficiaries prior to becoming fiduciaries; for example trustees of family trusts are often related to the beneficiaries or have known them for many years. And in other cases, fiduciaries may develop meaningful relationships with their beneficiaries over the course of acting as a fiduciary. However, fiduciaries are bound by the full panoply of fiduciary duties and liabilities at the moment they become fiduciaries and, in the vast majority of cases, they become fiduciaries because they made a contractual or similar undertaking to act in the interests of individuals who were previously strangers. The trustees in charge of managing commercial trust funds typically do not meet the fund's beneficiaries prior to agreeing to act; indeed, in many cases such trustees will never meet the beneficiaries or even know their names (for example, where the beneficiaries are members of a pension fund). Company directors are often in a similar position. Yet in such cases trustees and directors become fiduciaries in the full sense from the moment they take on these roles. In short, in the vast majority of fiduciary relationships it is simply not possible for fiduciaries to act loyally or disloyally; therefore, it is not possible for the law to care whether they act loyally or disloyally.

The second core feature of loyalty that stands in the way of a loyalty-based explanation of fiduciary law is that acting loyally always involves acting for a particular kind of motive.[8] It is not possible to act loyally—or disloyally—by accident or when one is sleepwalking.[9] Even acts that are intended to benefit individuals with whom one has the kind of relationship that makes loyalty possible are not instances of loyalty unless they are performed at least in part because of that relationship. My decision to offer my best friend a job is not an instance of loyalty, if I make the offer because my friend's uncle threatened me or because my boss ordered me to make the offer or because, having contractually promised to make the offer, I am afraid of the legal liability that I might incur if I do not make it.

[7] See Daniel Markovits, 'Promise as an Arm's Length Relation' in Hanoch Sheinman (ed), *Promises and Agreements* (Oxford University Press, 2011).

[8] 'Loyalty is the attitude and associated pattern of conduct that is constituted by an individual taking something's side, and doing so with a certain sort of motive ... [Loyalty always requires] an attitude of positive regard': Keller (n 4) 21. See also Penner (n 1) 161–62; and Stephen Galoob and Ethan Leib, 'Intentions, Compliance, and Fiduciary Obligations' (2014) 20 Legal Theory 1.

[9] In contrast, it is possible to keep a promise by accident: see ibid 5–10.

To count as an instance of loyalty an action must be motivated at least in part by the actor's prior commitment (in the sense explained earlier) to the action's beneficiary. Conversely, it is possible to display loyalty towards another while acting against that person's interests. Friends who go to great lengths to try to support you and who do so because they are your friends are displaying their loyalty even if it turns out that their actions do not achieve their intended results. If I were tasked with managing my parent's investments, I would do so loyally but, in all likelihood, ineffectively. Although it is not possible to act loyally without acting, an action can be loyal (or disloyal) regardless of its outcome. In short, in order to act loyally towards another one must be in a certain kind of relationship with that person *and* one's actions with respect to that person must be motivated at least in part by that relationship. When we talk of acting 'out of a sense of loyalty' it is this motivation to which we are referring.[10]

Loyalty's dependence on motive is fatal to any attempt to explain fiduciary law in terms of loyalty because the core rule of fiduciary law—the no-conflict rule—is unconcerned with motive.[11] The no-conflict rule prohibits fiduciaries from entering transactions without the beneficiary's consent in situations where the fiduciary's duty to the beneficiary (with respect to the execution of the trust, provision of legal services, etc.) may conflict with his or her own interests.[12] To be sure, fiduciaries that enter into conflicts of interest often do so precisely because they wish to promote their interests over those of the beneficiary. But the no-conflict rule is not restricted to such cases. The rule is doubly strict: not only is it no defence that the transaction was in the beneficiary's best interests, it is no defence that it was done for the purest of motives.[13] A breach of the no-conflict rule may be committed 'with perfect good faith'.[14] In short, the most loyal of fiduciaries may run afoul of the no-conflict rule.[15]

[10] 'A true friend has to see loyalty as in itself sufficient reason to bear a burden': Thomas Scanlon, *What We Owe Each Other* (Belknap Press, 1998) 62. The fact that loyalty requires fidelity to one's commitments helps to explain why we normally regard loyalty as a virtue, notwithstanding that the object of one's loyalty might be a horrible person. Though not identical to keeping a promise or a vow, acting loyally shares with these actions the idea of being true to one's commitments, broadly understood: see Raz (n 4) 354; Andrew Gold, 'The Loyalties of Fiduciary Law' in Andrew Gold and Paul Miller (eds), *Philosophical Foundations of Fiduciary Law* (Oxford University Press, 2014) 180–81.

[11] As noted above, I regard the other core rule of fiduciary law—the no-profit rule—as a part of the no-conflict rule. However, my objection to loyalty-based explanations of fiduciary law does not depend on this classification since the no-profit rule is equally unconcerned with motives: *Keech v Sandford* (1726) 25 ER 223.

[12] *Aberdeen Railway Co v Blaikie Bros* (1854) 1 Macq 461, 471. For reasons explained in Section 4, I support the conventional view that the no-profit rule imposes a duty to avoid acting in unauthorized conflicts (as opposed merely to imposing a condition for the valid exercise of a fiduciary power). However, my objection to loyalty-based explanations of fiduciary law does not depend on this view: the no-conflict rule is unconcerned with motive regardless of whether it is classified as a duty-imposing or condition-imposing rule.

[13] *Boardman v Phipps* [1967] 2 AC 46; *Regal (Hastings) Ltd v Gulliver* [1967] 2 AC 134n.

[14] *Bray v Ford* [1896] AC 44, 48.

[15] It is true that fiduciaries who are inclined to act disloyally will be more likely to act on this inclination in situations where they can personally profit. The no-profit rule may therefore reduce the number of instances in which fiduciaries act disloyally. However, the rule only has this effect with respect to fiduciaries who have committed themselves to their beneficiaries in such a way that it is possible for them to act disloyally. More importantly, the no-conflict rule also reduces—and in all likelihood to a greater extent— the number of instances in which fiduciaries who are inclined to act loyally can act on

The possibility of fiduciary relationships arising between strangers, together with the strictness of the no-conflict rule, is sufficient reason to reject loyalty-based explanations of fiduciary law. However, it may be useful to flag two other respects in which such accounts appear to be inconsistent with the law.[16] First, it is unclear what role loyalty could possibly play in the common situation where the fiduciary's primary mandate is to allocate benefits between multiple beneficiaries.[17] The law rightly requires that fiduciaries act fairly, not loyally (whatever this might mean), in such cases. Second, if fiduciaries had duties to act loyally those duties would frequently conflict with their primary mandates. Most fiduciaries have a duty to use proper care and skill when performing their mandates (for example, to act reasonably—or more strictly 'prudently'—when investing on the beneficiary's behalf). This duty often requires different actions than those that would be required by a duty of loyalty. For example, in cases where the fiduciary's primary mandate is to invest on the beneficiary's behalf, fiduciaries who are bound to act loyally (assuming that loyal behaviour is even possible) must presumably purchase investments that they believe will maximize the fund. Yet the loyal fiduciary may be mistaken in this belief. In such a case, the investment chosen by the loyal fiduciary may be one that a prudent fiduciary would not have chosen. To be sure, the loyal, but mistaken, fiduciary will not realize that she is acting unreasonably, but here, as elsewhere in the law, reasonableness is assessed according to an objective standard. Thus, a duty to act reasonably and a duty to act loyally may conflict. Indeed, these duties would conflict in most cases where fiduciaries are found not to have performed their mandate properly since in most such cases the fiduciary presumably did not intend to act unreasonably. In the typical cases in which fiduciaries have breached their duty to perform their mandate, the breach was not intentional.[18]

their inclinations. The no-conflict rule prohibits both disloyal and loyal fiduciaries from acting in conflict situations. And since the latter are almost certainly more common than the former, on balance the no-conflict rule dissuades, rather than promotes, loyal actions.

16 Other reasons for rejecting a loyalty-based account of fiduciary law are discussed in Conaglen (n 2) (though not explicitly presented as such, nearly the entirety of Conaglen's book amounts to a critique of such accounts). As mentioned earlier, I regard the no-profit rule as part of the no-conflict rule, but whether or not this interpretation is correct the no-profit rule cannot be explained in terms of a concern for loyalty because this rule applies irrespective of motive and the nature of the parties' relationship (see Section 4).

17 See Evan Fox-Decent, *Sovereignty's Promise: The State as Fiduciary* (Oxford University Press, 2012) 34.

18 In his loyalty-based account of fiduciary law, Lionel Smith places significant weight on the rule that a transaction may be set aside if it was not made in what the fiduciary subjectively thought were the beneficiary's best interests: Smith (n 1) 611–12. Outside of the United States, most commentators regard the 'subjective best interests' doctrine as part of the law governing 'proper purposes' (or perhaps part of the law on good faith) as opposed to part of fiduciary law: see eg, Conaglen (n 2) 44–50 (on American law, see Andrew Gold, 'The New Concept of Loyalty in Corporate Law' (2009) 43 UC Davis L Rev 457). But even if this doctrine is part of fiduciary law, it is not about loyalty. As I noted earlier, loyal fiduciaries must not only act in what they believe is the beneficiary's best interests, they must also act *for this reason* (Lionel Smith disagrees: see 'Can We Be Obliged to Be Selfless' in Andrew Gold and Paul Miller (eds), *Philosophical Foundations of Fiduciary Law* (Oxford University Press, 2014) 141, 152). Fiduciaries who act in what they believe is the beneficiary's best interests only because they have promised to do this or because they may be fired if they don't do it are not acting loyally (nor are they acting disloyally: their actions are neutral so far as loyalty is concerned). Further, the subjective best

II. Fiduciary Law Should not Care about Loyalty

For the reasons just explained, the question of whether a fiduciary has acted loyally does not even arise in the context of most fiduciary relationships. Most fiduciaries cannot act loyally, or disloyally, even if they wanted to. However, it might be thought that the question courts should be asking is not whether it is possible for fiduciaries to act loyally but whether, assuming it were possible for them to act loyally, they acted as a loyal fiduciary would act. In other words, it might be thought that fiduciaries should be assessed according to whether they are acting as loyal fiduciaries would act—regardless of whether they were in fact in a position to act loyally.

If this suggestion is intended to assist in understanding the positive law then an immediate objection is that it cannot explain the strictness of the no-conflict rule. If the law cared about loyalty (even in the hypothetical sense just described), it would care about the fiduciary's motives. A further reason to reject this suggestion is that 'acting as a loyal fiduciary would act' has little value in fiduciary relationships. Stated differently, it would be surprising if the law cared whether fiduciaries acted as loyal fiduciaries would act. The vast majority of beneficiaries do not care whether their fiduciaries act as loyal fiduciaries would act. As already mentioned, most fiduciary relationships arise in commercial settings: fiduciaries are typically paid to act as fiduciaries. In particular, fiduciaries are typically paid to perform particular tasks—for example to invest funds, seek business opportunities, or provide legal services—and the main thing, if not the only thing, that most beneficiaries want from a fiduciary is that those tasks be performed properly. Of course, if the parties are in fact in the kind of relationship in which issues of loyalty can arise, the beneficiary may care whether the fiduciary acts loyally and, therefore may care about the fiduciary's motives. But most fiduciary relationships are strictly commercial and in these cases what beneficiaries care about are outcomes, not motives. If I transfer funds to a trustee to invest on my behalf, what I care about is whether the trustee invests the assets productively—not whether she invests with the right motive. My dog is loyal to a fault, but I would not want him managing my assets.

Admittedly, few beneficiaries would be happy to learn that their assets were managed by a fiduciary with no interest at all in their well-being. But aside from cases involving family-member fiduciaries and the like, the reason they would be unhappy is not that they care what fiduciaries think of them, but that they would worry that a fiduciary with no interest in their well-being would be unlikely to do a good job performing their mandate. What beneficiaries ultimately care about are

interests doctrine can be explained on the same basis as the no-conflict rule (see below)—namely that it helps to prevent breaches of the fiduciary's mandate. While it is possible for fiduciaries to act other than in what they believe is the beneficiary's best interest and to still perform their mandates to the appropriate standard, in practice this combination is unlikely.

outcomes. Indeed, because duties of loyalty and care may conflict (as explained earlier) there are situations where beneficiaries would prefer that the fiduciary act as a disloyal fiduciary would act. Suppose that I transfer funds to a financial advisor to invest on my behalf. Unbeknownst to me, the advisor has a high risk tolerance; much higher than my own (though the advisor is also unaware of the difference). Given this tolerance, the advisor might honestly believe that a risky investment is in my best interest. In such a case, I might well want the advisor to act disloyally, say by personally purchasing the more risky investment and then choosing an investment for me that the advisor believes is not in my best interests. More generally, what I want is an advisor that picks investments that are in my best interests. Whether the advisor does this because she genuinely cares about me, or because her boss will fire her if she doesn't do it, or because she purchases for herself what she believes are the best investments is irrelevant to me.

In theory, there might be reasons that the law should care—even if beneficiaries do not care—whether fiduciaries act in the way that loyal fiduciaries would act even if beneficiaries do not care. For example, it might be thought that 'acting loyally' has a social value that is distinct from whatever value beneficiaries place upon it. Attempts to justify private law duties and liabilities on the basis of social values should be approached with caution but, even accepting the possibility of such a justification, it is not clear how a concern for loyalty could be so justified. Loyalty has little, if any, inherent value.[19] It is entirely possible, and in practice not uncommon, for individuals to be loyal to evil people, and for these individuals to do horrible things—lying, stealing, killing—because of their loyalty. Many beneficiaries are no doubt horrific people: displaying loyalty towards them is not a virtue. Of course, where fiduciaries have undertaken to act on behalf of such persons fiduciaries normally have a moral and legal duty to fulfil their undertaking (save where the undertaking requires them to do something immoral or illegal). But in such cases there is no value in performing the undertaking loyally; on the contrary, it is detrimental to act loyally in such cases. These observations are not meant to deny that most fiduciary relationships are valuable. But they are valuable for the same reason that contracts are valuable: they allow individuals to do things that they could not do otherwise or at least not easily.

Finally, even if there were reasons for the law to care whether fiduciaries act as loyal fiduciaries would act, there is little, if anything, that the law—or at least the private law—can do to promote such actions. To act as a loyal fiduciary would act, a fiduciary must act with a certain disposition towards the beneficiary. If fiduciaries are not already inclined towards such dispositions there is little the law can do to induce them to develop the disposition. The law can alter our reasons for action, but it cannot change our dispositions towards others. Fortunately, it is actions, not dispositions, that fiduciary law should care about.[20]

[19] See Penner (n 1).

[20] Because acting loyally requires that one actually act, the law may be able to reduce the number of disloyal actions by imposing sanctions on such actions. However, as explained in note 14, such sanctions also decrease the possibility of acting loyally. To the extent that a fiduciary acts in the beneficiary's interest because of an incentive, the fiduciary is not acting loyally (or disloyally)— the action is neutral so far as loyalty is concerned: see Galoob and Lieb (n 8).

III. A Legal Term of Art?

The law often attaches special meanings to ordinary English words. The meaning of 'consideration' in the common law of contract is different than its meaning in ordinary language (though the meanings are related). The features of loyalty defended above are part of its ordinary meaning. It might be thought, then, that whatever that account's accuracy, the account itself is irrelevant when trying to understand the law because the law uses the term 'loyalty' in a special sense. In other words, when courts and commentators talk about loyalty, they do not mean loyalty in the ordinary sense.

This view of loyalty's legal meaning must be correct. Or at least it must be correct if the preceding account of loyalty's ordinary meaning is accurate. If loyalty is only possible in a sub-class of fiduciary relationships, and if acting loyally always involves acting for the right kind of motives, then when courts and commentators say that a duty of loyalty lies at the heart of fiduciary law, they must be understood as using the term in a special sense.

Nonetheless, it is important to state clearly—as I have tried to do above—that fiduciary law has nothing to do with loyalty in the ordinary sense of the word. It is important, first, because with rare exceptions courts and commentators do not make clear that, when they refer to loyalty, they are using the term in a special sense.[21] Courts and commentators typically employ the term without qualification. Further, in contrast to a concept like consideration, the concept of loyalty is not typically applied directly to the facts of a dispute. Rather, loyalty is typically introduced, usually at the beginning of a court's or commentator's discussion of fiduciary law, as a core value or principle or foundation of the law.[22] The implication is that the concept of loyalty explains or at least describes the particular rules that are discussed afterwards and which, in legal decisions, are applied directly to the facts. In short, the way that courts and commentators employ the concept of loyalty suggests that the concept is meant to carry its ordinary meaning.

The confusion engendered by associating fiduciary law with loyalty in the ordinary sense would not matter if fiduciary law's foundations were well established. If this were the case, then it would be obvious that fiduciary loyalty is different from ordinary loyalty. But as the contributions to this book make clear, fiduciary law's foundations are generally thought to be something of a mystery. About the only thing that most (but not all) commentators agree upon is that fiduciary law

[21] See, eg, the examples cited in note 1. Exceptions include Paul Miller, 'Dimensions of Fiduciary Loyalty' in D Gordon Smith and Andrew S Gold (eds), *Research Handbook on Fiduciary Law* (Elgar, forthcoming). However, while Miller argues that the concept of loyalty at work in fiduciary law differs from the 'moral' conception, he concludes that rather than abandoning the concept (as argued for in this chapter) we should simply recognize that fiduciary loyalty is a distinctive kind of loyalty.

[22] Ibid.

is different in significant ways from contract or tort law. This view may well be correct. However, the assumption that fiduciary law is qualitatively different from contract and tort law makes the constant references to loyalty dangerous. When loyalty is understood in its ordinary sense, its value (such as it is) is qualitatively different from the values that we normally associate with contract, tort, and other core private law areas. Loyalty is a virtue, not a duty, and it involves particular attitudes or dispositions towards others. The risk, then, is that the assumed distinctiveness of fiduciary law may be thought to be explained in some way by the equally distinctive value of loyalty; all while forgetting that this value is tied to features of the ordinary meaning of loyalty that are not present in the legal conception. In short, there is a temptation to try to understand fiduciary law in terms of values that would be appropriate only if the law actually cared about loyalty in the ordinary sense of the term. More broadly, courts' and commentators' constant references to loyalty indirectly support the common assumption that fiduciary law cannot be explained using the kinds of principles and values traditionally employed to explain private law. As I hope to demonstrate below, this assumption should be resisted.

IV. The No-Conflict Rule Imposes a Prophylactic Duty

If the no-conflict rule is not intended to protect or promote or otherwise support loyalty (in the ordinary sense of the term), what is its purpose? The answer suggested by the preceding comments is familiar: the no-conflict rule is prophylactic. The no-conflict rule makes it less likely that fiduciaries will breach their mandates (eg, their duties to execute trusts, advance the interests of a company, provide legal services, etc) by prohibiting them from acting in situations where there is a heightened risk of such a breach. The common-sense idea underlying this suggestion is that even fiduciaries with the best intentions will be prone to breaching their mandates if they act in conflict situations: '[H]uman nature being what it is, there is danger, in such circumstances, of the person holding a fiduciary position being swayed by interest rather than by duty, and thus prejudicing those whom he is bound to protect.'[23] As explained by Lionel Smith:

> When a person exercises judgement in a conflict situation, it is impossible for that person to be certain that they have excluded extraneous considerations. A professor would not wish to grade an examination written by his own child; the professor could never be sure whether love for the child was leading towards a too-high grade, or whether the effort to exclude this was leading to overcompensation and a too-low grade. And if the professor, in perfectly good faith, cannot be certain, then of course no one can. The problem cannot be solved by any amount of evidence.[24]

[23] *Bray v Ford* [1896] AC 44, 51 (Lord Herschell). The 'circumstances' to which Lord Herschell refers are the fact that fiduciaries acquire powers that, while they are meant to be used for the beneficiary's benefit, can easily, and with little risk of detection, be applied to other uses.

[24] Smith (n 1) 624. See also Conaglen (n 2) 69–70; Penner (n 1) 168; Peter Birks, 'The Content of Fiduciary Obligation' (2000) 34 Israel L Rev 3, 10; Irit Samet, 'Guarding the Fiduciary's

The prophylactic explanation of the no-conflict rule follows from the preceding analysis of loyalty because if the only value at stake in fiduciary relationships is fulfilling the fiduciary's mandate, then the only possible reason not to act in a conflict situation is prophylactic. Acting in a conflict situation is not itself a breach of the fiduciary's mandate or otherwise wrongful. However, acting in a conflict situation makes it more likely that fiduciaries will unintentionally breach their mandates. On the reasonable assumption that it is desirable for fiduciaries to perform their mandates, it is also desirable for them to avoid situations in which they are likely, even with the best intentions, to fail to perform them.

Some writers who accept that the no-conflict rule is prophylactic nonetheless reject the idea that the rule imposes a *duty* to avoid conflicts. Lionel Smith, in particular, argues that the no-conflict rule merely expresses a *requirement* for the valid exercise of a fiduciary power.[25] According to this view, there is no duty to avoid conflicts, but if a fiduciary acts in a conflict the transaction may be set aside. In Sections VI and VII, I examine certain features of fiduciary law remedies that appear to support this view. In this Section, I consider briefly whether there is anything odd in principle about the concept of a prophylactic duty.

Prophylactic duties appear odd when compared to the kinds of duties typically recognized by tort law, at least as those duties are conventionally understood. In that understanding, most duties in tort law are outcome-dependent. For example, it is not a wrong to place oneself in a position where one is likely to commit a trespass; the wrong of trespass is only committed if one actually trespasses. Nor is it possible, according to the conventional view, to breach the duty not to act negligently without actually harming someone. Notwithstanding that taking reasonable care to try to avoid harming others is a good way to reduce the likelihood of actually harming others—in other words, notwithstanding that taking reasonable care is a good prophylactic against harming others—the conventional view of the duty in negligence is that it is not breached unless a particular outcome—harm—has occurred. This understanding of tort law, and in particular the tort of negligence, may be queried (see Section VIII), but for present purposes it is sufficient to note that many other private law duties are not outcome-dependent. Contractual duties, in particular, are

Conscience—A Justification of a Stringent Profit-Stripping Rule' (2008) 28 Oxford Journal of Legal Studies 763. A different version of the prophylactic view supposes that the no-conflict rule is designed to prohibit fiduciaries from acting in situations where it will be difficult for beneficiaries to determine if the fiduciary has breached a non-fiduciary duty: 'To relax standards for situations where the defendant allegedly acted "properly" cannot be allowed because most of the relevant evidence will be peculiarly within the defendant's knowledge and control, so making it very difficult for the disadvantaged plaintiff to know whether or not they have a case for saying the defendant acted "improperly": DJ Hayton and CCJ Mitchell, *Hayton & Mitchell's Commentary and Cases on the Law of Trusts and Equitable Remedies* (12th edn, Sweet and Maxwell, 2005) 6–24. The arguments that follow are consistent with either version of the prophylactic argument.

[25] James Penner also rejects the duty formulation, but on a different basis: for Penner there is neither a duty nor a requirement to avoid conflicts, but merely a liability to disgorge profits if one obtains them while acting in a conflict: Penner (n 1) 171–72. It is difficult to assess Penner's argument because (if I have understood correctly) he has yet to explain why the liability arises.

typically not outcome-dependent. For example, contractual duties to take care may be breached regardless of whether harm ensues. Further, and directly on point, there is nothing odd about prophylactic contractual duties. Suppose that I want to hire you to deliver goods by ship from India to England by a specified date. Let us assume that most ships making such a delivery would avoid traveling near the coast of Somalia because of the risk of piracy. However, I worry that you, a well-known risk taker, might nonetheless be tempted to take this route. I am aware that I can sue you for damages if you fail to deliver by the contractually-specified date but for obvious reasons I would prefer that you simply arrived on time. In these circumstances, I might well decide to include a clause in our contract stipulating that you may not use a route that takes you near the Somali coast. I would express this clause as a duty, rather than a mere condition (whose non-fulfilment would allow me to cancel the contract), because I would not want to leave you the option, if you decided to take the risk, of travelling by Somalia in the hope that I would not cancel the contract. What I want is for you to have a contractual duty not to travel by the Somali coast. As I discuss in Section VI, such a clause raises interesting remedial issues. It might also be queried whether it is ever appropriate for the law to impose similar duties in non-contractual settings (see Section VIII). However, such a clause is perfectly rational and, as a matter of positive law, perfectly valid. If our contract contained such a clause you would have a contractual duty to avoid the Somali coast. This duty is prophylactic in the same way that the no-conflict duty is prophylactic.

V. The No-Profit Rule as Part of the No-Conflict Rule

Alongside the no-conflict rule, the other core fiduciary law rule is the 'no-profit' rule. According to the conventional understanding, the no-profit rule prohibits fiduciaries from profiting from their position unless expressly authorized to do so: 'It is an inflexible rule of a Court of Equity that a person in a fiduciary position … is not, unless otherwise expressly provided, allowed to make a profit.'[26] It is generally accepted that it is rare, if not impossible, for fiduciaries to profit from their positions without having acted in a conflict situation. Nonetheless, courts and commentators are divided over whether the no-profit rule is distinct from the no-conflict rule.[27] And as was true of the no-conflict rule there is also a debate as to whether the no-profit rule imposes a duty (in this case a duty to avoid making

[26] Lord Herschell in *Bray v Ford* [1896] AC 44, 51.

[27] Courts and writers who view the no-profit rule as part of the no-conflict rule include: *Bray v Ford* [1896] AC 44, 51 (Lord Herschell); *Boardman v Phipps* [1967] 2 AC 46, 123 (Lord Upjohn); *New Zealand Netherlands Society v Kuys* [1973] 1 WLR 1126, 1129 (Privy Council); Penner (n 1) 168; and (with small qualifications) Conaglen (n 2) 124–25. Examples of the opposing view include: *Chan v Zacharia* (1984) 154 CLR 178, 198 (Deane J); *Queensland Mines Ltd v Hudson* (1978) 52 AJLR 399, 401; Smith (n 1). For a detailed analysis of the relevant cases, see Conaglen (n 2) 114–25.

unauthorized profits) or merely stipulates that certain consequences follow if such profits are made (in particular that the fiduciary must disgorge the profits).[28]

The preceding analysis suggests that the no-profit rule is part of the no-conflict rule and, like the no-conflict rule, is duty-imposing. Like the no-conflict rule, the no-profit rule is doubly strict: it applies regardless of the fiduciary's motivations and regardless of whether the fiduciary's mandate is properly performed. The rule precludes fiduciaries from making unauthorized profits even when they act with the purest of motives and even when the profit is an incidental by-product of an action that promotes the beneficiary's interests. It follows that the no-profit rule is no more concerned with fiduciaries' loyalty than is the no-conflict rule. Further, and again like the no-conflict rule, it is difficult to think of any reason that beneficiaries—or the law—would care whether fiduciaries make profits except for the fact that in situations where fiduciaries have the opportunity to make profits there is a significant risk that they may fail to perform their mandate properly. In other words, the only reason to care whether fiduciaries make profits is prophylactic. Finally, for the same reason that it makes sense to interpret the no-conflict rule as imposing a duty to avoid conflict, it makes sense to interpret the no-profit rule as imposing a duty to avoid making unauthorized profits. The rationale for both rules is to prevent fiduciaries from breaching their mandates. The obvious way to give effect to this rationale is for fiduciaries to avoid acting in the situations contemplated by these rules. If the no-profit rule merely provided that where fiduciaries make profits the relevant transaction may be rescinded and/or fiduciaries may be required to disgorge their profits, then fiduciaries would be legally free to enter transactions in which they profit so long as they are willing to hand over those profits. It is difficult to think of any reason that beneficiaries—or the law—would take an interest in whether fiduciaries make profits, yet be indifferent as to whether fiduciaries are obliged to avoid making profits as opposed to merely being obliged to hand over their profits if the beneficiary so requests. In any event, the prophylactic justification for the no-profit rule clearly supports a duty to avoid making profits: the prophylactic reason is a reason for fiduciaries to avoid acting in situations where they may make a profit.[29]

[28] See Smith (n 1); Penner (n 1); and Section VI below.

[29] Lionel Smith correctly observes that a beneficiary's power to rescind transactions between the fiduciary and a third party cannot easily be explained as a remedy for breach of a no-conflict duty: Smith (n 1) (criticizing Conaglen (n 2) 76). However, it does not follow from this observation that the no-conflict rule is not a duty: it only follows that rescission must be otherwise explained. The explanation is admittedly not obvious; it is not clear why individuals should have the power to rescind transactions to which they were not a party. One possible explanation is that the power arises from a limitation on the powers granted to the fiduciary. By analogy to the rule that agents may only bind their principals when acting within the scope of their authority, it might be thought that fiduciaries only have powers to enter transactions in which they are not conflicted. However, if this explanation were correct we would expect that, as in cases where agents act outside their authority, the impugned transactions would be void, not (as is true in fiduciary law) voidable: Smith (n 1) 612. A second explanation, developed by Lionel Smith, is that the beneficiary's power to rescind is analogous to the power held by a contracting party who has entered a contract under duress or mistake. In such cases, the law allows contracting parties to set aside the contract if they so choose because their consent was impaired: Smith (n 1) 612. But the fact that a fiduciary has acted in a conflict does not show that the beneficiary's consent was impaired. More importantly, it is unclear why a 'defect' (however defined) in the relationship between the fiduciary and the beneficiary should allow the beneficiary to rescind a

VI. Disgorgement of Profits

If fiduciaries are legally obliged not to act in conflict situations without authorization—as I have argued—we would expect the law to provide a remedy to beneficiaries when this obligation is breached. In this Section, I argue that the 'disgorgement rule'—the rule that holds fiduciaries liable to disgorge to the beneficiary any profits that they have made while acting in conflict situations if the beneficiary so demands[30]—sets out this remedy. However, before making that argument I consider two alternative explanations of the disgorgement rule.

A. Disgorgement as a deterrent

The most common explanation of the disgorgement rule views disgorgement as a deterrent.[31] Writers who defend this view typically describe disgorgement as a remedy, but they do not regard disgorgement as a remedy in the usual sense, that is, as an award that is intended to redress, repair, undo, or otherwise remedy a wrong. According to the deterrence theory, the justification for awarding the fiduciary's profits to the beneficiary is that the threat of having to disgorge profits will deter future fiduciaries from acting in conflict situations without authorization. If the deterrence theory is correct, disgorgement is not a remedy. However, the theory should be rejected. As other writers have noted,[32] the deterrence theory is vulnerable to two serious objections. First, disgorgement is a poor deterrent because it leaves fiduciaries in the same position they were in prior to the wrong. Second, the deterrence theory cannot explain why the fiduciary's profits are given to the plaintiff rather than to the state.

B. The primary-right explanation of disgorgement

Two leading critics of deterrence theories—Paul Miller and Lionel Smith—have recently developed alternative theories of the disgorgement rule.[33] Although Miller and Smith's theories differ in important respects,[34] each regards the disgorgement

contract between the fiduciary and a third party. In the end, the beneficiary's ability to rescind contracts with third parties is not easy to explain.

30 *Regal (Hastings) Ltd v Gulliver* [1967] 2 AC 134n; *Murad v Al-Saraj* [2005] EWCA Civ 959.

31 See, eg, James Edelman, *Gain-Based Damages: Contract, Tort, Equity and Intellectual Property* (Hart Publishing, 2002) 212, 216, 244; IM Jackman, 'Restitution for Wrongs' (1989) 48 Cambridge LJ 302; Conaglen (n 2) 76.

32 See in particular Lionel Smith (n 1) 621; Lionel Smith, 'Deterrence, Prophylaxis and Punishment in Fiduciary Obligations' (2013) 7 J Equity 87; Miller (n 1) 590–94.

33 Lionel Smith (n 1); Paul Miller (n 1).

34 Amongst other differences, Miller believes that fiduciaries have duties to avoid conflicts and to avoid making profits, while Smith, as we have seen, believes that the no-conflict and no-profit rules merely impose requirements for the valid exercise of fiduciary powers. Given this difference, Miller could in theory support an explanation of the disgorgement rule similar to mine (namely as a way of placing a proportionate value on the beneficiary's infringed right). However, as I hope to show, Miller's

rule as giving effect to a beneficiary's primary right to the profits.[35] For both Miller and Smith, fiduciaries must disgorge their profits because these profits always belonged to the beneficiary or at least should be seen as having always belonged to the beneficiary.

But why does the beneficiary have such a right? If I have understood correctly, Miller and Smith's theories explain this right as part of a beneficiary's property-like right to the means that the fiduciary used to make the profits.[36] On this view, the rule providing that fiduciaries must disgorge their profits is broadly analogous to the rule providing that defendants who have infringed the plaintiff's intellectual property rights must disgorge the profits they realized through the infringement.[37] To be clear, neither Smith nor Miller suggests that fiduciary profit-making is directly analogous to such cases. As they are aware, cases in which fiduciaries must disgorge profits arising from the use of fiduciary 'opportunities' or arising from advice that they gave in a fiduciary capacity cannot easily be explained using a simple property analogy. Further, if it were the case that beneficiaries had rights to any profits arising from the use of property managed on their behalf, they would presumably also have a right to profits made by third parties in transactions where the third party acquires such property. Such profits are not subject to the disgorgement rule.

If I have understood correctly, the analogy to the intellectual property cases operates at a higher level. For both Miller and Smith, the essence of a fiduciary relationship is that the fiduciary has acquired powers—decision-making powers—that are normally held by the beneficiary. In Miller's words, 'Power is the key definitive formal property of the fiduciary relationship … [it] is a form of authority derived from the legal capacity of another person.'[38] Similarly, for Lionel Smith, '[t]he fiduciary relationship is characterised by the acquisition by the fiduciary of part of the autonomy—part of the choice-making ability—of the beneficiary.'[39] Importantly, these powers are not simply transferred wholesale to the fiduciary; instead they are delegated to the fiduciary so that the fiduciary may manage them on the beneficiary's behalf. It follows for Miller and Smith that, just as in cases where physical assets are held by a trustee for a beneficiary, the ownership of the beneficiary's

explanation rests ultimately not on the fiduciary's wrongdoing but, like Smith's, on the beneficiary's anterior right to whatever profits the fiduciary makes through exercising his or her fiduciary powers.

[35] '[W]hen the fiduciary, through the use of the levers of control that he holds over the beneficiary's autonomy, is able to extract some wealth or value, the law ascribes it to the beneficiary as a matter of primary right': Lionel Smith (n 1) 628. 'Wherever a fiduciary takes property, profits, or opportunities for same in the execution of a fiduciary mandate, she violates the beneficiary's implied right to those gains. Her wrong necessarily involves appropriation of that to which the beneficiary was entitled as a matter of primary right': Miller (n 1) 617.

[36] '[D]isgorgement reflects the quasi-proprietary nature of the beneficiary's right to loyalty: Miller (n 1) 617.

[37] See generally, Andrew Burrows, *Remedies for Torts and Breach of Contract* (3rd ed, Oxford University Press, 2004) 384–90.

[38] Miller (n 1) 607.

[39] Smith (n 1) 628. Smith refers to 'choice-making ability' rather than 'powers' in this quotation, but elsewhere in the article he describes this ability as a power ('Thus, if you acquire powers to make choices *for* another person, you are bound by the requirement of loyalty': ibid 615).

powers remains, in an important sense, with the beneficiary. Miller writes: 'Being derived from the legal personality of another, fiduciary power must be understood as a means belonging rightfully to that other (or her designated beneficiary) for it is but an extension of her legal personality.'[40] In a similar vein, Smith writes: 'Our autonomy belongs to us, in a non-legal sense. The law seeks, so far as it can, to give effect to this.'[41] It further follows for Miller and Smith that just as owners should retain the rights to unauthorized profits made from their property, beneficiaries should retain the rights to any profits that arise from the fiduciary's use of the beneficiary's delegated powers.[42] Stated differently, the powers exercised by the fiduciary are ultimately the beneficiary's powers, and therefore any profits made through the use of these powers are rightly attributed to, or properly held by, the beneficiary. Miller and Smith summarize their arguments as follows:

Where the fiduciary receives an unauthorized profit from the exercise of fiduciary power, she treats the power as a means of her own. Yet, in law, it is a means of the beneficiary. The beneficiary is entitled to have fiduciary power exercised for her benefit alone. The fiduciary is required to avoid conflicts so that nothing might interfere with the exclusivity of her claim. This suggests that the primary right to loyalty should be interpreted as including an implied entitlement to profits realized through the exercise of fiduciary power. The fiduciary is not obliged to produce value for the beneficiary. But to the extent that value is realized, the fiduciary is obliged to see to it that the beneficiary alone receives it.[43]

[T]he fiduciary relationship is characterised by the acquisition by the fiduciary of part of the autonomy—part of the choice-making ability—of the beneficiary. Our autonomy belongs to us, in a non-legal sense. The law seeks, so far as it can, to give effect to this. Thus, when the fiduciary, through the use of the levers of control that he holds over the beneficiary's autonomy, is able to extract some wealth or value, the law ascribes it to the beneficiary as a matter of primary right.[44]

The 'primary-right' explanation of disgorgement is the most sophisticated attempt yet to explain the disgorgement rule. However, it is vulnerable to two objections. The first is that the explanation proves too much. There are countless situations in which individuals are delegated powers to make decisions that normally belong to the delegator, but where those individuals are not required to disgorge profits that they make from their position. When I give my car to a mechanic or hire someone to paint my house or consent to a surgeon operating on me, I delegate decision-making powers that normally belong to me. The mechanic, the painter, and the surgeon are authorized to make choices that, absent the delegation, I would make myself. The same is true of nearly every employment relationship: the employer gets to choose what employees do, where they do it, and when they do it. Yet in none of these cases is the delegate required to disgorge profits that they have made through the exercise of their delegated powers. To be sure, these examples differ in

40 Miller (n 1), 610. 41 Smith (n 1), 628.

42 'Should retain' because aside from the intellectual property cases, defendants who have wrongly used another's property are normally required to pay only the market rental rate (as opposed to disgorging their entire profits): see the cases cited in notes 50, 52, 53.

43 Miller (n 1) 615. 44 Smith (n 1) 628.

important ways from typical fiduciary relationships. The mechanic, the painter, and the surgeon typically have less discretion than fiduciaries with respect to how they use their delegated powers, and that discretion is usually limited to unimportant matters.[45] But they have discretion. The mechanic can choose which of your car's wheels to replace first, the painter can choose to place tape on your walls or not, and the surgeon can decide to tie a ligature more or less tight. Thus, these relationships all share the feature of fiduciary relationships that the primary-right explanation focuses upon: they are situations in which one person has acquired decision-making abilities—powers—that normally belong to another.

The second objection to the primary-right explanation is more general. The primary-right explanation interprets the right to disgorgement as flowing from the fiduciary's acquisition of powers normally belonging to the beneficiary. This acquisition normally arises from a voluntary transfer by the beneficiary or a third-party benefactor, although in some cases it appears to arise from operation of law, either legislative or judge-made. It would be prima facie odd to learn that one of the implications of such a grant was inconsistent with the reasons that the grant was made or with the interests of those whom the grant was meant to serve. Yet the primary-right explanation presumes such an inconsistency. The primary-right explanation supposes that an implication of the grant of power that creates a fiduciary relationship is that the beneficiary retains a primary right to profits arising from the power's exercise. As we have seen, there is typically no reason—aside from the prophylactic reason discussed earlier (and rejected by the present argument)—for those who grant fiduciary powers to fiduciaries to care whether fiduciaries make profits. As I explained earlier, the only thing that most beneficiaries (and benefactors) care about is whether fiduciaries properly perform their mandates. Insofar as beneficiaries care about fiduciaries making profits, they care about them for the same prophylactic reason that (as I have argued) they care about fiduciaries acting in conflict situations. The law takes (or at least should take) the same position.[46]

[45] Lionel Smith argues that roofers are not fiduciaries, and so not bound to act loyally, because their obligations are 'objectively articulated' by a contract: Smith (n 1) 615. However, even roofers have discretion to exercise powers that normally belong to the homeowner. For example, roofers can choose which side of the house to lean a ladder against or which side of the roof to begin removing old shingles. To be sure, homeowners usually do not care how roofers make such choices: all homeowners usually care about is the final result (which is indeed articulated by the contract). This indifference may explain why roofers are not fiduciaries. However, it remains the case that roofers have the power to make choices that normally belong to homeowners.

[46] In contrast to Smith, Miller does not view disgorgement as a consequence or 'encumbrance' of the grant of power, but rather views it as implication of the nature of the fiduciary's primary duty—which he sees as a duty that requires fiduciaries to ensure that their actions only benefit the beneficiary: Miller (n 1), 615. The above objection is therefore ultimately an objection to how Miller understands the fiduciary's duty. Specifically, the objection is that there is no reason—aside from the prophylactic reason—for beneficiaries or the law to want to hold fiduciaries to a duty to avoid making profits, even in cases where that profit is an incidental or even necessary side-effect of actions that maximally promote the beneficiary's interests.

C. Disgorgement as a remedy for breach of the no-conflict duty

If fiduciaries have legal duties not to make unauthorized profits—as I have argued—then the natural explanation of the disgorgement rule is that it stipulates a remedy for the breach of this duty. Disgorgement of profits is admittedly an unusual private law remedy. However, prophylactic duties are not standard private law duties. It is true, as my example of the shipper's promise to avoid the Somali coast illustrates, that there is nothing odd in principle about prophylactic duties. But prophylactic duties are unusual in one important respect: the breach of a prophylactic duty never results in a loss that is not otherwise compensable. By definition, the purpose of a prophylactic duty is to reduce the risk that another duty—the primary duty—will be breached. It follows that any loss that arises from the breach of a prophylactic duty *and* that falls within the prophylactic duty's scope can equally be attributed to a breach of the primary duty. In my shipping example, a breach of the promise to avoid the Somali coast will only cause a compensable loss if it leads to a breach of the duty to deliver by the contractually specified date. Similarly, in the case of a fiduciary breaching a prophylactic no-conflict duty, the only losses arising from such a breach that fall within the duty's scope will be losses that are also attributable to breach of the fiduciary's non-fiduciary duty.

It follows that a consequence of the subsidiary nature of prophylactic duties is that they can be breached without regard to the risk of paying compensatory damages. More generally, insofar as monetary remedies are limited to compensatory awards, the subsidiary nature of prophylactic duties means that they are effectively unenforceable duties: in a world of exclusively compensatory damage awards, prophylactic duties can be breached with impunity. This possibility should give rise to concern. While it is true that many private law duties may be breached in particular circumstances without incurring anything more than a liability to pay nominal damages, it is difficult to think of other private law duties that can be systematically breached without ever incurring a risk of liability that would not otherwise arise. Stated differently, it is difficult to think of private law duties that can consistently be breached with impunity. Fortunately, or at least fortunately for anyone who finds this possibility troubling, private law damages are not always or even primarily compensatory. In brief—a full discussion would require another paper if not a book—while damages for consequential losses arising from a breach of duty are indeed compensatory, damages awarded for the breach of a duty itself are not typically compensatory. Rather, they are an attempt—always imperfect—to put a value on the right.[47] The primary purpose of such damages is to express in tangible terms

[47] I discuss this understanding of damages in more detail in 'Remedies for Breach of Contract: One Principle or Two?' in G Klass, G Letsas, and P Saprai (eds), *Philosophical Foundations of Contract Law* (Oxford University Press, 2014) 341 and 'Duties, Liabilities, and Damages' (2012) 125 Harv L Rev 1727. See also (with some caveats) Robert Stevens, *Torts and Rights* (Oxford University Press, 2007) esp Ch 4; Robert Stevens, 'Damages and the Right to Performance: *A Golden Victory* or Not?' in J Neyers, R Bronaugh, and S Pitel (eds), *Exploring Contract Law* (Oxford University Press, 2009) 171; and (with more caveats and focusing exclusively on tort law), John Goldberg and Benjamin Zipursky, 'Rights and Responsibility in the Law of Torts', in Donal Nolan and Andrew Robertson (eds), *Rights*

that the defendant has wronged the plaintiff and, at the same time, to symbolically redress that wrong.

The most obvious examples of non-compensatory damages are nominal damages, punitive damages, and damages for pain and suffering.[48] Closer to present concerns, the standard award of damages for the loss, destruction, or non-delivery of goods is not compensatory.[49] In such cases, damages for the breach (as opposed to damages for the losses consequential to the breach) are typically set at the good's market value[50]—notwithstanding that in many cases the plaintiff's loss is less than that value.[51] Similarly, the standard award of damages for failing to perform a contractual service is the market cost of providing the performance.[52] And this market price is awarded, exceptional cases aside,[53]regardless of whether the plaintiff has done the work (or will do it) or has otherwise suffered a tangible loss.[54] A third example is the award issued where the defendant has trespassed on the plaintiff's land or used the plaintiff's property. In such cases, the plaintiff is normally awarded the market rental rate—and again this award is normally available regardless of whether it corresponds to the plaintiff's actual loss.[55] In all these cases, the market rate is used not because it equals the plaintiff's loss, but because it is an objective, representative, and proportionate valuation of the right that was infringed. Like statutory criminal fines, the market rate is a way of embodying in tangible form what is ultimately intangible.

Cases in which the infringed right has no market value raise special problems. Short of concluding that the right has no value, the courts must devise another way of valuing the plaintiff's right. The courts have indeed done this, though, perhaps unsurprisingly, their approach has not been perfectly consistent. In cases such as *Wrotham Park Estate Co v Parkside Homes*[56] (breach of a covenant restricting building on purchased land), *Bracewell v Appleby*[57] (trespass on the defendant's road), and *Experience Hendrix LLC v PPX Enterprises Inc*[58] (breach of a contractual promise to return goods), the plaintiff was awarded a portion (though not always the same portion) of the defendant's gain. In contrast, in *Ministry of Defence v*

and Private Law (Hart Publishing, 2011) 251; Benjamin Zipursky, 'Civil Recourse, Not Corrective Justice' (2003) 91 Georgetown LJ 695.

[48] Pain and suffering is not a loss; it is something that victims endure.

[49] This example and the others mentioned in this paragraph are discussed in more detail in Stevens (n 47).

[50] Sale of Goods Act 1979 s 53(3).

[51] See eg, *William Bros v Ed T Agius Ltd* [1914] AC 510.

[52] Eg, *Radford v De Froberville* [1977] 1 WLR 1262.

[53] Eg, *Ruxley Electronics and Construction Ltd v Forsyth* [1996] AC 344.

[54] Eg, *Darlington Borough Council v Wiltshier Northern Ltd* [1995] 1 WLR 68, 80 (Steyn LJ); *Alfred McAlpine Construction Ltd v Panatown Ltd* [2001] 1 AC 518, 557 (Lord Goff). His Lordship held that the intention to do the work was relevant to the reasonableness of the plaintiff's claim, but did not suggest that it was a condition of such a claim.

[55] *Strand Electric Engineering Co Ltd v Brisford Entertainments Ltd* [1952] 2 QB 246; *Penarth Dock Engineering Co Ltd v Pounds* [1963] 1 Lloyd's Rep 359; *Inverugie Investments Ltd v Hackett* [1995] 1 WLR 713.

[56] [1974] 1 WLR 798. [57] [1975] Ch 408. [58] [2003] 1 ALL ER 830.

Ashdown[59] (where the defendant wrongfully occupied Royal Air Force housing) and *Attorney-General v Blake*[60] (where a former MI5 agent published a book in breach of a confidentiality covenant), the plaintiff was awarded the entirety of the defendant's profits. In the recent case of *Lawrence v Fen Tigers*,[61] Lord Neuberger went so far as to suggest that the latter award should generally be considered an appropriate measure of a defendant's property right, or at least of a defendant's right to the reasonable enjoyment of their property:

> It seems to me at least arguable that, where a claimant has a prima facie right to an injunction to restrain a nuisance, and the court decides to award damages instead, those damages should not always be limited to the value of the consequent reduction in the value of the claimant's property. While double counting must be avoided, the damages might well, at least where it was appropriate, also include the loss of the claimant's ability to enforce her rights, which may often be assessed by reference to the benefit to the defendant of not suffering an injunction.[62]

Against this background, an award of profits is a reasonable way for courts to place a value on the beneficiary's right that the fiduciary not make an unauthorized profit. As noted, the breach of this duty will never support a separate award of consequential damages since any losses within the duty's scope can also be attributed to the breach of the fiduciary's non-fiduciary duty. Nor is a market-value approach to assessing damages possible in such cases because there is no market for the actions contemplated by prophylactic duties. On the other hand, an award of profits is an objective and proportionate representation of the infringed right. The award is objective because the sum is not left to a judge's discretion but instead fixed at the measure of the defendant's profits. It is proportionate because by definition it will never exceed the defendant's gain. Further, profits represent or 'embody' the breach in the obvious sense that they represent the very thing that the defendant was meant not to do.[63] Finally, an award of profits is linked to the breach in the sense that they represent the monetary value of the action that the defendant failed to carry out, namely to obtain the beneficiary's consent. As we have seen, acting in a conflict is not intrinsically wrongful: the wrong is (merely) the wrong of not obtaining authorization from the beneficiary. This characterization explains why the no-profit rule is rarely described in terms of a simple duty 'not to profit': the rule is normally described as upholding a duty 'not to make an *unauthorized* profit'. It follows that an award of profits is linked to the duty breached in the sense that it represents the largest amount that the beneficiary might reasonably have been expected to obtain in exchange for authorizing the profit. Of course, the courts usually have

[59] [1993] 32 EGLR 102.
[60] [2001] 1 AC 268. See also *Esso Petroleum Co Ltd v Niad* [2001] All ER (D) 324.
[61] [2014] UKSC 13. [62] Ibid at para 128.
[63] Though he approaches the issue from a different starting point, Ernest Weinrib reaches a similar conclusion when he writes that 'gains can be regarded as the material embodiment of the breach of the duty … Seen in this light, the fiduciary's liability to disgorge profit … [is] the remedial consequence that reflects the nature of the obligation owed by the fiduciary': Ernest J Weinrib, 'Restitutionary Damages as Corrective Justice' (1999) 1 Theor Inq L 1, 33–34.

no way of knowing (and in any event do not ask) whether the beneficiary would have demanded the profits in exchange for authorization or whether the beneficiary would have agreed to authorize profits at all. In many cases, the beneficiaries undoubtedly would not have authorized the conflict. However, the possibility that such a deal could have been struck means that an award of profits can play a broadly similar role to that played by the market rate awards in the cases discussed earlier. It is an objective, proportionate, and representative valuation of the beneficiary's right to refuse authorization. Unless the law is to allow such rights to be breached with impunity, it must place a value on them. To be consistent with the rule of law, that value must be objectively ascertained. Finally, fairness demands that the value be broadly proportionate to the wrong. In the unusual case of prophylactic duties, the breaching party's profit is a reasonable valuation of the plaintiff's right.[64]

VII. Fiduciary Law as Contract Law

A final implication of my analysis of loyalty is that fiduciary law should be understood, in most cases anyway, as a branch of contract law, broadly understood.[65] Prophylactic duties are by definition subsidiary in the sense that they exist to protect another 'primary' duty. In the case of the no-conflict rule (understood here to include the no-profit rule) the primary duty is typically a contractual duty, again broadly understood. Most fiduciary relationships are straightforwardly contractual in the sense that the fiduciaries are contractually obliged to fulfil their mandate. But even where the fiduciary's mandate is not contractual in the strict sense (say because the fiduciary is not paid), it is normally contractual in the broad sense, in that it was voluntarily undertaken. The vast majority of fiduciaries voluntarily undertake to perform the mandates that the no-conflict duty protects. In Millet J's oft-quoted words from *Bristol & West Building Society v Mothew*:[66] 'A fiduciary is someone who has undertaken to act for and on behalf of another in a particular matter in circumstances which give rise to a relationship of trust and confidence.'[67]

The observation that fiduciaries typically undertake their mandates does not prove that fiduciary duties—and specifically no-conflict duties—are themselves

[64] I am unaware of non-fiduciary cases where courts have directly addressed the issue of damages for breach of a prophylactic duty. However, I suspect—and here I am arguing against interest—that if cases existed in which the courts had awarded a gain-based remedy for the breach of a prophylactic duty, they would be well-known. The famous, or perhaps infamous, decision in *City of New Orleans v Firemen's Charitable Association*, 9 So 486 (1891)—in which the defendants' breach of a contractual duty to keep ready a certain number of horses, carts, etc. for the purpose of fighting fires did not lead to a loss—is the closest example of breach of a prophylactic duty that comes to mind. The plaintiff was awarded only nominal damages.

[65] Other supporters of this view include Edelman (n 3); Frank H Easterbrook and Daniel R Fischel, 'Contract and Fiduciary Duty' (1994) 36 JL & Econ 425; John H Langbein, 'The Contractarian Basis of the Law of Trusts' (1995) 105 Yale LJ 625; Robert H Sitkoff, 'The Economic Structure of Fiduciary Law' (2011) 91 BUL Rev 1039.

[66] [1998] Ch 1, 18.

[67] See also *Galambos v Perez*, 2009 SCC 48; Conaglen (n 2) 257; Virgo (n 1) 484.

typically voluntarily undertaken. It may be that in most cases the no-conflict duties are similar to mandatory implied-in-law contractual duties (for example, an employer's mandatory duties to provide vacation time) and, as such, are contractual only in the sense that their existence depends upon, and that they are implied into, contracts or at least into voluntary undertakings. However, it seems reasonable to assume that in most cases in which fiduciaries undertake their mandates voluntarily the no-conflict duty is also voluntarily undertaken. The argument for this assumption is developed in detail by James Edelman in a recent paper,[68] so I will restrict myself to four supporting comments.

First, a term may be implied 'in fact' into an undertaking notwithstanding that the relevant party did not have that term in mind when making the undertaking or, indeed, that the party had never given the term any thought at all. The implication of in fact terms is part of the broader task of interpreting the meaning of what has been said or otherwise communicated. This task is an objective exercise. The meaning of an undertaking is established by what the undertaking is reasonably understood to mean, not what the relevant party subjectively intended or was thinking at the time.[69] Thus, when determining whether a term should be implied in fact into an undertaking, the question, broadly understood, is whether, given the context of the negotiations and the particular aims of the undertaking, such a term might be said to 'go without saying'.

Second, what must go without saying for the no-conflict duty to qualify a term that is implied in fact is the nature of the duty; not the remedy for its breach. This distinction must be stressed. Indeed, some commentators have criticized the idea of implied in fact fiduciary duties on the basis that parties would not voluntarily subscribe to the stringent remedies attached to breach of the no-conflict duty.[70]

Third, it is reasonable to assume that a requirement to obtain the beneficiary's consent before acting in a conflict of interest would indeed 'go without saying' in most cases where the fiduciary's mandate is voluntarily undertaken. The principle that one should seek authorization before acting in a conflict situation is commonplace. Individuals who agree to judge or referee a competition would typically consider it a matter of course that they should notify the relevant authority if they learn that a family member will take part in the competition. If the parties to a fiduciary relationship were asked directly whether the fiduciary should be allowed to act in a conflict of interest without authorization, they would almost always give a negative answer. Further, even in cases where they would give an affirmative answer, it would be rare that such an answer would have been expected (and therefore rare that it would follow as a matter of interpreting the undertaking).

Finally, even if it cannot be assumed that the no-conflict duty can be implied in fact into every voluntary fiduciary relationship, it is not unreasonable for the law to presume such an implication. The obvious advantage of such a presumption is

[68] Edelman (n 3).

[69] Hilary Putnam, 'Meaning and Reference' (1973) 70 J of Philosophy 699; Stephen A Smith, *Contract Theory* (Oxford University Press 2004) 271–74.

[70] Eg, Conaglen (n 2) 217.

that it saves the parties—and more importantly the courts—from having to make detailed inquiries in every case as to whether the implied in fact duty arises on the facts. Unless the parties say otherwise—and of course the parties are free to say otherwise—the effect of such a presumption is that it will be assumed (for the reasons described earlier) that they implicitly agreed to the duty. The law frequently presumes in fact implications of this kind.[71] The warranty implied by Section 39(1) of the Marine Insurance Act, 1906 that a ship for which insurance is sought is seaworthy merely gives statutory form to a warranty that had long routinely been implied in fact into most marine insurance contracts. Similarly, most of the non-mandatory implied terms in the Sale of Goods Act 1979 are terms that courts had routinely implied in fact into most contracts of sale prior to the passing of the original Sale of Goods Act and which courts would have continued to routinely imply whether or not the Act was passed. It goes without saying that in a normal sales contract the goods will be of 'satisfactory quality' and that the vendor will 'deliver the goods'. Indeed, most non-mandatory statutorily implied terms are similar: they are generalized versions of individualized implied in fact terms. The terms in such cases are implied as a matter of law, but the basis for the implication is the factual presumption that the parties in such cases will in fact have normally agreed, albeit implicitly, to them.

VIII. Non-Contractual Fiduciaries

It is obviously not possible to explain no-conflict duties as implied in fact contractual terms in cases where the entire fiduciary relationship is involuntary. Exactly how many fiduciary relationships fall into this category is a matter for debate, but most courts and commentators assume that at least some fiduciary relationships are of this kind.[72] In such cases, the no-conflict duty is not subsidiary to a contractual duty, so it should not be classified as contractual. Whether the duty is classified as 'tortious', or 'equitable', or simply imposed by law depends on how the fiduciary's primary mandate is explained.

The conclusion that no-conflict duties may be contractual or extra-contractual depending on the circumstances is consistent with the duty's prophylactic nature. By definition, prophylactic duties are subsidiary to other duties; thus, it follows that their proper classification depends, in every case, on the classification of the primary duty.

However, the possibility of extra-contractual no-conflict duties might be thought to raise a different objection to this chapter's arguments. In Section IV I introduced the example of a shipper's promise not to travel by the Somali coast to show that there is nothing odd in principle about prophylactic duties. But I also noted

[71] See Stephen Smith (n 69) 309–10.

[72] See eg, Lionel Smith (n 1) 615; Virgo (n 1) 482. However, it is difficult to identify non-controversial examples.

that it might be thought that there is something odd, indeed something objectionable, about non-contractual prophylactic duties. Contracting parties are generally free to agree to whatever duties they choose. But it might be thought improper for the law, or at least for the private law, to *impose* duties on individuals to avoid doing things that merely lead to a risk of injury. Prophylactic duties, it might be thought, are like pre-emptive interferences with liberty: they impose duties on persons to avoid doing things that, it may well turn out, are not wrongs in any sense of the word. Further, such duties might be thought inconsistent with the positive law of tort. Although engaging in risky behaviour increases the risk that others will be injured, it is not possible, according to the conventional view, to commit the tort of negligence without injuring the plaintiff. Similarly, it is not a tort to put oneself in a position where one is likely to commit a trespass (say by riding one's bicycle on the very edge of another property): the tort of trespass is not committed unless one actually trespasses. It is true that it is possible, in the appropriate circumstances, to obtain an injunction—a 'quia timet' or 'preventative' injunction—that commands the defendant not to engage in an activity that, while not wrongful in itself, is likely to lead to a wrong in the near future. For example, a court might order a defendant to repair a wall that is in danger of falling onto the plaintiff's property.[73] Such injunctions are prophylactic. However, they are rare and conventionally understood as part of remedial law, not substantive law.[74] In short, notwithstanding that there are many things that individuals could do to avoid being in positions where they are likely to injure others, commit trespasses, and so on, it appears that the substantive private law never imposes duties to avoid being in such positions.

This objection invites two possible responses. The first is simply to accept that imposed-in-law prophylactic duties cannot be justified. If this response is adopted then it follows that this chapter's arguments do not account for all fiduciary duties, as currently understood. Whether this admission is sufficient reason to reject a theory of fiduciary law based on these arguments depends on the frequency of non-contractual fiduciary relationships and the centrality of such relationships to our understanding of fiduciary law. I won't attempt to answer any of these questions here, but my sense is that the number of truly involuntary fiduciaries is relatively small and that these instances are not generally regarded as core examples of fiduciary law.[75] Further, it is far from clear whether the no-conflict rules do or should apply in these cases. In Canada, the parent–child relationship is held to be fiduciary (and is frequently cited to show the possibility of non-contractual fiduciaries),[76] but so far as I am aware the no-conflict rules have never been be applied to parents. Indeed, it is not clear how they could be applied: parents must constantly balance their own interests (in their jobs, relationships, hobbies, and so on) against those of their children. These observations are not meant to deny that non-contractual

[73] See eg, *Hooper v Rogers* [1975] Ch 3.

[74] Not everyone agrees with this classification. In particular, Peter Birks and other scholars who accept that traditional civil law view that judicial orders necessarily replicate substantive duties must believe that quia timet orders replicate prophylactic duties: Peter Birks, *English Private Law* (Oxford University Press, 2000) xxxvi.

[75] See Penner (n 1) 244–48; Virgo (n 1) 482–85.

[76] *M(K) v M(H)* [1992] 3 SCR 6.

fiduciaries owe duties to act, broadly speaking, in the beneficiaries' best interests. The question is whether the strict no-conflict duty should apply in such cases.

The other possible response, toward which I am inclined, though I cannot fully defend it here, is to argue that imposed-in-law prophylactic duties are defensible in principle.[77] As noted earlier, the common law has long recognized the possibility of prophylactic court orders. Further, it is arguable that the substantive law implicitly recognizes prophylactic duties. Consider again the tort of negligence. As noted earlier, it is not possible according to the conventional view to commit the tort of negligence unless one inflicts an injury on another. It follows, in this view, that the 'negligence duty' must be understood as a duty 'not to commit harm through failing to take proper care to try not to commit harm.' This formulation only needs to be said out loud to appreciate its oddness. On the one hand, insofar as the duty is meant to provide a guide for conduct, the requirement of 'not committing harm' is superfluous. From the perspective of guiding conduct, a duty 'to try not to commit harm' is identical to a duty 'not to commit harm through failing to try'. Adding the qualification that one should not commit harm to the first duty is superfluous since we cannot control whether our efforts to avoid harm are successful. The conduct-lesson to draw from each duty is identical: one should try not to commit harm.

On the other hand, insofar as the duty is meant to identify wrongful actions, there is a straightforward sense in which failing to try properly to avoid harming another is a wrong regardless of whether harm occurs. If I carelessly expose you to a serious risk, then I fail to treat you with proper, that is to say equal, concern and respect. For example, if I carelessly fire a gun in your direction then I have placed my interest in firing guns above your interest in bodily safety. Indeed, what makes firing a gun in your direction unreasonable is that it shows that I do not treat your interest in bodily integrity as worthy of respect. And such actions show disrespect regardless of whether I actually harm you. To be sure, if I do harm you, and then subsequently fail to apologize or attempt to repair the harm, I will have shown you further disrespect. Further, the fact that one has breached a duty to try not to harm another need not, standing alone, attract sanctions or liability of any kind. It is perfectly reasonable for the law to say that while failing to take reasonable care is a wrong, it should only attract liability in the case that it leads to actual harm.[78] Nonetheless, my failing to take care to try not to harm you, regardless of its outcome, is itself a distinct way of failing to show you proper respect and concern.[79]

[77] I explore the issues discussed below in more detail in S Smith, 'Duties to Try and Duties to Succeed' in A Dyson, J Goudkamp, and F Wilmot-Smith (eds), *Defences in Tort* (Hart Publishing, 2015) 63.

[78] See ibid 73.

[79] There is also a straightforward sense in which harming another, regardless of whether one caused the harm carelessly or intentionally, is a wrong. Suppose that through no fault of my own I run over your foot with my car. The blamelessness of my action does not change the fact that it would have been better had I not run over your foot. There is a straightforward sense in which we can say that I ought not to have run over your foot. Stated differently, there is a straightforward sense in which I have committed a 'wrong'. This sense is what is intended when we say that we took a 'wrong turn' when driving or that we took the 'wrong' umbrella from a stand—notwithstanding that our actions were, in the circumstances, entirely blameless. These actions are wrongs because they bring about the wrong

It is arguable, therefore, that the basic duty recognized by the tort of negligence is prophylactic: it is a duty to take reasonable care to try not to harm another. On this view, the fact that one caused harm is relevant only at the stage of assessing liability. Fiduciaries' duties to seek authorization before acting in conflict situations may be similar in this regard. A fiduciary who fails to obtain such authorization fails to treat the beneficiary with proper respect. Where the fiduciary profits from that failure it is not unreasonable to hold him or her liable for that profit.

These observations only skim the surface of a deep and complex issue. However, they are sufficient to cast doubt on the assumption that the law never does, and never should, recognize imposed-by-law prophylactic duties.

IX. Conclusion

In this chapter, I have argued that fiduciary law is unconcerned with loyalty, or at least that it is unconcerned with loyalty as this concept is normally understood. Of course, the law frequently attaches special meanings to ordinary words. But in this case, the difference is at once large and easy to miss. The law is not merely unconcerned with whether fiduciaries act as loyal fiduciaries would act; in most cases it is not possible for fiduciaries to act loyally—or disloyally—even if they wanted to. At the same time, courts and commentators rarely indicate that they are employing 'loyalty' in a special—and especially denuded—sense. What they say, typically without qualification, is that a concern for loyalty lies at the core of fiduciary law. Consciously or not, such statements invite us to try to understand fiduciary law using ideas that are tied to loyalty's ordinary meaning. And since loyalty, in the ordinary understanding, has little in common with the concepts that courts normally employ when they decide private law disputes, such statements invite us to explain fiduciary law using ideas that are rarely employed by private law scholars. Firmly rejecting this invitation, this chapter has asked how we might explain the main features of fiduciary law if we begin by acknowledging clearly that fiduciary law has nothing to do with loyalty. The end result is admittedly less inspiring—or at least is couched in less-inspiring language—than some accounts of fiduciary law. However, it has the advantage of fidelity to the law, or so I hope to have shown.

outcome. The puzzling feature of the duty in negligence, as conventionally understood, is therefore not its focus on outcomes or its focus on efforts to avoid an outcome: the puzzling feature is that the tort of negligence combines an 'outcome wrong' with an 'effort wrong': see Stephen Smith (n 77), 76–79.

10

Triangular Torts and Fiduciary Duties

John CP Goldberg and Benjamin C Zipursky***

I. Introduction

A century ago, *MacPherson v Buick* held that a manufacturer is obligated to be vigilant of the life and limb of a consumer of its products even absent privity between them.[1] Across the US, the privity rule fell quickly. In 1941, William Prosser reported that *MacPherson* had been widely accepted.[2] In 1960, he declared it to be the law of every state.[3]

In fact, Prosser saw in *MacPherson* a deeper and broader lesson. It had not merely jettisoned a narrow rendering of the duty owed by manufacturers to consumers. It had rejected the idea that 'duty'—as that term is normally understood—plays a meaningful role in the tort of negligence.[4]

On the surface, of course, Cardozo's opinion held that Buick owed MacPherson a duty of care. But this was just a nod to the traditional language of the law. What Cardozo (supposedly) had come to realize is that the 'duty' question has little or nothing to do with obligation and everything to do with 'policy'. The duty element, on this view, is but a placeholder that gives judges the opportunity to determine whether policy considerations favour or disfavour the imposition of negligence liability in a particular class of cases. With the 'true' nature of the duty question exposed, Prosser looked forward to the day when courts would put aside the narrow, moralistic question of whether a certain kind of actor owed vigilance to a potential

* Eli Goldston Professor of Law, Harvard Law School.

** Professor of Law and James H Quinn '49 Chair, Fordham University School of Law. For very helpful comments on earlier drafts, thanks to Andrew Gold, Bruce Green, Scott Hershovitz, Ethan Leib, David Luban, Michael M Martin, Paul Miller, Russell Pearce, and Victor Tadros, and to the participants in the Contract, Status and Fiduciary Law Conference held at McGill University in November 2015.

[1] 111 N.E. 1050 (N.Y. 1916).

[2] William L Prosser, *Handbook of the Law of Torts* (West Publishing, 1941) 678.

[3] William L Prosser, 'The Assault Upon the Citadel (Strict Liability to the Consumer)' (1960) 69 Yale LJ 1099, 1100. Prosser allowed that there was some uncertainty as to whether two states had fully embraced *MacPherson*. Ibid.

[4] See John CP Goldberg and Benjamin C Zipursky, 'The Moral of *MacPherson*' (1998) 146 U Pa L Rev 1733, 1762–69.

victim, and instead would ask whether, on balance, society would be well-served by allowing or blocking negligence liability for recurring injury-producing scenarios.

Things both have and have not played out as Prosser might have hoped. Following the example set by the California Supreme Court in the 1950s and 60s,[5] courts routinely talk the Prosserian talk.[6] But they do not consistently walk the walk. Duty remains an element of negligence in all US jurisdictions. And it is neither a formality, nor—despite judicial rhetoric to the contrary—does it operate exclusively or even typically as a 'hook' for macro-level policy analysis.[7] A plaintiff who sues for negligent infliction of emotional distress might well find her claim dismissed on the ground that the defendant was *not obligated* to take steps to avoid distressing her. Whether society is, on balance, well served by such a liability limitation is rarely if ever the driving force behind such a decision. The same is true for a plaintiff who sues for negligence causing economic loss, as well as for negligent failures to warn, rescue, or protect.

The continued centrality of duty to negligence is also on display in claims brought against professionals. For there is a stark contrast in how courts treat, on the one hand, claims brought by a patient against her physician or a client against her lawyer and, on the other hand, a claim brought by a nonpatient or a nonclient. When a patient sues her doctor for negligence, the doctor will have almost no hope of prevailing on a no-duty argument. Yet such an argument has a good chance of prevailing when the plaintiff is not a patient. In other words, something like the privity limitation is alive and well as the default rule in cases of professional misconduct that injures third parties. We will refer to these cases as *triangular torts*.[8] While plaintiffs sometimes win triangular tort cases—*Tarasoff* being perhaps the most famous example[9]—they tend to lose on the ground that the defendant did not owe them a duty of care.

As scholars who have been keen to defend the place of duty in negligence law against Prosserian efforts at deconstruction, we might be expected to be positively inclined toward cases that continue to recognize no-duty limitations on negligence. Alas, matters are not so simple for us. As we read it, the basic lesson of

[5] See John C P Goldberg and Benjamin C Zipursky, 'Shielding Duty: How Attending to Assumption of Risk, Attractive Nuisance, and Other "Quaint" Doctrines Can Improve Decisionmaking in Negligence Cases' (2006) 79 S Cal L Rev 329, 329–30.

[6] Thus, it is routine for modern courts to begin their analysis of duty questions by asserting that duty raises a question of policy, and by invoking Prosser's quip about duty not being 'sacrosanct in itself'. See Prosser (n 2) at 180 ('[D]uty is not sacrosanct in itself, but only an expression of the sum total of those considerations of policy which lead the law to say that the particular plaintiff is entitled to protection').

[7] John CP Goldberg and Benjamin C Zipursky, 'The Restatement (Third) and the Place of Duty in Negligence Law' (2001) 54 Vand L Rev 657.

[8] Although this chapter will focus on triangular tort claims against medical providers, it will also examine under that same rubric certain claims against attorneys. See Section III, *infra*. In a well-known article published almost thirty years ago, Professor Hazard examined what he referred to as 'triangular' lawyer relationships. Geoffrey Hazard, 'Triangular Lawyer Relationships: An Exploratory Analysis' (1987) 1 Geo J Leg Ethics 15.

[9] *Tarasoff v Regents of the University of California*, 551 P.2d 334 (Cal. 1976) (recognizing a duty owed by a treating therapist to take steps to warn an identifiable third party of a patient's intention to harm the third party).

MacPherson—much like the lesson of *Heaven v Pender*[10] before it, and *Donoghue v Stevenson*[11] after it—is that the question of whether one is obligated to be vigilant of another person's well-being does not turn exclusively or even primarily on the directness of one's relationship to them, does not turn on status, and does not turn on contract. Thus for us, as for most other scholars, negligence decisions that adopt or maintain something like a privity limitation on duty warrant scepticism.

Still, this scepticism can be overcome. The abandonment of privity in the context of liability for injuries caused by carelessly made products might be fully consistent with continued reliance on privity in the professional malpractice context. The key question—one to which we have not given adequate attention—is whether there are special considerations at work in malpractice law that warrant a departure from the now well-entrenched notion that the duty of care is something we owe to others as 'neighbours' (to use Lord Atkin's famous turn of phrase in *Donoghue*) or fellow human beings.

Perhaps fittingly, given the context in which we are writing, we conclude that the maintenance of privity-like rules in the malpractice setting is defensible, and that the key to their justifiability—as well as to an appreciation of their proper limits—resides in the recognition that professionals owe *fiduciary duties* to those who retain them. The fiduciary aspects of the doctor–patient relationship go a long way toward explaining why a physician's obligation of vigilance only stretches so far.

In Section I we present a triangular tort scenario that has given rise to a number of appellate decisions. In this scenario, a child (an adolescent or young adult daughter, typically), through therapy, purports to recover memories of sexual abuse at the hands of a parent. The child's parent (or parents), insisting that the 'memories' are false, sues the therapist for harming the parent(s) through negligent treatment of the child. Courts faced with these cases have split on the question of whether, in such situations, the therapist owed a duty of care to the parent(s), though a majority has concluded that no such duty is owed.

Section II demonstrates that the tendency of courts to conclude that a therapist does not owe a duty of care to her patient's parents is consistent with a larger though admittedly complex pattern of decisions concerning duties owed by physicians to non-patients. This pattern in turn reflects the idea that the fiduciary aspect of the physician–patient relationship frequently—but not inevitably—precludes the recognition of certain duties of care to non-patients. It is *because* professionals owe heightened solicitude for the relevant interests of their patient or client that they are generally deemed not to owe conflicting duties of care to others.

Section III suggests that a similar pattern, with a similar explanation, can be found in decisions concerning the duties of lawyers to non-clients. Finally, in Section IV, we address the significance of the foregoing analysis from a jurisprudential point of view, examining whether judicial reasoning about duty is best understood on instrumental or non-instrumental terms.

[10] 11 Q.B.D. 503 (Eng. C.A. 1883). More precisely, we refer here to MR Brett's opinion in *Heaven*.

[11] [1932] AC 562.

II. Parent–Therapist Cases

Roberts v Salmi, a case that the Michigan Supreme Court first agreed to hear but then, after oral argument, declined to decide, illustrates a now frequently litigated triangular tort claim.[12]

Lale and Joan Roberts discovered that a friend of the family had engaged in inappropriate sexual contact with their 17-year-old daughter K. In response, they arranged for Salmi to provide counselling to K. Almost as soon as the counselling began, K claimed to remember that her father, Lale, had sexually abused her. After arranging a group counselling session at which K confronted her parents with the allegations of abuse, Salmi reported the allegations to the Michigan Department of Human Services ('DHS'). DHS and State Police investigated, but concluded that there was no evidence of abuse, and no basis for taking action against Lale or Joan.

Lale and Joan sued Salmi, alleging that Salmi breached a duty owed to them to 'not improperly implant, or reinforce false memories of physical and sexual abuse in K's mind by use of hypnosis, age regression and other psychotherapy techniques.'[13] Their complaint further alleged that, as a result of Salmi's treatment, K had severed all ties with them, caused them to be subjected to civil and criminal investigations, and harmed their standing in their community. Salmi responded by denying that she used hypnosis, repressed or recovered memory therapy, or other suggestive techniques. She also argued that, under Michigan common law, she owed a duty of care only to K, not to K's parents.

The trial court dismissed the parents' claim as a matter of law on no-duty grounds. However, the Michigan Court of Appeals—the state's intermediate appellate court—reversed, holding 'that a mental health professional owes a duty of care to his or her patient's parents arising from the treatment of the patient'.[14] Salmi took an interlocutory appeal to the Michigan Supreme Court, and, in September 2015, that court agreed to review the lower court's decision. However, after briefing and oral argument, the high court in May 2016 vacated its decision to entertain the appeal.

As noted, *Roberts* is by no means the first US case involving parents who sue their child's therapist for damage allegedly arising from the therapist having negligently induced the child to make false allegations of sexual abuse. Of the seven state high courts to have addressed the issue, five (Connecticut, Illinois, Maine, Pennsylvania, and Texas) have held that a therapist does *not* owe a duty of care to a patient's parents, whereas two (New Hampshire and Wisconsin) have held that the therapist does owe the parents such a duty. If one counts intermediate appellate courts that have addressed the same issue, and state supreme courts addressing closely related issues, a similar pattern is found: a majority leans against finding a duty, while a non-trivial minority is willing to recognize a duty of care owed to parents.

The Michigan appellate court's analysis of the duty issue in *Roberts* begins on the now-standard Prosserian note: 'the ultimate inquiry in determining whether a legal

[12] 866 N.W.2d 460 (Mich. App. 2014), appeal granted, 868 N.W.2d 911 (Mich. 16 September 2015), order granting appeal vacated, 877 N.W.2d 903 (Mich. 6 May 2016).

[13] Ibid at 464 (quoted source not identified).

[14] Ibid at 473.

duty should be imposed is whether the social benefits of imposing a duty outweigh the social costs of imposing a duty.'[15] However, the court, like most courts, quickly qualified this crudely instrumentalist formulation by identifying a list of relevant policy 'factors' that gives prominence to considerations that have little to do with social benefits and costs, and a lot to do with the question of obligation. In particular, the court indicated that it would give great weight to 'the relationship of the parties [and] the foreseeability of the harm …'[16]

The court's application of the relationship factor—although murky and inconsistent—came to a plausible conclusion: while something like privity sets the rule of duty for physicians and other health care providers, it is a rule that has tolerated and can tolerate exceptions. The court's lengthier discussion of the foreseeability factor provided it with an opportunity to review the entire genre of recovered memory therapy (RMT).

> As there developed a heightened awareness of the prevalence of child sexual abuse, some mental health professionals began to subscribe to the position that a wide variety of problems, such as sleep and eating disorders, had their origin with repressed memories of sexual abuse during childhood. These mental health professionals adopted the theory—referred to as 'recovered memory theory'—that persons suffering from these disorders can best be helped by awakening the dormant memories through recovered memory therapy and then confronting their abusers. Therapists who subscribe to this theory might employ a wide range of tools—including drugs, hypnosis, guided fantasy, automatic writing, support groups, suggestion, interpersonal pressure, and appeals to authority—in order to cause the patient to recover the memories of sexual abuse, if the patient has no memory of abuse.[17]

After indicating that a variety of experts have cast doubt upon the legitimacy and reliability of RMT, the court concluded that it is entirely foreseeable that the use of such techniques carries a risk that parents will be falsely accused of abuse and will suffer serious harms as a result.

With foreseeability squared away, and with the absence of a direct relationship between therapist and parent deemed not fatal to the parents' claim, the court next considered relevant policy considerations. In particular, it considered whether recognition of a duty to the parents might unduly interfere with the performance of the therapist's duty to her patient, or might generate too many false negative diagnoses, with resulting harm to misdiagnosed patients and others.

While acknowledging that a therapist under duties both to patients and parents might face conflicting incentives, the court concluded that the conflict was manageable and warranted in light of the foreseeability and severity of the harm accompanying false memories of sexual abuse. The court reached this conclusion largely on the assumption that therapists can discharge their duties to parents merely by avoiding resort to demonstrably unreliable therapy methods. Thus, even given the recognition of the duty owed to parents, a therapist would still

[15] Ibid at 465. [16] Ibid (quoted authority omitted).
[17] Ibid at 467 (citations omitted).

have the full array of therapeutic techniques at his or her disposal, subject only to the duty to treat his or her patient in a way that minimizes the risk that the patient will develop false memories of childhood sexual abuse ... While the burden on a mental health professional can be minimized with a carefully crafted duty, the failure to recognize that duty might encourage the continued use of questionable therapeutic techniques on uninformed patients. This might continue despite the fact that there is plainly no social benefit to the creation of a false memory in a patient.[18]

The Michigan court's weighing of policy considerations followed closely the New Hampshire Supreme Court's analysis in its 1998 *Hungerford* opinion:

Imposing a duty of care on therapists who elect to publicize accusations of sexual abuse against parents, or who encourage patients to do so, should not unreasonably inhibit sexual abuse diagnosis or therapy. Recognizing such a duty where parents are implicated, however, should result in greater protection for parents and families from unqualified or unaccepted therapeutic diagnoses. While imposition of this duty may impair societal efforts to bring some sexual abusers to justice, we recognize its need due to the increased foreseeability and devastating consequences of publicized false accusations against parents.[19]

In *Sawyer v Midlefort*,[20] Wisconsin's Supreme Court also followed New Hampshire's lead, concluding that 'none of the public policy considerations identified by the defendants should preclude the imposition of liability in this case.'[21]

Contrary to *Roberts, Hungerford*, and *Sawyer*, the majority of state high courts who have engaged in policy-balancing on the question of a therapist's duty to a patient's parents have concluded that policy considerations favour a finding of no duty. The reasoning of the Pennsylvania Supreme Court's *Althous* decision is representative:

There are certainly compelling arguments that a person falsely accused of child abuse should have a remedy in law and our decision today would not prevent all such actions against liable parties. However, the societal interest in encouraging treatment of child abuse victims and maintaining the trust and confidentiality within the therapist/patient relationship dictates against the imposition of a duty of care beyond that owed to the patient.[22]

Similarly, the Supreme Court of Texas, in *Bird v W.C.W.*,[23] concluded that any harm to patients' parents is outweighed by the superior abuse prevention that can be expected to follow from greater abuse detection, which in turn can be expected to follow from a no-duty rule that grants mental health professionals broad leeway to diagnose abuse.[24]

[18] Ibid at 472. [19] *Hungerford v Jones*, 722 A.2d 478, 482 (N.H. 1998).
[20] *Sawyer v Midlefort*, 595 N.W.2d 423, 435 (Wisc. 1999) (citing and quoting *Hungerford*).
[21] Ibid at 436.
[22] *Althaus v Cohen*, 756 A.2d 1166, 1171 (Pa. 2000) (footnotes and citation omitted).
[23] *Bird v W.C.W.*, 868 S.W.2d 767, 769 (Tex. 1994). [24] Ibid.

III. Healthcare Professionals and Triangular Torts

A. The place of fiduciary duty

1. The problem

For reasons we will explain, we believe that the majority position—rejecting parental claims of negligence against their child's therapist—is correct. Yet even if the majority rule were to take hold in more jurisdictions, we might still be troubled. The problem would not be with the prevailing rule of law but with the reasoning that courts have employed to reach it.

Whether recognizing or refusing to recognize a duty owed by a therapist to a patient's parents, courts have purported to resolve the issue on the basis of consequentialist judgement as to which of the two following scenarios is preferable: (i) a world in which therapists experience fewer conflicts between duties and face less litigation, and in which sexual abuse is likely to be more often reported and treated; or (ii) a world in which parents enjoy greater protection from, and redress against, false accusations, and in which therapists are likely to be better incentivized to use more reliable treatment methods. In our view, there is another way—and a better way—to decide these cases: one that is less indeterminate and more consistent with the judicial role. We will elaborate upon it throughout the remainder of this Section.

2. The relationship between healthcare professionals and patients

We begin with a characterization of the physician–patient relationship and other, similar relationships. Two preliminaries are in order. First, we will assume that, in describing the physician–patient relationship, we are offering a serviceable model not just for medical doctors and psychiatrists, but also for clinical psychologists and trained therapists—hence our use of the phrase 'healthcare professionals'.[25] Second, this characterization aims in the first instance to be sociological rather than a description of the legal rights and duties attending these relationships. For now, we aspire to give a rough description of ordinary, everyday understandings of the physician–patient relationship. (Obviously, however, legal rules governing this relationship have had, and continue to have, a significant influence on those understandings.)

Physicians hold themselves out to be uniquely qualified to be entrusted with the essential task of attending to their patients' physical and mental wellbeing. On this basis, patients place a trust and confidence in their physicians that goes well beyond

[25] Our description is obviously of an ideal type. Moreover, we do not mean to suggest that by including 'clinical psychologists and trained psychological therapists' we have exhausted the category of healthcare professionals (eg, nurse practitioners). Nor do we assume that the generic description of the physician–patient relationship offered in this section applies without qualification to all such professionals.

the trust and confidence they place in other persons with whom they regularly or repeatedly interact. Physicians come to know things about their patients that few others do, including even close family members. They often interact with patients on terms that are intimate and embarrassing.

These common understandings include a picture of the duties physicians owe to patients. Most familiar, perhaps, is the duty to provide competent care. In addition, however, the physician is under duties that are fairly characterized as fiduciary, though other terms are sometimes used to describe them.[26] These include a duty to maintain confidentiality, and, more fundamentally, a duty of scrupulous attention to the wellbeing of the patient.

The latter duty—which is sometimes described as a duty of loyalty—manifests itself in various ways. Patients do not regard physicians as self-abnegating altruists. Nonetheless, they expect their physicians to be committed, if not devoted, to their best interests. Though a physician is entitled to fair compensation for services rendered, she may not place her financial self-interest above the interests of her patient. A physician who, for her own profit, induces her patient to undergo an entirely harmless but unnecessary treatment has acted unprofessionally. By contrast, a prospective seller in an arm's length commercial transaction—so long as he does not use misrepresentations or other unfair practices—is free to encourage a buyer to buy something that the seller knows will be of no use to the buyer (or, in some cases, even harmful to the buyer).

A physician is likewise required to be highly attentive to the possibility of abusing or exploiting a patient's trust and gratitude. Even absent coercion or undue influence, a physician must refrain from sexual relations with a patient. More mundanely, a physician ought not to accept a gift from a patient beyond a modest token of appreciation.

In contrasting a physician's duty of competence with her fiduciary duties, we do not mean to suggest that these constitute mutually exclusive categories. The same conduct might simultaneously be a breach of the duty of competent care and a breach of fiduciary duty. A disturbing example of this sort of overlap is *Norberg v Wynrib*.[27] The plaintiff, a young woman addicted to painkillers, acceded to the defendant-physician's demands for sexual favours in return for receiving the drugs she craved. While the Canadian Supreme Court Justices disagreed as to how to characterize the defendant's wrong, it seems to have been both flagrant malpractice (an utter failure to provide competent medical care) and a flagrant breach of fiduciary duty (a physician using his office—including his privilege to dispense medication—to pursue base self-interest in disregard of the patient's well-being).

[26] See, eg, Peter Bartlett, 'Doctors as Fiduciaries: Equitable Regulation of the Doctor–Patient Relationship' (1997) 5 Med L Rev 193; Maxwell J Mehlman, 'Why Physicians are Fiduciaries for their Patients' (2015) 12 Ind Health L Rev 1; Michelle Oberman, 'Mothers and Doctors' Orders: Unmasking the Doctor's Fiduciary Role in Maternal-Fetal Conflicts' (2000) 94 Nw U L Rev 451.

[27] [1992] 2 SCR 266 (SCC).

3. The core claim

Returning now to triangular torts, and to the therapist cases in particular, we can state our core claim. *Given settled understandings of the therapist–patient relationship as including a duty of loyalty to the patient, the therapist is not correctly described as owing a duty of care to parents.* It is part and parcel of these understandings that licensed psychiatrists—and, by extension, clinical psychologists as well as licensed therapists who hold themselves out to be trained professionals providing individualized treatment of psychological problems—do not normally regard themselves as duty-bound to adjust their treatment decisions to avoid generating negative consequences for other persons, including family members.

For example, suppose that a medically appropriate course of therapy, if successful, might foreseeably induce a patient to divorce her spouse. While the therapist obviously must take into account the prospect of the marriage's dissolution for her patient's wellbeing,[28] it would be inappropriate for her to take into account the effect of the dissolution purely on the wellbeing of the nonpatient spouse. This is for a reason. Therapists understand themselves to owe a duty of loyalty to their patients, not simply a duty of care. And they are understood by patients to have such a duty: that is part of how our institutions have (thus far) crafted the therapist–patient relationship.

Cases like *Roberts* do not pose the question of how to strike a balance between two duties of the same kind—ie, two duties to take care not to cause injury to another. There is a qualitatively different kind of legal duty on one side of this imagined ledger, and it is the sort of duty that, given the present state of the law, requires courts to decline to recognize a duty on the other side. To the extent that courts articulating duties of care are not simply creating duties and imposing them, but rather recognizing them as existing and articulating them, the therapist's fiduciary duty to the patient precludes the recognition of a duty of care to the patient's parents.[29]

[28] A negative impact on a spouse that in turn generated a negative impact on the patient would thus be inside the range of considerations the therapist would have a duty to consider.

[29] An important premise of our account in this chapter relates to structural aspects of a negligence claim that we have discussed at length elsewhere and will therefore not dwell upon here. Briefly, the duty element in negligence is linked to a standing-like requirement: a plaintiff who can prove that the defendant acted carelessly so as to cause his injury is not entitled to recover unless he further proves that the defendant breached a duty of care *owed to him*. Goldberg and Zipursky (n 7) at 709–12. We have argued that Cardozo's famous *Palsgraf* opinion can be understood as a compelling defence of this understanding of negligence, which refuses to take a reductive approach to the standing-duty linkage. See, eg, Benjamin C Zipursky, 'Rights, Wrongs and Recourse in the Law of Torts' (1998) 51 Vand L Rev 1. By contrast, as we noted at the outset of this chapter, many courts and scholars, including Prosser, have followed Judge Andrews' *Palsgraf* dissent in adopting a reductive, policy-making approach to duty, according to which answers to duty questions are reverse-engineered from an account of who should be able to sue in order for liability to promote objectives such as deterrence and compensation.

In cases like those explored in this chapter, the difference in the two approaches to duty is illustrated by an objection to our analysis put to us by several colleagues: 'If recovered therapy treatment is so unreliable that its administration can be deemed careless and harmful *to the patient*, there can be no conflict associated with the recognition of a duty of care to the patient's parent, and indeed no reason not to permit the parent to recover on a negligence claim against the therapist.' We do not credit this objection because we believe that tort law is structured such that a plaintiff must establish that the defendant

We will have more to say in Section IV about the nature and substance of this claim, and particularly its reliance on a characterization of the duties therapists actually owe their patients as the ground for identifying duties that they do not owe. Before proceeding to that discussion, however, we will review related case law that will bolster our descriptive and doctrinal claim that doctors owe fiduciary duties to their patients, and that these duties set limits on the duties they owe to others.

4. The legal duties of physicians

Here we review tort doctrines suggesting that: (i) among the duties owed by physicians to patients, some are distinctively fiduciary, and (ii) the recognition of these fiduciary duties helps to explain both the general adherence to something like the privity rule in doctor–patient cases, as well as certain recognized exceptions.

(i) *Duties to Nonpatients Outside of Triangular Torts.* Evidence that the law recognizes fiduciary duties running from physicians to patients (and, by extension, from therapists to patients), can be found in decisions that, ironically, sometimes make it more difficult for physicians to invoke a no-duty argument to defeat liability to a nonpatient.

A familiar litigation scenario involves a prospective employer contracting with a physician to assess a prospective employee's health. The physician's examination reveals a health problem unrelated to the employer's concerns, but that would be important for the prospective employee to know. However, the physician does not tell the prospective employee. Some time later, the prospective employee discovers the problem—which by then has advanced in a way that could have been prevented—and sues the physician for not informing her of it. The physician in turn argues that the plaintiff was not her patient, and therefore was owed no duty of care.

In these cases, the full-blown physician–patient relationship is absent. More precisely, the physician, acting as contractor for the prospective employer, owed no duty of *loyalty* to the plaintiff. However, it is a fallacy to assume that the absence of the core fiduciary duty means there were no duties at all running from the physician to the prospective employee. The prospective employee properly can claim that the physician owed her a duty of care simply because the physician undertook to apply professional expertise to the examination of her health.[30] Certainly attending to the wellbeing of the plaintiff would not conflict with any duty owed to the employer.

wronged her. In the context of a negligence claim this means establishing that the defendant owed a duty to the plaintiff to be vigilant as to *her* well being, and breached *that* duty. A duty of care owed by the therapist to the parent cannot be established merely by the putative fact that harm to the parent would have been averted if the defendant had taken adequate care as to the well-being of the patient.

[30] See, eg, *Stanley v McCarver*, 92 P.3d 849 (Ariz. 2004) (*en banc*) (recognizing existence of duty of care). Although some other states take the same position as *Stanley*, a larger number probably refuse to recognize a duty of care in this context. See generally Dan B Dobbs, Paul T Hayden, and Ellen M Bublick, *The Law of Torts* (2d ed, West Publishing, 2011) § 286.

In short, the absence of a fiduciary duty in certain non-structured, non-physician-patient relationships does not entail the absence of a duty of care.

(ii) *Intentional Torts, Privileges, and Compromise*. Negligence is not the only kind of tort claim brought against professionals by family members who claim to have been harmed by false charges of child abuse. In numerous cases from around the United States (and the common law world), therapists, social workers, physicians, and counsellors have been sued for defamation based on reports alleging that the plaintiff parents abused their children (who are typically patients of the defendant). Slander and libel are intentional torts—the gravamen of these wrongs is that one person has intentionally spoken ill of another, not that he acted carelessly toward her. Appropriately, this difference sometimes makes a difference to the treatment of nonpatient (or nonclient) claims, opening a small window of possible recovery.

There is no precise analogue in the torts of slander and libel to the duty element of negligence. Historically, a defamation plaintiff was not required to prove that the defendant owed her a duty to take care against defaming her. This is not to say that common law would impose strict liability upon a therapist for reporting suspected child abuse to authorities. Rather, it is to note that defamation law has a different structure, one in which many of the important limits on liability are set not within the description of the wrongs of libel and slander, but instead the recognition of various privileges and immunities that, in effect, allow speakers and writers to defame others.

For example, if a therapist were to state her suspicions of abuse in an affidavit as part of a judicial proceeding to terminate parental rights, she would face no liability because statements made in connection with legal proceedings enjoy an absolute immunity. In the more common case, in which a care provider shares her suspicions with another family member, or an agency charged with protecting child welfare, there is not absolute immunity, but instead a qualified or conditional privilege. Many states have enshrined this qualified privilege in a statute.[31]

By virtue of common-law and statutory privileges, a plaintiff claiming to have been defamed by a therapist's accusation of child abuse (outside the setting of a judicial proceeding) will not be able to recover, or even go to trial, (at least) without offering substantial evidence of malice or lack of good faith on the part of the therapist.[32] And, while it is the rare plaintiff who can meet this burden, the common law clearly contemplates the possibility of defamation liability.[33] This raises for us a puzzle: if the therapist's fiduciary duty to the patient fully forestalls a negligence claim on no-duty grounds, why does it not fully cut off defamation liability, at least in the traditional understanding of the common law?

[31] Some statutes grant absolute immunity in this context as well. See generally, 'Validity, Construction, and Application of State Statutes Requiring Doctor or Other Person to Report Child Abuse' (1989 & Cumulative Supp.) 73 A.L.R. 4th 782 § 15.

[32] See, eg, *Bol v Cole*, 561 N.W.2d 143, 149–51 (Minn. 1997).

[33] See, eg, *J.E.B. v Danks*, 785 N.W.2d 741, 751 (Minn. 2010) (reversing grant of summary judgment to a defamation defendant given a factual dispute as to whether defendant acted with malice in asserting that plaintiff committed sexual abuse).

Our answer hinges on the distinctive nature of the wrongs of negligence and defamation. At its core, negligence consists of a failure to adjust one's conduct in a manner that attends appropriately to aspects of other persons' wellbeing. Defamation, by contrast, consists of acting in a way that one ought not to act, full stop. It is not wrong to drive, but only wrong to drive carelessly. By contrast, it is wrong—though sometimes permitted—to speak ill of another person.

The fact that the defamation torts consist, at their core, of prohibitions on conduct rather than rules about how one must engage in permitted conduct, explains why and how the conflict between the recognition of a therapist's duty of loyalty to her patient and her duty not to defame nonpatients is *manageable* in a way that the conflict between her duty of loyalty and a duty of care to nonpatients is not. To recognize a duty of care running to nonpatients invites the physician/therapist to consider adjusting her treatment of the patient in light of the possible consequences for non–patients. This is the sense in which such a duty interferes with the therapist's duty of loyalty to her patient. With defamation, there is no equivalent 'grey area' to navigate with respect to what constitutes proper or improper therapy. Indeed, the issue has nothing to do with the patient's treatment. The issue instead is whether, because of information obtained by the therapist during treatment, the therapist should or must do something that otherwise would quite clearly be wrongful and a basis for liability.

It is wrong to say of another person that he has sexually abused his child. Yet, for very good reason, the law permits (and sometimes requires) certain persons to say such things. To enable this to happen, the law has carved out a well-defined safe harbour for reports of this sort. In doing so, it allows therapists to overcome the injunction not to speak ill of others in the name of protecting their patients' interests.

(iii) *Triangular Torts that Generate Liability to Nonpatients.* Our core claim is that the duty issue raised by triangular torts involving therapists alleged to have carelessly harmed nonpatients is elegantly resolved by observing that physicians and other healthcare providers owe fiduciary duties to their patients and clients. The alleged duty to take care with nonparties, such as the patient's parents, is—we argue—inconsistent with the duty of loyalty owed to the patient or client. The point is not simply that one would create a conflict if one imposed such a duty to the nonpatient. It is that, given the fiduciary duty, it is simply not true that there is a duty of care to the nonpatient.

This claim leaves us with an obvious explanatory burden. For it is not as if courts *never* recognize duties of care running from healthcare providers to nonpatients. We now aim to meet that burden by explaining what distinguishes triangular torts involving healthcare providers that do generate liability to nonpatients.

Consider a physician who places a patient on a strong allergy medication that the physician knows, or should know, might cause the patient to experience a sudden onset of severe drowsiness, yet neglects to inform the patient of this possible side effect. Under the influence of the medication, the patient falls asleep while driving, injuring a pedestrian. If the pedestrian sues the physician for negligence in failing to warn his patient of the risk of drowsiness, the physician will surely argue that he owed no duty of care to the nonpatient pedestrian. Yet in most American jurisdictions the argument will fail. In these 'patient-driver' cases, physicians are held to have owed a duty of care to nonpatients.

It may be tempting to suppose that the basis for these 'yes-duty' decisions is the foreseeability of harm to persons such as the pedestrian. But foreseeability can't be doing the work. Even where harm to patients' parents is a foreseeable consequence of therapy, therapists are held by the majority of courts to owe no duty to the parents. Moreover, while it is a requirement of negligence law that the defendant's conduct be not merely negligent 'in the air', but negligent *as to* the victim, a physician's failure to warn a patient of the possibility of sudden, severe drowsiness *is* arguably careless as to pedestrians (unless, perhaps, the physician has reason to believe that a particular patient is not going to be engaged in ordinary activities such as driving).

At a superficial level, perhaps the largest difference between the patient-driver and therapist cases appears to be that the defendant in the patient-driver cases has a less impressive policy argument. Indeed, it is difficult to see anything comparable to the good of unmasking sexual abuse that will somehow be undermined by imposing liability on a prescribing physician who fails to warn of side effects. And yet it is not that difficult to craft a policy argument against liability. One might argue, for example, that some mixture of first- and third-party private and public insurance would be a far more efficient way to cover such car accident costs than processing claims through the notorious tangle of medical malpractice law.

A better account of the difference between the therapist cases and the patient-driver cases requires that we turn away from the inevitably indeterminate terrain of policymaking and instead focus on duties—specifically, the physician's fiduciary duties. In doing so, one recognizes almost immediately a salient difference between the two kinds of case. In the patient-driver cases there is no conflict between the physician's duty to attend scrupulously to the patient's wellbeing and a duty of care to the nonpatient. Loyalty to the patient, conduct in conformity with the patient's unqualified trust in the physician, and full focus by the physician on the patient's health are in no way inconsistent with the recognition of a need to take reasonable steps to protect those at potential risk from such driving. Ironically, the consistency of such vigilance with a fiduciary duty to the patient explains the presence of a duty of care to the nonpatient, just as its inconsistency explains the absence of such a duty in the therapist cases.

A nuanced decision by the Tennessee Supreme Court nicely brings this contrast to light by examining a variation of the typical patient-driver case. In *Burroughs v Magee*,[34] the defendant doctor prescribed potentially disorienting drugs to a patient, who, while taking the medication, drove through a red light and struck the plaintiffs' car. With respect to the plaintiffs' claim against the prescribing physician, the Court entertained two alternative theories of liability: (i) that the physician was negligent for having prescribed the drugs, in light of both their addictiveness and the potential for harm to third parties; and (ii) that, having chosen to prescribe the

[34] 111 S.W.3d 323 (Tenn. 2003).

drug, the physician was negligent in failing to warn the patient of their dangerous side effects.

The Court concluded that theory (i) failed for lack of duty but that theory (ii) was viable. As to theory (i), the court reasoned that a physician's treatment choice cannot be dictated by potential harm to third persons. To take into consideration the wellbeing of others would be inconsistent with the physician's fiduciary duty to his patient.

> A physician's first loyalty must be to his patient. Imposing a duty on a physician to predict a patient's behavioral reaction to medication and to identify possible plaintiffs would cause a divided loyalty. Were we to impose a duty on a physician to consider the risk of harm to third persons before prescribing medication to a patient, we would be forcing the physician to weigh the welfare of unknown persons against the welfare of his patient. Such an imposition is unacceptable. The physician has the duty to his patient to decide when and what medication to prescribe the patient, and to inform the patient regarding the risks and benefits of a particular drug therapy. He should fulfill that duty without fear of being exposed to liability to unknown, unidentified third persons.[35]

However, once a course of treatment has been decided upon that includes the administration of certain medications, the need to supply appropriate warnings for the patient is not only important for the patient's safety, but also for the safety of third parties. More to the point, protecting the wellbeing of third parties is among the reasons that appropriately weigh on the physician when she or he makes a decision about which warnings to provide and how fulsome they must be. It is not simply that the patient and the injured third party would both have benefited from the physician's warning. It is that, more broadly, there is no tension between vigilance about the plaintiff's wellbeing and a physician maintaining a single-minded focus on the patient in advising and treating the patient.

The Massachusetts Supreme Judicial Court faced another variation on the patient-driver case in *Medina v Hochberg*.[36] As in the medication cases, the patient injured the plaintiff because of negligent driving caused by his physical or mental condition. And, as in those cases, the court was willing to assume that the physician was or should have been aware of the patient's compromised ability to drive because of his condition, and failed to explain these risks to the patient or provide adequate warnings. However, in *Medina*—by contrast with the cases we have so far surveyed— the patient's impaired condition was not a result of medication. Rather, the patient's impairment was produced by a seizure caused by a brain tumour.

A unanimous court in *Medina* rejected the plaintiff's claim, holding that the physician owed no duty of care to the nonpatient plaintiff. Distinguishing *Coombs v Florio*,[37] an earlier decision recognizing a duty owed to non-patients in a standard patient-driver case involving a physician's failure to warn of drug side effects, the Court focused on the fact that the driver's impairment in *Medina* did not result from treatment. The brain tumour that led to the seizure and the accident was a natural

[35] Ibid at 334 (quoting *Webb v Jarvis*, 575 N.E.2d. 992, 995 (Ind. 1991)).
[36] 987 N.E.2d 1206 (Mass. 2013). [37] 877 N.E.2d 567 (Mass. 2007).

occurrence, while the impairment in *Coombs* was a result of medication prescribed by the defendant physician. *Medina*, too, emphasized that a physician's duty is to focus on the patient's well-being, and that liability to third parties, or even threat of such liability, for injuries resulting only from a patient's diminished condition stand to interfere with the physician's primary duty to the patient.

The Massachusetts court was in our view correct to conclude there was no duty to the plaintiff in *Medina*, and correct to emphasize the treatment/condition distinction. It is, however, possible to misread the significance of that distinction. *Medina* states that the physician's duty to a third party is different when the risk to that party is generated by the physician's affirmative act of prescribing medication. This might be taken to suggest that: (a) there is a powerful doctrinal account of the patient-driver cases that has little do with fiduciary duty but really turns on the misfeasance–nonfeasance distinction; and (b) in deciding whether to prescribe the somnolence-inducing medication to the patient at all, the physician has a duty of care running to third parties. A different way of putting the point—one that we aim to refute below—is that one cannot use the distinction between acting to create a risk and failing to control for a preexisting risk to distinguish the *Medina* fact pattern, unless one is prepared to reject the analysis of Tennessee Supreme Court in *Burroughs* that the physician owes no duty of care to third parties with respect to the decision about whether to medicate, but does owe a duty of care with respect to warning the patient of a prescribed drug's dangerous side-effects.

This objection is misguided, but useful nonetheless. Patient-driver cases are not 'clean' misfeasance cases. They are probably best characterized as affirmative duty-to-protect cases based not on a special relationship between defendant and plaintiff, but rather on a duty to take steps to control a specific peril that one has helped to create, even nonwrongfully. In the words of the Third Torts Restatement: 'When an actor's prior conduct, even though not tortious, creates a continuing risk of physical harm of a type characteristic of the conduct, the actor has a duty to exercise reasonable care to prevent or minimize the harm.'[38]

The key point is that one's role in generating a risk need not be wrongful in order for it to generate a duty to protect what would not otherwise exist. There was no duty to take steps to protect in *Medina*, the brain tumour case, because the physician has not generated any risk at all. By contrast, cases in which the physician, by prescribing a course of treatment, has helped to generate a certain risk of harm to third parties are ones in which courts could, consistent with general tort principles, recognize a duty of care. Yet when it comes to risks resulting from treatment decisions, the courts still hold that no duty is owed. They do so because the fiduciary duty owed by physician to patient undermines the plausibility of thinking that the decision whether to prescribe the medication turns on the risks to others.[39] Only when the physician's negligence does not concern treatment decisions, but instead

[38] Restatement (Third) of Torts: Liability for Physical and Emotional Harm § 39 (2012).

[39] Of course, this is not to say that a physician is entitled to conspire with a patient to break the law by so diminishing the patient's driving abilities as to render him an unlawful driver.

concerns matters such as a failure to warn the patient of side-effects from treatment, are the courts prepared to recognize a duty to nonpatients.

5. Nearby frameworks allowing for liability

As will be clear from the foregoing, our goal is not to establish that a medical provider can never be held liable for breaching a duty owed to a nonpatient. Rather, we aim to expose some reasons relating to fiduciary duty that tend to provide a special argument against the existence of a duty of care to nonpatients in various settings. We believe that the recovered memory case law nicely illustrates this structural point, but it is implicit in our broader general position that the nonpatients in these cases (typically parents of a child who has undergone treatment by the defendant) might find ways to articulate a plausible tort claim. Below we sketch how some of these might go. The point is not to backtrack on our position about the relationship between fiduciary duties to a patient and the lack of a duty of care owed to others. On the contrary, it is to suggest that to the extent that a plaintiff advocate's position appears to be compelling in particular cases, it is not because our structural account is wrong, but because of special features of such cases.

(i) *Family Practice.* There is a well-known field of family therapy, in which two or more members of a family are among the patients of the therapist. Even apart from the case of 'family therapists' so-called, there are plenty of instances in which a therapist takes on the care of more than one family member. One might suppose that this shows that fiduciary duties owed to individual patients are not inconsistent with duties of care to the family members of such patients. And of course it does show that, at one level. But it proves too much, for it is part of how a responsible therapist would engage in family therapy that each member would (or should) be aware that the therapist's duties of loyalty and care are modified to each in a manner that accommodates the duties of care owed to the others. Most obviously, duties of confidentiality are not wholly waived because of the presence of third persons; rather, they are modified to remain consistent with third-party family members being privy to revelations. Therapists and physicians (like lawyers) need to structure in advance the departures from default rules of loyalty when multiple family members are simultaneously patients. In cases like *Roberts*, where it does not appear that there was any such advance structuring to accommodate potential conflicts, there is *a fortiori* no accommodation built into the content of the fiduciary duty.

(ii) *Intentionality and Recklessness.* As our discussion of defamation indicated, intentional torts committed by medical care providers against nonpatients call for distinct treatment. This difference, moreover, extends to instances of recklessness, which, in various tort contexts (eg, punitive damages, waivers of liability, intentional infliction of emotional distress) falls within the rubric of intentional torts. Indeed, if a therapist is reckless in bringing his minor patient to the point of (falsely) believing that her parent committed serious criminal acts against her, and is reckless in urging the patient to confront family members with clearly ungrounded accusations and to contact police or public health officials, thereby resulting in injury to the parent, many states' tort law would regard the therapist's injuring of the parent as falling within the domain of intentional torts. A hypothetical example helpfully posed to us by Scott Hershovitz graphically illustrates the point. A psychiatric patient is obsessed with fantasies of stabbing her husband in the middle of the night. Her therapist believes that the patient's neurosis can be cured if the patient is made to confront directly the reality of what she is contemplating. The therapist thus instructs the patient to hold a knife to her husband's throat while he is sleeping (though she also instructs the patient not to injure him). Unfortunately, when the patient does so, the husband wakes up and is traumatized by the perception of his wife apparently about to slash his throat.

Hershovitz suggests that this therapist can be held liable for the emotional harm of the husband, and that, moreover, it is implausible to suggest that the therapist's duty of loyalty to her patient forecloses such liability. We agree. The husband's tort claim would not be in negligence, however, but in assault (and perhaps intentional infliction of emotional distress). And it would not simply be a claim against his wife, but also against the therapist as a joint tortfeasor, given that the therapist conceived of and directed the wife's conduct. Duties not to commit intentional torts and duties not to injure through failure to use care are treated quite differently in tort law, and for good reason. Intentional torts prototypically involve discrete kinds of interests and discrete interferences with those interests. This makes it possible for them to sit alongside of, and constrain, fiduciary duties to individuals without undermining the special salience of those duties. Duties of care in negligence law are otherwise; it is part of what is special about them that they are pervasive, general, and incremental. The point of a duty of loyalty is in part to cut through the pervasiveness of not only self-interest, but of duties of care owed to others. Like clear-cut duties under statutory and regulatory law, the duties not to commit intentional torts can play a framing role for fiduciary duties without subsuming them.

(iii) *Quackery, Professionalism, and the Public.* A professional's fiduciary duties are not simply framed by criminal, regulatory, and intentional tort law, but by duties and norms recognized within the profession itself. Providers of medical care, for example, are required to maintain certain standards of conduct by professional organizations with disciplinary authority and, in less formal ways, by their peers. Members of the profession and private parties benefit in various ways from having these relationships so structured. But theirs are not the only interests served.

To some extent, norms of professional conduct also serve the public interest. Just as the protections afforded to patent holders by patent law can be understood as advancing science and technology in the long run, so, for example, the privacy norms that physicians must observe with respect to their patients arguably serve the public in the long run by allowing the profession to deal effectively with patients who might otherwise be reluctant or unwilling to seek treatment. It was on this basis that dissenting justices in *Tarasoff* argued against the recognition of a duty on the part of a therapist to warn a third party of the risk of being attacked by the therapist's patient. Far from protecting potential victims, these dissenters argued, the warning regime implemented by the majority, by creating a significant exception to confidentiality, would discourage dangerous patients from seeking treatment and undermine the effectiveness of therapy, thus increasing the likelihood of attacks.[40]

The larger point is two-fold: (i) many of the norms applicable to professional communities exist at least in part because of public welfare concerns; (ii) even the understanding of physicians as owing a duty of loyalty to their patients exists against the backdrop of physicians being deemed to be responsible members of an important, learned profession in which education and compliance with norms of scientific rationality play a significant role. In this context, society accepts a special privileging of the professional–patient relationship as one that allows the professional to be in some respects narrowly focused on the wellbeing of her patient rather than focused directly on the public good. But this acceptance is conditioned on, among other things, a genuine commitment to professionalism. Professionals escape more formal regulation in part because they impose and accept a certain amount of formal and informal self-regulation.

Within this larger context, the question arises as to how one should treat professionals who deviate substantially from the norms of their profession but still enlist the heightened trust of their patients or clients. Our view is that the privilege of professionals to focus on their patients and clients rather than the public good (where the two might conflict) turns, in part, on their belonging to a community whose members in general enjoy such privileges. A putative professional whose conduct within her professional relationship violates public-oriented norms of the profession therefore stands in a potentially compromised position with respect to her claim to be free of duties to third parties.

Perhaps because we are lawyers, it is easiest to see this point within the legal profession. Imagine a lawyer for a pharmaceutical company who plays a part in the company's preparation of an incomplete and misleading application for approval of a drug to the Food and Drug Administration. There is a powerful argument that, in litigation against the company, the attorney is not shielded from subpoena by a confidentiality privilege. This is so even beyond the matters that he knew or believed were wrongful. The basic idea is that the lawyer's role carries special treatment only because society values the creation and performance of such roles; if a lawyer is not authentically occupying that role, she is not entitled to that special treatment.

A person who holds herself out as a professional therapist does not thereby qualify automatically as someone entitled to say that her fiduciary duty squeezes out her duty of care to nonpatients. We recognize therapists' relationships with their patients as special (and fiduciary in nature) in part because of a set of values and expectations associated with being a therapist as a profession—a profession that utilizes knowledge and methodologies that our legal system regards as a legitimate and effective means of assisting people to cope with (and heal from) psychological or psychiatric conditions. If, in fact, the putative knowledge is fabricated and

[40] *Tarasoff v Regents of the Univ. of California*, 551 P.2d 334, 359–60 (1976) (Clark, J, dissenting, joined by McComb, J). We merely offer this argument as an example; we take no position on its merits.

the methodology is unfounded according to norms of the professional community upon which our legal system relies, then it is not at all clear that the privileging of the relationship (or the therapist) is warranted. Put more bluntly, if putative health-care professionals are actually inauthentic as professionals—if they are engaged in quackery rather than medicine—their putative fiduciary relationships are not entitled to occlude the duties to third parties.

We believe that recovered memory therapy cases have raised such a difficult legal issue in part because the therapy remains controversial as a methodology and controversial in its foundations (to put the point gently). Some leading psychologists and psychiatrists as well as whole professional organizations have expressed reservations about its legitimacy. Nonetheless, it does not appear that one can regard the practice[41] as having been wholly discredited as a matter of professional knowledge and methodology.[42]

If this were so, however—if recovered memory therapists are rightly regarded as not merely negligent, but as quacks (and if, hypothetically, courts were justified in taking judicial notice that this was so)—courts would have much less reason to declare that they owe no duty of care to family members and other nonpatients. For while patients might place the same level of trust in a recovered memory therapist as in any other (credible) therapist, the system need not shield and privilege that relationship and that trust in the same way.[43]

[41] A related problem is that it remains unclear which aspects or sorts of therapy count as relying unjustifiably on recovered memories.

[42] The American Psychiatric Association's official position on recovered memory therapy is equivocal. American Psychiatric Association, 'Position Statement on Therapies Focused on Memories of Childhood Physical and Sexual Abuse' (reaffirmed July 2013), <http://www.psychiatry.org/file%20 library/about-apa/organization-documents-policies/policies/position-2013-memories-child-abuse. pdf> (last visited, 14 February 2016). The APA statement's most negative passage reads as follows:

> Some therapeutic approaches attempt specifically to elicit memories of childhood abuse as the central technique for relieving emotional distress. The validity of such therapies has been challenged. Some patients receiving this treatment have later recanted their claims of recovered memories of abuse and accused their therapists of leading or pressuring them into such ideas.
>
> Research has shown that memory does not always record events accurately.

Ibid. On the other hand, the statement's narrative portion concludes: 'It is well documented that both dismissing true accounts, and accepting false accounts, can harm patients and possibly others.' Ibid.

[43] Although our focus in this chapter is on fiduciary duties in the professional context, it bears mention that a parallel set of concerns applies in the corporate context. Many courts and scholars today regard it as naïve to suppose that the fiduciary duties of corporate directors are owed exclusively to shareholders. See Paul B Miller and Andrew S Gold, 'Fiduciary Governance' (2015) 57 Wm & Mary L Rev 513, 535–39. But even if one were to suppose that corporate fiduciaries owe loyalty exclusively to shareholders and that this duty exerts pressure against fiduciaries' consideration of the well-being of other stakeholders, the state law that creates the corporate form exists for public-oriented reasons that may explicitly or implicitly generate limits on the extent to which those fiduciaries may act with indifference to the welfare of third parties or the public. We take no position on these issues here. Our point is that it is one thing to recognize that duties of loyalty in the fiduciary context have some exclusionary force with regard to duties to others, and another to say that the state may not condition the privileging of fiduciary relationships in a variety of ways aimed at promoting the welfare of other stakeholders. In corporate law, as in the law governing the professions, we accept the first proposition while rejecting the second.

(iv) *Summary of Possible Exceptions.* With regard to recovered memory therapists, we have generally argued that they do not owe a duty of care to the parents of their patients, and that therefore they do not face liability for negligence in lawsuits brought by parents. In this section, we have indicated why there might still be some powerful arguments for plaintiffs in such cases. First, family members are sometimes patients too, and then quite obviously there may be a negligence claim. Second, a therapist who intentionally or recklessly defames the parent or causes them massive emotional harm might indeed be liable under an intentional tort claim. And third, therapists who are engaging in quackery are not entitled to claim the privileges and protections that go along with the provision of certain kinds of professional services.

IV. Lawyers' Duties to Clients and Nonclients

Section III argued that a physician's fiduciary duties to her patient account for the general absence of a duty of care owed to non-patients, as well as exceptions to that rule. To bolster this account, we now turn to a closely related area of law—legal malpractice. We aim to show that the same pattern is also at work here. Although courts confronted with duty questions tend to speak in Prosserian terms, something close to the privity rule remains the default. Both the rule and its exceptions, we contend, demonstrate that the courts' decisions and reasoning have much more to do with their understanding of the fiduciary nature of duties owed by lawyers to their clients than with the open-ended policy analysis in which they purport to engage.

A. Duty, loyalty, and privity

Just as it is easy to lose sight of privity-like limitations on the liability of physicians to nonpatients, so it is with respect to the liability of lawyers to nonclients. The most memorable decisions in these areas, and the ones most frequently taught and written about, are those that articulate exceptions. Moreover, these same cases, as we noted in the Introduction, often are written in a way that falsely suggests that the duty element, in every case, invites judges to partake of all-things-considered, consequentialist policy analysis.

The California Supreme Court's *Tarasoff* decision obviously fits the foregoing description to a 't'. But so too do a pair of decisions on legal malpractice. In *Biakanja v Irving*[44] and *Lucas v Hamm*,[45] the court allowed malpractice claims, absent privity, by intended beneficiaries of wills who were prevented from inheriting under the wills because of defendants' negligence. Although today *Tarasoff* is probably the better-known decision, it is *Biakanja* and *Lucas*—decided fifteen years

[44] 320 P.2d 16 (Cal. 1958). [45] 364 P.2d 685 (Cal. 1961).

earlier—that first embraced the Prosserian deconstruction of duty into an assortment of policy factors. As the Court wrote in *Biakanja*:

the determination whether in a specific case the defendant will be held liable to a third person not in privity is a matter of policy and involves the balancing of various factors, among which are the extent to which the transaction was intended to affect the plaintiff, the foreseeability of harm to him, the degree of certainty that the plaintiff suffered injury, the closeness of the connection between the defendant's conduct and the injury, and the policy of preventing future harm.[46]

Despite this open-ended language, and notwithstanding the recognition of important exceptions, it remains the case even today that a broad array of claims by nonclients with plausible allegations of having been injured by attorney carelessness fail because of the absence of a duty of care owed by the defendant attorney to the nonclient plaintiff.

The most obvious cases in which nonclients are not permitted to recover involve direct conflicts of interest. A person who sues her spouse's lawyer in divorce proceedings on a claim that the lawyer acted with careless disregard for her interests will lose as a matter of law. And she will lose for the obvious reason. A lawyer does not owe a duty of care to her client's adversary in litigation. Quite the opposite, a lawyer's duty of loyalty to her client frequently requires that the lawyer *not* act in pursuit of her adversary's wellbeing. A duty of care carries with it a norm of acting for the advantage of the person to whom the duty is owed.

It is possible, of course, to have a duty of care to multiple parties simultaneously. The question is whether the scenario is one in which the duty of care to the nonclient is or is not consistent with the duties owed to one's own client. Where there is conflict, the lawyer's fiduciary duty to her client prevails.

B. Nonclients outside of the triangular tort context

In Section III, the distinction between duties of care and fiduciary duties allowed us to clarify an important class of cases in which non-patients have viable claims against physicians, namely, those involving misdiagnoses within health screenings provided by prospective employers. In these cases, we argued, the duty issue does not turn on whether the plaintiff could establish a full-blown physician-patient relationship. Although the relationship with the patient was plainly not a fiduciary one, it is quite plausible to suppose that the physician owed a duty of competent treatment.

A similar account applies to the question of whether lawyers can be sued for negligence by prospective clients in cases in which the client or the lawyer declines representation. It is well recognized today that the answer is *yes*. The existence of a duty of care does not turn on whether the whole package of attorney obligations, including a fiduciary duty, is applicable.

[46] 320 P.2d at 19.

To give a fairly straightforward example, an attorney who turns down a personal injury case that a reasonable attorney would recognize to be running up against the relevant limitations period may well be obligated to inform the prospective client of the impending time-limit.[47] This, at least, is the view taken by the Restatement of the Law Governing Lawyers,[48] though American jurisdictions are split on the issue.[49] Our analysis suggests that the Restatement view is certainly not ruled out by nonprivity in the way that classic nonclient claims are. If courts are going to decline to recognize a duty of care here, they will need a very strong reason.[50]

C. Intentional Torts

We saw in the sexual abuse cases that a small subset of libel and slander claims by parents can prevail even if negligence claims fail categorically because the duty element cannot be satisfied. Recognized privileges to report abuse will make a parent's claim of defamation very difficult, but a clear showing of bad faith or malice will enable recovery.

Legal malpractice works analogously. If a businessperson believes she is being sued for fraud because her adversary's lawyer did not adequately research the allegations in a complaint, the businessperson's negligence claim will fail as a matter of law on the duty element. But if she can establish, for example, that both the adversary and the adversary's lawyer manufactured the allegations in a complaint solely or primarily to inflict harm on her, she can prevail.

As with defamation claims, the premise of a malicious prosecution suit is not that counsel had a duty to be vigilant for the wellbeing of his client's adversary. The tort is not about failing to take care not to injure another. It involves instead a prohibition of affirmative acts of a certain kind, namely, the bringing of a lawsuit. Of course, lawyers bring suits, and are expected to bring suits, all the time. Hence the law gives very broad leeway for them to do so. It is only if the suit is known to be groundless and/or fueled by malice that the privilege to sue is lost.[51] Because the tort involves an affirmative act of attacking the plaintiff (maliciously and groundlessly), there is no conflict with the fiduciary duty to the client.

47 *Miller v Metzinger,* 154 Cal. Rptr. 22 (Ct. App. 1979).

48 Restatement (Third) of the Law Governing Lawyers § 51(1) (2000).

49 See, eg, *Allen v Steele*, 252 P.3d 476, 479 (Colo. 2011) (*en banc*) (rejecting the Third Restatement's position on duties to prospective clients).

50 Cf *Flatt v Superior Court*, 885 P.2d 950, 951 (Cal. 1994) (attorney's duty of loyalty to client precluded recognition of duty owed to a prospective client to inform the prospective client of the limitations period applicable to a claim by the prospective client against the existing client).

51 Ronald E Mallen with Allison Martin Rhodes, *Legal Malpractice* (Thomson Reuters 2015) § 6:22 ('To establish the tort of malicious prosecution, the claimant must plead and prove that the damage occurred because the attorney prosecuted a claim with malice and without probable cause, and that the proceeding ended in the claimant's favor') (citation omitted).

D. Viable triangular tort claims against lawyers

There are now a few well-established categories of attorney duties of care to nonclients. These are nicely laid out by the Restatement of Law Governing Lawyers.[52] The best-established domain of liability to nonclients, however, lies in the area of estate law. As mentioned above, tort liability to nonclients basically started in the United States with the California Supreme Court's decision in *Lucas v Hamm*, which extended the court's earlier decision in *Biakanja v Irving* from a notary authorized to practice law to licensed lawyers.[53] In *Lucas*, the testator's attorney drafted a will in a manner that violated the Rule against Perpetuities, and the would-be beneficiaries of a trust intended by the testator had to settle with those beneficiaries who benefitted from the drafting error. Notwithstanding the lack of privity between the beneficiaries and the testator's lawyer, the California Supreme Court allowed the plaintiffs to recover from the attorney the $75,000 that was lost in the settlement.

The great majority of states recognize a cause of action for plaintiffs who can prove that they were intended by a testator to inherit under the will, with New York and Texas being the most notable exceptions.[54] *Lucas* itself spells out two different rationales for recognizing a duty. One is an early version of California's skepticism about whether there really is any support for a duty 'limitation' of directness or privity in the first place. The other treats the plaintiffs in cases such as these as intended beneficiaries of an undertaking made by the attorney to the testator-client. Courts following *Lucas* have frequently discussed both rationales. There are some courts that have rejected negligence or legal malpractice causes as such, but permitted plaintiffs to recover in contract under a third-party beneficiary rationale.

The intended-beneficiary rationale for recognizing duty within negligence law makes sense on two levels. From the point of view of explaining why the attorney should not be indifferent to the wellbeing of the plaintiffs (since they are not his client), it provides a clear answer: loyalty to the client itself requires attentiveness to those whom the client wishes to benefit. For the same reason, there appears to be no conflict with the attorney's fiduciary duty to the client. The fact that the client has sought out professional assistance with the aim of providing a benefit to nonclients is also pivotal in the other major area of liability to nonclients—namely, cases involving opinion letters commissioned by a client expressly for the benefit of a designated nonclient.[55]

[52] Restatement of Law Governing Lawyers (n 49) § 51.

[53] Prior to this time, disappointed intended beneficiaries were sometimes able to obtain remedies through will contests and restitutionary remedies. John CP Goldberg and Robert H Sitkoff, 'Torts and Estates: Remedying Wrongful Interference with Inheritance' (2013) 65 Stan L Rev 335, 343–55.

[54] *Estate of Schneider v Finmann*, 15 N.Y.3d 306 (N.Y. 2010); *Barcelo v Elliott*, 923 S.W.2d 575 (Tex. 1996).

[55] Restatement of Law Governing Lawyers (n 49) § 51(3) & cmt e.

E. Complexities in triangular torts involving legal malpractice

Even in the supposedly straightforward area of triangular tort claims against estate lawyers, remarkably thorny legal issues have arisen.[56] For this reason, it is not surprising that New York and Texas have chosen not to go down this road. Within those jurisdictions that have recognized nonclient claims for negligent estate lawyering, there are indeed difficult lines to be drawn.

Rydde v Morris concerns the sad case of a woman named Knight who died intestate after a lengthy hospitalization.[57] A month prior to her death, Knight hired the defendant, Morris, to write her will. In response to Morris' questionnaire about to whom she wished to leave her estate, she identified Rydde and others. Morris prepared documents and returned them to Knight, who did not immediately execute them. A week later she died without having executed the documents. Rydde and others named in the questionnaire sued Morris for legal malpractice, arguing that: (a) the evidence clearly showed that they were intended beneficiaries; (b) Morris was careless in delaying the execution of the will, given the grave circumstances and Knight's expressed desire to move expeditiously; and (c) they had suffered financial losses as a direct result of Morris' carelessness.

The South Carolina Supreme Court rejected Rydde's claim. Reasoning that the 'imposition of a duty on an attorney to a prospective beneficiary of a nonexistent will would wreak havoc on the attorney's ethical duty of undivided loyalty to the client and force an impermissible wedge into the attorney–client relationship',[58] the Court concluded that the privity rule should not be relaxed. And yet five years later, in *Fabian v Lindsay & Lindsay, LLC*,[59] the same court held that a nonclient can sue an attorney in an estate context, at least where the plaintiff was an intended beneficiary named in a valid will.

South Carolina's combination of views is common, even if the order in which it reached them was not. Today that jurisdiction—like many—permits nonclient claims by intended will beneficiaries, but draws a line in cases where the breach asserted is a failure to execute the will at all (or a failure to have a second will executed, etc). This limitation may seem odd, especially given the strong showing in *Rydde* that the nonclient was indeed an intended beneficiary who suffered harm only because the defendant lawyer had not pushed to have the testator execute a will that she desired to execute. Nonetheless, when the issue is considered with attention to the fiduciary dimension of an attorney's duty to his client, the logic of *Rydde* comes into view.

A fiduciary duty to the client/testator *is* potentially inconsistent with a duty of care to nonclients who lack independent evidence that they were intended beneficiaries. More forcefully, if we describe the failure to execute or change a will as a breach of a duty of care to the ultimately injured party, we are saying that the lawyer

[56] Goldberg and Sitkoff (n 53) at 365–79 (discussing decisions allowing, with various limitations, tort claims by disappointed beneficiaries for intentional interference with inheritance).

[57] 675 S.E.2d 431 (S.C. 2009). [58] Ibid at 435. [59] 765 S.E.2d 732 (S.C. 2014).

owed it to these persons to have the will executed. In refusing to recognize such a duty, the *Rydde* court quoted from the Connecticut Supreme Court's prior analysis of the same issue:

A central dimension of the attorney-client relationship is the attorney's duty of '[e]ntire devotion to the interest of the client.' This obligation would be undermined were an attorney to be held liable to third parties if, due to the attorney's delay, the testator did not have an opportunity to execute estate planning documents prior to death. Imposition of liability would create an incentive for an attorney to exert pressure on a client to complete and execute estate planning documents summarily. Fear of liability to potential third party beneficiaries would contravene the attorney's primary responsibility to ensure that the proposed estate plan effectuates the client's wishes and that the client understands the available options and the legal and practical implications of whatever course of action is ultimately chosen. These potential conflicts of interest are especially significant in the context of the final disposition of a client's estate, where the testator's testamentary capacity and the absence of undue influence are often central issues.[60]

In this context, one cannot expect lawyers, who have a fiduciary duty to their clients, to comply with that duty while also remaining vigilant that things will turn out well for nonclients. The law instead is that they do not have a duty to take care that things turn out well for the nonclients.[61]

V. Duty, Policy, and Jurisprudence

We have maintained that courts faced with triangular tort cases involving medical and legal malpractice have, quite sensibly, adopted broad no-duty rules, and certain exceptions to those rules. Yet we have also suggested that they have done so almost in spite of themselves. In their general pronouncements about the analysis of the duty element of negligence, courts invoke Prosser's duty-qua-policy approach. Precisely because that approach calls for indeterminate, multi-factor policy analysis, one would not expect it to generate categorical majority rules. That courts have hit on such rules strongly suggests that they are working within an analytic approach that does not (despite what they sometimes say) reduce the relevance of a professional's fiduciary duties merely to one among myriad policy considerations. Rather, in keeping with widely shared understandings of the norms governing doctor–patient and lawyer–client relationships, the fiduciary nature of professionals' duties is given dispositive or near-dispositive weight.

Prosserians will no doubt be resistant to this aspect of our argument. To it, they are likely to respond as follows:

The statement about whether there is or is not a duty in a case of negligence, at least as made by a judge in a case of first impression, cannot be a purely descriptive one. The descriptive

[60] *Rydde*, 675 S.E.2d at 434 (quoting *Krawczyk v Stingle*, 543 A.2d 733, 736 (Conn. 1988) (internal citations omitted)).

[61] Ibid (noting that a majority of courts to consider the issue have adopted the same rule).

part—characterizing the way members of the profession and their patients currently understand their roles and their duties—is at most relevant to determining the framework of expectations and performance into which a judicial decision would be received. It does not supplant the need for a decision. When faced with the issue of the care owed to non-patients, courts will naturally and appropriately find themselves asking a question that is at once descriptive, empirical, and normative. Given how therapists currently understand their duties, would the imposition of a duty of care to the parents create a conflict of interest for the therapist, and, if so, how serious a problem would that be? Answering this question requires policy analysis. Will recognition of a previously unrecognized duty to parents cause therapists to take fewer cases or to provide less efficacious treatment? Will the failure to recognize such a duty generate false positive diagnoses that harm both patients and their families? Thus are courts led, inevitably, back into instrumental reasoning.

While the foregoing critique is imagined, it is not difficult to find judicial opinions that seem to conform to its key contentions. Consider, for example, the Illinois Supreme Court's opinion in *Doe v McKay*, another decision wrestling with the question of a therapist's duty of care to a nonpatient plaintiff. *Doe* does indeed focus on the nature of the duties owed by a therapist to her patient:

> Concern about how a course of treatment might affect third parties could easily influence the way in which therapists treat their patients. Under a rule imposing a duty of care to third parties, therapists would feel compelled to consider the possible effects of treatment choices on third parties and would have an incentive to compromise their treatment because of the threatened liability. This would be fundamentally inconsistent with the therapist's obligation to the patient.[62]

However, the Court explicitly situates these considerations in the context of conducting a multi-factor, consequentialist analysis of the duty issue. Indeed, its analysis commences with the following framing of the question: 'In deciding whether a duty exists in a particular case, a court will consider the foreseeability of the plaintiff's injury, the likelihood of the occurrence, the magnitude of the burden of guarding against it, and the consequences of placing that burden on the defendant.'[63] The block quotation above is one part of a larger policy argument against the imposition of a duty.

In this last section, we offer a relatively modest response to the imagined Prosserian rejoinder. It is modest in that we do not aim to show that all courts' analyses of duty issues are or must be distinct from the policy-factor approach. Rather, we will establish the converse—that not all such analyses must be consequentialist. An alternative, categorical approach is available and attractive. An example from the law governing lawyers will help us to explain the nature of our response.

In *State v Gonzalez*,[64] a public defender had been assigned to represent a murder suspect (Gonzalez). However, she was permitted to decline that representation on the ground that another client had revealed that she (the other client) intended to lie when called to testify in the Gonzales prosecution. While the assigning judge

[62] 700 N.E.2d 1018, 1023–24 (Ill. 1998).
[63] Ibid at 1021–22.
[64] 234 P.3d 1 (Kan. 2010).

accepted the public defender's refusal to represent Gonzalez, an assistant District Attorney subpoenaed her to identify the client who had stated an intention to commit perjury. The public defender refused to comply with the subpoena on the ground that the other client's communication was protected by the attorney–client privilege. The lower court rejected the privilege argument, reasoning that either that client was seeking advice on committing the crime of perjury and defrauding the court (in which case an exception to the privilege was applicable), or she was not seeking legal advice at all (in which case the privilege was inapplicable).

The Supreme Court of Kansas reversed, reasoning that there was no evidence that the client sought legal advice for assisting her in perjury—stating an intention to perjure oneself and seeking advice for perjury are different. Implicitly, the court concluded that the right of the client to trust in the confidentiality of what she told her lawyer attached to the whole conversation unless the client was seeking help in committing a crime or fraud, which she was not.

The Court in *Gonzalez* could of course have framed the issue differently. Would it be best, in this case and in cases like it, for the privilege to be compromised as to statements evincing an intention to commit perjury? There is, after all, a risk that the criminal nonclient (Gonzalez) would be falsely convicted based on the perjurer's testimony, or that a prosecution of an actual offender would fail because of a perjured alibi. It is far from clear that a privilege somewhat diminished by a slightly enhanced crime-fraud exception would really be worse. And, indeed, it is not crystal clear just what the dimensions of the crime-fraud exception are—to some extent, the Supreme Court of Kansas was ruling on its dimensions, and not simply reiterating clear positive law on the question.

It would not be correct, however, to characterize *Gonzalez* as having made a 'policy' decision in the sense that Prosserians use that term. The Kansas Court looked to attorneys' and clients' understanding of the scope of the privilege (and, to some degree, to the scope of the right of confidentiality). The fiduciary duty of the lawyer creates a right of confidentiality, a right from which our evidentiary system then derives a privilege. In other words, the court treated the public defender as both entitled and obligated to refuse to reveal information because it *interpreted* her relationship and her duty to cover this sort of case. To be sure, a legislature might well have the power to alter the dimensions of the privilege. Arguably, a court could also do so, within limits. But this decision was not about the justifiability or unjustifiability of *altering the scope of the privilege*; it was about applying the privilege as it is understood to exist. The unidentified client had the right to her lawyer being shielded from testifying, and the Kansas Supreme Court was enforcing that right, not deciding which dimensions to grant it from a policy perspective.

In a similar manner, the defendant therapist in a case like *Doe v McKay* or *Roberts v Salmi* is not arguing, first and foremost, that it would be a policy problem to impose liability. The argument is that there *is* no duty of care to parents, not that *courts have not yet imposed one* or that *it would be a poor policy choice* to impose one. There is a fiduciary duty to the patient, and it is part of what it is to have such a duty (properly understood) that the duty-holder is obligated to prioritize the well-being of the patient in a manner that is sufficiently strong and exclusive to defeat any suggestion of a duty of care owed to the parents. This is not to say that there is no possibility of crafting or interpreting the fiduciary duty so that it is weaker—just as one might have interpreted the attorney–client privilege more narrowly in the *Gonzalez* case.

If this account of decisions like *Doe* and *Roberts* were accepted, one might next conclude that, when it comes to the actual 'policy' question of what therapist's duties to patients and non-patients ought to look like (as opposed to the question of what those duties actually are), one ought to look in the first instance to legislatures rather than courts. Interestingly, this is precisely the claim of the dissenting judge in *Roberts v Salmi*,[65] who quoted from a similar decision by the California Court of Appeals: 'If therapists are to be put in what is so obviously an untenable position, it should be by the Legislature, not the legal fiat of appellate judges.'[66]

One can of course doubt that legislatures really are in a better position to alter the law in the name of policy. For now, our point is simply that courts facing parental claims against a child's therapist need not regard the analytic task at hand as one of policymaking or factor-balancing. The recognition of the existence and nature of a therapist's fiduciary duty to the patient is itself a strong categorical reason for concluding that the therapist does not have a duty of care to the parent. It may also present a good reason of policy for declining to *impose* a duty of care to the parent, but that is a different question.

VI. Conclusion

Moral and legal thinkers have always taken seriously the possibility that our non-promissory duties to others may vary depending on the nature of the relationships we have to them. In the 1970s, however, the philosopher Bernard Williams offered a critique of impartial morality that pushed this observation one step further. He suggested not only that the character of certain personal relationships (such as between spouses) might ratchet up the duties we owe to certain persons, but also that the converse might be true.[67] That is, certain relationships might, in effect, render it permissible not to act for the benefit of others, at least in some scenarios. Schematically, *X*'s special relationship to *Y* might not only intensify *X*'s duties to *Y*, but might also diminish what would otherwise be *X*'s duties to *Z*. Many scholars have since elaborated Williams' claims.

Our examination of triangular torts in professional malpractice has for the most part brought us to a similar point. Certain relationships come with special kinds of duties. In particular, many professional relationships, including doctor–patient and attorney–client, come with fiduciary duties. Forged in public not private

[65] *Roberts v Salmi*, 866 N.W.2d 460, 476 (Mich. App. 2014) (Sawyer, J, dissenting), appeal granted, 868 N.W.2d 911 (Mich. 16 September 2015), order granting appeal vacated, 877 N.W.2d 903 (Mich. 6 May 2016).

[66] Ibid at 478 (quoting *Trear v Sills*, 82 Cal. Rptr. 2d 281 (Ct. App. 1999)).

[67] Bernard Williams, 'Persons, Character and Morality' in *Moral Luck: Philosophical Papers 1973–80* (Cambridge University Press, 1980) 1.

settings, these are relationships of trust and loyalty. While not exactly of the sort that Williams had in mind (he focused on the sort of loving relationships that tend to stand at the centre of one's life), these relationships exist to ensure that important needs are met, and in a manner strongly protective of individuals' wellbeing as against vulnerabilities to illness and injury, legal and financial woes, and mistreatment at the hands of professionals themselves.

Tort law's treatment of professionals provides an analogue for legal duties to Williams' claim about the significance of special relationships for moral duties. In some cases in which a professional's careless conduct injures a person, that person may not have a negligence claim, even if the injury was foreseeable, because of the professional's fiduciary duty to her patient or client. The fiduciary aspects of a professional's relationship with those whom she treats or counsels simultaneously intensifies the duties owed to them while diminishing certain duties that might otherwise be owed to others.

PART IV

CONTRACT AND STATUS WITHIN THE FIRM

11

Exit, Choice, and Employee Loyalty

*Aditi Bagchi**

I. Introduction

Courts disagree whether employees are fiduciaries of their employers. Although that was the traditional rule, most jurisdictions now hold that employees owe a 'duty of loyalty' that is not fiduciary unless the individual is a higher-level 'key' employee of 'confidence'. Other jurisdictions continue to describe all employees as fiduciaries. One way to understand the split is that while some jurisdictions regard the duty of loyalty as contractual, others continue to attach the duty by virtue of employee status.

This chapter will argue that the employee duty of loyalty should be regarded as contractual rather than fiduciary.[1] In particular, it is best understood as derived from the general duty of good faith performance. As a mandatory duty applied to the (generally) less informed and less powerful party to a contract, it should be narrowly construed where job duties and terms of exit are unspecified in an employment contract *ex ante*. The upshot is that the duty of loyalty, like the contractual duty of good faith of which it is an instantiation, is indeed universal. But it is usually, and appropriately, weak. The contractual paradigm helps explain why and how the scope of the duty varies even among non-fiduciaries.

The argument in this chapter for a contractual reading of the duty of loyalty is limited to the employment context, though it may have broader implications. Some of its assumptions are forgivable in its domain, though they may raise controversy as general propositions. For example, the fiduciary version of the duty of loyalty is taken here to attach by virtue of an employee's status. This is not to imply that the facts of employment do not inform the application of a fiduciary duty of

* This chapter benefited from comments at the conference on Contract, Status, and Fiduciary Law at McGill University. Additional thanks to Paul Miller and John Goldberg for written comments.

[1] It might be useful to refer to the contractual duty as a 'duty of fidelity' to distinguish it more easily from the fiduciary duty of loyalty. But the duty under discussion is in fact referred to as a duty of loyalty by even those courts that do not regard it as a fiduciary duty, so I retain their nomenclature here.

loyalty; to the contrary, as discussed *infra*, the fiduciary form of the duty is highly sensitive to fact in its scope. And there are surely circumstances where fiduciary duties, including the duty of loyalty, attach in the absence of any status occupied by a fiduciary. Indeed, even under a contractual approach, some employees would be subject to fiduciary duties by virtue of the facts of their situation. But for purposes of this chapter, under consideration is a fiduciary duty of loyalty that applies to all employees just by virtue of their status as employees.

It is such a model that is rejected here. Although employment is undeniably an important status-based category in the law, with many legal rights attaching to employees by virtue of status, the modern notion of employment status is justified only where it is protective of employees, in recognition of their inability to contract for socially acceptable levels of safety and compensation on the market. It is critical that employment law be responsive to status hierarchies in society and in the workplace or else it will fail in its essential purpose, that is, mitigating the tendency of that hierarchy to entrench and suffocate. As discussed by Paul Miller in this volume, legal statuses need not always interact with social status in this way.[2] But in light of the distinctive purpose that status-concepts serve in the context of modern employment law, status-based employee *liabilities* are highly anomalous.

Of course, a contractual paradigm carries its own risks. This chapter concludes that these risks are less acute than they might at first appear. It examines several contractual conceptions of the duty of loyalty, including those in which it is treated as a duty imputed by public policy or a duty inferred as an element of party agreement. It ultimately argues that understanding the duty as an instance of the general duty of good faith makes the best sense of a historically suspect obligation. This understanding not only redeems the duty of loyalty as a reasonable obligation of employees but also generates guidance on how the duty can be construed in the most normatively satisfactory way.

On a contractual account, two features of employment should figure in determining the scope of the duty of loyalty in any given case: employer discretion and the terms of employee exit. *Employee* discretion on the job is usually regarded as essential to ascertaining the nature and scope of the duty of loyalty because it speaks to employee power. Employee power is central to a fiduciary paradigm, since it is what would justify designation of employees as fiduciaries.[3] However, the contractual paradigm offers an alternative, better, explanation for the significance of employee discretion: it is the space unoccupied by employer discretion. The latter is an entitlement that employers preserve by contract. The scope of mandated loyalty

[2] Paul B Miller, 'The Idea of Status in Fiduciary Law' at p 25 in this volume.
[3] Paul B Miller, 'Justifying Fiduciary Duties' (2013) 58 McGill LJ 969, 987.

should depend on such contract terms because the employee duty of loyalty, like the general duty of good faith of which it is a part, helps to fill out the contract that the parties made. The duty prohibits opportunistic behaviour by employees, and what qualifies as opportunistic depends on the particular bargain that an employer has specified, as an employee reasonably understands it.

Employers usually have wide discretion over the content of employees' duties. In part because employee obligations are unspecified *ex ante*, the primary mechanism by which performance is monitored and induced is the threat of termination. Employers can specify employees' duties *ex ante* but choose not to. Where they are prepared to give notice of such duties, such as a duty not to disparage an employer on social media, they can; in some cases, it might require that they pay some offsetting compensation. A mandatory default is inequitable for its asymmetry and likely absence of notice on the part of employees. There is also no reason to believe that employers would not impose those duties themselves where their cost was justified. As discussed *infra*, we should impute only the loyalty requirements that are implicitly required under contract to preserve value for the employer in the face of potential opportunism. Even absent an independent norm of reciprocity or equivalence in exchange, ordinary principles of construction suggest an inverse relationship between employer discretion and the scope of employees' implied duty of loyalty in a given employment contract.

The second feature of employment to which courts should regularly look in order to calibrate the duty of loyalty is employee exit. Most employees are at-will and have no rights to notice, severance, or any other procedural or substantive protection. The at-will default is publically justified by reference to a public interest in a dynamic business environment and the formal symmetry of a 'right of free exit' on the part of both employers and employees. Both of these considerations point to a light version of the duty of loyalty, and one that is minimally demanding for at-will employees. The duty is essentially an interpretive gap-filler. Employers should not be rewarded with enforceable expectations of robust loyalty where they choose to leave employee's substantive duties in employment unspecified, and the conditions under which they can be terminated unconstrained. Any default obligations imputed to employees should be minimized to those that are actually incompatible with provision of services. Other restrictions on employees should be noticed and, in principle, compensated by way of express terms. Again, we can arrive at this interpretive stance without reliance on any exogenous commitment to substantive equality as between the parties' rights and obligations.

The more general imperative is to complete the contractualization of employees' obligations to employers. Once we are clear about the conceptual basis for those obligations, courts will be less likely to arbitrarily impose obligations that employers choose not to include in the employment contract.

II. The Nature of Employees' Duty of Loyalty

Employees bear a duty of loyalty to their employers. Courts throughout the United States are divided on whether this amounts to a fiduciary duty but the trend is to hold that only 'key employees' or employees of 'confidence' are fiduciaries. Other lower level employees bear some watered down version of the fiduciary duty. In some cases, breach of that lighter duty is not an independent cause of action but merely justifies termination by an employer.

The nature of the free-standing ('non-fiduciary') employee duty of loyalty is unclear. There are several ways we might understand it. First, it might be imputed to employment contracts as a matter of public policy. Even at-will employees are said to operate by some contract, albeit not a term contract. The term requiring loyalty might be imputed by virtue of public policy, in the manner of the default at-will term. It might be imputed because productive employment, including the trust necessary to efficiently delegate duties and the incentive to train employees, depend on it.

Alternatively, the duty might be imputed because of a general consensus that certain behaviours by employees are unfair or morally wrongful. This would reflect a judgment about the ethics of the employment relationship and what constitutes a violation of its norms. Arguably, the doctrine of the 'faithless servant' invokes such judgement, reflecting social assumptions we would no longer endorse. Even if the doctrine is not a misguided rejection of insubordination but rather a morally sound rejection of vice, we would need some further account of why it is properly a mandatory element of employment contracts.

Still another possibility is that the duty is implied by the operation of the employment relation. That is, the facts of employment might in each case result in a mutual understanding between employer and employee that the latter bears a duty of loyalty, just as in rare cases their mutual understanding is that the employee will be terminated only for cause.[4] In this conceptualization, the duty is the product of actual agreement. Since the duty is acknowledged without any factual evidence of agreement, courts may reason that the employment contract simply does not make sense without the duty, such that it must be part of the agreement whether the parties would have said so or not—just as the duty of good faith and fair dealing might be imputed to every contract on the theory that parties would not rationally agree to proceed without it.

How best to understand the duty of loyalty, in light of these varied options? This part will examine the conceptual possibilities and recommend one contractual approach.

[4] The mutual understanding may not be rare but legal recognition of it is. See Jonathan Fineman, 'The Vulnerable Subject at Work: A New Perspective on the Employment at-Will Debate' (2013) 43 Sw L Rev 275 (at 290: 'implied contract claims are not a significant challenge to the dominance of the at-will rule for both practical and structural reasons'). See also Lauren B Edelman and others, 'Professional Construction of Law: The Inflated Threat of Wrongful Discharge' (1992) 26 Law & Soc'y Rev 47.

A. The fiduciary duty of loyalty

In the United States, employees are usually regarded as agents of their employers.[5] Agents are generally fiduciaries of their principals.[6] From the perspective of agency law, then, employees are presumptively subject to fiduciary duties.[7]

Indeed, the Restatement (Third) of Agency Law includes employees in a list of fiduciary-agents.[8] In part to align itself with the Restatement of Agency Law, as well as its author's reading of relevant case law, the recent Restatement (Third) of Employment Law holds that all employees may bear a duty of loyalty but not all employees are *fiduciaries*.[9] After significant controversy,[10] the Restatement seems to have backed off the blanket assertion in an earlier draft that 'employees owe a duty of loyalty to their employers in matters related to the employment relationship' and expressly provides that the rigour of the duty will vary depending on the type of employee and her level of discretion and access to confidential information. In its final form, the Restatement holds that most employees, even if subject to an 'implied contractual' duty of loyalty, do not have fiduciary duties to their employers. Fiduciary duties attach only to those who exercise substantial discretion or are entrusted with trade secrets.[11]

Some jurisdictions maintain, however, that all employees are fiduciaries based on the logic of agency law.[12] This contrast is real but perhaps not so great as it appears at first blush, given that the implications of fiduciary status vary.[13] Even where all employees are considered fiduciaries, they are not subject to the same duties; the duty of loyalty will require more of an employee positioned to inflict greater economic harm on her employer.[14]

[5] Restatement (Third) of Agency § 1.01 cmt. c (2006); Deborah A DeMott, 'Disloyal Agents', (2007) 58 Ala L Rev 1049 (at 1051: 'agents for purposes of common law agency include … employees').

[6] Restatement (Third) of Agency § 1.01 (2006) ('Agency is the fiduciary relationship that arises when one person (a "principal") manifests assent to another person (an "agent") that the agent shall act on the principal's behalf and subject to the principal's control, and the agent manifests assent or otherwise consents so to act'); *Walton v United States*, 80 Fed. Cl. 251, 273–74 (Fed. Cl. 2008).

[7] See *Nat'l R.R. Passenger Corp. v Veolia Transp. Servs.*, Inc., 791 F. Supp. 2d 33, 47 (D.D.C. 2011).

[8] Restatement (Third) of Agency Sec. 1.01 cmt. c (2006).

[9] Restatement (Third) of Employment Sec. 8.01 (2014).

[10] See Michael Selmi, 'The Restatement's Supersized Duty of Loyalty Provision' (2012) 16 Employee Rights and Employment Policy J 395, 404 (citing and criticizing initial draft of Section 8.01).

[11] Ibid at Sec. 8.01 cmt. a.

[12] See ABA Section of Brian M Malsberger and others (eds), *Labor & Employment Law, Employee Duty of Loyalty: A State-by-State Survey* (3rd ed, Bloomberg BNA, 2004); *Astra USA Inc. v Bildman*, 914 N.E.2d 36 (Mass. 2009); *St. Paul Fire & Marine Ins. Co. v Hoskins*, No. 5:10cv087, 2012 U.S. Dist. LEXIS 30770, at *15 (W.D. Va. 7 March 2012); *Williams v Dominion Tech. Partners, LLC*, 576 S.E.2d 752, 757 (Va. 2003); *Pure Power Boot Camp, Inc. v Warrior Fitness Boot Camp, Inc.*, 813 F. Supp. 2d 489, 521–22 (S.D.N.Y. 2011); *Graphic Directions, Inc. v Bush*, 862 P.2d 1020 (Colo. Ct. App. 1993); *Cenla Physical Therapy & Rehab Agency, Inc. v Lavergne*, 657 So. 2d 175, 176–77 (La. Ct. App. 1995).

[13] See, eg, *Cameco, Inc. v Gedicke*, 724 A.2d 783, 789 (N.J. 1999).

[14] Bret L Grebe, 'Fidelity at the Workplace: the Two-Faced Nature of the Duty of Loyalty under Dalton v. Camp' (2002) 80 North Carolina L Rev 1815 (at 1819: 'the employment-agency relationship gives rise to some fiduciary duty, the breadth and scope of which depends on the nature of the employment relationship').

Given the flexibility allowed within the fiduciary concept, the consensus that the duty of loyalty must vary by employee type does not preclude applying fiduciary status to all employees. Indeed, even the Restatement (Third) of Agency, which appears most demanding of employees, allows that the fiduciary duty owed by agents to their principals is not 'monolithic'.[15] In fact, the logic of fiduciary law explains why and how the substance of the duty is responsive to ground level facts about the relationship it governs.

Agents are fiduciaries where they are entrusted with property or power and where neither the principal nor the market can ensure that they will use the property or power to benefit the principal.[16] An agent's duty of loyalty requires what cannot be independently secured, that is, that the agent act for the exclusive or at least primary benefit of the principal.

In the context of employment, an employee-fiduciary would be required to exercise judgement and direct resources to the sole benefit of her employer. Her duty is understood to apply only within the scope of employment. That restriction is not inevitable; one can imagine a more all-encompassing duty that would require employees to advance the interests of their employer in the course of all their actions, insofar as the interests of the employer are implicated one way or another. But perhaps as a concession to the movement from status to contract in employment, courts do not apply so demanding a duty to employees, one that would seem to subsume the employee more wholly under the wing of her employee than employment is now understood to do. Instead, employees are expected to make decisions in the course of employment with a sole eye to their employer's interests.

'Key employees' or employees 'of confidence' are sometimes characterized as those called upon to make more decisions, or more consequential ones, for their employers. But even low-level employees make myriad decisions of great consequence for their employers. Consider a truck driver who must decide whether to obey a traffic rule, or just how fast to drive. Or a delivery person who must decide whether to leave a package in front of a home or attempt delivery on another date. Or a customer service representative who must decide whether to permit a discount that a customer requests. Made poorly over time, each of these employees is in a position to significantly undermine employer interests. But they are prototypical examples of employees subject to the weakest duty of loyalty. Testing for decisions of consequence does not deliver as clear a result as either our common sense or the common law.

The role of fiduciary law in policing just those decisions that cannot be effectively policed by private actors alone points to a better way to identify those employees

[15] Restatement (Third) of Agency Sec 8.01 cmt. c (2006).

[16] See Tamar Frankel, *Fiduciary Law* (Oxford University Press, 2011) 6. See also Paul Miller, 'The Fiduciary Relationship' in Andrew Gold and Paul B Miller (eds), *Philosophical Foundations of Fiduciary Law* (Oxford University Press, 2014) at 69 (defining a fiduciary relationship as one in which the fiduciary 'exercises discretionary power over the significant practical interests of' the beneficiary).

who should be subject to the more rigorous fiduciary duty: employees whose decisions cannot be regulated by way of clear decision-rules in advance, and whose decisions—including their consequences—are either not easily appraised by employers or not easily traced to those who made them. Only elite employees will have a *fiduciary* duty to their employers under this standard.

Although some employees are fiduciaries, the universal employee duty of loyalty is improperly regarded as fiduciary in nature. Employees should not be regarded as fiduciaries as a matter of status. Those employees who are fiduciaries bear heightened responsibilities by virtue of specific powers they possess; their formal status as employees should be regarded as essentially incidental. Employees generally should not be regarded as fiduciaries both because they are not situated in the power relation that gives properly rise to fiduciary duties and because they cannot plausibly be required to comply with the fiduciary duty of loyalty as it is normally articulated.

The fiduciary duty of loyalty requires employees to advance their employers' interests exclusively. This requirement is unduly burdensome and cannot sensibly be extended to most employees. It is inevitable that employees will take into account their own interests and sometimes balance them against those of their employer. It is also clearly permissible—and desirable—that they do so.

Most fiduciary roles occupy a limited space within the fiduciary's life. Lawyers are fiduciaries to multiple clients and trustees do not usually dedicate most of their days to maintenance of a single trust. But employment dominates the life of most employees, and often they are accountable to a single employer. The way than an employee conducts her work affects her daily quality of life. The decisions that affect her employers' interests deeply affect her own. Often, making decisions exclusively with an eye only to her employer's interests would undermine her own simply because it would make work more burdensome than it tends to be already. Although employees are not free to direct material resources to their own benefit, they can choose to be more or less careful, diligent, or thrifty with the employer's resources. Of course, a better employee will be more careful, diligent, and protective of her employer's interests. But it is hardly a violation of a legal duty to be less than an exemplary employee. Employees are free as a legal matter to be mediocre where they decide it is just not worth it to be better. They are still subject to the price employers will extract or withhold for that choice.

The remarkable favour that fiduciary law shows beneficiaries only makes sense when fiduciaries are not themselves vulnerable to the decisions they are making on their beneficiaries' behalf. This point relates, of course, to the more fundamental problem with applying the fiduciary framework to employees. The power relation between employers and employees is not such as to require protection of employers.

As agents, employees do exercise power over their employers. Many are in a position to take advantage of their employers. But fiduciary law offers effective protection against such exploitation only where employers learn of a violation. In those cases, most employers are able to protect themselves absent a fiduciary duty as well. They may discipline or terminate an employee *ex post*, and importantly, they may contract in advance both to entitle themselves to appropriated profits and compensatory liquidated damages. Given the ready availability of self-help, there is no need to subject employees to fiduciary duties.

Imposing a fiduciary duty of loyalty is perverse given the actual power dynamic between employees and employers. As compared to other advanced industrialized democracies, employers in the United States enjoy unrivaled prerogative to terminate employees at-will and unilaterally alter their terms and conditions of employment.[17] With a low social wage (ie, resources available to persons by virtue of citizenship or residency), employees are radically dependent on their employers for basic resources.[18] If fiduciary duties apply to agents whose power cannot be checked by principals or markets, employees stand in almost the opposite condition. Their conduct vis-à-vis employer-principals is highly conscribed by their employers directly and by labour markets indirectly.

Most states in the United States have abandoned the fiduciary model of employment. Although the best alternative is debatable—and the question of the next sections—on its own terms the fiduciary duty of loyalty is inapt. Employees whose actions cannot be effectively controlled, either by clear *ex ante* rules or *ex post* assessment, may rightly be held to be fiduciaries of their employers. But employees should not be subject to any fiduciary duty to their employers by virtue of their employment per se.

B. Contract-based models of the employee duty of loyalty

An alternative model for understanding employees' duty of loyalty is that of employment contract. One might worry that this is not an alternative at all since contract is always (now) the basis for employment, such that a fiduciary duty that attaches by virtue of one's job must indirectly depend on the underlying contract. However, though fiduciary duties usually attach only where contracts put fiduciaries in their positions of power, the content of those duties does not derive from the underlying contract. Just as a consumer contract may create a relationship between a customer and a boat operator and yet subject the boat operator to non-contractual obligations in tort, so an employment contract can be the basis for the employment relation yet to give rise to fiduciary obligations. As discussed *infra*, it is commonplace to subject employers to a range of duties irrespective of the content of employment contracts. Might the employee duty of loyalty be of this type? This section first considers the

[17] Marian Riedy and Kim Sperduto, 'At Will Fiduciaries? The Anomalies of a "Duty of Loyalty" in the Twenty-First Century' (2014) 93 Nebraska L Rev 267 (at 285: 'the employment relationship is the mirror-image of the fiduciary relationship').

[18] Gosta Esping-Anderson, *The Three Worlds of Welfare Capitalism* (Princeton University Press, 1990) 115 (defining social wage as 'the share of a nation's resources that is distributed according to social rather than strict market criteria').

question of how a contract-based duty differs in principle from a status-based conception. It then explores several variants of the contractual alternative.

1. The contract difference

Fundamentally, the choice between the contract and status-based models of the employee duty of loyalty turns on whether the law aims to recognize an obligation that employees undertake in exchange for compensation, or whether it instead regulates the employment relationship for ends outside those that the parties pursue. This characterization of the choice may be jarring since, as a formal matter, fiduciary duties protect beneficiaries, not third parties. Nevertheless, mandatory duties imposed on a contractual relationship for the benefit of one party are best understood as indirectly advancing some public interest, broadly conceived.

Duties imposed on *employers* are often status-based. Minimum wage requirements are not about enforcing bargains. The employees who benefit from these requirements are not usually in the position to bargain for much. They are rather 'takers' of the price for their labour, and given their alternatives it is plausible that they would agree to work for less than minimum wage.

Employment laws nevertheless impose duties on the employer beyond what employees can extract bilaterally. Regulations reflect social ends that include but are not limited to the particular ends that motivate a given employee in her contract. The social purposes of employment law range from the advancement of distributive justice to maintaining community living standards to increasing consumer demand. Promoting the welfare of particular employees is often incidental to regulation but not its primary purpose. Thus, even where a particular employee would prefer to work on terms noncompliant with background regulation (for example, where she cannot obtain a position at the higher, legally-imposed price of her labour), she is not permitted to pursue her own welfare in this way at the expense of the social purposes of the relevant regulation.

Employees could be subject to duties for social ends too but it is rightly rare and probably should be rarer. Interventions in the employment relationship that grant employees rights against employers are intended to correct for the negative social externalities of contracts that are hard or highly restrictive on employees. Cumulative individual contract fails to protect employees adequately as a class. The long-term result is entrenchment and reinforcement of disadvantages borne by low-wage employees. Employers are not similarly disadvantaged over the aggregate. Interventions that protect their interests are likely to preserve or reinforce the advantages of their status in the existing socio-economic hierarchy. A few duties or restrictions on employees are responsive to coordination limitations among employers. For example, employees may not collectively boycott or picket against 'secondary employers' under American labour laws. But the sense of this restriction, if it is sensible, lies in the social interest in preventing the diffusion of industrial conflict.

An employee duty of loyalty justified by reference to social ends would have to denote some social benefits it delivers beyond the interests of individual employers. Possibly, the duty makes it more likely that employers will invest in employee training, resulting in a more productive workforce. In the absence of coordinating institutions among employers, as exist in some countries where employer associations set up apprenticeship and university-based programs, regulations that lower the probability of employee defection might be a mechanism for inducing employers to train their own employees more than they otherwise would.

But an employee duty of loyalty is a poor means to that end. Understood this way, it must impair employee mobility to serve its purpose. Yet case law on the duty of loyalty aims expressly to limit its effects on employee mobility, which is regarded not only as an important right of individual employees but also an objective of public policy, because it ensures competitive labour markets. The duty is also substantially broader than this end requires; though it limits employees' ability to compete with employers while in employment, it also prevents employees from pocketing corporate opportunities and trading in the property of the employer, independently reasonable prohibitions that do not directly serve the end of motivating employers to train employees.

An employee duty of loyalty probably does allow employers to entrust employees with more powers than they would otherwise, generating social efficiencies. But employers can contract for specific duties sufficient to allow expanded delegation of power—and this gets at the crux of why the duty should be conceived of contractually. The efficiencies of the duty of loyalty all benefit employers in the first instance. Since employers determine employees' substantive duties, they are well positioned to contract for an over-arching protective duty such as the duty of loyalty if that is what they need.

We might nevertheless grant employers a right to employee loyalty if the duty were morally compulsory in the way that many people regard some employee rights as necessary to render the employment relationship morally acceptable. But intuitions about the morality of individual employment transactions ultimately turn on context, and the justice of employment more broadly. Outside of physical endangerment, most unacceptable employment conditions are unacceptable only by reference to background markets and other social institutions. Historically, the sense that employees owed employers loyalty as a matter of morality similarly depended on quasi-feudal ideas about the social hierarchies that the duty of loyalty helped to uphold. Having abandoned those sensibilities, the duty of loyalty plays no role in supporting a just social order.[19] Whatever its merits, the advantages it confers operate in the first instance to the benefit of the more advantaged and powerful party to the employment transaction. We can make sense of these private benefits only if they are privately secured through contract.

[19] Benjamin Aaron and Matthew Finkin, 'The Law of Employee Loyalty in the United States' (1999) 20 Comp. Labor Law & Pol'y J 321 (at 340: identifying a 'sea change in public attitude' that may undermine 'implied obligation of respectful obedience').

A contractual model of duty of loyalty faces a few immediate obstacles. First, it might appear to unduly limit remedies. Second, it might suggest that courts are not free to construe the content of the duty in light of ground-level facts. Finally, it might threaten to render the duty more burdensome for low-level employees due to manipulation by employers. The contractual model can, however, overcome each of these obstacles.

If understood as a contract-based obligation, remedies for disloyalty by employees would normally be limited to expectation damages. In many cases, employers might have no demonstrable damages.[20] Specific performance, in the form of an order of loyal service, is not an option. In some cases, a negative injunction would be possible to stop an employee or former employee from continuing to engage in the 'disloyal' conduct. But the typical remedy of disgorgement for disloyal conduct in a fiduciary regime is anomalous on a contractual understanding of the duty.[21]

Disgorgement is sometimes an intuitively appropriate remedy in cases of employee disloyalty, as where a disloyal employee has converted property or opportunities for profit. If an employee trades a company discount for something of value to herself, it is not clear that (or at least, what) the company has lost, since the customer using the discount might not otherwise have made the purchase. If an employee uses confidential information to compete with a former employer, the employer will have difficulty showing how much business was lost as a result. But in the former case, the employer would be able to show the value that the employee extracted in exchange for the company discount, or in the latter case, the profits that the employee earned using the confidential information.

Courts could, of course, simply marry a contractual understanding of the underlying right of action with a nonstandard contractual remedy. Restitution is not outside the bounds of contract remedies, after all.[22] But it would certainly cast a doubt on a contractual conception of the employee duty of loyalty if at the all-important remedial stage the contractual basis for the obligation ceased to do work.

There is, however, an alternative approach to remedies that would over time offer remedies comparable to those now available, albeit on distinct grounds. A combination of liquidated damages, broadly conceived expectation damages, and restitution in exceptional cases would achieve common sense restoration. Under the contract model, employers can specify damages where they would be difficult to establish.

[20] See Charles Sullivan, 'Mastering the Faithless Servant?: Reconciling Employment Law, Contract Law, and Fiduciary Duty' (2011) Wisconsin L Rev. 777 (at 793: 'normal contract remedies are often either legally or practically inadequate when an employee breaches').

[21] Conventional wisdom holds that disgorgement is not among the usual remedies in contract. See Restatement (Second) of Contracts § 344 (listing protected interests as expectation, reliance, and restitution). Farnsworth drafted the Restatement and defends the exclusion of disgorgement in E Allan Farnsworth, 'Your Loss or My Gain? The Dilemma of the Disgorgement Principle in Breach of Contract' (1985) 94 Yale LJ 1339. See also Dan B Dobbs, *Law of Remedies* Vol 3 (2nd ed, West Publishing, 1993) §12.7(4) at 171. Disgorgement is not wholly absent in contract law, however, and may play an important role on the margins. See Melvin Eisenberg, 'The Disgorgement Interest in Contract Law' (2006)105 Mich L Rev 559.

[22] See James Edelman, *Gain-Based Damages: Contract, Tort, Equity and Intellectual Property* (Hart Publishing, 2002) 149–89.

Of course, they would not be entitled to disgorgement per se on this approach. But the defendant's profits might be the best *ex ante* estimate of the loss the employer expects to suffer, and therefore qualify as enforceable liquidated damages. Where the employee's gains are not a plausible estimation of employer losses, it is not clear why the employer should be entitled to them anyway.

In some cases, even though an employer would not be entitled to disgorgement, she may be entitled to a different compensatory remedy. In the above example, where an employee has traded on a company discount, courts could apply a presumption that sales would have taken place absent the discount and employers could recover the value of the discount. Employees could rebut the presumption where they have evidence that the sales would not otherwise have taken place. Similar causal presumptions would allow for recovery of expectation damages in a variety of situations where courts now order disgorgement.

Some cases will remain intractable from the standpoint of ordinary contract remedies, in that expectation damages, reliance damages, and specific performance are all inapt. In those cases, courts could proceed with disgorgement of the value usurped by the disloyal employee. The upshot would be a remedial regime that is not unlike the one presently applied in employee duty of loyalty cases, but more firmly rooted in contract.

The second is that the contract model appears to assign little weight to ground-level facts about the employment relationship that arise after the time employment begins. The terms of contracts are generally set at the moment of formation. If the content of a duty of loyalty turns on agreement, then the ongoing evolution of the relationship will not inform the contract. By contrast, under the fiduciary model what counts as loyalty changes and the underlying relationship and circumstances change.[23] As Daniel Markovits has argued, this reflects a fundamental difference in the normative presuppositions underlying contractual and fiduciary duties.[24]

There are, however, two major exceptions to the general principle that contract terms are set at formation: course of performance can be used to interpret ambiguous terms in the original agreement, and terms can be modified. The ground-level facts of employment can be used to interpret the duty of loyalty where employers have failed to specify its contents *ex ante*. And where *ex ante* specification of the duty is at odds with practice, employees (or employers, for that matter) can argue that it has been impliedly modified. In this way, facts about the degree of access employees have to confidential information, the level of discretion they are afforded, or the extent of monitoring and control to which they are subject—all of which appropriately inform how rigorous their duty of loyalty should be—will still be taken into account.

Ambiguity and modification need only be relied upon where an express agreement exists. In the vast majority of cases, employees are at-will and have no written

[23] See, eg, *Rash v J.V. Intermediate, Ltd.*, 498 F.3d 1201, 1207–09 (10th Cir. 2007). See also Leslie Larkin Cooney, 'Employee Fiduciary Duties: One Size Does Not Fit All' (2010) 79 Miss LJ 853, 868.

[24] See Daniel Markovits, 'Sharing *Ex Ante* and Sharing *Ex Post*' in Gold and Miller (n 16).

employment agreement. In these cases, the employment contract is recreated daily. It is here even more plausible that the mutual understanding of employer and employee can be reconstructed only by reference to the operational facts of employment. Consideration of these facts does not imply that employees' legal obligations transform over time; rather, facts are used to reveal the nature of the obligation that employees plausibly undertook to begin with.

The concern about consideration of ground-level facts gives rise to a final, more substantial risk of the contract paradigm. If the duty of loyalty is a contractual term, it is subject to specification by the parties. And it will usually be the employer who details its scope and perhaps the remedy for its breach, as suggested *supra*. This might lead to a perverse expansion of the duty for the vast majority of employees who take the terms of their employment without negotiation, and without the ability to shop around for better terms.

The ability of employers to impose onerous duties on employees is a real one, but it is not a byproduct of conceptualizing the duty of loyalty as contractual. Employers are already able to specify what employees must or must not do within few statutory bounds. The duty of loyalty serves only to clarify that certain conduct is prohibited even where the employer has not expressly so provided. Because it is a gap filler, parties are able to reduce the size of the gap irrespective of the normative basis for the filler. Conceiving of the duty of loyalty in contractual terms will no more enable party control over employment terms than the general duty of good faith and fair dealing can be said to enable freedom of contract more generally.

This section has had two aims in some tension with each other. My first aim was to describe the conceptual difference between contract and status-based employee of loyalty. My second was to show that certain intuitively attractive aspects of the duty of loyalty could persist in a contractual paradigm. The next part will explore several different forms the contractual approach might take. The next section will consider some of the doctrinal consequences of a shift to the best contractual approach.

2. *Variations on the contractual duty of loyalty*

There is more than one way to conceive of the employee duty of loyalty in contractual terms. The following discussion is intended to identify more precisely the contractual basis of the duty, and is thus relevant even to those jurisdictions which already recognize it as an implied contract term.[25] All of the forms I consider here share an important feature of the existing doctrinal duty: they are mandatory. Every employee is subject to the duty of loyalty.[26]

[25] See *CRC-Evans Canada Ltd. v Pettifer* (1997) 26 C.C.L. (2d) 294 (Alta. Q. B.) at 303; James Oakley, 'Employee Duty of Loyalty—A Canadian Perspective' (1999) 20 Comp. Labor Law & Pol'y J 185, 187, 189; Manfred Weiss, 'Employee Loyalty in Germany' (1999) 20 Comp. Labor Law & Pol'y J 237, 238–39.

[26] In part because the nature of the duty is highly contested and unsettled, it is not actually clear that all jurisdictions recognize a universal employee duty of loyalty. However, it looks as though the

a. Duty of public policy

The first two ways to understand the duty of loyalty interpret it as an implied term of public policy. They differ in the grounds of public policy invoked: economic policy, and public morality, respectively. Courts might hold employees to a duty of loyalty because it makes workers more productive directly (an indirect argument will be considered shortly). Firms presumably perform better when their employees advance their employers' interests. This logic is akin to that behind the at-will rule, which is supposed to support business flexibility. But it goes much further because the at-will rule is only a default.

Further justification would be needed to explain why employees should be held to the duty without the possibility to opt-out. Scholars have suggested additional indirect economic benefits of employee loyalty. The duty arguably provides employers with the assurance necessary to invest in employee training, and to efficiently delegate work and share business information.

Many employees, however, receive no training with the duty securely in place. The other two economic benefits are conferred in the first instance on the employer alone and are for that reason not properly conceived as reasons of public policy. Only terms that benefit third parties are imputed as a matter of public policy, especially in mandatory form. There is little reason to think that employers would undervalue efficient workplace operations in configuring work conditions.

The alternative public policy justification would turn to shared understandings about the ethics of employment. The duty at issue, after all, is that employees should be loyal. Loyalty is regarded as a virtue in many relationships.[27] Assuming it is at least sometimes a virtue, is the employment relation properly one to which it applies? And is cultivation of virtue a proper aim of public policy in contract law?

The employee duty of loyalty appears to be an outgrowth of the master-servant framework of employment. The 'faithless servant' doctrine allows employers to recover for just those behaviours that constitute violations of the duty of loyalty.[28] It has been scaled back substantially over time. For example, employees are permitted to prepare to compete with employers during their employment as long as they do not actually compete until they have left employment. Employer claims that an employee has used confidential information are scrutinized for evidence of access and use. I will assume that the conduct that the duty of loyalty now prohibits is deplorable well outside the semi-feudal mindset that led to the original doctrinal framework.

Nevertheless, it is doubtful that the conduct is any more morally deplorable than other opportunistic behaviour by contracting parties known to each other. The employment relationship may be uniquely emotionally ridden because, especially in small work settings, employer and employee spend large amounts of time

jurisdictions that plausibly do not recognize any duty for low-level employees are really rejecting application of a fiduciary duty to those employees.

[27] See Alan Wolfe, *Moral Freedom: The Search for Virtue in a World of Choices* (W W Norton & Company, 2001) 21; Simon Keller, *The Limits of Loyalty* (Cambridge University Press 2007) 21–23, 218 (though sceptical, casting loyalty as practically necessary). But see James Penner, in Gold and Miller, *supra* note 16.

[28] See Sullivan, *supra* note 20.

together and depend on each other in myriad small and big ways. But the moral fabric of employment relationships varies considerably. In some, there is closeness and camaraderie. In others, there is sharp distrust and resentment. The ethics of what employees owe their employers are responsive to how the employer has treated its employees. But the cases on employees' duty of loyalty are not. Although courts look to ground-level facts to determine the content of a duty of loyalty, the relevant facts are the extent of delegation and access to confidential information. Courts do not inquire what loyalty a particular employer properly commands from a given employee from a moral point of view. Furthermore, it is highly anomalous to 'moralize' the duty of loyalty in this way where there is no comparable legal interest in the ethics of employer behaviour. Absent symmetry, the alleged moral foundation of the duty of loyalty appears to rest not on any formal principle of private obligation but just those parochial norms specific to employment that render an employee duty of loyalty suspect in the first place.

Both public-policy-based understandings of the employee duty of loyalty also face a separate, common obstacle. Although the duty is mandatory, as noted *supra*, employers can specify more particular duties or damages. Moreover, where employers are prepared to authorize particular behaviours that might plausibly qualify as violations of the duty, those authorizations operate to narrow the duty and preempt its application. To the extent the duty of loyalty is motivated by social interests outside those of the parties to a contract, it is unclear why the parties should be able to pare it down as it suits their particular interests.

b. Duty of implied agreement

Instead of imputing the duty of loyalty as a matter of public policy, courts might read it into agreements as an implied term. That is, they might infer the duty because the words and conduct of the party imply its existence. Of course, on this theory of the duty, courts would have to 'read' it into every employment agreement. Implied terms are not usually universal to a contract type in this way. But perhaps there is something about the employment relationship, a universal or inevitable dynamic that is characteristic of every employment relationship, that justifies constructing each of them as embodying a voluntary commitment on the part of the employee to comport with certain norms of loyalty.

The problem with this approach is that it has difficulty accounting for the mandatory character of the duty. To be sure, it is the most contractual of the contractual approaches for precisely this reason: it turns on the mutual understanding of the parties. But though the voluntary character of contract is its usual appeal as an alternative to status-based duties, it is an obstacle when explaining mandatory duties. Even if we could imagine that employees implicitly undertake a duty of loyalty to their employers, the fact that such a commitment could in principle be avoided puts it at odds with the duty as we know it. We cannot explain the duty as it exists in this way.

c. Duty of loyalty as derivative of the duty of good faith

The final and best method for accounting for the duty of good faith within the contract paradigm is as a corollary of the duty of good faith and fair dealing. The duty of good faith is a mandatory duty applicable to all contracts. It is in some ways a hybrid of the two types of contract terms considered above. Although formally closer to a duty of public policy, it is not required for the benefit of third parties. But nor is it open to exclusion by the parties, as an implied term must be. It is mandatory but nevertheless regarded as inevitably implicit in parties' mutual agreement.

Contracts do not make sense without the duty of good faith and fair dealing. No party would rationally agree to proceed without it. This is because good faith requires only that the parties perform as expected, without attempting to usurp opportunities or reclaim value that was forfeited. It is by definition consistent with party agreement, even if it does not derive from it. Although it has a moral cast, it is the morality of an arms-length relation that does not depend on or even take interest in the interpersonal dynamic between the parties. It is sufficiently thin that it is assumed at the outset of every contract, yet what is required by way of compliance may turn on facts that arise after formation. It is efficient in that it prevents parties from undertaking wasteful protective measures but it need not rely on this economic rationale for its justification. Its inevitability in the logic of agreement is sufficient to explain its universal applicability.

In all of these respects, the duty of good faith and fair dealing resembles the employee duty of loyalty, which is best understood as an instantiation of the more general duty of good faith in the particular context of the employment relationship. There is a moral wrong in disloyal conduct by employees, but it is a wrong that does not turn on employees' status or any personal relationship between the parties. The duty enhances the efficiency of employment and is an element of well-designed employment, but it does not primarily promote amorphous public interests in efficient employment practices. It can be assumed to be a point of agreement between employees and employers, and their express terms determine its content in any given agreement; but it is beyond their power to reject. It does not make sense for employees to undertake job responsibilities for an employer only to reserve the option of undermining the employer in the very course of those job functions.

Importantly, understood as an aspect of the duty of good faith, the duty of loyalty is malleable. Parties can, and do, fill in its content by requiring that employees perform particular tasks and foreswear from certain conduct. Parties do not opt out of the duty of loyalty when they detail these job duties, any more than ordinary contract obligations depart from the duty of good faith. Just as all substantive contract terms minimize the gaps to be filled with the general duty of good faith, substantive terms of an employment contract leave less work to be done by the employee duty of loyalty.

III. The Narrow Reading of the Duty of Loyalty

Thus far this chapter has assessed several conceptions of the employee duty of loyalty, in and out of a contract paradigm, and recommended understanding it as an implication of the more general duty of good faith and fair dealing in contract. In this part, I suggest how the duty should evolve when viewed in this way. Specifically, I recommend a narrow reading that does not impose obligations on employees that employers are well positioned to secure expressly. The open-ended character of the duty of loyalty[29] creates the risk of opportunistic assertions of employee disloyalty by employers. Employers can allege disloyal conduct without hope of ultimately prevailing, forcing some employees to bear the cost and stigma of defending themselves and perhaps causing others to foreswear even permissible behaviour in an abundance of caution. As always, courts should avoid rewarding strategic gaps that permit employer overreach after the fact. Although the status hierarchy that permeates the employment relation does no direct work in this analysis, the related asymmetry of power and information motivates the argument for a narrow default duty of loyalty.

Courts are ill positioned to assess power and information asymmetries directly. They should look instead to features of the employment contract that might indicate how expansive or narrow the duty of loyalty should be in a given case. Two features will be considered here: the terms of exit and the specification of substantive duties. The absence of these provisions—in the case of at-will contracts for employees over whom employers enjoy total discretion—cuts in favour of the narrowest reading of the duty of loyalty.

A. Exit

Most employees in the United States are at-will, which means that they can be terminated for 'a good reason, bad reason or no reason'.[30] They are not entitled to either notice or severance. This policy is justified primarily by reference to business interests in flexibility, but one of its defensive justifications is that it respects a formal equality in the employment relation. Employees are free to exit at will too. Both justifications of at-will employment point in favour of a weak duty of loyalty as applied to cases involving preparation for competition, one of the major categories of employee loyalty cases.

Business flexibility is said to be an essential advantage of American businesses.[31] Firms can quickly build up and build down, adapting to dynamic markets. Markets remain dynamic, though, only if firms are subject to robust competition, with firms not only growing and shrinking but with new firms entering and exiting the marketplace. The higher the barriers to entry, the less dynamic and competitive we can expect a market to be.

A strong duty of employee loyalty can be expected to raise barriers to entry for some of those best positioned to compete. People who have worked in an industry are an important class of potential competitors, and an important source of know-how for other potential competitors. In order for employees to compete upon exit

[29] See Deborah A. DeMott, 'Beyond Metaphor: An Analysis of Fiduciary Obligation' (1988) Duke LJ 879, 879; Lawrence E Mitchell, 'The Death of Fiduciary Duty in Close Corporations' (1990) 138 U Pa L Rev 1675, 1696.

[30] See Pauline T. Kim, 'Bargaining with Imperfect Information: A Study of Worker Perceptions of Legal Protection in an At-Will World' (1997) 83 Cornell L Rev 105, 107.

[31] Richard A Epstein, 'In Defense of the Contract At Will' (1984) 51 U Chi L Rev 947, 982.

from their present positions, they must be able to make detailed arrangements or bear the high cost of a gap between employment and the start of their new businesses. Once in a new position, employee-entrepreneurs should also be able to take advantage of expertise they developed in a prior position; otherwise, they will not pose the meaningful competitive threat that a dynamic economy requires. The same interest in business flexibility that justifies at-will employment justifies a narrow construal of the duty of loyalty. Employers who avail themselves of the at-will default can be understood to subject their employees to a complementary regime of limited duties of loyalty.

The other, defensive justification for at-will employment points in the same direction. Both employees and employers are equally entitled to end an at-will employment relationship. But in reality firms are freer to terminate than most employees are to exit.[32] Most employees do not have the economic wherewithal simply to quit an unpleasant job without thought to future income. Most will apply for other jobs first. But a few will either attempt to start a new business of their own, or join others who are setting up a new firm and taking colleagues with them. Restrictions that make this process more burdensome and risky undermine freedom of exit from employment. Policymakers have long resisted notice and severance obligations for employers on a similar logic, ie, that these would unduly burden the valuable right to end the employment relationship. Because the duty of loyalty burdens employee exit, it too should be construed narrowly. Again, this presumption applies with greatest force where the employer retains the right to terminate at will.

These considerations are defensive, in that they aim to show that the justifications for the at-will default in legal discourse are consistent with associating at-will employment with a narrow duty of employee loyalty. The affirmative case for the proposed association, that is, treating at-will employment as an indication that the parties have agreed upon a limited employee duty of loyalty, is that in these cases we have no reason to think that employers have contracted for a more exacting one. An employer's ability to terminate an employee without explanation or recourse is sufficiently disciplining of employee behaviour. Courts can assume that employers with that prerogative will not pay for a robust duty of loyalty. Parties do not rationally bargain for redundant contractual protections because people do not rationally buy things they do not need. The affirmative case for a weak duty of loyalty is an exercise in rational reconstruction of the parties' agreement, and is not underwritten by first-order reliance on substantive policy preferences.

[32] There is a debate outside the scope of this essay about whether corporate directors and officers should owe a duty of loyalty to the corporation's employees. See, eg, Terry O'Neill, 'Employees' Duty of Loyalty and the Corporate Constituency Debate' (1993) 25 Conn L Rev 681; Marleen A O'Connor, 'Restructuring the Corporation's Nexus of Contracts: Recognizing a Fiduciary Duty to Protect Displaced Workers' (1991) 69 NC L Rev 1189, 1259–60; Katherine Van Wezel Stone, 'Employees as Stakeholders Under State Nonshareholder Constituency Statutes' (1991) 21 Stetson L Rev 45, 48.

Some employers go beyond the at-will default to require that employees arbitrate any claims against the employer, claims most likely to arise upon termination of the relationship by either side.[33] Employers may also prohibit class actions by employees, further burdening the right to litigate.[34] These provisions make the employee even more vulnerable than the at-will default because they make it difficult to challenge even unlawful termination by the employer, as in cases of discrimination. They also locate the employment relationship on the fringes of the law, almost outside the bounds of the courts. The employee duty of loyalty should be read accordingly. Just as employees enjoy little public recourse for employer violations when subject to terms requiring arbitration and prohibiting class actions, employers should have little recourse beyond termination for employee violations of the duty of loyalty.

B. Discretion

The second set of contract features that often justify a narrow reading of the duty of loyalty relates to the degree of discretion enjoyed by the employer over the employee's job functions. This aspect of an employment contract is more elusive than terms covering exit. It speaks to the level of control exercised by the employer over the employee's daily activities. High-level employees, even if at-will, may enjoy considerable control over how they discharge their responsibilities. Their performance may be strictly evaluated but their methods and efforts subject to less scrutiny. Lower level employees may find their every move subject to the most rigid control. Variation in this aspect of the work experience is one of the most startling and disturbing inequalities in the day-to-day lives of working people.

High-level employees entrusted with more sensitive information are already subject to a more rigorous duty of loyalty. The argument I advance here supports this approach but for different reasons, emphasizing the significance of control over trust. It is intuitive to say, as the cases do, that employees in whom employers have placed greater trust should be held to a higher standard. But it remains ambiguous what trust entails, and it is likely that courts assessing the degree of 'trust' in a particular employee will tend to focus on whether her judgement is relied upon.

The approach here focuses instead on the presence or absence of contract terms that specify job duties, effectively restricting the employer in what it can expect from the employee. Where a contract is silent on this and the employer is unconstrained in what it may require of an employee, including the hours and locations she is expected to work, or the output demanded of her, the employer can be regarded as having deliberately left a gap with respect to employees' substantive duties. That

33 See Marcy Greenwade, 'The Future of Mandatory Employe Arbitration Agreements' (2014) J Disp Resol 135 (discussing legal status and controversy over employment arbitration agreements).

34 See Stephanie Greene and Christine Neylon O'Brien, 'The NLRB v. The Courts: Showdown Over the Right to Collective Action in Workplace Disputes' (2015) 52 Am Bus LJ 75 (discussing legal status and controversy over prohibitions against collective action in employment agreements).

gap may be rational, even efficient; but the employer ought not to be able to pair the advantages of such open-endedness with highly forgiving defaults in her favour.

Viewing the duty of loyalty through the lens of good faith reveals it to be just another poorly specified obligation of employment. Where an employer has avoided specification of the conditions and expectations of employment to its own advantage, its withholding of information from the employee over its expectations warrants a penalty default that limits the employer's entitlement under the background duty of loyalty. Courts should not correct an employer's failure to specify an employee's obligations, including duties of forbearance, where that silence is intended to preserve maximum flexibility for the employer at the expense of employee security and stability of expectations.

It is important to note that, though the duty of loyalty is mandatory, employers can avoid the narrow reading proposed here. They need only avoid the contract terms that trigger a lighter duty.[35] Doing so will provide at least formal notice, and may even trigger compensation if the obligation is priced. Of course, we can expect that few employers will opt out of loyalty-lite where doing so requires that they forego valuable discretion with respect to job duties and termination. The duty of loyalty is worth less to employers as a legal obligation than the various prerogatives they would need to forego in order to win a stronger loyalty entitlement. As it is, the duty of loyalty's disciplining effect may lie in its ambiguity, or the general sense that employees owe something to their employers beyond the particular tasks assigned to them; something in their basic orientation to the firm. The few improvements in clarity of mutual expectations that we might see where an employer seeks to avoid a weak loyalty default would be valuable. A gradual shift away from the amorphous sentiment of general obligation that the duty of loyalty appears to demand of employees would be more valuable still.

IV. Conclusion

The contract paradigm in employment has its limits. Its language of a voluntary bargain may fail to resonate with many employees. Its focus on the two parties to a transaction misses much of the social import of work. Nevertheless, there were enormous moral gains achieved in the move from status to contract. The move helped to usher a broad cultural shift in our perceptions of workplace entitlements, and that sea change set the stage for subsequent status-based interventions on behalf of employees in modern employment law. The result is overlapping legal frameworks, and we would benefit from an overarching analytic scheme that allocates questions

[35] Contrast the practice of specifying substantive duties in order to avoid the light form of the duty, about which I speculate here, with the possibility of contracting out of the duty. The latter would be impossible on the reading proposed here, just as parties may not contract out of the duty of good faith more generally. Cf J Dennis Hynes, 'Freedom of Contract, Fiduciary Duties, and Partnerships: The Bargain Principle and the Law of Agency' (1997) 54 Wash & Lee L Rev 439.

arising in the context of employment among those frameworks. For now, we should hesitate to grant employers private claims against their employees for which they have not contracted. This requires that we locate a universal employee obligation such as the duty of loyalty in a universal feature of contract—the general duty of good faith in performance—and adjust its scope and content accordingly.

12

Firms and Fiduciaries

*D Gordon Smith**

I. Introduction

The first task of fiduciary law is to distinguish fiduciary and non-fiduciary relationships. Most fiduciary relationships 'are treated as such as a matter of status or convention'.[1] These so-called 'categorical' fiduciary relationships are varied, including relationships between trustees and beneficiaries, agents and principals, directors and corporations, and guardians and wards. Other relationships may be treated as fiduciary on an informal or ad hoc basis.[2] Whether categorical or ad hoc, fiduciary relationships—and the distinctive duty of loyalty that is imposed on such relationships—call out for justification.[3]

In prior work, I have argued that economists who study the theory of the firm draw a line between firms and markets that corresponds to the line lawyers draw between fiduciary and non-fiduciary relationships.[4] Inspired by the property-rights theory of the firm,[5] I proposed the Critical Resource Theory (CRT), which holds that the distinguishing feature of fiduciary relationships is that 'a fiduciary exercises discretion with respect to a critical resource belonging to the beneficiary, whereas

* Glen L. Farr Professor of Law, J. Reuben Clark Law School, Brigham Young University. Special thanks to Deborah DeMott, Andrew Gold, Christine Hurt, Matt Jennejohn, Peter Klein, Paul Miller, Jeff Schwartz, and Julian Velasco for comments, and to Daniel Lyman and Tyson Prisbrey for research assistance.

[1] Andrew S Gold and Paul B Miller, 'Introduction' in Andrew S Gold and Paul B Miller (eds), *Philosophical Foundations Of Fiduciary Law* (Oxford University Press, 2014) 1, 2.

[2] See Deborah A DeMott, 'Relationships of Trust and Confidence in the Workplace' (2015) 100 Cornell L Rev 1255, 1261 ('courts impose ad hoc or fact-based fiduciary duties when although the parties' relationship was not categorically fiduciary, its characteristics nonetheless justified one party's expectation of loyal conduct from the other').

[3] For leading accounts, see Tamar Frankel, *Fiduciary Law* (Oxford University Press, 2011); Paul B Miller, 'Justifying Fiduciary Duties' (2013) 58 McGill L J 1014; D Gordon Smith, 'The Critical Resource Theory of Fiduciary Duty' (2002) 55 Vand L Rev 1399.

[4] Smith, *Critical Resource Theory* (n 3) at 1404–05.

[5] See generally Oliver Hart, *Firms, Contracts, and Financial Structure* (Oxford University Press, 1995) 29–55; Sanford J Grossman and Oliver D Hart, 'The Costs and Benefits of Ownership: A Theory of Vertical and Lateral Integration' (1986) 94 J Pol Econ 691; Oliver Hart and John Moore, 'Incomplete Contracts and Renegotiation' (1988) 56 Econometrica 755; Oliver Hart and John Moore, 'Property Rights and the Nature of the Firm' (1990) 98 J Pol Econ 1119.

most contracting parties exercise discretion only with respect to their own performance under the contract.'[6] Under this account, 'the duty of loyalty that is the essence of fiduciary duty protects beneficiaries against opportunistic behavior by fiduciaries.'[7]

Economists and lawyers are interested in the distinction between markets and firms for different reasons.[8] Where economists are keen to compare the allocation of resources through the price mechanism with the allocation of resources through 'managed coordination',[9] lawyers are interested to know when courts should impose the distinctive duty of loyalty that accompanies fiduciary service. The feature of firms that distinguishes managed coordination—namely, the authority that one person exercises over the resources of another—is the same feature that motivates the imposition of a duty of loyalty to channel the use of that authority.

In this chapter, I refine the description of 'resources' under CRT using the resource-based view of the firm (RBV) and extend the analysis of CRT to two important implications flowing from the basic structure of fiduciary relationships: (1) while some features of fiduciary relationships are traceable to the logic of contract and some features are traceable to the logic of property, fiduciary relationships are unique hybrid institutions; and (2) the distinctive duty of loyalty that is imposed on fiduciary relationships is designed to protect the beneficiary's property-like interest in critical resources. Section II offers a brief history of the theory of the firm, showing how arm's-length contracts differ structurally from multi-person firms. Section III revisits the concept of 'resources' under CRT and compares it with the more capacious conception of resources under RBV. Section IV shows that firms are not merely a special form of contract or property, but a unique hybrid organization. Section V discusses the implications of this analysis for the duty of loyalty and the remedy of disgorgement.

[6] Ibid at 1403. Paul Miller offers an account that is similar to CRT. In this account, instead of exercising discretion over the 'critical resources' of the beneficiary, the fiduciary 'enjoys discretionary power over the significant practical interests of another'. Paul B Miller, 'A Theory of Fiduciary Liability' (2011) 56 McGill LJ 235, 283. See also Paul B Miller, 'The Fiduciary Relationship' in Andrew S Gold and Paul B Miller (eds), *Philosophical Foundations of Fiduciary Law* (Oxford University Press, 2014) 63. In Section II of this chapter, I will revisit the concept of 'resources' and compare this concept to Miller's 'significant practical interests'.

[7] Smith, *Critical Resource Theory* (n 3) at 1402.

[8] Chief Justice Cardozo's renowned opinion in *Meinhard v Salmon* is one of many judicial opinions to frame the issue by contrasting markets (arm's-length contracts) and firms (fiduciary relationships). See *Meinhard v Salmon*, 164 N.E. 545, 546 (N.Y. 1928) ('Joint adventurers, like copartners, owe to one another, while the enterprise continues, the duty of the finest loyalty. Many forms of conduct permissible in a workaday world for those acting at arm's length, are forbidden to those bound by fiduciary ties').

[9] Harold Demsetz, *The Economics of a Business Firm: Seven Critical Commentaries* (Cambridge University Press, 1996) 15.

II. Firms

Neoclassical price theory explains how markets allocate resources through a series of exchange transactions. Under this theory, the firm is a 'black box', with resources flowing into the firm and goods coming out.[10] The internal workings of the firm are a mystery. Theories of the firm aim to open the black box, explaining the existence, boundaries, and internal structure of multi-person economic organizations.[11]

In 'The Nature of the Firm', Ronald Coase set out to provide a clear definition of the word 'firm'.[12] Coase started from the simple proposition that markets direct resources into production using the price mechanism, which operates through a series of exchange transactions.[13] Within the firm, by contrast, an entrepreneur directs resources into production,[14] suggesting that 'the distinguishing mark of the firm is the suppression of the price mechanism.'[15] In this story, therefore, the price mechanism and the entrepreneur perform the same essential function, the former in the market and the latter within the firm.[16] According to Coase, the decision to organize production within a firm makes sense only if the costs associated with firm production are less than those required by the price mechanism.[17]

[10] Harold Demsetz, 'The Firm in Economic Theory: A Quiet Revolution' (1997) 87 Am Econ Rev 426.

[11] See Nicolai J Foss, Henrik Lando, and Steen Thomsen, 'The Theory of the Firm' in Boudewijn Bouckaert and Gerrit de Geest (eds), *Encyclopedia Of Law And Economics, Volume III: The Regulation of Contracts* (Edward Elgar, 2000) 631, 632.

[12] Ronald H Coase, 'The Nature of the Firm' (1937) 4 Economica 386, 386.

[13] Ibid at 387–88.

[14] Ibid at 388 ('Outside the firm, price movements direct production, which is co-ordinated through a series of exchange transactions on the market. Within a firm, these market transactions are eliminated and in place of the complicated market structure with exchange transactions is substituted the entrepreneur-co-ordinator, who directs production').

In a later reflection on 'The Nature of the Firm', Coase disclaimed any intention to suggest that his 'firm' was a sole proprietorship and explained his use of the word 'entrepreneur' as follows: 'What I meant by the entrepreneur is the hierarchy in a business which directs resources and includes not only management but also foremen and many workmen. It is not a particularly good term, but this was the normal usage in England at that time.' Ronald H Coase, 'The Nature of the Firm: Meaning' (1988) 4 JL Econ & Org 19, 31.

[15] Coase (n 12) at 389. [16] Ibid at 389.

[17] Ibid at 390. This is a point on which there has been some confusion among readers of Coase. In a later reflection on the article, he attempted to clarify his position:

> There is … one misunderstanding that, I fear, is both widespread and serious, one that relates to the very heart of my thesis. This concerns the source of the gains which accrue through the existence of the firm. My view is, of course, that they come from a reduction in transaction costs. But the main transaction costs that are saved are those which would otherwise have been incurred in market transactions between the factors now cooperating within the firm. It is the *comparison* of these costs with those that would have to be incurred to operate a firm which determines whether it would be profitable to establish a firm.

Coase, 'Meaning' (n 14) at 32.

Richard Langlois has observed that the most prominent costs associated with the price mechanism—the costs of discovering prices and concluding contracts—'exist only under circumstances of novelty and change. If nothing changes in my pattern of transacting, I won't need to keep searching, and I can continue to trade with the same partners over time.' Richard N Langlois, 'The Entrepreneurial Theory of the Firm and the Theory of the Entrepreneurial Firm' (2007) 44 J Mgmt Stud 1107, 1110.

Harold Demsetz has argued that this explanation for the existence of firms does not necessarily bear on the internal organization of firms,[18] but Coase illustrated his theory of the firm using an employment relationship, comparing the costs of coordination between an employer and employee with the costs of coordination among arm's-length market participants. He later called this the 'key idea' in his article.[19] Thus, although his main purpose was to explain the existence of firms,[20] Coase felt that managed coordination among multiple participants in the firm was a necessary implication of his theory.[21]

Coase was keen to describe the costs of using the price mechanism, but he was less attentive to the costs of managed coordination. In making the comparison of markets and employment relationships, Coase seemed to assume that the employer could transmit a complete set of instructions to the employee, whose only choice occurred at the formation of the employment relationship, when the employee agreed to obey the employer.[22] But all contracts, including, and perhaps especially, employment contracts, are incomplete. Focusing his attention on the coordinating power of the entrepreneur, Coase did not acknowledge the inevitable incompleteness of the employer's instructions and the concomitant discretion left to the employee. This does not undermine the power of Coase's fundamental insight regarding the importance of comparing the costs of the price mechanism with the costs of managed coordination in explaining the existence of firms, but it raises another question posed by Harold Demsetz relating to the boundaries and internal organization of firms: 'if the contractual arrangements between a firm and its suppliers share characteristics with the contractual arrangements between a firm and its workers, and if these characteristics respond to the same types of forces, why should we distinguish between them?'[23]

The answer to this question depends in part on a simple but profound insight from Oliver Williamson, who observed that cooperation among market participants may be facilitated by vertical integration. Williamson used *transactions* as 'the basic unit of analysis',[24] and, building on Coase, asked why firms had a comparative

[18] See Demsetz (n 9) at 1 (1996) (arguing that '[m]odern treatments of the firm do not cleanly separate the organization of the firm from the question of its existence' and contending 'that mixing these two issues is a source of confusion').

[19] Ronald H Coase, 'The Nature of the Firm: Influence' (1988) 4 J L Econ & Org 33, 38.

[20] Ibid at 47.

[21] Cf Demsetz (n 9) at 15 (noting, 'a reduction in the cost of transacting is viewed not only as a source of vertical integration … but also as a substitution of the firm for the market, which comes close to identifying managed coordination as the essence of the firm').

[22] Coase, 'Nature of the Firm' (n 12) at 391 ('It is important to note the character of the contract into which a factor enters that is employed within a firm. The contract is one whereby the factor, for a certain remuneration (which may be fixed or fluctuating), agrees to obey the directions of an entrepreneur *within certain limits*. The essence of the contract is that it should only state the limits to the powers of the entrepreneur. Within these limits, he can therefore direct the other factors of production'). See also, Steven NS Cheung, 'The Contractual Nature of the Firm' (1983) 26 JL & Econ 1, 5 (arguing that a firm involves 'a form of contract that binds the input owner to follow directions instead of determining his own course by continual reference to the market prices of a variety of activities he may perform').

[23] Demsetz (n 9) at 16.

[24] Oliver E Williamson, *The Economic Institutions of Capitalism* (Simon & Schuster, 1985) 18.

advantage over markets in organizing some transactions and not others.[25] Unlike Coase,[26] Williamson placed *opportunism*—which he famously defined as 'self-interest seeking with guile'[27]—at the heart of his account of firms.[28] In a world where human agents suffer from *bounded rationality*,[29] contracts are incomplete, leaving the door open to opportunism. The risks associated with opportunism are particularly acute when one of the parties to a transaction owns assets that cannot be moved from one use to another without losing productive value, a problem that Williamson describes as *asset specificity*.[30]

[25] Williamson described this as a choice between 'markets' and 'hierarchies.' See Oliver E Williamson, 'Hierarchical Control and Optimum Firm Size' (1967) 75 J Pol Econ 123; Oliver Williamson, 'Markets and Hierarchies: Some Elementary Considerations' (1973) 63 Am Econ Rev 316; Oliver E Williamson, 'The Vertical Integration of Production: Market Failure Considerations' (1971) 61 Am Econ Rev 112. Similar work was being done at the same time by Benjamin Klein. See, eg, Benjamin Klein, 'Contracting Costs and Residual Claims: The Separation of Ownership and Control' (1983) 26 JL & Econ 367, 367–68; Benjamin Klein and Keith B. Leffler, 'The Role of Market Forces in Assuring Contractual Performance' (1981) 89 J Pol Econ 615; Benjamin Klein, 'Transaction Cost Determinants of "Unfair" Contractual Arrangements' (1980) 70 Am Econ Rev 356, 361–62; Benjamin Klein and others, 'Vertical Integration, Appropriable Rents, and the Competitive Contracting Process' (1978) 21 JL & Econ 297, 308–10. Benjamin Klein has applied transaction-cost economics in several specific contractual relationships. See, eg, Roy W Kenney and Benjamin Klein, 'The Economics of Block Booking' (1983) 26 JL & Econ 497; Benjamin Klein and Lester F Saft, 'The Law and Economics of Franchise Tying Contracts' (1985) 28 JL & Econ 345.

[26] See Demsetz (n 9) at 20:

> Opportunistic behavior is not a problem that is mentioned by Coase in his famous paper, but it is clear from his later writings ... that he does not believe opportunism offers a *special* justification for vertical integration. Therein lies a difference between Coase and those who see opportunism as an important source of vertical integration. Coase believes that there is a wide variety of coordination problems, of which opportunism is only one, and that all of these are candidates for resolution through managed coordination *or* through contractual arrangements made across markets. Which institutional arrangement seems best requires a judgment about the tradeoff between transaction and management costs, even in the case of opportunism.

This difference in view has important implications for the ability of economists to explain *why* vertical integration exists. Demsetz seems right when he observes that vertical integration has many explanations other than opportunism, including monopoly, 'continuity of operations', and 'informational advantages accruing to managed direction of activities'. Ibid at 21. Nevertheless, this debate is wholly beside the point when using the concept of firms to distinguish fiduciary and non-fiduciary relationships. One of the main rationales for imposing fiduciary duties is to combat opportunism, but the potential for opportunism need not completely justify the existence of a firm. As long as the potential for opportunism exists in firms and that potential is not completely addressed by governance mechanisms, fiduciary law has a purpose.

[27] Oliver E Williamson, 'Transaction-cost Economics: The Governance of Contractual Relations' (1979) 22 J L Econ 233, 234 n 3 ('Opportunism is a variety of self-interest seeking but extends simple self-interest seeking to include self-interest seeking with guile').

[28] Ibid at 234 ('opportunism is a central concept in the study of transaction costs').

[29] This is the notion that, try as they might, people cannot foresee all future contingencies. The term 'bounded rationality' was coined by Herbert Simon. See Herbert A Simon, *Models of Man* (Wiley, 1957) 198 (describing the 'principle of bounded rationality'). Williamson traces the recognition of this idea even further back, to the work of Chester Barnard. See Chester I Barnard, *The Functions of the Executive* (Harvard University Press, 1938) 12–45.

[30] Oliver E. Williamson, *The Mechanisms of Governance* (Oxford University Press, 1996) 59. Elsewhere, Williamson notes, 'it is the condition of asset specificity that distinguishes the competitive and governance contracting models.' Ibid at 42. For another well-known perspective on asset specificity, see Benjamin Klein and others, 'Vertical Integration, Appropriable Rents, and the Competitive

According to Williamson, the type of opportunism that motivates the creation of a firm is the 'holdup problem'.[31] When one party to an incomplete contract has invested in assets that are specific to the relationship, the counterparty will be tempted to take advantage of the situation by threatening to withdraw from the relationship unless the investing party renegotiates the deal. The creation of a new firm through vertical integration eliminates the potential for holdup opportunism. Under this view, the firm is a *governance mechanism*, the function of which is to eliminate the risk of holdup opportunism by placing the ownership of all resources in the hands of a single entrepreneur.

Sanford Grossman, Oliver Hart, and John Moore were also concerned about incomplete contracts and the potential for opportunism, but they noted that vertical integration resolved these problems only partially by moving relationships from market coordination to managed coordination. Grossman and Hart observed, 'given that it is difficult to write a complete contract between a buyer and seller and this creates room for opportunistic behavior, the transactions cost–based arguments for integration do not explain how the scope for such behavior changes when one of the self-interested owners becomes an equally self-interested employee of the other owner.'[32] In other words, for all of their substantial contributions, the Coasean and Williamsonian firms each remained a black box.

Grossman, Hart, and Moore opened that black box by focusing on *asset ownership*. In a market transaction, Party A and Party B interact at arm's length, each managing its own resources and fulfilling duties in accord with the contract. Of course, the contract is incomplete, and this incompleteness could motivate the parties to integrate into a single firm. For example, Party A might acquire the assets belonging to Party B. In the wake of this transaction, Party A would become the 'owner' of the assets of the firm, and Party B would become the 'employee' who manages those assets.[33]

In forming this new relationship, the two parties enter into a new contract (an employment agreement), but that contract would also be incomplete.[34] And so we come to the central insight of this so-called 'property rights theory' of the

Contracting Process' (1978) 21 JL & Econ 297, 298–302. For a sceptical view of asset specificity, see Yoshiro Miwa and J Mark Ramseyer, 'Rethinking Relationship-Specific Investments: Subcontracting in the Japanese Automobile Industry' (2000) 98 Mich L Rev 2636.

[31] See, eg, Williamson, *Economic Institutions* (n 24) at 78 (noting that '[m]arket contracting gives way to bilateral contracting, which in turn is supplanted by unified contracting (internal organization) as asset specificity progressively deepens').

[32] Sanford J Grossman and Oliver D Hart, 'The Costs and Benefits of Ownership: A Theory of Vertical and Lateral Integration' (1986) 94 J Pol Econ 691, 692.

[33] This stylized transaction is inspired by the hypothetical ones described in Oliver Hart, *Firms, Contracts, and Financial Structure* (Oxford University Press, 2003) 29. If Party B did not become the employee of Party A, some other party would be hired to manage the assets in the multi-person firm.

[34] The incompleteness in an employment relationship—and in other fiduciary relationships—is often intentional. D Gordon Smith and Jordan C Lee, 'Fiduciary Discretion' (2014) 75 Ohio St L J 609, 610–11 ('We contend that the grant of discretion in fiduciary relationships is not merely an artifact of human weakness, but a crucial part of the fiduciary bargain. To borrow an expression from software design, contractual incompleteness is not a bug, it's a feature').

firm: allocating residual control rights (ownership) over the assets of a firm to Party A reduces the likelihood that Party B will act opportunistically. Under this view, Party A, as owner of assets of the firm, may deter opportunistic behaviour by threatening to dismiss Party B from employment, hiring someone else to manage the assets.

According to Nicolai Foss and others, the property rights theory of the firm is 'the first to provide a formal model that could explain both the advantages and the disadvantages of firm-organization, that is, a theory that could convincingly establish the boundaries of the firm.'[35] Perhaps not surprisingly, the property rights theory of the firm has become the 'arguably dominant contemporary approach to the economics of the firm.'[36]

Coase, Williamson, and the property rights theorists each make distinct contributions to our understanding of the firm, but all of them describe the firm by reference to managed coordination among multiple participants. In light of these contributions, the answer to Demsetz's question—why should we distinguish between employees and suppliers?—should be apparent: an employee exercises discretion with respect to the resources of the entrepreneur, while a supplier exercises discretion only with regard to its own resources. The existence of a person who exercises discretion with respect to the resources of another is an essential feature of multi-person firms.[37]

Lawyers are also keen to understand the distinction between arm's length relationships and firms because relationships at arm's length are generally regulated under contract law and related doctrines, while fiduciary law supplements contract law in regulating relationships within a firm. Contract law suffices when all parties to the relationship exercise discretion only with regard to their own resources, but when one or more of the parties in the relationship exercises discretion with respect to resources belonging to other parties, additional protection of those resources is warranted. The role of fiduciary law is to channel the resource manager's exercise of discretion through the imposition of fiduciary duties.

[35] Foss and others (n 11) at 642.

[36] Kirsten Foss and Nicolai Foss, 'Coasian and Modern Property Rights Economics: A Case of Kuhnian Lost Content' (Working Paper 2014).

[37] Despite this emphasis on managed coordination, many have argued that multi-person organization is not essential to our understanding of 'firms'. Certainly, if a firm is nothing more than 'an institution that specializes in the production of goods for others', Demsetz (n 9) at 15, or 'human activity that transforms inputs into outputs', Christos Pitelis, 'Edith's Garden and a Glass Half-full: Further Issues' in *The Growth of the Firm: The Legacy of Edith Penrose* (Oxford University Press, 2002) 309, 313, then a single person could constitute a firm. See Demsetz (n 9) at 15 ('A single person can constitute a firm, producing goods for the use of others'). Although these definitions could be interesting for some purposes, they would not be helpful in understanding the questions that motivate much of the modern literature on firms.

III. Resources

Under the property rights theory of the firm, 'the defining characteristic of the firm is the collection of physical assets that are jointly owned.'[38] The reference to 'physical assets' is not intended to distinguish tangible property from intangible property. Rather, the term 'physical assets' is used simply to denote 'nonhuman assets'.[39] Oliver Hart contends that something 'as little as a place to meet' or 'even just ... the difficulty [the firm's] workers face in coordinating a move to another firm' might serve as the 'property' around which a firm organizes. Thus, the property rights theory of the firm does not invoke any particular legal notion of 'property', but relies instead on a less formal notion like the concept of 'resource' in CRT.[40]

Under CRT, a 'resource' is something that belongs to the beneficiary and 'provides the fiduciary with the occasion to act opportunistically'.[41] This latter attribute suggests that the resource is capable of being managed by the fiduciary. Resources may be tangible or intangible.[42] The 'owner' need not have legally enforceable rights in the same way that an owner of property has such rights, but the owner of a resource often has a right to exclude other people from accessing the resource.[43] In the final analysis, the 'owner' must have practical control over the resource.[44]

Like the definition of 'physical assets' under the property rights theory of the firm, the foregoing description of 'resources' in CRT extends well beyond legal notions of 'property'. It also bears some resemblance to 'resources' under the resource-based view (RBV), which is the dominant theoretical approach of organizational strategy research.[45] RBV is not a theory of the firm in the sense described

[38] Raghuram G Rajan and Luigi Zingales, 'Power in a Theory of the Firm' (1998) 113 Q J Econ 387, 388.

[39] Oliver Hart, 'An Economist's Perspective on the Theory of the Firm' (1989) 89 Colum L Rev 1757, 1765.

[40] See Smith, *Critical Resource Theory* (n 3) at 1404:

> The term 'critical resource' is introduced here to avoid the pitfalls associated with relying on the legal concept of 'property'. In many instances, a critical resource will be something that is widely recognized as property – for example, money or land that is placed in trust. In other instances, a critical resource will be something valued by the beneficiary but not ordinarily considered property – for example, the confidential information shared by a client with an attorney. For purposes of articulating a theory of fiduciary duty, an exact definition of the boundaries of the term 'critical resource' is not required. The important point is that something lies at the core of the fiduciary relationship and binds the fiduciary to the beneficiary.

[41] Smith, *Critical Resource Theory* (n 3) at 1444.

[42] Ibid at 1444.

[43] Pamela Samuelson, 'Privacy as Intellectual Property?' (2000) 52 Stan L Rev 1125, 1130 (noting that 'individuals generally have a legal right to exclude other people from access to their private data', even though such data is not 'property').

[44] Smith, *Critical Resource Theory* (n 3) at 1444.

[45] See, eg, Jeroen Kraaijenbrink, Nikos J-C Spender, and Aard J Groen, 'The Resource-Based View: A Review and Assessment of Its Critiques' (2010) 36 J Mgmt 349 (observing that RBV 'has become one of the most influential and cited theories in the history of management theorizing'); Sharon A Alvarez and Lowell W Busenitz, 'The Entrepreneurship of Resource-based Theory' (2001) 27 J Mgmt 755, 756 (noting that RBV has become 'a dominant paradigm for strategic management research').

above because it does not attempt to explain the existence, boundaries, and internal structure of multi-person economic organizations,[46] but RBV is complementary to the property rights theory of the firm.[47] Thus, a comparison of resources under CRT and RBV is instructive in understanding the nature of resources for purposes of fiduciary law.

RBV scholars study the ways in which organizations use tangible and intangible resources to gain sustained competitive advantage.[48] In his seminal work on RBV, Jay Barney defined 'firm resources' as 'all assets, capabilities, organizational processes, firm attributes, information, knowledge, etc. controlled by a firm that enable the firm to conceive of and implement strategies that improve its efficiency and effectiveness.'[49] The breadth of this definition is viewed by Barney as a strength, but others have argued that it 'is surely a weakness so long as it drives the theory toward tautology.'[50] An important feature that limits the concept of 'resources' under RBV is that they are controlled by the firm, and this is also a feature of resources under CRT.

Whether any resource under RBV could be the basis of a fiduciary relationship under CRT depends not only on whether the resource is subject to the beneficiary's practical control, but on whether the resource 'provides the fiduciary with the occasion to act opportunistically' towards the beneficiary.[51] Under CRT fiduciary relationships arise from the exercise of discretion by a fiduciary over resources

[46] See Joseph T Mahoney, 'A Resource-based Theory of Sustainable Rents' (2001) 27 J Mgmt 651, 655 ('resource-based theory is a theory of firm rents and transaction costs theory is a theory of the existence of the firm'). See also Richard L Priem and John E Butler, 'Is the Resource-based "View" a Useful Perspective for Strategic Management Research?' (2001) 26 Acad Mgmt Rev 22, 25 (declining to address whether RBV is a theory of the firm because 'key issues explained in theories of the firm are not addressed' by RBV). But see Kathleen R Conner, 'A Historical Comparison of Resource-Based Theory and Five Schools of Thought within Industrial Organization Economics: Do We Have a New Theory of the Firm?' (1991) 17 J Mgmt 121, 144 ('resource-based theory comprises a new theory of the firm').

[47] See Mahoney (n 46) at 655 ('resource-based theory and transaction costs theory are complementary'). See also, Nicolai J Foss and Peter G Klein, *Organizing Entrepreneurial Judgment: A New Approach to the Firm* (Cambridge University Press, 2012) 151 ('capabilities and contractual approaches are complements, rather than substitutes').

[48] Jay Barney, 'Firm Resources and Sustained Competitive Advantage' (1991) 17 J Mgmt 99, 100–01. Barney's definition of resources is not offered as a workable understanding of resources for purposes of CRT, but merely as an illustration of the broad range of things beyond legal 'property' that might be controlled by an organization and provide a fiduciary of that organization the occasion to act opportunistically, thus justifying the imposition of fiduciary duties. Some of these resources could be owned or controlled by an individual outside of the organizational context, while others would exist only within organizations. 'Resources' under CRT must be understood to be broad enough to describe fiduciary relationships involving individuals or organizations.

[49] Ibid at 101. Barney's version of RBV has been criticized for being tautological because he defines 'competitive advantage' as a value creating strategy, and he defines the 'resources' in terms of their ability to improve efficiency and effectiveness. Priem and Butler (n 46), at 27–28. Barney rejects this criticism. Jay B Barney, 'Is the Resource-based "View" a Useful Perspective for Strategic Management Research? Yes' (2001) 26 Acad Mgmt Rev 41, 42 (contending that 'all strategic management theories are tautological in the way Priem and Butler describe').

[50] Kraaijenbrink and others (n 45) at 358 (noting additionally, 'there is nothing strategically useful associated with the firm that is not a resource').

[51] Smith, *Critical Resource Theory* (n 3) at 1444.

belonging to the beneficiary, so a key attribute of 'resources' is that a person other than the 'owner' can exercise discretion over them in a self-interested manner. As illustrated below, some resources under RBV are simply incapable of delegated use.

Money and tangible assets are clearly resources under RBV, and they lie at the heart of many fiduciary relationships, including trusts, business organizations, executorships, receiverships, etc. In these relationships, the assets belong to a beneficiary and are susceptible to the opportunistic exercise of discretion by a fiduciary. Some intangible assets—including intellectual property and confidential information—also clearly qualify as resources under this same principle.

On the other hand, human capital—such as training, experience, intelligence, judgement, and insight[52]—may fail to qualify as a resource under CRT, even though it would certainly count as a resource under RBV.[53] As conceived here, human capital is not severable from an individual.[54] Thus, human capital may belong to an individual who is purported to be a beneficiary in a fiduciary relationship, but if the purported fiduciary cannot as a practical matter exercise discretion with respect to the other individual's human capital, there is no fiduciary relationship.[55] In other words, the beneficiary's human capital would not be a resource under CRT.

Of course, the beneficiary may have the right to deploy the human capital of another person through an employment agreement, and the rights to performance under such an agreement may be a resource under CRT.[56] Even when employees

[52] Human capital is a variegated concept. Economists and legal scholars often describe human capital as the present value of future wages. See, eg, Joseph Bankman and Daniel Shaviro, 'Piketty in America: A Tale of Two Literatures' (2015) 68 Tax L Rev 453, 499 ('We define human capital, for our purposes, as the present value of one's remaining lifetime earning ability'). A more expansive definition, also framed in terms of valuation, holds that human capital is 'equivalent to the present value of the flow of future satisfactions that an individual can command in the course of his life.' Paul B Stephan III, 'Federal Income Taxation and Human Capital' (1984) 70 Va L Rev 1357, 1358. For purposes of CRT analysis, it is preferable to focus on the source of value, such as knowledge or skills. See, eg, Orly Lobel, 'The New Cognitive Property: Human Capital Law and the Reach of Intellectual Property' (2015) 93 Tex L Rev 789, 835 ('Human capital is the stock of knowledge in all its multiple forms that contributes to productive work, including knowledge that is noncodifiable as well as knowledge that expresses itself in skills and know-how, in relationships and networks, in creativity and motivation, and in the ability to disrupt and energize').

[53] Barney (48) at 101. Strategy scholars have a very expansive understanding of resources, asserting that 'beliefs about the value of resources are themselves resources.' Alvarez and Busenitz (n 45) at 756.

[54] See Gary S. Becker, 'Investment in Human Capital: A Theoretical Analysis' (1962) 70 J Pol Econ 9, 9 (describing 'investing in human capital' as 'activities that influence future real income through the imbedding of resources in people').

[55] One might say that human capital, when possessed by an employee of a firm, also belongs to the firm in an informal way. See Rajan and Zingales (n 38) at 388 (arguing that employees 'belong' to an organization in the sense that there is an expectation that they will benefit if the organization benefits). This perception may enable 'acqui-hiring'. See John F Coyle and Gregg D Polsky, 'Acqui-hiring' (2013) 63 Duke LJ 281, 311 (arguing that a cluster of social factors, not litigation risk, encourages large technology companies to acquire smaller firms to hire some or all of the at-will employees).

We recognize a limit to the principle that a person is not a resource in the cases of guardianships or parent–child relationships, where a person may be viewed as the resource to be managed. Smith, *Critical Resource* (n 3) at 1415 n 63 and 1454–55.

[56] For example, in the well-known case of *Bancroft-Whitney Company v Glen*, 411 P.2d 921 (Cal. 1966), the Supreme Court of California held that a corporate officer breached his fiduciary duty by misleading his employer about the recruitment of personnel by another company, suggesting salary increases for those personnel that would facilitate this recruitment, and disclosing confidential

have no legal obligation to continue working for an employer—that is, even for at-will employees—the employment relationships may constitute a resource for purposes of fiduciary law because a fiduciary could exercise discretion over these relationships in a self-interested manner.[57]

Organizational capital—including a firm's routines, leadership structure, legal personality, or other design-oriented features—also presents a mixed case. Organizational capital unquestionably belongs to a firm (beneficiary) and counts as a resource under RBV.[58] If a purported fiduciary could exercise discretion in a self-interested manner with respect to organizational capital, the management of this capital should be regulated by fiduciary law.

Confidential information is often treated as a resource under CRT, but the mere sharing of one's confidential information with another typically is not enough to give rise to fiduciary duties.[59] CRT is particularly helpful in explaining why counselling relationships (such as those between lawyers and clients, doctors and patients, clergy and parishioners) are not thoroughgoing fiduciary relationships, but fiduciary only in part: when 'the fiduciary is given access to confidential information regarding the client ... the advice-giver assumes a non-fiduciary obligation to maintain confidentiality, as well as a fiduciary obligation to refrain from using the information for personal advantage.'[60] Within the past decade, commentators have suggested an extension to the logic of these counselling cases, applying fiduciary law to 'information fiduciaries',[61] such as companies running search engines and online merchants.[62]

information regarding salaries to the other company in order to facilitate the recruitment. Ibid at 936–7. When a fiduciary no longer has the ability to exercise discretion over employment agreements, there typically is no breach of fiduciary duty associated with the recruitment of personnel. See, eg, *Reeves v Hanlon*, 95 P.3d 513, 515 (Cal. 2004) ('one commits no actionable wrong by merely soliciting or hiring the at-will employee of another').

[57] See, eg, Robert W Hillman, 'Loyalty in the Firm: A Statement of General Principles on the Duties of Partners Withdrawing from Law Firms' (1998) 55 Wash & Lee L Rev 997 ('A partner planning to withdraw from a firm may not recruit (that is, persuade to leave) staff of the firm prior to giving the partnership notice of withdrawal').

[58] Barney (n 48) at 101.

[59] See, eg, Restatement (Second) of Contracts § 161(d), cmt. f (1981) ('Even where a party is not, strictly speaking, a fiduciary, he may stand in such a relation of trust and confidence to the other as to give the other the right to expect disclosure. Such a relationship normally exists between members of the same family and may arise, in other situations as, for example, between physician and patient); Restatement (Third) of Trusts § 2 cmt. (b)(1) (2003) ('Thus, a confidential relation may exist although there is no fiduciary relation and is particularly likely to arise between family members or close friends or on the basis of the confidence that arises between physician and patient or priest and penitent').

[60] Smith, *Critical Resource Theory* (n 3) at 1460.

[61] The term seems to have been coined by Kenneth C Laudon, 'Markets and Privacy' (1996) 39(9) Comm ACM 92, 93 ('Like banks, they would accept deposits of information from depositors and seek to maximize the return on sales of that information in national markets or elsewhere in return for a fee, possibly a percentage of the total returns').

[62] See, eg, Neil M Richards, 'Intellectual Privacy' (2008) 87 Tex L Rev 387, 436 ('Just as we do not rely merely on market forces and goodwill to mandate confidentiality from our lawyers or librarians, so too should information fiduciaries like search engines and online bookstores be subject to meaningful requirements of confidentiality to safeguard the vitally important interests at stake'); Jack M Balkin, 'Information Fiduciaries and the First Amendment' 49 UC Davis L Rev 1183 (arguing that 'many

Paul Miller objects to the emphasis on 'resources' in CRT on the ground that they are 'not well-defined',[63] though he inaccurately states, 'We are told nothing about the character of a resource other than that, like property, it encompasses tangible and intangible things.'[64] As noted above, a 'resource' under CRT has the following attributes: it belongs to the beneficiary; it 'provides the fiduciary with the occasion to act opportunistically';[65] it may be tangible or intangible; and the owner of a resource must have practical control over the resource.[66]

In a similar vein, Deborah DeMott has argued that 'identifying the core "critical resource" within some conventional fiduciary relationships taxes the theory considerably.'[67] DeMott contends, for example, that an agent's power to affect the principal's legal relations requires courts 'to assign a meaning to the term 'resource' distinct from its more intuitive meaning in contexts in which a fiduciary necessarily controls property for the benefit of another'.[68] While there is no question that agents are fiduciaries,[69] '[f]iduciary duty does not necessarily extend to all elements of an agency relationship, and does not explain all of the legal consequences that stem from the relationship.'[70] The ability of one person to affect the legal relations of another is traditionally referred to as 'power',[71] and a person holding such power need not be a fiduciary.[72] Thus, an agent's power to affect the principal's legal relations does not arise under fiduciary law and does not require analysis under CRT.

online service providers and cloud companies who collect, analyze, use, and distribute personal information should be seen as information fiduciaries toward their customers and end-user').

[63] Miller, *Justifying* (n 3) at 990. [64] Ibid.

[65] Smith, *Critical Resource Theory* (n 3) at 1444.

[66] Miller also argues that 'fiduciary relationships feature objects that cannot plausibly be construed as resources, including persons.' Miller, *Justifying* (n 3) at 990. As noted above in the cases of guardianships and parent–child relationships, 'nothing prevents us from viewing the person as a critical resource.' Smith, *Critical Resource* (n 3) at 1455.

[67] Deborah A DeMott, 'Breach of Fiduciary Duty: On Justifiable Expectations of Loyalty and Their Consequences' (2006) 48 Ariz L Rev 925, 935.

[68] Ibid at 935–36.

[69] Restatement (Third) of Agency § 1.01 ('Agency is the fiduciary relationship that arises when one person (a 'principal') manifests assent to another person (an 'agent') that the agent shall act on the principal's behalf and subject to the principal's control, and the agent manifests assent or otherwise consents so to act').

[70] Ibid at § 1.01 cmt. e.

[71] The distinction between 'power' and 'authority' was prominent in the Restatement (Second) of the Law of Agency. See Restatement (Second) of Agency § 6 (1958) (defining 'power' as 'an ability on the part of a person to produce a change in a given legal relation by doing or not doing a given act'); ibid at § 7 (defining 'authority' as 'the power of the agent to affect the legal relations of the principal by acts done in accordance with the principal's manifestations of consent to him'). The Restatement (Third) of the Law of Agency retains a distinct notion of 'power' in a separate title describing 'Irrevocable Powers'. Restatement (Third) of Agency Title C.

[72] See Restatement (Third) of Agency § 3.12 cmt. b ('A power given as security does not create a relationship of agency … because it is neither given for, nor exercised for, the benefit of the person who creates it. The holder is not subject to the creator's control and the holder does not owe fiduciary duties to the creator'); Restatement (Second) of Agency § 6 cmt. d ('There are a number of situations in which a power to bind another is sometimes expressed in terms of agency power … In these situations, however, the one holding the power is not a fiduciary for the one giving it and is not acting for the latter's benefit; he does not hold the power because he is an agent and such power cannot be controlled or terminated by the one who is subjected to liability by his conduct').

DeMott also objects to CRT on the ground that an advisor may breach a fiduciary duty through self-serving conduct that itself involves no misuse of the advisee's confidential information.[73] She points to the example of a lawyer who breaches 'a fiduciary duty to the client set forth in § 16(3) of the Restatement (Third) of The Law Governing Lawyers. The fiduciary duty specified in Section 16(3) requires a lawyer to 'comply with obligations concerning the client's confidences and property, avoid impermissible conflicting interests, deal honestly with the client, and not employ advantages arising from the client-lawyer relationship in a manner adverse to the client.'[74] While DeMott is correct in noting that 'to establish that a lawyer breached a fiduciary duty owed to a client does not require that the client establish the lawyer's possession or misuse of confidential information of the client',[75] confidential information is not the only basis for a fiduciary relationship between a lawyer and a client. As noted in my earlier work, an 'attorney will often be privy to extensive information about a client's assets and investment preferences that would typically not be disclosed in an arm's-length transaction.'[76] If a lawyer attempts to use this information to obtain a benefit for herself, fiduciary law rightly plays a role in checking that lawyer's self-interested action.

Rather than relying on 'resources', Miller prefers the notion of 'significant practical interests', which he defines as follows: 'An interest is practical where it connotes a real, ascertainable matter of personality, welfare, or right in relation to which one person may be uniquely and materially susceptible to the exercise of authority by another.'[77] Miller claims that the typology of 'personality, welfare, or right' is 'capable of accommodating and explaining the protection afforded by fiduciary law to a variety of interests of a range of beneficiaries, from children and patients to corporations and *cestui que trust*'.[78]

While it seems plausible that these features would be present in every fiduciary relationship, it also appears that they might be present in non-fiduciary contexts, thus making Miller's account of fiduciary relationships over-inclusive. For example, 'matters of personality include aspects of the actual and legal personality of incapable and artificial persons, including the determination of the ends or interests of persons as such.'[79] This broad invocation of fiduciary law for matters relating to parents and their children may fit the Canadian jurisprudence, but the parental role is not necessarily viewed as that of a fiduciary in the United States.[80]

[73] DeMott (n 67) at 935–36.

[74] Restatement (Third) of The Law Governing Lawyers § 16(3) (2000). These duties are identified as 'fiduciary' in Section 49. Ibid at § 49.

[75] DeMott (n 67) at 936 n 54.

[76] Smith, *Critical Resource* (n 3) at 1462.

[77] Miller, *Theory* (n 6) at 276.

[78] Ibid.

[79] Ibid.

[80] See, eg, *Economopoulos v Kolaitis*, 528 S.E.2d 714, 718 (Va. 2000) ('A parent-child relationship, standing alone, is insufficient to create a confidential or fiduciary relationship'); *Roybal v Morris*, 669 P.2d 1100, 1105 (N.M. App 1983) (same). See also Elizabeth S Scott and Robert E Scott, 'Parents as Fiduciaries' (1995) 81 Va L Rev 2401 (developing an informal model of the parent as fiduciary).

It is also worth noting that in Australia, 'parent/child relationships are not recognised as giving rise to fiduciary obligations.' Margaret Fordham, 'Sexual Abuse and the Limitation of Actions in Tort—A Case for Greater Flexibility?' (2008) Sing J Legal Stud 292, 303.

Similarly, Miller states that '[m]atters of right include decisions relating to the legal rights, obligations, powers and liabilities of natural and artificial persons, including those in relation to contract and property',[81] which seems much too broad to provide guidance for courts in the United States. For example, attorneys often make decisions relating to the legal rights of their clients, but only certain actions of an attorney are governed by fiduciary law in the United States.[82] This chapter is not the right venue for a thorough analysis of how 'significant practical interests' would be treated under the jurisprudence of the United States, but these examples coupled with the foregoing analysis of 'resources' show how CRT may be a better fit for US fiduciary law.

IV. Fiduciaries

CRT observes that firms under the property rights theory of the firm have the same structure as fiduciary relationships in law,[83] suggesting that economists and lawyers are partaking of a shared intuition about the nature of these organizations. Both economists and lawyers distinguish between arm's-length contracting (markets) and employment (firms) in the same way: arm's-length contracting parties exercise discretion over their own resources, but employees exercise discretion over resources belonging to their employer.[84] Thus, the distinctiveness of multi-person firms—and, therefore, of fiduciary relationships—is attributable to the relationships between resource owners and resource managers. As discussed below, these relationships have some features that are traceable to the logic of contract and some features that are traceable to the logic of property, but they are unique hybrid institutions, ultimately defined in law only as 'fiduciary'.

Instead of looking to the property rights theory of the firm, many fiduciary law scholars have relied on principal–agent models of the firm, which highlight incentive conflicts between fiduciaries and their beneficiaries.[85] Although these models draw on an analogy to legal agency relationships, which are fiduciary by definition,[86] the principal–agent models of the firm in economics are fundamentally

[81] Miller, *Theory* (n 6) at 276.

[82] See, eg, Restatement (Third) of The Law Governing Lawyers § 16 (2000) (listing many duties that a lawyer owes to a client, only some of which are fiduciary in nature). For a recent examination of lawyers as fiduciaries under Canadian law, see Alice Woolley, 'The Lawyer as Fiduciary: Defining Private Law Duties in Public Law Relations' (2015) 65 U Toronto LJ 285.

[83] Smith, *Critical Resource Theory* (n 3) at 1404–05 (noting that fiduciary relationships bear a 'strong resemblance' to firms under the property rights theory).

[84] Cf Foss and others (n 11) at 641 ('The basic distinction between an independent contractor and an employee, that is to say, between an inter-firm and an intra-firm transaction, turns on who owns the physical assets which the person utilizes in his work. An independent contractor owns his tools, and so on, while an employee does not').

[85] See, eg, Robert H Sitkoff, 'The Economic Structure of Fiduciary Law' (2011) 91 BU L Rev 1039; Robert Cooter and Bradley J Freedman, 'The Fiduciary Relationship: Its Economic Character and Legal Consequences' (1991) 66 NYU L Rev 1045; Frank H Easterbrook and Daniel R Fischel, 'Contract and Fiduciary Duty' (1993) 36 JL & Econ 425.

[86] Restatement (Third) of Agency §1.01 ('Agency is the fiduciary relationship that arises when one person (a "principal") manifests assent to another person (an "agent") that the agent shall act on the

contractual. For example, the most influential of these models in legal scholarship has been the nexus-of-contracts approach,[87] which treats the firm as a 'legal fiction'.[88] Under this view of the firm, legal status may have important economic implications—including, in the corporate context, perpetual existence, limited liability, and free transferability of interests—but the firm is essentially a special kind of market contracting.[89] While contracts play an important role in structuring organizations, models that are based entirely on contracts cannot distinguish the firm from the market, and this distinction is necessary to explain the boundaries of the firm and the existence of fiduciary relationships.

The distinctive structure of fiduciary relationships shows that they are not merely a special kind of contractual relationship, as often assumed.[90] Indeed, the crucial feature of all fiduciary relationships arises from the property-like nature of resources: the exercise of discretion by the fiduciary over resources belonging to the beneficiary. While the beneficiary and fiduciary often have a contractual relationship, the duties imposed on the fiduciary are not designed to fill gaps in that contract, but rather to protect the resources of the beneficiary.

principal's behalf and subject to the principal's control, and the agent manifests assent or otherwise consents so to act').

[87] See, eg, Kenneth Ayotte and Henry Hansmann, 'A Nexus of Contracts Theory of Legal Entities' (2015) 42 Int'l Rev L & Econ 1; Stephen M Bainbridge, 'The Board of Directors as Nexus of Contract' (2002) 88 Iowa L Rev 1.

[88] Michael Jensen and William Meckling, 'Theory of the Firm: Managerial Behavior, Agency Costs and Capital Structure' (1976) 3 J Fin Econ 305, 311 (describing the firm as a 'legal fiction which serves as a nexus for contracting relationships and which is also characterized by the existence of divisible residual claims on the assets and cash flows of the organization which can generally be sold without permission of the other contracting individuals'). Other foundational pieces in agency theory include Eugene F Fama, 'Agency Problems and the Theory of the Firm' (1980) 88 J Pol Econ 288; Eugene F Fama and Michael Jensen, 'Separation of Ownership and Control' (1983) 26 JL & Econ 301; Michael Jensen, 'Agency Costs and Free Cash Flow, Corporate Finance, and Takeovers' (1986) 76 Am Econ Rev 323. For early formal explications of agency theory, see Bengt Holmstrom, 'Moral Hazard and Observability' (1979) 10 Bell J Econ 74; and Stephen Ross, 'The Economic Theory of Agency: The Principal's Problem' (1973) 63 Am Econ Rev 134.

[89] See Foss and others (n 11) at 636. The other major principal–agent model—team production—also treats the firm as a special form of contracting. See Armen A Alchian and Harold Demsetz, 'Production, Information Costs, and Economic Organization' (1972) 62 Am Econ Rev 777. Team production occurs when two or more people work jointly, and their respective inputs are 'unobservable'. In other words, an outsider would find it impossible to reward team members based on the quantity or quality of their inputs for the simple reason that direct observation of each team member's performance is impossible or prohibitively costly, or because the inputs of one team member are indistinguishable from the inputs of other team members. Alchian and Demsetz argued that shirking by team members could be reduced by subjecting the team to outside monitoring. Such monitoring would be performed by a principal, who specialized in monitoring, and the monitor's incentives would derive from the fact that he was entitled to the residual earnings of the team. Ibid at 781–82. One of the problems with the team production model—aside from the impossibility of monitoring unobservable behaviour—is that a monitor does not need to be a principal of the firm, but could be hired through market contracting. Thus, the theory of team production does not offer a theory regarding the boundary of the firm. See Foss and others (n 11) at 637.

[90] See, eg, Ronald H Coase, 'The Nature of the Firm: Meaning' (1988) 1 J L Econ & Org 19, 28 ('A number of economists have said in recent years that the problem of the firm is essentially a choice of contractual arrangements. I have never thought otherwise').

Thomas Merrill and Henry Smith have described the trust—the quintessential fiduciary relationship—as an institution that straddles contract and property.[91] The trustee (fiduciary) holds legal title to the trust property and 'exercises managerial authority over the trust corpus, much in the way an owner would: The trustee exercises the right to exclude others, determines when and if to transfer the assets of the trust to third parties, and so forth.'[92] But the trustee is not in a position akin to an ordinary owner of property because the managerial authority (ie, discretion) must be exercised on behalf of the beneficiary of the trust. According to Merrill and Smith, therefore, 'we can think of a trust as the transfer of *in rem* rights associated with ownership, subject to a set of *in personam* duties designed to fulfill the settlor's intentions toward the beneficiary.'[93]

Every relationship that rightly bears the designation 'fiduciary' has a similar combination of property and contract features. The fiduciary exercises discretion similar to an owner over resources belonging to the beneficiary,[94] and the exercise of authority is constrained by duties that are personal to the fiduciary. Although all fiduciary relationships are hybrid institutions, not every hybrid institution is a fiduciary relationship because other hybrid institutions do not involve discretionary authority of the type exercised by a fiduciary on behalf of the resource owner.[95]

V. Loyalty and Disgorgement

Although fiduciary relationships have the unique structure described in Section IV of this chapter, most fiduciary relationships are also contractual relationships. As a result, a fiduciary who is a contracting party is subject to non-fiduciary duties under the contract, and a fiduciary who breaches this contract would typically be called to answer for expectation damages. The same fiduciary also has an obligation

[91] Thomas W Merrill and Henry E Smith, 'The Property/Contract Interface' (2001) 101 Colum L Rev 773, 843.

[92] Ibid at 844. [93] Ibid at 844.

[94] Paul Miller and Andrew Gold offer the example of charitable purpose trusts as an entity with trustees who have fiduciary duties but may have no definite or definitely ascertainable beneficiary. Paul B Miller and Andrew S Gold, 'Fiduciary Governance' (2015) 57 Wm & Mary L Rev 513, 528–30. The indefiniteness of the beneficiary in charitable purpose trusts does not undermine CRT, as the trust is established for the benefit of a community, a representative of which typically would be authorized to monitor the performance of the trustee. See Restatement (Third) of Trusts § 28 cmt c (2003) ('Charitable trusts are ordinarily enforceable upon suit by the Attorney General, as representative of the community, although there may also be beneficiaries with a special interest in the trust who can maintain a suit to enforce it'). This is the sort of practical control that any beneficiary must be able to exercise over critical resources.

[95] Merrill and Smith (n 91) identify three 'hybrid' institutions besides trusts, each 'partaking of some of the features of property rights and some of the features of contract rights': bailment, landlord–tenant, and security interests. Ibid at 777. Bailments involve a transfer of possession, but only for a specified purpose for which discretion is limited. Under landlord–tenant law, the tenant has the right to use and enjoy the premises but is not managing the property for the benefit of the landlord. A security interest entitles a lender to repossess property in the event of default, but, again, the lender exercises no managerial authority on behalf of the debtor.

not to harm the beneficiary, and a beneficiary who suffered actual harm—whether through breach of the fiduciary's duty of care or another tort duty—would be entitled to compensatory (and, sometimes, punitive[96]) damages.[97] The duty of loyalty that is distinctive to fiduciary relationships does not arise from a concern about breach of contract or harm from negligence or other tort, but about self-interested behaviour on the part of the fiduciary. Through the lens of CRT, therefore, the duty of loyalty arises out of a concern that the fiduciary will take advantage of his discretion over the beneficiary's resources.[98]

In addition to the core duty of loyalty, courts have identified myriad fiduciary duties, including the duty of care,[99] the duty of confidentiality,[100] the duty of candour,[101] the duty of obedience,[102] and the duty of good faith.[103] Commentators

[96] See Robert Cooter and Bradley J Freedman, 'The Fiduciary Relationship: Its Economic Character and Legal Consequences' (1991) 66 NYU L Rev 1045, 1069 ('Punishment for breach of fiduciary duty through the use of punitive damages is increasingly common'). See also, *Diversified Holdings, L.C. v Turner*, 63 P.3d 686, 697 (Utah 2002) ('The greater the trust reposed in a defendant, the greater will be the justification for a more significant award of punitive damages ... The breach of a fiduciary relationship also justifies higher punitive damages').

[97] Restatement (Second) of Tort § 274.

[98] Smith, *Critical Resource* (n 3) at 1408.

[99] See, eg, *In re Cornerstone Therapeutics Inc, Stockholder Litigation*, 115 A.3d 1173, 1177 (2015) ('the defendant directors were insulated from liability for monetary damages for breaches of the fiduciary duty of care by an exculpatory charter provision'); *Wilmot v Wilmot*, 58 P.3d 507, 516 (2002) ('a fiduciary duty of care requires that the statutory plaintiff and her lawyer act to protect the rights and interests of all beneficiaries who seek or may seek to assert their claims'). See also, Julian Velasco, 'A Defense of the Corporate Law Duty of Care' (2015) 40 J Corp L 647, 648 (arguing 'that the duty of care is not simply an ill-fitting appendage to the duty of loyalty, but rather an essential aspect of the singular fiduciary concept that also encompasses the duty of loyalty'). For arguments that the duty of care is not a fiduciary duty, see Christopher M Bruner, 'Is the Corporate Director's Duty of Care a "Fiduciary" Duty? Does it Matter?' (2013) 48 Wake Forest L Rev 1027 (describing several analytical problems associated with treating care as a 'fiduciary' duty); William A Gregory, 'The Fiduciary Duty of Care: A Perversion of Words' (2005) 38 Akron L Rev 181 ('The duty of care is a negligence concept quite unlike the duty of loyalty. Equating the duty of care with the duty of loyalty is bad law and worse semantics').

[100] See, eg, *Sorensen v Barbuto*, 177 P.3d 614, 618 (Utah 2008) ('Utah law recognizes a healthcare fiduciary duty of confidentiality'). Cf. *Doe 1631 v Quest Diagnostics, Inc.*, 395 S.W.3d 8, 11 (Mo. 2013) (where a statute already imposes a duty of confidentiality and creates a remedy for its breach, 'this Court will not create an additional equitable remedy by recognizing a separate fiduciary duty of confidentiality').

[101] See *Shenker v Laureate Education, Inc.*, 983 A.2d 408, 420 (2009) ('directors of Maryland corporations owe fiduciary duties of candor and maximization of shareholder value to their shareholders ... at least in the context of negotiating the amount shareholders will receive in a cash-out merger transaction'). See also, *In re Seidman v Office of Thrift Supervision*, 37 F.3d 911, 936 n.34 (3d Cir. 1994) ('A fiduciary's duty of candor is encompassed within the duty of loyalty').

[102] See, eg, *Cardwell v Gurley*, 2011 WL 6338813 at *9 (E.D. Tex. 2011) ('directors and officers of a corporation owe the fiduciary duties of obedience, care and loyalty to the corporation and its shareholders'). See also, Megan W Shaner, 'Restoring the Balance of Power in Corporate Management: Enforcing an Officer's Duty of Obedience' (2010) 66 Bus Law 27, 58 ('One way to achieve the goal of better corporate governance using fiduciary duties is through agency law's fiduciary duty of obedience'); Deborah A DeMott, 'The Mechanisms of Control' (1999) 13 Conn J Int'l L 233, 253 ('To impose a duty of obedience on directors, moreover, would conflict with the fundamental point that corporate law assigns ultimate managerial power and responsibility to directors').

[103] See eg, *Stone v Ritter*, 911 A.2d 362, 369–70 (Del. 2006) (describing the duty of good faith as part of the broader duty of loyalty); *Colo. Structures, Inc. v Ins. Co. of the West*, 167 P.3d 1125, 1233–34 (2007) ('The fiduciary relationship between the insurer and the insured is the source of the duty of good faith'). See also Melvin A Eisenberg, 'The Duty of Good Faith in Corporate Law' (2006) 31 Del

have attempted to classify fiduciary duties along various dimensions,[104] but for ease of explication, I suggest that a breach of fiduciary duty arises when a fiduciary wrongfully obtains a benefit from the beneficiary ('misappropriation') or wrongfully imposes a harm on the beneficiary ('harm'). Misappropriation by the fiduciary includes taking a resource (including a future opportunity) that belongs or should belong to the beneficiary or using the beneficiary's resources to generate profit for the fiduciary.[105] Cases of self-dealing by the fiduciary can also be viewed as forms of misappropriation. When acting as an adverse party to the beneficiary in a transaction or competing with the beneficiary over some 'economic advantage that the beneficiary is actually or potentially pursuing',[106] the fiduciary extracts resources from the beneficiary for personal gain. Regardless of the label used by courts, each act of misappropriation can be treated as a breach of the duty of loyalty. By contrast, when a fiduciary wrongfully imposes a harm on the beneficiary independently of any misappropriation, I treat this as a non-loyalty case or as a non-loyalty aspect of a case.

All forms of misappropriation discussed above are enabled by the fiduciary's exercise of discretion over the beneficiary's resources. Fiduciary law generally does not require the beneficiary to show that the fiduciary actually misused the beneficiary's resources. As observed in Restatement (Third) of Restitution and Unjust Enrichment, 'Many otherwise legitimate transactions are likewise condemned because of a potential conflict between the fiduciary's personal interest and the interest of the person that the fiduciary is bound to represent.'[107] Also, a fiduciary may be prohibited from taking resources that do not yet belong to the beneficiary, such as future profits earned in the wake of a misappropriation or misappropriation of a business opportunity.

As is evident from the analysis, the duty of loyalty in fiduciary relationships emanates quite naturally from the fiduciary's exercise of discretion over the resources of the beneficiary. It is perhaps not surprising, then, that the duty of loyalty in most fiduciary relationships contains a mandatory core that is not subject to waiver.[108]

J Corp L 1 ('good faith is an independent duty that gives rise to specific obligations not comprehended within the duties of care and loyalty').

104 See, eg, Julian Velasco, 'How Many Fiduciary Duties Are There in Corporate Law' (2010) 83 S Cal L Rev 1231.

105 Restatement (Third) of Restitution and Unjust Enrichment § 43 cmt. c (2011).

106 Ibid at cmt. d.

107 Ibid.

108 See Melanie B Leslie, 'Trusting Trustees: Fiduciary Duties and the Limits of Default Rules' (2005) 94 Geo L J 67, 69 (observing that 'trustees' fiduciary duties are not, and never have been, completely waivable'); Donald J Weidner, 'RUPA and Fiduciary Duty: The Texture of Relationship' (1995) 58 L & Contemp Probs 81, 89–93 (describing the 'mandatory minimum of fiduciary obligation' in partnership law); Jeffrey N Gordon, 'The Mandatory Structure of Corporate Law' (1989) 89 Colum L Rev 1549, 1551 (describing corporate fiduciary duties as 'an indispensable backdrop to corporate relationships, including protection against actions permitted by statute but nevertheless inequitable or overreaching'). The great exceptions to this observation are limited liability companies and limited partnerships in Delaware. In these instances, the exceptions prove the rule. But see Sandra K Miller, 'What Fiduciary Duties Should Apply to the LLC Manager After More Than a Decade of Experimentation' (2007) 32 J Corp L 565 (arguing for mandatory fiduciary duties in the LLC context).

If the beneficiary could waive all fiduciary protection, the fiduciary would be able to appropriate the beneficiary's resources or use those resources as the fulcrum for self-dealing. The mandatory core suggests that the purpose of the duty of loyalty is to protect the resources of the beneficiary and that this duty should not be viewed merely as a contractual gap filler.[109]

When a fiduciary obtains a benefit in breach of the duty of loyalty, the usual remedy is a form of restitution,[110] often referred to as 'disgorgement' or 'accounting'.[111] The remedial device for recovering identifiable property is a constructive trust,[112] but in many cases, a sum of money equivalent to the fiduciary's gain will suffice. Whatever the details of an actual remedial order, the purpose of disgorgement is to deprive the fiduciary of any gain obtained by misappropriation of the beneficiary's resources. Thus, even the remedial scheme in fiduciary law supports CRT.

VI. Conclusion

Theories of the firm distinguish economic activity in markets and firms. Motivated by these theories, CRT distinguishes fiduciary and non-fiduciary relationships. This chapter contributes to the development of CRT by refining the description of 'resources' using the resource-based view of the firm ('RBV'). In addition, this chapter extends the analysis of CRT by arguing that fiduciary relationships are unique hybrids of contract and property and that the duty of loyalty protects the beneficiary's property-like interest in critical resources.

[109] Cf Victor Brudney, 'Contract and Fiduciary Duty in Corporate Law' (1997) 38 BC L Rev 595, 627 (stating that 'fiduciary strictures are not designed like contract background rules to fill gaps in, or enforce, explicitly specified preferences or protective provisions that the parties selected').

[110] Restatement (Third) of Restitution and Unjust Enrichment § 43(a) (2011). Other remedies may be relevant to a breach of fiduciary duty. Ibid at § 43 cmt. a ('If the acts of the fiduciary have caused quantifiable injury to the beneficiary, the usual consequence is a liability in damages. If the challenged transaction remains executory, the beneficiary may be able to obtain relief by simple repudiation or by injunction').

[111] See Restatement (Third) of Restitution and Unjust Enrichment § 51(4) (2011) (specifying the unjust enrichment of a defaulting fiduciary as the 'net profit attributable to the underlying wrong', stating that the 'object of restitution in such cases is to eliminate profit from wrongdoing while avoiding, so far as possible, the imposition of a penalty', and noting that '[r]estitution remedies that pursue this object are often called "disgorgement" or "accounting"). Deborah DeMott refers to the imposition of a constructive trust and an accounting of profits as 'distinctively fiduciary remedies'. DeMott, *Relationships* (n 2) at 1268.

[112] See Restatement (Third) of Restitution and Unjust Enrichment § 55 (2011). The constructive trust was employed originally only in connection with 'some sort of relationship of trust, reposed and accepted, that parallels the fiduciary relationship an express trust creates between the trustee and the beneficiary.' H Jefferson Powell, '"Cardozo's Foot": The Chancellor's Conscience and Constructive Trusts' (1993) 56 Law & Contemp Probs 7, 11. Courts and commentators in the United States subsequently rejected this limitation on constructive trusts, now employing the remedy in any case involving unjust enrichment. Ibid at 14–15.

PART V

THE FIDUCIARY STATE AND THE INSTITUTION OF CONTRACT

13

The Fiduciary State and Private Ordering

Margaret Jane Radin

I. Introduction

In the United States, many firms are using mass-market fine print 'contracts' (boilerplate) to waive the remedies afforded by law to consumers and employees. Using the proliferation of mass-market rights deletions in the United States as a starting point, in this chapter I consider some implications for private ordering of viewing the State as a fiduciary for its populace. American courts have shown themselves willing to recognize boilerplate rights deletions as enforceable contracts. Moreover, firms are widely deploying arbitration clauses to preclude consumers and employees from accessing courts, and from undertaking aggregative legal actions.

Paul Finn has said that 'the most fundamental of fiduciary relationships in our society is that which exists between the community (the people) and the State and its agencies'.[1] In this chapter, I argue that by allowing firms to foreclose access to the courts and to legal remedies through boilerplate rights deletions, the American legal system is failing civil society, and its legal institutions are flouting their fiduciary obligation to the American people. In addition, I suggest that firms have an obligation not to deploy boilerplate so as to 'defect' unilaterally from the legal infrastructure that makes it possible for firms to function in civil society.

A. The American boilerplate problem

Boilerplate rights deletions have burgeoned exponentially in the networked digital environment. Exclusion clauses are prevalent in transactions for services, such as those provided by nursing homes, day care centres, fitness facilities, and summer camps. These clauses routinely purport to exclude any and all liability of the firm, no matter how culpable its behaviour. Many states enforce these clauses at least for negligence; and it seems that (to the extent that anyone reads them) they could deter legal action entirely. Even if legal action is brought against a service provider using

[1] Paul Finn, 'The Forgotten "Trust": The People and the State' in Malcolm Cope (ed), *Equity: Issues and Trends* (The Federation Press, 1995) at 131. This idea is elaborated in Evan Fox-Decent, *Sovereignty's Promise: The State As Fiduciary* (Oxford University Press, 2012).

a blanket exclusion clause,[2] plaintiffs will spend more time and money arguing for gross negligence. Also prevalent are mandatory pre-dispute arbitration clauses, which prevent class actions, thus precluding redress for recurring small harms. In practice, such arbitration clauses seem largely to preclude any relief.[3] Other prevalent clauses include choice of forum far from the place of domicile of the recipient,[4] one-sided unlimited modification clauses, curtailment of statutes of limitations, and other inventions of fertile legal minds.

In previous work I have argued that enforcement of these clauses entails a corruption of contract law that I called normative degradation.[5] The normative backdrop of contract law is the basic idea of voluntary agreement or consent between the parties to become mutually obligated to each other through contract.[6] This normative underpinning of contract is being degraded by various workarounds.

One workaround is the objective theory of contract. I call this doctrine 'as-if' consent: if a judge believes the situation would have seemed to an offeror like consent to his offer, the offeree is bound, as if she had consented. A further workaround is the idea that any time a recipient of fine print reasonably could have noticed it, the law will treat it 'as if' he saw and consented to it. I call this a double 'as-if' doctrine. These workarounds are of long standing in contract law, and they expose a fissure in contract doctrine between subjective normative underpinning and objective manifestation and implementation.[7] These doctrines largely developed in an earlier time, when traders probably knew each other, and understood each other's

[2] Exculpation of behaviour that causes personal injury to a consumer is prima facie unconscionable under the Uniform Commercial Code (UCC), a model statute that is enacted, with some variances, in all states. The UCC applies only to the sale of goods. There is no parallel statute governing services, and many service providers use blanket exculpatory clauses.

[3] See Judith Resnik, 'Diffusing Disputes: The Public in the Private of Arbitration, the Private in Courts, and the Erasure of Rights' (2015) 124 Yale Law Journal 2804. Mandatory pre-dispute arbitration clauses when massively deployed are particularly dangerous for the rule of law. They prevent collective remedies, and override relief provided by legislatures for small recurring injuries. Arbitration has no precedential value and the results are often secret, which undermines the common law system in practice and fails to deter a firm that loses a case from trying again, and again, against others seeking remedies. In essence, mandatory pre-dispute arbitration as it is massively deployed in the US is replacing the precedent system by a system of ad hoc unreviewable unreported decisions. See Margaret Jane Radin, *Boilerplate: The Fine Print, Vanishing Rights, And The Rule Of Law* (Princeton University Press, 2013) 130–35.

[4] I am using the term 'recipient' as shorthand for the employee, or consumer, or firm in the position of consumer, who is delivered boilerplate by a firm.

[5] Radin, *Boilerplate* (n 3); Radin, 'Boilerplate: A Threat to the Rule of Law?' in Lisa Austin and Dennis Klimchuk (eds), *Private Law and the Rule Of Law* (Oxford University Press, 2014) (<http://ssrn.com/abstract=2340005>); Radin, 'Access to Justice and Abuse of Contracts' (forthcoming, 2016 Windsor Yearbook of Access to Justice) (manuscript on file with author 2015).

[6] I take note that it is common for theorists to anchor contract in promising rather than in agreement per se, see, eg, Charles Fried, *Contract as Promise* (2nd ed, Oxford University Press, 2015). Perhaps I should characterize the normative basis of contract simply in voluntariness of exchange between willing parties, because that could be exchange of voluntary promises just as well as exchange of something else.

[7] I do not want to make too much of a subjective/objective dichotomy. Perhaps consent itself is neither subjective nor objective, but rather conditioned both by our own preconceptions and our social milieu. At any rate, consent is philosophically a difficult concept; and consent is often not an either/or decision for observers in practice.

behaviour in context. The use of fine print against employees and consumers and its exponential proliferation in the digital networked environment profoundly alters the picture.[8] Recipients are not fellow traders in the social milieu of firms, and firms have no basis to expect that recipients are signalling actual agreement to a particular offer. Furthermore, recipients are not making individual deals but are inundated with more boilerplate than anyone could read and understand.

B. Undermining the legal infrastructure

In previous work I also argued that firms that deploy mass-market deletions of remedies are undermining the legal infrastructure of contract.[9] They are privatizing what should remain public. This undermining of the state's legal infrastructure I have called democratic degradation.

When the State enforces a contract, it takes an entitlement from A against her will, and delivers it to B. For this involuntary redistribution to be consistent with legality, there must be a legal infrastructure of rules governing contract enforcement. Furthermore, this infrastructure must be one that participants recognize as existing for the benefit of all citizens, and which each is thereby committed to support. Hence the largely non-waivable legal requirement of good faith in contract performance. The infrastructure of contract recognition and enforcement is in the care of the State. The State depends upon contract participants to use and support the infrastructure in good faith. The State also depends upon contract participants to argue for and against enforcement where there is a dispute.

When firms deploy exclusions that eliminate or diminish rights of recourse that enable recipients to challenge their behaviour, and when courts as institutions of the State enable them to do this, each is at fault for undermining the infrastructure of private law. Just as parties under certain circumstances cannot waive the requirement of good faith, so too they should not be able to waive provisions that are critical to the legal infrastructure that supports the institution of contract. The possibility of a legal infrastructure for contract is still accepted as one of the reasons for exiting the state of nature, creating a political state, and submitting to its power. When firms undermine the infrastructure of contract, and are permitted by the apparatus of the State itself to do this, the rationale for the existence of the State is eroded.

Thus, it bears emphasis that the narrative of traditional liberalism implies that individuals cannot be divested of rights to redress of grievances without undermining the very structure of rights that the State is charged with maintaining in order to foster individual freedom. Freedom of contract is of course among these rights. To the extent that remedies for breach of contract are foreclosed, or sham contracts are treated as real and binding, the liberal ideal of private ordering cannot be implemented. In a sense, then, recipients of fine print exclusions who have lost their right to redress of grievances have been forced back into a *quasi* state of nature, where

8 Radin, *Boilerplate* (n 3) at 89–90; Radin, 'Access to Justice' (n 5).

9 Radin, *Boilerplate* (n 3) at 33–36.

they must fend for themselves rather than trust that they can rely upon the State for redress.[10]

C. Rights permanently in the care of the policy

On the basis of these arguments, I have argued that remedial rights should be market-inalienable, or at least that they should not be alienable on a mass-market basis. Market-inalienability refers to an entitlement that cannot be traded off by the holder, even if consideration is given and consent is impeccable.[11] The duty of good faith is an example of market-inalienability. The argument is that market-inalienable rights should remain permanently in the care of the polity.[12]

I take the area of remedial rights as the first avenue of analysis because I see no argument available that would affirm that a State can be justified in abolishing legal redress of grievances for its citizens. Again, making such remedies available has traditionally been treated as a primary rationale for the State's existence. More speculatively, below I will consider other matters that should remain permanently in the care of the polity. In this regard, I consider three areas of analysis that often overlap: implications of our commitment to the rule of law, protecting basic human rights, and situations in which a coordination problem means that the State must take responsibility. Matters that must remain permanently in the care of the polity must be so understood because of the fiduciary duties that the State owes to its people.

II. The State as Fiduciary and the Rule of Law

To the extent that the State forecloses access to remedies, it undermines the rule of law and the rationale for its own existence. Therefore, the State is obligated to maintain the legal infrastructure that supports redress of grievances. The obligation requires availability of redress in fact, in practice, not merely in theory. The State must recognize and make allowance for the fact that humans, being human, will make mistakes or act wrongly. A State that does not take account of actual—and perfectly ordinary—human frailties is only a pretense.

[10] See Radin, 'Boilerplate: A Threat to the Rule of Law?' (n 5).

[11] In practice, of course, it is hard to see what the consideration is for the exclusions. Proponents of the exclusions are likely to argue that the recipients are being compensated in lower prices for the product or service being purchased, and/or that recipients do not value remedies ex ante. As I have argued previously, insofar as these arguments rest on empirical assumptions, they cannot be true of all markets, and are probably false in many. Radin, 'From Baby-Selling to Boilerplate: Reflections on the Limits of the Infrastructures of the Market' (manuscript under submission 2015) at 36–41. As I have also argued previously, it does not follow from the fact that individuals do not subjectively value remedies before they are needed that the availability of remedies is not valuable to all individuals (ibid at 37). The existence of legal remedies is valuable to all individuals whether they realize that or not.

[12] See Radin, 'Boilerplate: A Threat to the Rule of Law?' (n 5). Note that I have not argued against standardized contracts per se, only those that interfere with market-inalienable rights.

A. Legal remedies and fiduciary duties regarding the rule of law

I regard access to legal remedies as a demand of the rule of law. In order for the State to honor its commitment to the rule of law, including the principle of equality before the law, all rights holders must have reasonable access to remedies.[13]

It is true that the rule of law is an ideal. But it is an ideal that structures relationships between a State and its subjects in the real world, a world in which complete fulfilment of ideals is never possible. For example, retroactive operation of law is presumptively inconsistent with the rule of law, because compliance with a rule cannot precede existence of that rule, but some measure of retroactivity can be tolerated before we conclude that a State in general has failed to abide by the rule of law. Nevertheless, there is a point at which deviations from rule of law norms become indefensible.

The rule of law is a contested set of ideas and ideals featuring various formal and substantive views. The formal views refer to the principles by which a system of law may be useful for governing human behaviour: a rule must exist in advance of the behaviour it is supposed to regulate; it must be understandable and susceptible of being followed by humans; and it must in some way promote human welfare. The substantive views refer to the principles by which a system can implement goods held to be essential to human flourishing, such as principles of democratic government, constitutional principles, and commitment to recognition of basic human rights.[14]

However the rule of law is construed, commitment to and maintenance of it is a responsibility of the State acting on behalf of its people. For these reasons, Evan Fox-Decent characterizes commitment to rule of law values as a matter implicating the fiduciary responsibilities of the State to its people.[15] Fox-Decent explains:

> [T]he state's overarching fiduciary obligation to its people is to secure legal order, to govern through the rule of law on behalf of the people ... As private parties, legal subjects cannot announce or enforce law, nor adjudicate their own disputes. A law-making public authority is required to specify the limits of permissible action. An administrative public authority is required to enforce the law. A law-interpreting public authority is required to judge alleged transgressions. The fiduciary principle entrusts the state to play these law-giving roles on behalf of the people, but at the same time encumbers the state with rule-of-law obligations to ensure that the state's agents govern impartially, as public authorities rather than as private parties.[16]

[13] It does not follow that a single breach of this principle means that a State is not justified. If a judge in one case wrongly deprives an individual of a right that should be recognized, the decision is itself wrong but absent a broader pattern of rights deprivations there is not necessarily an affront to the rule of law.

[14] I wrote more about the formal and substantive ways of thinking about rule of law in a 1989 article, 'Reconsidering the Rule of Law' (1989) 69 Boston U L Rev 781, in which I attempted to imagine what the rule of law would look like if we abandoned traditional conceptions of rules and instead think of rules in a holistic, social constructivist context. I did not mean to adopt the formal conception of rule of law, but rather to use it as the more challenging case for my social constructivist suggestion.

[15] Fox-Decent (n 1). [16] Ibid at 128.

I argue that at least one implication of a commitment to the rule of law—access to redress of grievances—must remain permanently in the care of the polity. Rights to redress ought not to be subject to exclusion: private parties should not be allowed to use instruments provided for the well-being of all against the rights of some by seeking to exclude rights on a mass-market basis. Where the State permits—and indeed, participates, in such significant derogation from rule of law principles, it fails to comply with its fiduciary responsibilities to its citizens and thereby undermines the legitimacy of its own claim to sovereignty.

Fox-Decent devoted much of his analysis to defending common law constitutionalism in light of the State's fiduciary relationship with its people, whereas I focus primarily on the State's duty to maintain access to public redress of private grievances. In particular, I claim that rule-of-law norms are violated where private entities are permitted, with the complicity of the State, to accomplish large-scale deletion of rights of access to remedies. This practice undermines the value of equality before the law and abrogates the responsibility of the State to prevent the exercise of arbitrary power. The State should insist that rights of access to remedies are market-inalienable in the context of mass-market deployment of boilerplate rights deletions. Even if they wished to do so, recipients may not *en masse* trade off remedial rights for money.[17]

An implication is that the courts should not focus exclusively on contractual formation and consent. They should instead focus first on the nature of the right that is the subject of exclusion. If the right is market-inalienable, consent to a purported exclusion is irrelevant. If courts accepted this responsibility, we could avoid arguments about whether clicking 'I agree' to a document one hasn't read—and wouldn't understand in any event—constitutes consent. We could also avoid arguments that the recipient, if reasonable, could have found and read a document, and that he therefore should be treated as if he had read, understood, and consented to it.[18] In the American context, the doctrine requiring aggrieved recipients of boilerplate rights deletions to prove both 'substantive' and 'procedural' unconscionability in respect of their 'decision' to exclude those rights could be bypassed.[19]

[17] In fact the 'trade-off' may be a ruse. See n 11 *supra*. It may yield no money to recipients, depending on the market structure and particularly its level of information asymmetry. In practice, it may often be the case that firms simply pocket their savings and pass on nothing to recipients in the form of lower prices. Also, I should note here that in the rule-of-law context I am speaking of mass-market pre-dispute relinquishment of remedies, not about settlement of disputes once initiated, and not about a *de minimis* individual case, unless it leads to proliferation.

[18] These are the kind of arguments that embarrass the law. I have never understood why anyone thinks that if I know a list of statements exists in my surroundings I have thereby agreed to it, but I am not debating this question here.

[19] I believe that this two-pronged view of unconscionability is borrowed from a widely adopted American approach. The doctrine requires both 'procedural' and 'substantive' unconscionability to be found in order to rule for the consumer. 'Procedural' means, roughly, does the court think there was adequate consent or agreement? If a court judges the recipient to have consented, even if by means of this 'double as-if' doctrine, it will not have to investigate whether the contract is substantively bad, including the question whether the recipient has signed away a right that is not subject to recipient choice because it is permanently in the care of the polity.

B. Human rights and public fiduciary duty

The responsibility to secure human rights might (and I think ought to be) considered part of the State's fiduciary duty toward its subjects.[20] Here I will only gesture at the issue of how far the State's fiduciary duty extends. Human rights may include individual autonomy, equality, dignity, and personal identity; freedom of expression, religion, and thought; freedom of movement; respect for privacy, and intimate and family relations; cultural or group identity; maintenance of the natural environment that supports human life; and satisfaction of basic human needs through access to resources including food, water, shelter.[21] In keeping with my emphasis here on the fiduciary responsibility of the State to create and appropriately administer the legal infrastructure of contract, I will briefly consider individual autonomy, freedom of speech, and privacy.

First, it seems clear that routine enforcement of boilerplate by the courts undermines autonomy and respect for individual choice. Freedom of contract is based on the idea of individual autonomy (freedom of the will) embodied in the notion of reciprocal agreement. Individual autonomy is not honoured when courts declare that recipients 'agreed' to contractual terms that they did not read and would not have comprehended had they done so.

Freedom of contract is the centrepiece of private ordering. Again, in traditional liberal theory, the need for impartial interpretation and enforcement of contracts is a basic reason for the State's existence. Thus, the exercise of coercive state powers to enforce (purported) contracts that derogate from values and principles underlying the institution of contract undermines the State's claim to commitment to individual autonomy. Doctrines attempting to assimilate agreement to consent, and consent to notice, and notice to constructive notice, attest ironically to the centrality of actual agreement in the justification of contract enforcement.

Second, consider freedom of speech. Relinquishment of freedom of speech may cause concern because of its fundamental importance as a human right in many legal and political systems. Boilerplate sometimes interferes with freedom of speech. Consider a clause providing that the recipient will not publish a critical comment on a product or service. Clauses invoking intellectual property can also significantly

[20] See Paul Finn, 'Public Trust and Public Accountability' (1994) 3 Griffith L Rev 224 at 232, asking to what extent the fiduciary idea limits Parliaments: 'Beyond any question of its [Parliament] merely acting unfairly or partially, does its trustee obligation to serve the people preclude it from acting so as to offend grievously against human rights deep rooted in the society we have created?' An answer to this question suggested by Evan Fox-Decent and Evan J Criddle is, 'Yes', according to a fiduciary theory of the obligations of public entities: 'The fiduciary theory views human rights as the consequence of persons' moral capacity as self-determining agents to place public institutions under legal obligations. Human rights protect individual dignity against state domination and instrumentalization by entitling all persons to be treated in certain ways by public institutions as a matter of right.' Evan Fox-Decent and Evan J Criddle, 'The Fiduciary Constitution of Human Rights' (2009) 15 Legal Theory 301.

[21] A starting point is the United Nations Universal Declaration of Human Rights of 1948. See <ohchr.org>.

restrict freedom of speech. For example, when a EULA declares that a user 'agrees' not to copy or distribute anything on a website, that 'agreement' supersedes the law of copyright. The law of copyright would have allowed not only fair use or fair dealing, but also copying of facts and ideas (rather than expressions of ideas). Courts faced with mass-market boilerplate that interferes with freedom of speech should at least be wary of enforcing it.

Third, consider individual privacy. Privacy is widely recognized as important to personal identity. Yet, individual privacy rights are especially sensitive to cognitive biases on the part of rights holders. People often do not understand the personal significance of privacy rights or the extent to which they might later regret waiving them.

Privacy waivers are of particular concern where a waiver scheme is widespread. Consider Facebook's Terms of Service. Facebook retains a right to use without consent certain materials relating to a user, even after the user has terminated her account. 'Information associated with your account will be kept until your account is deleted, *unless* we need the data to provide products and services.' Moreover, 'information that others have shared about you is not part of your account and will not be deleted when you delete your account.' In other words, Facebook will, if it chooses, feature your stories and photos in advertisements without your consent. We should not accept the proposition that, when Facebook posted new Terms of Service at the beginning of 2015, users who continued to use the service had thereby consented to everything in those terms.

C. Coordination issues and the state's fiduciary role

Sometimes a right enacted or protected by the State is a solution to a coordination problem. The purpose of this kind of right is defeated if it is alienable. In order to maintain the coordination solution, the State must generally disallow waivers (unless in an unusual situation a waiver is really *de minimis*). The rule about which side of the road to drive on is an easy example of a non-waivable rule that is essential to coordination, because without such a fixed rule chaos would ensue.

This reasoning can readily be extended to many kinds of rights that depend on coordination, including rights to clean air and water, and to amelioration of climate change. With rights of this sort, efforts at mass-market exclusion undermine collective commitment to rule-based social coordination. A State that takes seriously its fiduciary duties should not allow this to happen.

III. Duties of Firms to Support Background Legal Infrastructure

Firms that deploy boilerplate to rearrange the rights of recipients in ways they consider suitable for their own business goals are beneficiaries of the State's legal infrastructure themselves. Do they have any reciprocal duties toward the State, toward other market actors, and toward the general populace?

Of course they have a duty to obey the law. But I think that firms must also be precluded from derogating from legal infrastructure in ways that undermine the commitment of other firms to that structure and that undermine efforts by the State to maintain it. In competitive markets where boilerplate exclusions become common, its prevalence alone will undermine the commitment of competing firms to honour the State's legal infrastructure, because in a competitive market firms will be incentivized to offer worse terms[22] to avoid being driven from the market. Such a situation tends to lead to a race to the bottom. Firms must not be allowed to instigate this result, which undermines the infrastructure of private law, undermines the rule of law, and trenches upon rights that are permanently in the care of the polity.

A. An analogy: deceptive advertising

Seana Shiffrin has recently developed a parallel argument regarding deception in the law of commercial misrepresentation.[23] Consumers' misunderstanding of an advertisement may sometimes be considered deceptive even if deception was not purposeful or knowing. For example, an advertisement may not be purposely deceptive when it makes a truthful but artfully worded claim that causes some consumers to understand it mistakenly due to lack of attention or 'intellectual fault'.[24] Shiffrin points out that for many forms of liability for deception the law 'looks more to the effect of the speech on the audience than to the intent of the speaker.'[25] She explains: 'Statements that are true and might be meaningfully advanced for their literal truth may still be illegal because they have a tendency to mislead listeners.'[26]

Shiffrin suggests that there is an 'implicit picture of moral relations between speaker and listener embedded in the law'.[27] In support of this picture she argues that 'the listener is not welcome to become equally expert on the issues' and further that 'in a well-operating economic system, [the listener's] efforts would not importantly enhance the public dialogue but would detract from the achievement of the cooperative ends and the listener's individual chosen ends that our economic division of labor should facilitate.'[28] In the food product context, which gives rise to Shiffrin's discussion of deceptive advertising, people who buy food products have

[22] Firms could also meet the competitors' cost-saving bad terms by offering lower quality products, but this would probably be more obvious to customers.

[23] Seana Shiffrin, 'Deceptive Advertising and Taking Responsibility for Others' in Tyler Doggett, Anne Barnhill, and Mark Budolfson (eds), *Oxford Handbook Of Food Ethics* (forthcoming 2016); <http://ssrn.com/abstract=2658450>.

[24] Ibid at p 14 (draft). [25] Ibid p 8 (draft).

[26] Ibid p 13 (draft). For example, Gerber claimed its Fruit Snacks were made with 'real fruit juice and other all natural ingredients', which was true, but it was not true that all of their ingredients were natural, which a philosopher or logician would have realized and which the consumer could have found out by reading the nutrition label. A federal appellate court held that consumers do not have to look beyond the front of the box to be considered reasonable consumers. (And by implication, it seems, consumers do not have to be able to parse implicatures.) *Williams v Gerber Products Co.*, 552 F.3d 934 (2008).

[27] Shiffrin (n 23) p 17 (draft). [28] Ibid p 25 (draft).

to buy so many of them that it would be unduly time-consuming, and thus wasteful and detrimental to basic human projects, for them to investigate claims about those products. Furthermore, firms through manoeuvres such as 'ag-gag' laws make it more rather than less difficult to do so.

Thus, Shiffrin argues:

> Rather than expecting the parties to check one another and to stand in an adversarial relation to one another given that the non-expert party also has her hands tied behind her back, it makes more sense to complement the property right and the ability to exclude with a quasi-fiduciary duty towards the excluded who the property owner hopes to entice into a commercial relationship. *This quasi-fiduciary duty involves, among other charges, not providing the occasion in which one party might predictably make a mistake to the other party's benefit.*[29]

B. Deceptive boilerplate

I think that the same arguments about deception apply here, at least to the extent that recipients actually read the boilerplate.[30] Surely firms that deploy boilerplate rights exclusions are providing occasions 'in which one party might predictably make a mistake to the other party's benefit'. With fine print, it is not merely the case that the recipient will make a mistake about food ingredients, or about the superiority of one brand of painkiller over another. Instead, those who lose their right to redress may lose their homes or have to forego necessary medical care, or may find their children or elderly parents negligently injured by a firm whose exclusion clauses have diminished its responsiveness to legal deterrence.

With fine-print rights exclusions, it is not merely that recipients have 'intellectual faults' such as the inability to parse implicatures. Instead recipients are—we all are— subject to well-known and stubborn cognitive biases. There is now ample evidence that individuals are unable to reason well in certain circumstances.[31] There is also evidence that firms take advantage of cognitive biases.[32] In fact there is a relatively new field of marketing research and practice called neuromarketing, in which

[29] Ibid p 28 (draft) (emphasis supplied).

[30] Perhaps deployment of boilerplate should not properly be called deception when the boilerplate is not even read. Can someone be deceived by a text of which he is unaware? If so, this would be a different kind of deception than the kind Shiffrin is talking about. Perhaps deception in this situation is the mistaken trust the recipient may have that the firm would not use indecipherable fine print to divest core rights, coupled with the inference that firms know this. When the boilerplate is not read, the argument is also available that receipt of boilerplate is not a contract at all—unless we subscribe to the double as-if doctrine and charge the recipient both with having read and having understood the boilerplate. I think we should not subscribe to that doctrine; but if we did, perhaps we should further posit that the cognitive and other factors Shiffrin has identified suggest that we should also assume that the recipient would have been deceived.

[31] Please see Daniel Kahneman's masterful book, *Thinking, Fast and Slow* (Farrar, Strauss, and Giroux, 2011). See also, Richard H Thaler, *Misbehaving: The Making Of Behavioral Economics* (Norton, 2015), and George Akerlof and Robert J Shiller, *Phishing For Phools: The Economics Of Manipulation & Deception* (Princeton University Press, 2015).

[32] For example, upon opening a chequing account, John doesn't expect he will ever bounce a cheque, so even if he knows that the bank is making a large percentage of its profit on $45 fees for bounced cheques, John will accept their policy. Upon opening a credit card account, Sue doesn't expect to carry a balance, so she doesn't properly factor in big increases in interest rates on the card if she carries

market actors take advantage of customers' cognitive biases and other subconscious inclinations.[33] It does not seem far-fetched to speculate that knowledge developed for advertising is being, or will be, put to work in deployment of boilerplate rights deletions.

Recipients will be hampered by cognitive biases if they do try to read fine print. Firms know this. They learned by honing successful practices and dropping unsuccessful ones long before neuromarketing was developed. Most recipients do not try to read fine print because it is not a good use of their time. Firms that deploy fine print know this, too. In fact, in today's economy, many recipients cannot read much of anything (the illiteracy rate is high in the United States, and the innumeracy rate is even higher). Firms that deploy fine print know this as well. Even assuming we read boilerplate, we cannot spend our lives protecting ourselves from all of the self-exonerating firms we deal with. It is not merely that we have better uses for our time, as Shiffrin argues. If we are forced to protect ourselves and our families from harm caused by any of the many firms we deal with, there may be a point where no other use of our time would be possible.

We ought not to be required to go to such lengths to protect ourselves. We could not even do this well if we had to try. That is what the State is for. Especially in today's world in which recipients are inundated with boilerplate, it seems apt to consider recipients of boilerplate rights deletions as being in the position of the unfairly disappointed beneficiary of a fiduciary relationship. Hampered by cognitive biases and the burdens of life priorities, recipients of boilerplate are in a position of having their vulnerabilities catalogued and systematically exploited by firms. We should rightly expect that, rather than implicitly condoning this state of affairs, the State should live up to its fiduciary responsibilities.

C. Duties of market actors with regard to the state's fiduciary duty

Lest it be thought that the burden of responsibility falls on the State alone, it must be added that firms have responsibilities of their own. At the very least, they must not interfere with the State's fulfilment of its fiduciary responsibilities. It may be helpful to put this issue in terms of public choice theory: firms and other market actors are party to a general hypothetical bargain in which they are granted the advantages of participating in market activity in a civil society organized and maintained by the State by means of it underwriting an infrastructure of private law. Given that the hypothetical bargain relates to and provides benefits to all market actors, individual actors may not defect from it. Otherwise, the bargain would collapse.

a balance after the first few months. See Oren Bar-Gill, *Seduction by Contract* (Oxford University Press, 2012). (I am sorry Bar-Gill did not call the book *Deception by Contract*, but I suppose 'Seduction' was a more alluring title.)

[33] See, eg, Natasha Singer, 'Making Ads That Whisper to the Brain' *The New York Times* (New York, 13 Nov 2010).

This duty of firms dovetails with that of the State to maintain the recipients' right to the redress of grievances and other background rights that are critical to the infrastructure of private law. Firms are beneficiaries of these rights just as much as others. Under the rule of law, firms must accept that they are equal—but no more than equal—before the law. They cannot themselves rely on legal infrastructure to their own advantage while seeking to undermine that legal infrastructure (eg, contracts) to the disadvantage of others. The State should preclude the use of boilerplate to exclude market-inalienable rights. But equally, firms ought to recognize the dangerous hypocrisy involved in deploying these exclusions. If every firm were to do this, one of the key benefits of civil society would collapse; and if a substantial portion of firms do this, the same benefits would be seriously undermined.[34]

IV. Practical Considerations: What Should the State and Its Judicial, Legislative, and Administrative Branches Do?

Suppose one accepts the arguments that the State is a fiduciary of its people. Suppose further that one accepts that there is widespread lack of compliance by firms with their own civic duties, making it less possible for the State to fulfil its fiduciary responsibilities. What can the fiduciary State do in response to this problem?

A. (Back to) the American problem(s)

Perhaps the first thought is that the State should declare certain kinds of clauses unacceptable. A federal administrative agency—the US Federal Trade Commission (FTC)—has the power to declare certain behaviours an unfair method of doing business. So far the FTC has not declared that mass-market waivers of remedial rights are unfair. Why? That is a political, not a legal problem. Another federal agency—the recently organized Consumer Financial Protection Bureau (CFPB)—has been considering the use of onerous clauses in some industries, and some regulation may result, especially with regard to mortgages. But if the Republicans win

[34] A label on a product may be called 'disclosure', and terms of service may be called 'contracts', but whatever label is attached they are fine print that exclude market-inalienable rights and therefore undermine the legal infrastructure upon which markets and civil society depend. In *More Than You Wanted To Know: The Failure Of Mandated Disclosure* (Princeton University Press, 2014), Omri Ben-Shahar and Carl Schneider declared 'disclosure' of risks and limitations mandated by government entities (for example in mortgages) to be worse than useless, owing to many factors about American recipients, including overload and illiteracy, but did not recognize that the same critique applies to 'contracts' deployed by private parties without any government oversight. Given the reality that there often is no significant difference between fine print that is merely 'disclosure' and fine print that is labelled contractual, this book leads to the need to pay attention to the question whether (or when) fine-print terms that come with transactions should properly be enforced as contracts, a topic that the authors did not cover. The same facts that the authors marshal, about American illiteracy, innumeracy, lack of salience, and general fine-print overload apply to the many consumer contracts that (in the US) are largely enforceable. See Radin, 'Less Than I Wanted To Know: Why Do Ben-Shahar and Schneider Attack Only "Mandated" Disclosure?' University of Michigan Law and Economics Research Paper No. 14-012, online: <http://papers.ssrn.com/sol3/papers.cfm?abstract_id=2462818>.

the presidency in 2016, given that they are likely to retain majorities in Congress for at least two years, the CFPB is likely to be abolished, defunded, or diminished in power.

Meanwhile, in the European Union, the Commission promulgated a Directive in 1993 against unfair consumer contracts, with a list of terms that could be considered unfair. As Member States have worked toward compliance with this Directive, and as the EU has done more work on the problem, the regime has gotten stricter and more unified.[35] Other countries, such as Australia, have moved to ameliorate the situation consumers face, including providing for significant fines to be levied against firms that use illegal clauses.[36]

Given that federal administrative amelioration of the problem in the United States is uncertain at best, might the courts deal with the problem? Unfortunately, the prospects are rather grim. Federal courts seem to ignore due process in this field. Yet it seems clear that exclusions that undermine rights of redress should be analysed in this way. American constitutional law, under a principle of fundamental fairness, holds that every injured party must have her day in court. American constitutional law is in the guardianship of the federal courts. All people subject to US jurisdiction are supposed to be beneficiaries of that guardianship. Yet federal courts have failed to meet their fiduciary responsibilities as guardians of the constitution and its protections. Instead, they have held that many rights associated with due process, such as the right to jury trial, may be disposed of in indecipherable boilerplate.

Furthermore, often these issues do not come before a court; 'contractual' (boilerplate) arbitration clauses that deny jury trial, aggregative relief, and designate arbitrators whose impartiality is suspect, are widespread in the United States. The conservative activist majority of the United States Supreme Court has reinterpreted an early twentieth-century statute to essentially immunize arbitration clauses against consumers, employees, and businesses in the position of consumers. There is a pre-emption clause in the US Constitution providing that federal law is supreme, and state law conflicting with federal law cannot stand. The Supreme Court has interpreted that clause to mean that states do not have power to outlaw arbitration clauses, to treat them as prima facie unconscionable, or to subject them to stricter treatment of any sort.

Forced arbitration most of the time means no remedy,[37] especially since the Court has held that the 'contract' right to compel arbitration trumps state rights and other federal rights too (such as rights under competition law and antidiscrimination

[35] See, eg, Christian Von Bar and Eric Clive (eds), *Principles, Definitions and Model Rules of European Private Law: Draft Common Frame Of Reference (DCFR)*, 6 vols, prepared by the Study Group on a European Civil Code and the Research Group on EC Private Law (Acquis Group) (2010). See Jules Stuyck, 'Unfair Terms' in Geraint Howells and Reiner Schulze (eds), *Modernising and Harmonising Consumer Contract Law* (de Gruyter, 2009) 115 (providing a summary of the similarities and differences between the 1993 Directive, the DCFR, and the (then) proposed Consumer Rights Directive. The Consumer Rights Directive took effect in 2011).

[36] Australian Consumer Laws, Schedule 2 to the Competition and Consumer Act 2010, administered jointly by the Australian Competition and Consumer Commission (ACCC) and the State and Territory consumer protection agencies. A new law, effective 12 November 2016, extends protection against unfair terms in boilerplate to small businesses.

[37] For details on the Supreme Court rulings, and much more, see Resnik (n 3).

law).[38] Congress would have to amend the federal statute on arbitration to say, for example, that cases involving civil rights or anticompetitive behaviour cannot be made subject to arbitration. A bill that would do just that has been unsuccessfully submitted to Congress in each year since 2007.[39]

I don't know of another developed country that has the problem with mandatory pre-dispute arbitration clauses that the United States Supreme Court has enabled. In Canada arbitration is viewed favourably by the Canadian Supreme Court. Nevertheless, partly because Canada does not have the constitutional preemption provision that the United States has, the provinces have the power to decide whether mandatory pre-dispute arbitration provisions can be deployed against consumers. A few provinces have legislated against it.[40]

B. A tort of deprivation of basic legal rights

Under these circumstances it is worthwhile to consider whether there could be a remedy in tort against a firm deploying clauses that exclude access to redress. It is possible to view mass-market exclusion clauses as a deceptive business practice and thus a form of tortious behaviour. Indeed, it is more realistic to view mass-market rights deletions as a deceptive business practice than to view them as millions of separate identical contracts. If 'deceptive' is defined here as it is in the law of advertising, it would be possible to find many boilerplate exclusion clauses to be deceptive. It is clear that firms know what they are doing when they price mortgages or auto leases or cell phones the way they do.[41] They have honed these practices over a long time.[42] It is clear that firms know that consumers do not know what the firms are doing, and that it would be very difficult for consumers to find out and to act appropriately on that information.

The tort law analysis would be most convincing if there were evidence that firms are actually intending to deceive recipients of boilerplate. But do firms consciously intend to deceive? They do intend to persuade, and have manipulative methods of doing so. So far I have not found a smoking gun where a corporate principal

[38] *American Express v Italian Colors Restaurant*, 135 S.Ct. 2304 (2013) (restaurants subject to boilerplate arbitration clause could not bring class action for antitrust relief under federal law, even though no individual plaintiff would be able to afford the development of economic evidence that would be needed for the vindication of this federal right). Scalia, J, thereby elevated 'contractual' boilerplate over federal rights. As this chapter goes to press, the conservative activist majority on the US Supreme Court has been disrupted by the death of Scalia, J. How this may affect the Court's support of over-broad mandatory pre-dispute arbitration clauses is as yet unknown.

[39] Another such effort is pending as I write this.

[40] For a bit more on this, see Radin, 'Access to Justice and Abuses of Contract' (n 5) at 22–25.

[41] For example: even if you are a contracts professor, it is impossible to find out what an auto lease will cost either by reading the dealer's advertised price, or by hearing a quote on the telephone. Once you get to the dealership, where they want to have you, you will learn about some large fees that were not previously revealed, but you still won't know the actual price until you read all of the boilerplate that will be handed to you casually when the deal is complete (for example, the fact that the dealership will charge you a substantial fee when you return the car at the end of the lease if you do not lease another car from them).

[42] For literature on how advertising can be and has been used manipulatively in light of consumer cognitive biases, see Akerlof and Shiller, *Phishing for Phools* (n 29).

says something like: 'Let's deceive consumers about how we are secretly raising the aggregate price of our product and subjecting them to danger, while depriving them of viable methods of relief against us.'[43] We know that firms know about recipients' cognitive biases and make use of them. Perhaps a whistleblower will turn up with solid evidence of intent to deceive.[44] Though there are obstacles, I have not given up on the idea that boilerplate rights exclusions can be tortious.[45] Judges in some states, especially in California, might be receptive to this analysis, which suggests a way to get around the arbitration clause problem.[46]

V. Conclusion

If we grant that the State is a fiduciary of its people, the fiduciary frame of reference helps us to understand what is broadly and deeply problematic about privatization of public functions in the United States. Private armies, private prisons, private police, private housing compounds, private ownership of roads and bridges—all avoid the safeguards that the State is obligated to provide, and had previously attempted to provide in constitutional safeguards and other regulations. In the same way, excessive privatization of the legal infrastructure of contract law through widespread exclusion of recipients' rights to redress undermines the possibility of private ordering by contracts properly administered by the State. Privatization in this context means ceding powers that are properly public to private firms' self-interest, enabling the exertion of arbitrary power that the rule of law opposes. When the State condones excessive privatization, it condones arbitrary power, undermining the rule of law and the fiduciary foundation of its own claim to legitimate possession and exercise of public authority.

[43] There are other problems with considering use of boilerplate rights deletion as tortious. One is the economic loss doctrine, a judge-made doctrine precluding relief in tort for mere economic loss. I have attempted to reply to this and other doctrinal defenses; see *Boilerplate* (n 3) Ch 11.

[44] Analogously, Shiffrin found very useful quotes from industry managers about the high priority of minimizing customer service. As one quoted industry source said, avoiding phone calls and deflecting e-mails about customer issues would enable support workers to stop helping customers in order 'to spend time on cross-selling and up-selling.' Shiffrin (n 22) p 26 (draft).

[45] In addition to the deception analysis discussed above, judges could consider a product that comes with onerous clauses attached to it that harm the recipient (and the public system of redress of grievances) to be a unified defective product capable of harming the recipient (and the public system of redress of grievances). The idea that the physical product and its boilerplate can be amalgamated and considered a composite product stems from a law-and-economics view. (Of course, that law-and-economics view does not say that the composite product might be defective. That is my addition.) See Radin, 'Access to Justice and Abuses of Contract' (n 5) 7–10 (draft); Radin, *Boilerplate* (n 3) Ch 6.

[46] See Resnik (n 3).

Index